ST. LOUIS COUNTY
COVERAGE

Kittson

Roseau

Lake of the Woods

Koochiching

ARROWHEAD REGION

Cook

Marshall

Pennington

Beltrami

Lake

St. Louis

Red Lake

GRAND RAPIDS & BEMIDJI AREA

Polk

Clearwater

Itasca

Norman

Mahnomen

Hubbard

Cass

DETROIT LAKES & OTTERTAIL

LEECH LAKE

Clay

Becker

BRAINERD AREA

Carlton

Wadena

Crow Wing

Aitkin

Wilkin

Otter Tail

Pine

Mille Lacs

Kanabec

Todd

Morrison

EAST METRO

Grant

Douglas

ALEXANDRIA AREA & WEST CENTRAL

Benton

Traverse

Pope

Stearns

Isanti

Chisago

Stevens

Sherburne

Anoka

Washington

Big Stone

Swift

Kandiyohi

Meeker

Wright

WEST METRO AREA

Ramsey

Chippewa

Hennepin

Lac qui Parle

Renville

McLeod

Carver

Yellow Medicine

Scott

Dakota

Sibley

Goodhue

Lincoln

Lyon

Redwood

Nicollet

Le Sueur

Rice

Wabasha

Brown

SOUTHERN MINNESOTA

Steele

Dodge

Olmsted

Winona

Pipestone

Murray

Cottonwood

Watonwan

Blue Earth

Waseca

Rock

Nobles

Jackson

Martin

Faribault

Freeborn

Mower

Fillmore

Houston

TABLE of CONTENTS

See back cover for alphabetical listing of lakes
MAPS IN THIS GUIDE ARE NOT FOR NAVIGATION

TABLE of CONTENTS

St. Louis County Fishing Map Guide
by Sportsman's Connection

Editor and Publisher *Jim Billig*

Senior Editor *Dave Landahl*

Editorial/Research *Kristin Landahl, Steve Meyer, Jack Tyllia, Joe Verdegan, Jon Wisniewski, Mike Billig*

Creative & Production Director *Kurt Mazurek*

Production Coordinator *Shelly Wisniewski*

Senior Cartographer/GIS Specialist *Eric McPhee*

Cartographers *Hart Graphics, Linda Hollinday, Andrew King-Scribbins, Mandy Shaw*

Information Systems Manager *Jon Fiskness*

ISBN-13: 978-1-885010-32-2

Sportsman's Connection
Superior, Wisconsin 54880
800-777-7461

www.scmaps.com

FOREWORD

Many books have been written about fishing. Most are of the "how-to" variety, focusing on certain species, offering tips regarding the best lures or baits and the best techniques for using them. Few books focus on the fishing waters, offering not just information on how to catch a particular fish species, but on where to catch them.

Where to catch fish in St. Louis County, Minnesota is what this book is all about. We've attempted to be as comprehensive as possible, giving readers an in-depth view of the area's best and most notable fishing prospects. Included is information on more than 190 waters of local, regional or state-wide significance.

This, of course, is not a complete picture of the region, or any given body of water. Nor, probably, should it be. Our purpose in publishing this book is to serve the angling public. We've tried, first and foremost, to give our readers information on waters they can use. And we've avoided, we believe, those waters that the public cannot fish.

As we've compiled this book, we've tried to be as accurate as possible in our depiction of each lake, stream or river. Within the limits of the source materials we were able to locate, we believe we have been. We have, in fact, relied not only upon our own expertise, but on the experience and knowledge of many others.

In all cases, we've used the best and most-recent data available. In some instances, however, the available data are several years old and may not accurately reflect the current situation. Readers should bear this in mind before relying solely on the information given for a lake; check the date provided with each table.

Regulations change from year to year. Be sure to consult current state and site-specific regs before fishing any new lake or river.

Readers should also be aware that data tables and management information focus primarily on the sport fishery. We believe this emphasis accurately reflects the interests of our readers. However, maintaining this focus has sometimes meant that data on less-desirable species has been sacrificed in order to present more comprehensive information on game species. The absence of rough fish or other less-desirable species in the information presented, therefore, does not mean these species are not present.

Refer to the "Reader's Guide to Using this Publication" (facing page) for terminology definitions and a map legend that will help you maximize the practical use of this publication.

We've received considerable assistance from a number of public and private agencies, each of which generously and courteously contributed material or knowledge to our work. These people help us develop a better understanding of the region and the resources. Thanks to the U.S. Geological Survey, National Oceanic and Atmospheric Administration and the Minnesota Department of Natural Resources.

Be respectful, please, of the fishery and the land, both public and private. Be especially aware of the growing problem the spread of exotic fish, plants and other aquatic species has on our fisheries, many of which are changing with alarming speed and irreversible consequences. Remove all vegetation from boats and motors, drain live wells and take other precautions before you leave the lake or river. Preserve the recreational opportunities lands, lakes and rivers offer for us all to enjoy.

Special thanks to all agencies, businesses and individuals who contributed to this effort:

Minnesota Department of Natural Resources
Al Anderson, DNR Assistant Area Manager
Lynn Bergquist, Fisheries GIS
Deserae Hendrickson, Fisheries Manager
Ted Halpern, Fisheries Biologist
Tom Jones, Fisheries Specialist
Timothy Loesch, GIS Operations Supervisor
Kevin E. Peterson, Area Fisheries Supervisor
Don Schreiner, Fisheries Manager
Allen Stevens, Lake and Stream Survey Program Cons.
Maggie Gorsuch, Data Manager - DNR Fish and Wildlife

Wisconsin Department of Natural Resources
Dennis Pratt, Fisheries Biologist
St. Louis County
Andrew Hayden, GIS Specialist
Mark Eyre, Contractor for St. Louis County
David Phillips, Undersheriff
Jeff Storlie, GIS Specialist
Iron Range Resources
Dan Jordan, Ray Svatos

Anderson Sports Port, Highway 53, Orr, MN 218-757-3411
Bimbo's Octagon Restaurant & Motel, George Pernat, Box 397, Side Lake, MN, 218-254-2576
Chalstrom's Bait & Tackle, 5067 Rice Lake Road, Duluth, MN, 218-726-0094
Crestliner Boats, John Janousek, 609 13th Avenue NE, Little Falls, MN 56345, 320-632-6686 *www.crestliner.com*
Fisherman (The), Jerry Snyker, 100 Memorial Drive, International Falls, MN, 218-283-9440
Fisherman's Corner, Scott VanValkenburg, 5675 Miller Trunk Hwy., Hermantown, MN 218-729-5369
Fredenberg Minno-ette, 5109 Fish Lake Road, Fredenberg, MN, 218-721-4800
Gander Mountain, 4275 Haines Road, Hermantown, MN, 218-786-9800

Lake Superior Sportfishing Charters, Captain Steve Johnson, 800-531-FISH (3474), *www.LakeSuperiorFishing.com*
Marine General, Russ Francisco, 1501 London Road, Duluth, 55812, 800-777-8557, *www.MarineGeneral.com*
Meyer's Minnows, Gas & More, 3302 Hwy. 53, Orr, MN, 218-757-3411
Skube's Bait & Tackle, 1810 E. Sheridan St., Ely, MN, 218-365-5358
Virginia Surplus Store, Doug Ellis, 105 3rd Ave., Virginia, MN 218-741-0331
Walleye Waters Guide Service, Captain Blaine Johnson, Jr., 218-590-9094, *www.WalleyeWatersGuide.com*
Western Lake Superior Trollers Assn., *www.wlsta.com*

Thank you to our fellow sportsmen who contributed their knowledge and expertise:
Retired Captain Bob Smith, David Yapel (local angler)

READER'S GUIDE *to* USING *this* PUBLICATION

Your fishing map guide is a thorough, easy-to-use collection of accurate contour lake maps along with geographic and biologic statistical information to help you locate a lake and enjoy a successful day out on the water of one of Minnesota's excellent fisheries.

The heart of this book is the **contour lake map**. Copyrighted maps are used with permission from the Minnesota Department of Natural Resources and are not intended for navigation. The lakes selected for this guide are confined to those that are accessible to the public.

Each map is accompanied by a **detailed write-up**. In each piece, you'll find fishing tips and hot spots specific to the body of water you're planning to fish.

Lake **stocking records** and **management comments** are provided courtesy of the Minnesota Department of Natural Resources and summarized to reflect management trends and objectives for each fishery represented. Please keep in mind that annual fish stocking aspirations are directly affected by state hatchery production levels and sometimes the numbers available for stocking fluctuate considerably.

Detailed **area road maps** (1:150,000 scale) and **lake access** information is provided to help you plan your route to the lake. If there is more than one access point on a body of water, the GPS coordinates refer to the primary access. To locate a lake on these road maps, simply use the alphabetical lake listing on the back cover. Turn to that page to find the area road map page and coordinates for the lake. As a cross-reference, the area road maps include numbers on or adjacent to featured lakes, which designate the pages of the lake maps and information. Streams and rivers are also referenced in these area road maps.

While every effort is made to create the most accurate maps possible, the process of merging existing DNR maps with the latest GPS information will cause some slight differences to occur. (Especially on larger, more complicated lakes.) Please use the GPS grids provided in this book only as a guideline.

GLOSSARY OF TERMS

Gill net: This is the main piece of equipment used for sampling walleye, northern pike, yellow perch, cisco, whitefish, trout, and salmon. The standard gill net is 6 feet tall by 250 feet long, with 5 different mesh sizes. Gill nets are generally set in off shore areas in water deeper than 9 feet. Nets are fished for a period of 24 hours. Fish are captured by swimming into the net and becoming entangled. Fisheries workers record length and weight data from each fish, determine the sex, look for parasites or disease, and remove several of the fishes scales for determining the fishes age. Most of the fish taken in gill nets are

killed, but only a small portion of the lakes fish population is sampled during an individual survey event. The number of gill nets set during a survey is dependant on the lake acreage.

Trap net: This is the main piece of equipment used for sampling bluegill, crappie, and bullheads. The standard trap net is 4 feet tall by 6 feet wide with a 40 foot lead. Trap nets are generally set perpendicular to shore in water less than 8 feet in depth. Nets are fished for a period of 24 hours. Fish are captured by swimming into the lead and following it towards the trap. Most of the fish collected in trap nets are returned back to the water as soon as the necessary biological data is recorded. The number of trap net sets during a survey is dependant on the lake acreage.

Electrofishing: This is a specialized type of equipment that is most often used for sampling largemouth bass, smallmouth bass, and young of the year walleye. A boat-mounted generator is used to induce electrical current into the water that stuns the fish, allowing fisheries workers to net the fish for placement in live wells. Most of the fish caught by electrofishing recover rapidly and are promptly returned to the water after the necessary biological data is recorded.

CPUE: An acronym representing "Catch Per Unit of Effort," a way of representing the density of a species population. Readings are in fish captured per hour or minute of surveying. The higher the CPUE value, the greater the number of fish present.

PSD: An acronym for "Proportional Stock Density," which is a way of representing the size structure of fish populations. It represents the percentage of "quality-size" fish within a given population. In arriving at this figure, one considers only fish of "stock" length (the size at which members of a given species reach sexual maturity) or greater. Young-of year fish are not included in the calculation. The higher the PSD number, the greater the percentage of "quality" fish within a particular population.

RSD-12 (or -10 or -14, etc.): An acronym for "Relative Stock Density," which is yet another way of representing the size structure of fish populations. This corresponds to the percentage of fish at a given length or larger within a population. Hence, an RSD-14 reading of 25 for largemouth bass indicates that 25 percent of sexually mature bass are at least 14 inches in length. On another measurement scale, the RSD- values could be stated as "preferred," "memorable," or "trophy."

YAR: An acronym for "Young-(to)-Adult Ratio." This refers to the proportion of young-of-year fish in relation to adult or "quality-size" fish within a particular population. For balanced populations, the index should be about 1-to-10. In smaller waters, 1-to-3 is considered a reasonable ratio.

Secchi Disk: Used in measuring water clarity, it is a white-colored, plate-size device submerged on the end of a line until it reaches a point where it's no longer visible; the depth at which this occurs is measured and recorded. In this book, secchi disk readings are given in English measure. Of course, many factors influence water clarity, and secchi disk readings vary according to season, growth of vegetation, weather, location in a lake, even human activity. Hence the readings given are approximations for any lake—snapshots of the water clarity at a given time and in a given location.

LEGEND

Boat Ramp	Fishing Area	Rocks	GPS Grid
Carry Down Access	Boat tie-up	Submerged Culvert	
Access by Navigable Channel	Reservoir Outlet	Submerged Ruins	Red & Green Channel Buoys
Public Fishing Access	Reservoir Inlet	Marsh	
Access Information Marker	Marina	Emergent Vegetation	White Hazard Buoy
Campground	Lilly Pads	Manmade Canal	River Mile
Picnic Area	Submergent Vegetation	Marked Fishing Spots	Daymarker
Handicap Accessible	Emergent Vegetation	Submerged Rail	Light & Daymarker
Fishing Dock (Pier)	Stumps	Submerged Road	County Road
Shore Fishing	Flooded Timber	Bridge	State Highway
Fish Attractors		Submerged Riverbed	US Highway
Shipwreck			Interstate

LENGTH TO WEIGHT CONVERSION SCALE

Inches	Inland Lakes Species				Inland Trout				Lake Superior Species				
	Northern Pike	Walleye	Largemouth Bass	Crappie	Brook Trout	Brown Trout	Rainbow Trout	Lake Trout	Atlantic Salmon	Chinook Salmon	Coho Salmon	Lake Trout	Steelhead
8				0.4									
9				0.6									
10				0.8	0.06								
11				1.1	0.08								
12			1.0	1.4	0.11	0.10	0.10		0.50	0.60	0.66	0.45	0.59
13			1.3	1.8	0.14	0.30	0.20		0.64	0.77	0.81	0.59	0.75
14		1.0	1.7	2.2	1.02	1.01	1.00		0.81	1.00	0.98	0.75	0.93
15		1.2	2.1	2.8	1.06	1.05	1.03	1.00	1.00	1.18	1.16	0.94	1.14
16		1.5	2.5	3.4	1.11	1.09	1.07	1.04	1.22	1.44	1.36	1.17	1.38
17		1.8	3.0	4.1	2.00	1.14	1.12	1.08	1.47	1.73	1.60	1.44	1.64
18		2.2	3.6		2.07	2.04	2.01	1.13	1.75	2.06	1.83	1.74	1.94
19		2.5	4.2		2.14	2.11	2.07	2.30	2.07	2.43	2.10	2.08	2.28
20		3.0	5.0		3.06	3.02	2.14	2.90	2.42	2.84	2.39	2.47	2.65
21		3.4	5.7		3.15	3.10	3.05	3.00	2.81	3.29	2.70	2.91	3.05
22		3.9	6.6		4.80	4.03	3.13	3.80	3.25	3.80	3.04	3.40	3.50
23		4.5	7.6		5.03	4.12	4.06	4.00	3.73	4.34	3.40	3.95	3.99
24	3.9	5.1			5.15	5.07	5.00	4.90	4.25	4.94	3.78	4.55	4.52
25	4.4	5.7			6.12	6.03	5.11	5.04	4.82	5.60	4.19	5.22	5.09
26	5.0	6.5			6.15	6.06	5.15	5.44	6.30	4.63	5.95	5.71	
27	5.6	7.2			7.13	7.20	6.11	6.11	7.06	5.09	6.75	6.38	
28	6.2	8.1			8.12	8.00	7.08	6.83	7.89	5.57	7.62	7.10	
29	7.0	9.0			9.11	8.15	8.70	7.61	8.78	6.09	8.57	7.87	
30	7.7				10.12	10.00	9.60	8.45	9.73	6.63	9.60	8.69	
31	8.5						10.70	9.35	10.75		10.71	9.57	
32	9.3						11.80	10.31	11.84		11.92	10.50	
33	10.2						12.90	11.34	13.00		13.21	11.49	
34	11.2						14.00	12.43	14.23		14.60	12.54	
35	12.2						15.50	13.59	15.55		16.08	13.65	
36	13.3						16.12	14.83	16.94		17.67	14.82	
37	14.5							16.14	18.41		19.37		
38	15.7							17.52	19.96		21.17		
39	16.9							18.98	21.60		23.09		
40	18.3							20.52	23.33		25.14		
41	19.6							22.14	25.15		27.30		
42	21.2							23.85	27.06		29.59		
43								25.64	29.07		32.00		
44								27.53	31.17		34.57		
45								29.50	33.38		37.27		

Average Weight (pounds)

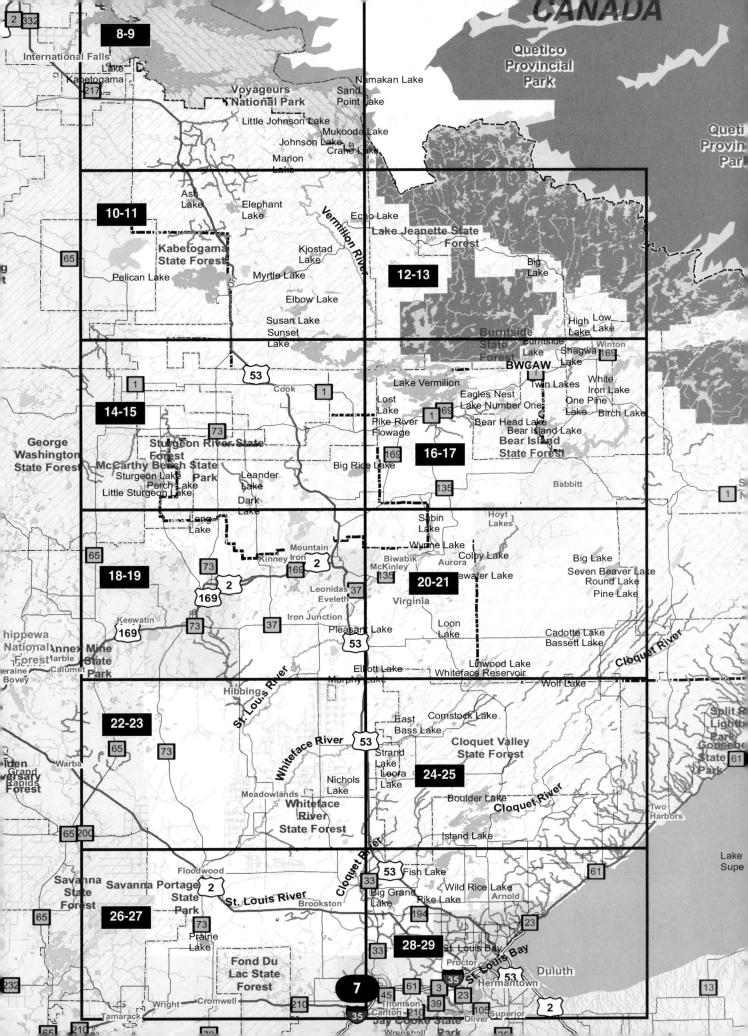

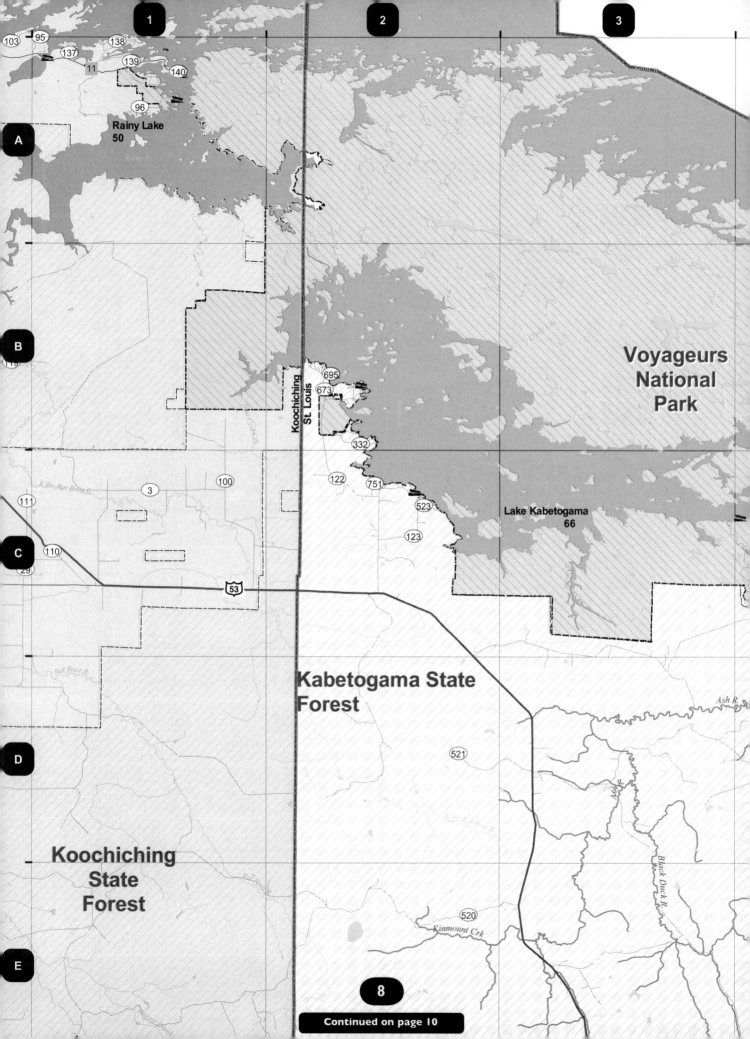

A

103
95
138
137
11
139
140
96

Rainy Lake
50

Rainy R.

B

Voyageurs National Park

Koochiching
St. Louis

695
673

332

119

F. Br. Rat Root R.

3
100

751
122

111

523

Lake Kabetogama
66

123

C

110

29

53

Rat Root R.

Kabetogama State Forest

Ash R.

D

521

Koochiching State Forest

Ash R.

Black Duck R.

520

Kinmount Crk

E

Continued on page 10

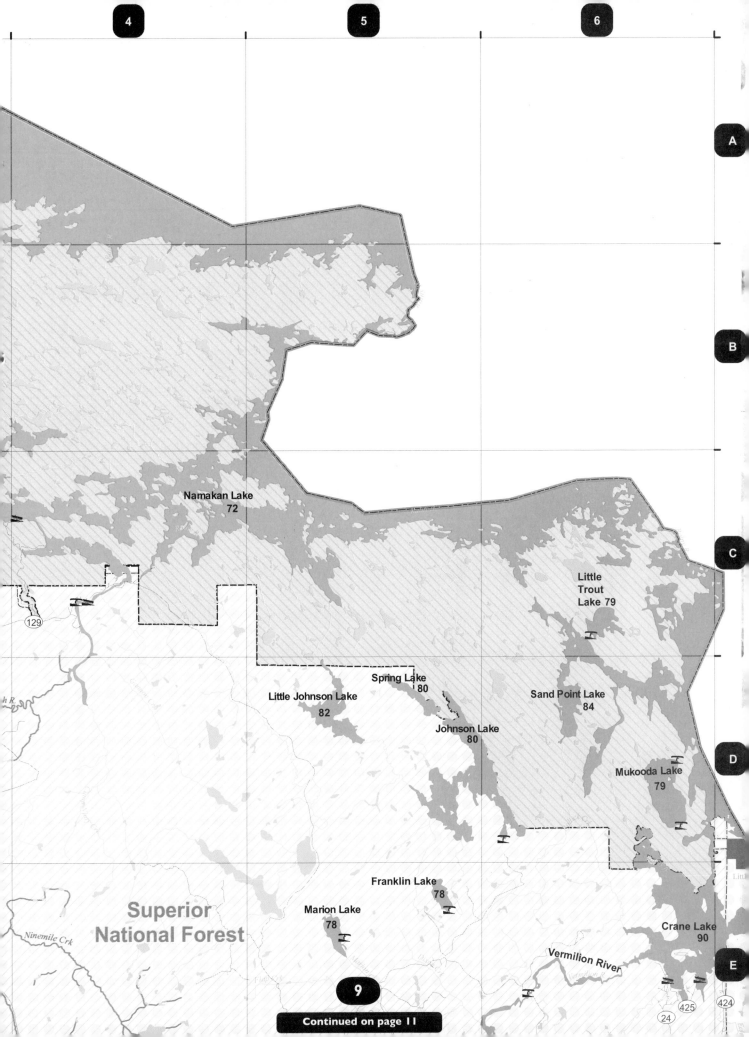

A

B

C

D

E

Namakan Lake
72

Little
Trout
Lake 79

Spring Lake
80

Little Johnson Lake
82

Sand Point Lake
84

Johnson Lake
80

Mukooda Lake
79

129

h R.

Franklin Lake
78

Superior
National Forest

Marion Lake
78

Crane Lake
90

Ninemile Crk

Vermilion River

425

424

24

Continued on page 11

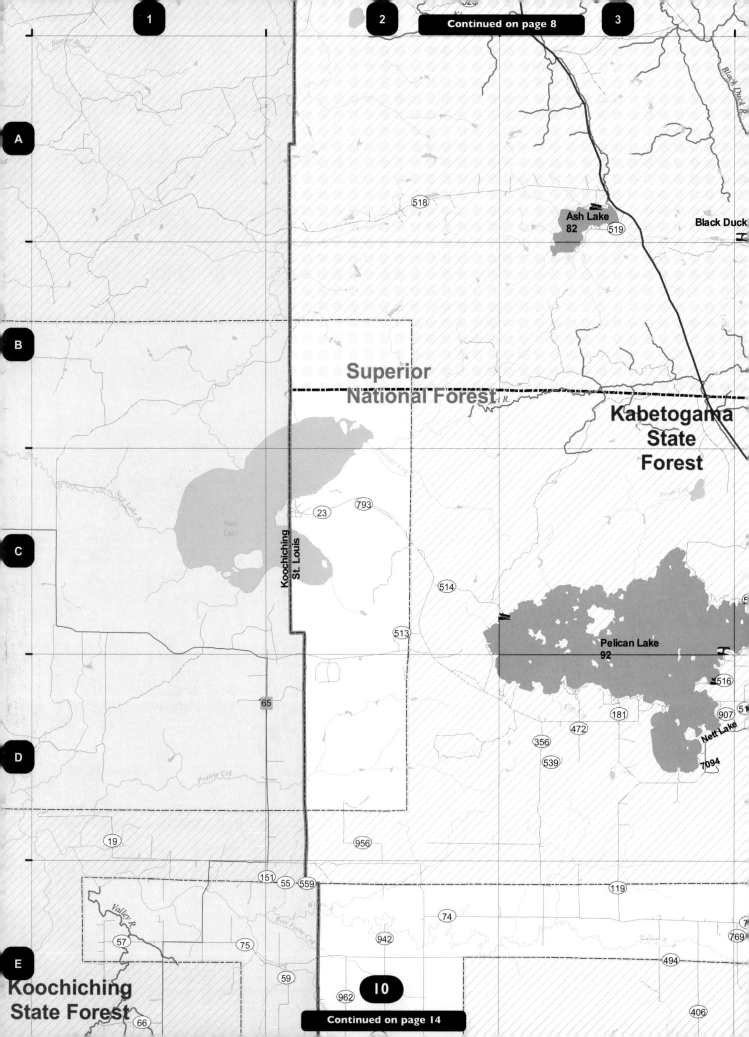

Continued on page 8

A

518

Ash Lake
82

519

Black Duck

B

Superior
National Forest

**Kabetogama
State
Forest**

Nett Lake R.

Nett
Lake

793

23

Koochiching
St. Louis

C

514

Pelican Lake
92

516

65

181

907

472

356

D

539

7094

Prairie Crk

19

956

E

151 55 559

119

Valley R.

74

57

75

942

769

59

494

**Koochiching
State Forest**

962

406

66

Continued on page 14

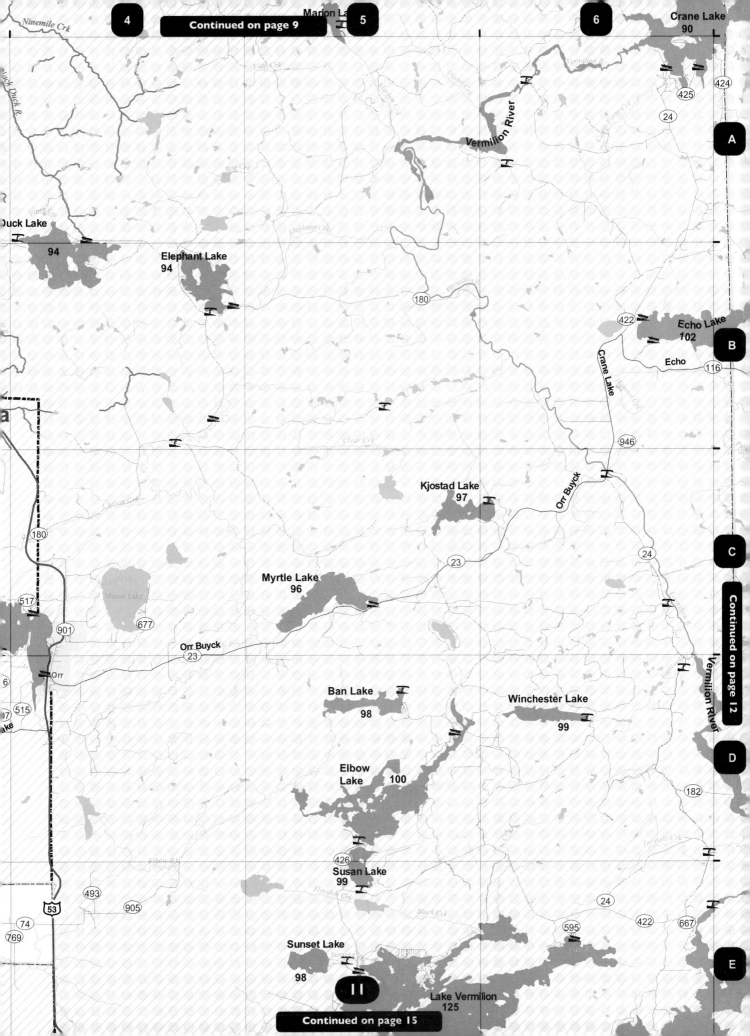

Continued on page 9

Marion La

Crane Lake
90

Ninemile Crk

A

424

425

24

Vermillion River

Duck Lake

94

Elephant Lake
94

Echo Lake
102

422

B

Echo

116

180

Crane Lake

Clear Crk

946

Kjostad Lake
97

Orr Buyck

24

C

a

180

Moose Lake

23

Myrtle Lake
96

517

901

677

Orr Buyck
23

Vermillion River

6

Orr

Ban Lake

98

Winchester Lake

99

515

D

17

ake

Elbow
Lake   100

182

426

Susan Lake
99

493

905

24

53

595

74

422

667

769

Sunset Lake

II

98

E

Lake Vermilion
125

Continued on page 15

Continued on page 12

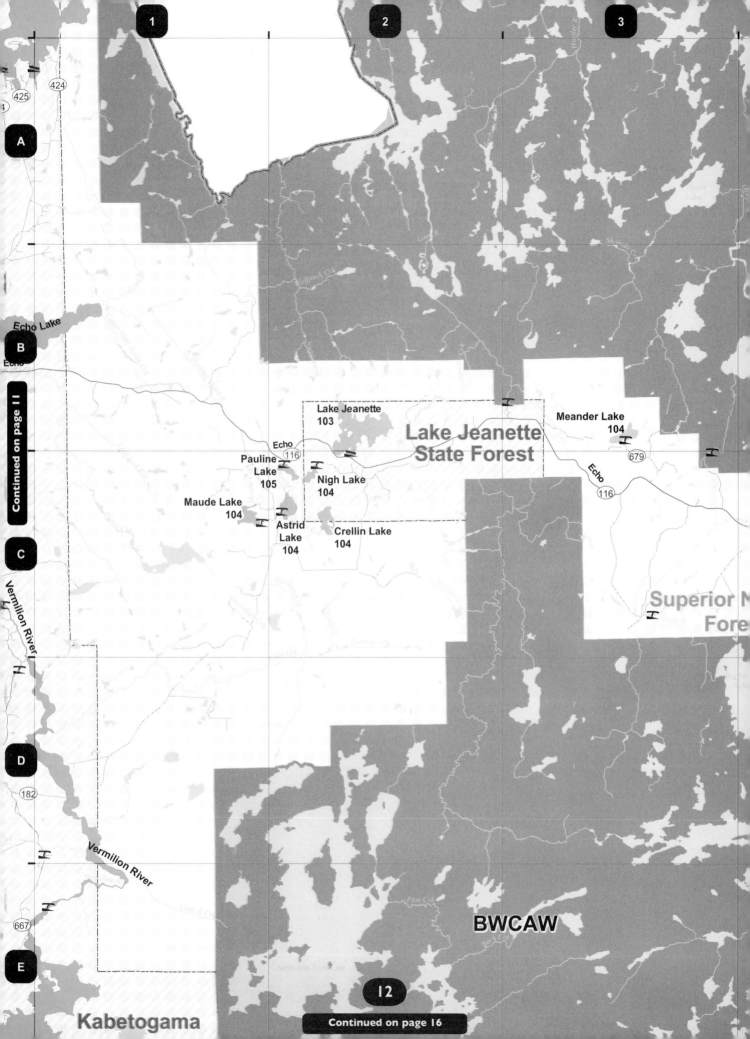

A

(424)
(425)

Echo Lake

B

Echo

Continued on page 11

Lake Jeanette
103

Meander Lake
104

Echo
116

Lake Jeanette
State Forest

Pauline
Lake
105

(679)

Echo
116

Nigh Lake
104

Maude Lake
104

Astrid
Lake
104

Crellin Lake
104

C

Vermilion River

Superior N
Fore

D

(182)

Vermilion River

(667)

E

BWCAW

12

Kabetogama

Continued on page 16

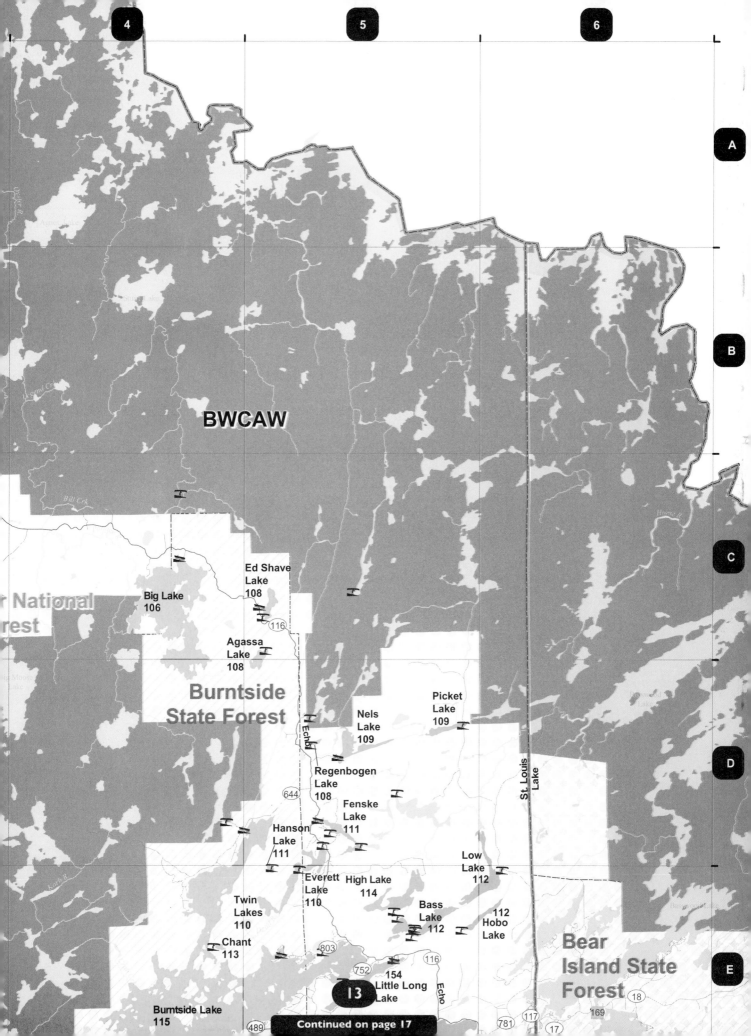

A

B

BWCAW

C

r **National**

rest

Ed Shave
Lake
108

Big Lake
106

116

Agassa
Lake
108

**Burntside
State Forest**

Picket
Lake
109

Nels
Lake
109

Echo

D

Regenbogen
Lake
108

644

Fenske
Lake
111

St Louis Lake

Hanson
Lake
111

Low
Lake
112

Everett
Lake
110

High Lake
114

Twin
Lakes
110

Bass
Lake
112

112
Hobo
Lake

**Bear
Island State
Forest**

Chant
113

803

18

752

116

E

154
Little Long
Lake

Echo

13

Burntside Lake
115

489

Continued on page 17

781   117

169

17

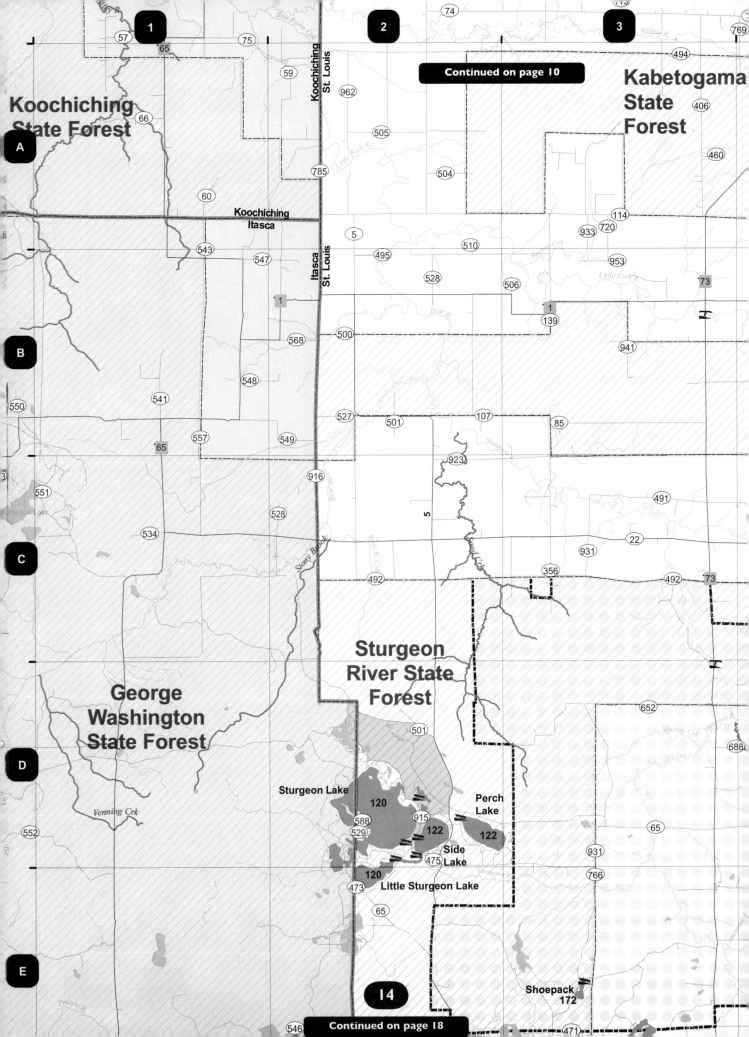

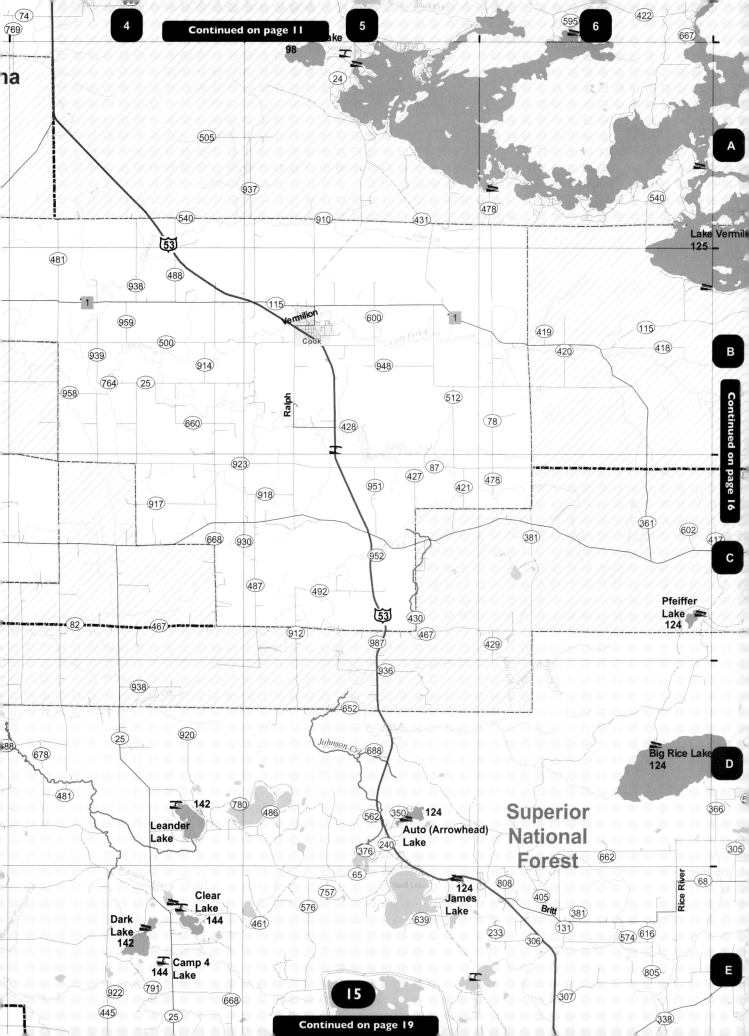

Continued on page 11

98

74
769

505

937

540

910
431

478

540

$\textbf{53}$

481

938

488

115

Vermilion
Cook

600

1

115

B

419

420

418

959

500

939

914

948

512

78

764
25

958

660

Ralph

428

87

951
427

421

478

361

602
417

923

917

918

361

C

668
930

381

487

492

952

Pfeiffer
Lake
124

$\textbf{53}$
430

82
467

912
467

429

987

936

938

652

920

Johnson Crk

688

Big Rice Lake
124

D

678

481

25

142
Leander
Lake

780

486

562

350
124
Auto (Arrowhead)
Lake

**Superior
National
Forest**

366

305

888

376
240

662

Rice River

68

Clear
Lake
144

65

757

576

Sand Lake

124
James
Lake

808

405
Britt
381

131

574
616

Dark
Lake
142

461

639

233

306

805

Camp 4
Lake
144

922
791

445

25

668

Continued on page 19

307

338

Continued on page 16

Lake Vermil
125

A

24

422
667

595

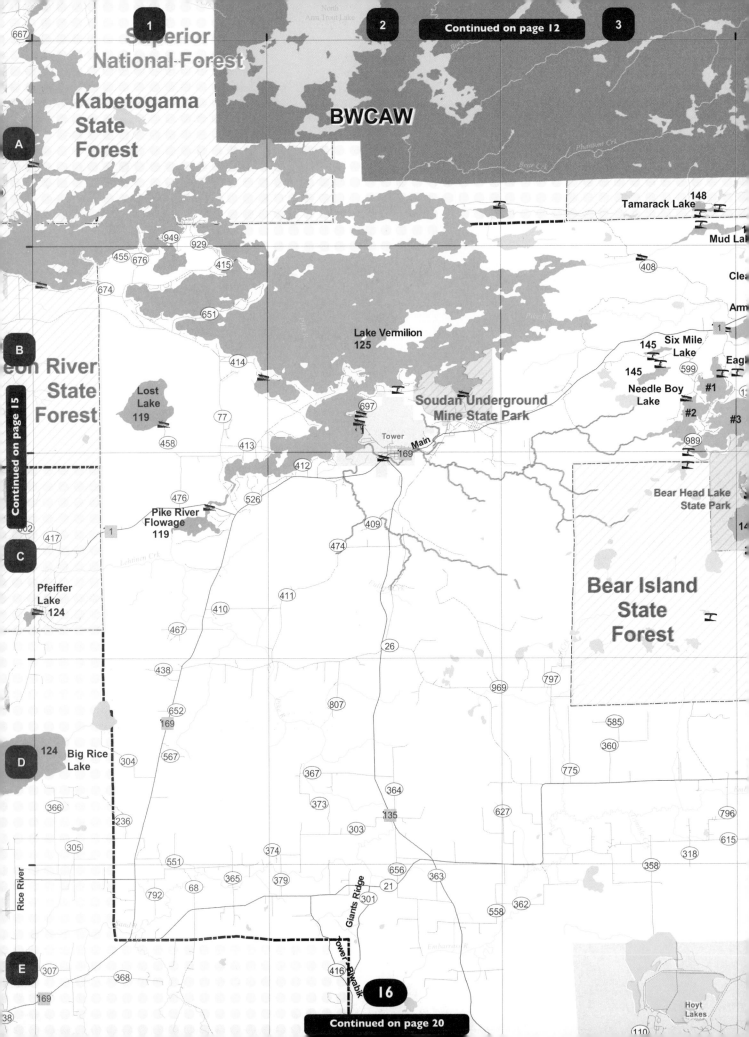

667

Superior National Forest

Kabetogama State Forest

A

BWCAW

148

Tamarack Lake

Mud Lak

949

929

408

Clea

455 676

415

674

651

Arm

1

B

Lake Vermilion 125

145

Six Mile Lake

Eag

eon River State Forest

414

145

599

#1

1

Lost Lake 119

77

697

Soudan Underground Mine State Park

Needle Boy Lake

#2

#3

458

413

Tower

Main

989

412

169

Continued on page 15

Bear Head Lake State Park

476

526

Pike River Flowage 119

409

02

417

1

474

C

Pfeiffer Lake 124

411

410

Bear Island State Forest

467

14

438

26

969

797

652

807

169

585

360

304

567

775

D

124 **Big Rice Lake**

367

364

366

373

627

796

236

303

135

615

305

374

358

318

Rice River

551

365

656

379

792

68

21

363

Giants Ridge

301

558

362

E

307

368

416

Tower Biwabik

Hoyt Lakes

38

169

110

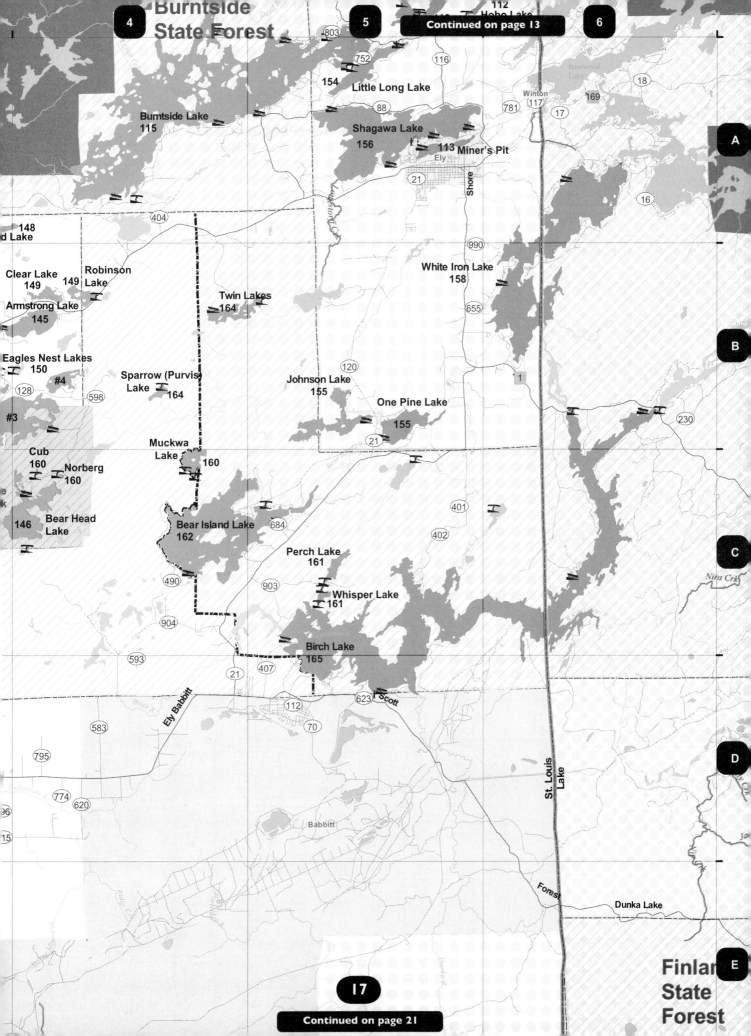

Continued on page 13

Burntside
State Forest

803

752

116

154

Little Long Lake

88

A

Winton
117

781

17

169

18

Burntside Lake
115

Shagawa Lake
156

113 Miner's Pit

Ely

21

Shore

16

404

990

148
d Lake

White Iron Lake
158

Clear Lake
149

149

Robinson
Lake

655

B

Armstrong Lake
145

Twin Lakes
164

Eagles Nest Lakes
150

120

#4

Johnson Lake
155

128

Sparrow (Purvis)
Lake
164

One Pine Lake

230

598

155

#3

21

Muckwa
Lake
160

Cub
160

Norberg
160

401

402

684

Bear Island Lake
162

490

146

Bear Head
Lake

Perch Lake
161

903

C

Nira Crk

Whisper Lake
161

904

593

Birch Lake
165

407

21

623 Scott

Ely Babbitt

112

583

70

St. Louis Lake

D

795

774

620

Babbitt

96

15

Forest

Dunka Lake

Finla
State
Forest

E

Continued on page 21

Continued on page 14

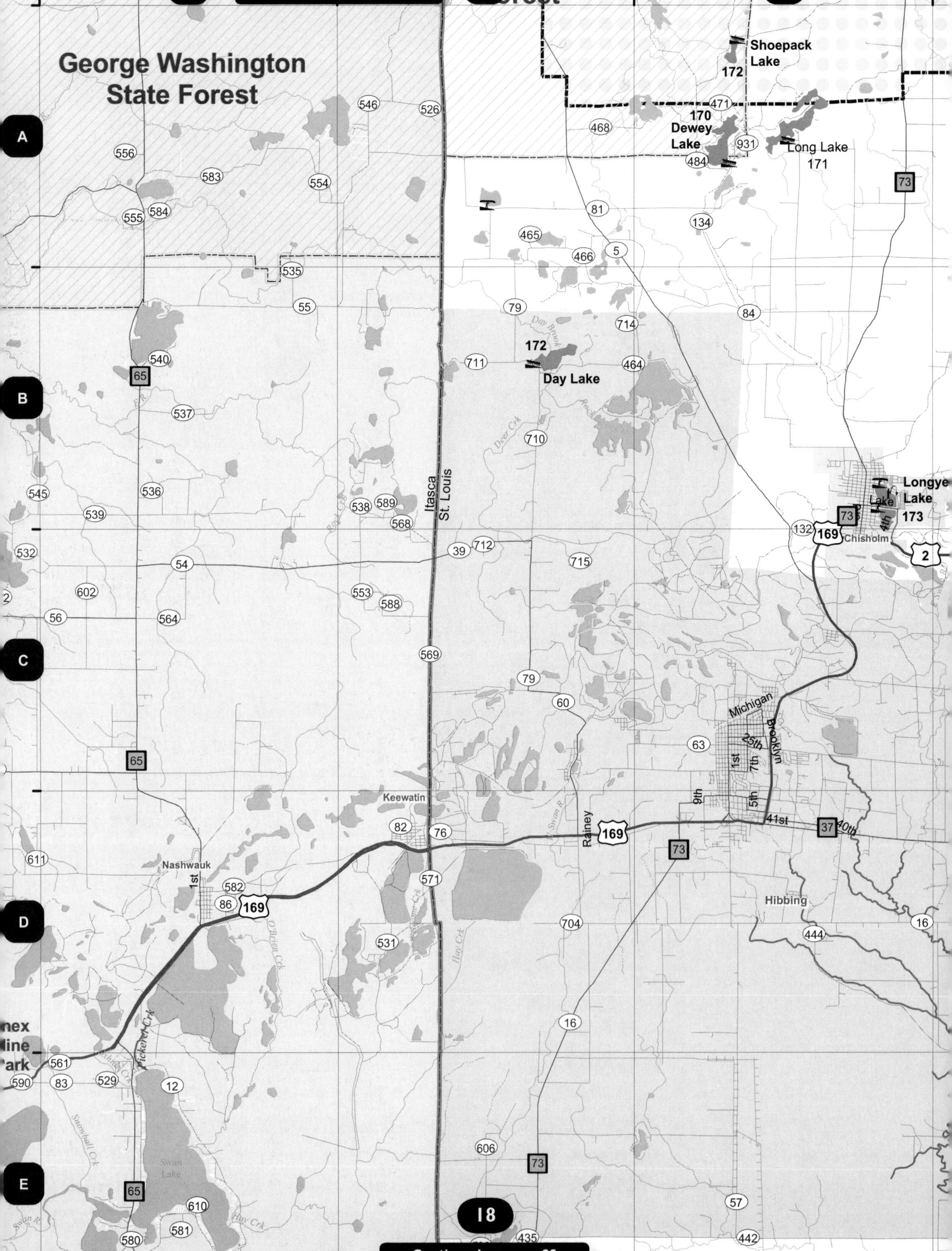

State Forest

George Washington State Forest

A

556

583

554

546 526

555 584

535

55

540

65

537

B

Shoepack Lake

172

471

170 Dewey Lake

931 Long Lake 171

484

468

73

134

465

466 5

81

84

79

714

172

Day Lake

464

711

710

Deer Crk

St. Louis

Itasca

545

536

538 589

568

532

54

712

39

715

Longye Lake 173

4th Lake

132 73

169 Chisholm

2

602

56

564

553 588

569

C

79

60

63

Michigan

Brooklyn

25th

7th

1st

5th

9th

82 76

Keewatin

Rainey

169

41st 40th

37

611

Nashwauk

1st

582

571

169

86

531

704

Hibbing

444

16

D

16

nex
ine
ark

561

590 83 529 12

73

606

Swan Lake

65

610

57

580 581

442

E

18

73

435

Continued on page 22

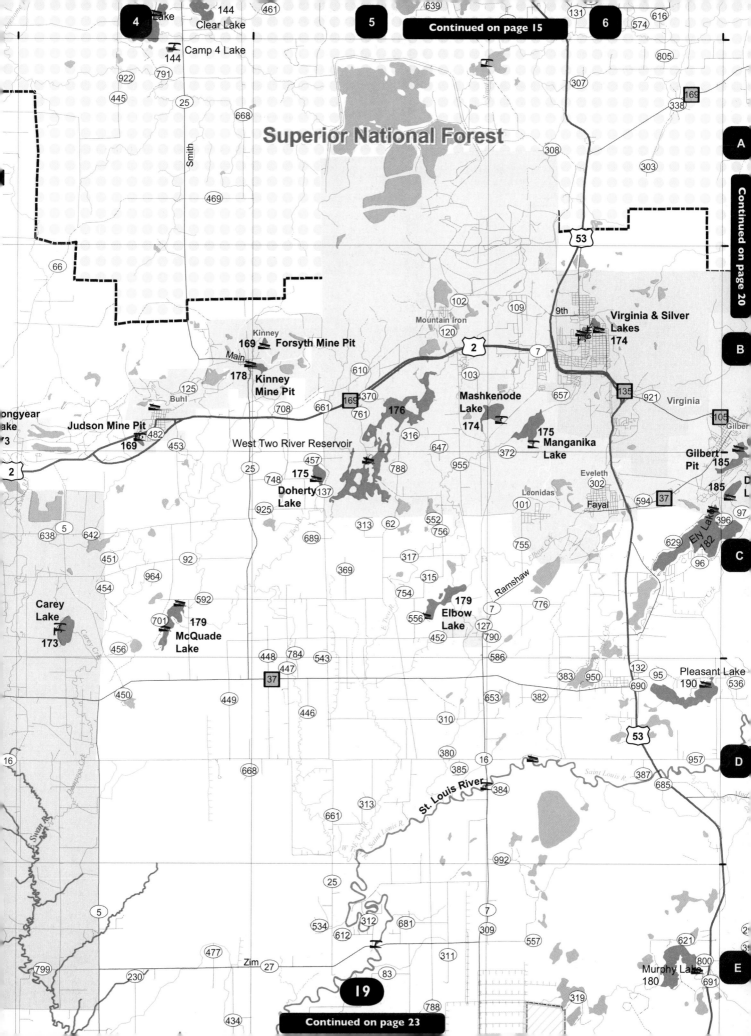

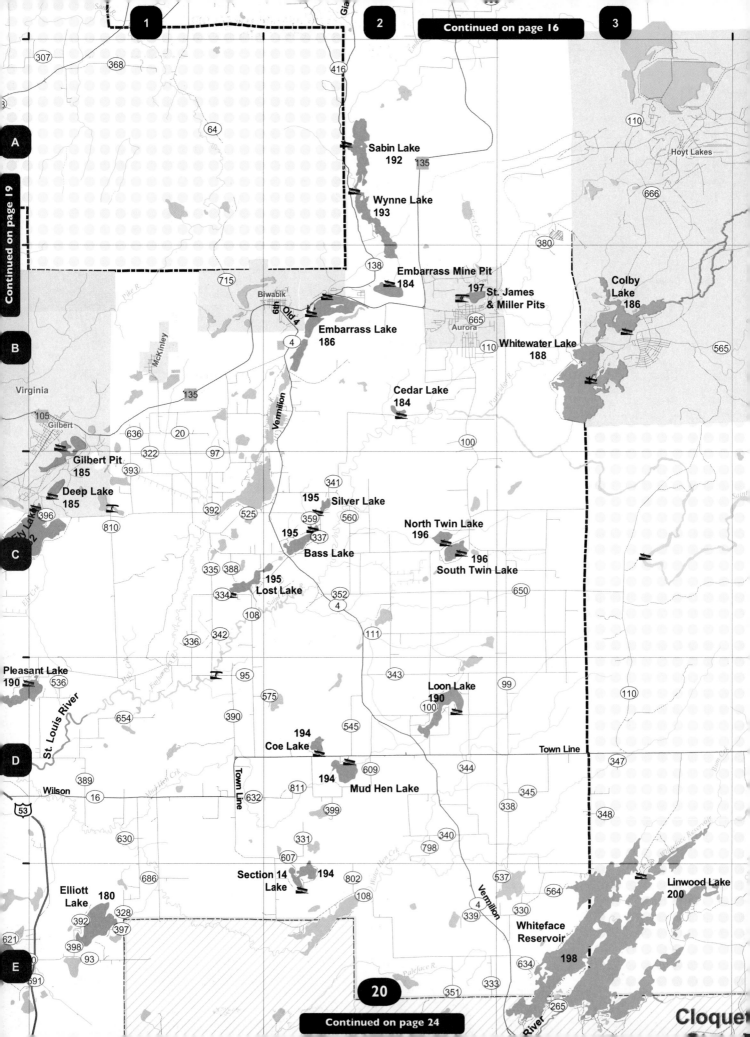

307
368
(3)
64
416

A

Continued on page 19

Sabin Lake
192
135

Wynne Lake
193

110

Hoyt Lakes

666

138

715
Biwabik
380

6th
Old 4

Embarrass Mine Pit
184
197 St. James
& Miller Pits

Colby
Lake
186

B

McKinley

Virginia

Embarrass Lake
186
4
Aurora
665
110

Whitewater Lake
188

565

135

Cedar Lake
184

Vermilion

105
Gilbert

636
20

322
97

100

393

341

Gilbert Pit
185

195 Silver Lake

392
525
359
560

North Twin Lake
196

Deep Lake
185
396

195
337

810

Bass Lake

196
South Twin Lake

C
Ely Lake
2

335 388

195
Lost Lake

334
352
4

650

108

336 342

111

St. Louis River

Pleasant Lake
190
536

95

343

Loon Lake
190
100

99

110

575
545

390
654

Coe Lake
194

609

Town Line

347

D

Town Line

389
Wilson
632
811

194
Mud Hen Lake

344
345

338

348

53
16

399

630

340
798

331

607

Section 14
Lake
194
802

537

Vermilion

Linwood Lake
200

686

Elliott
Lake
180

392 328
397

108

564

4

330

53

Whiteface
Reservoir
198

398
93

339

634

621
591

351

333

265

Cloquet

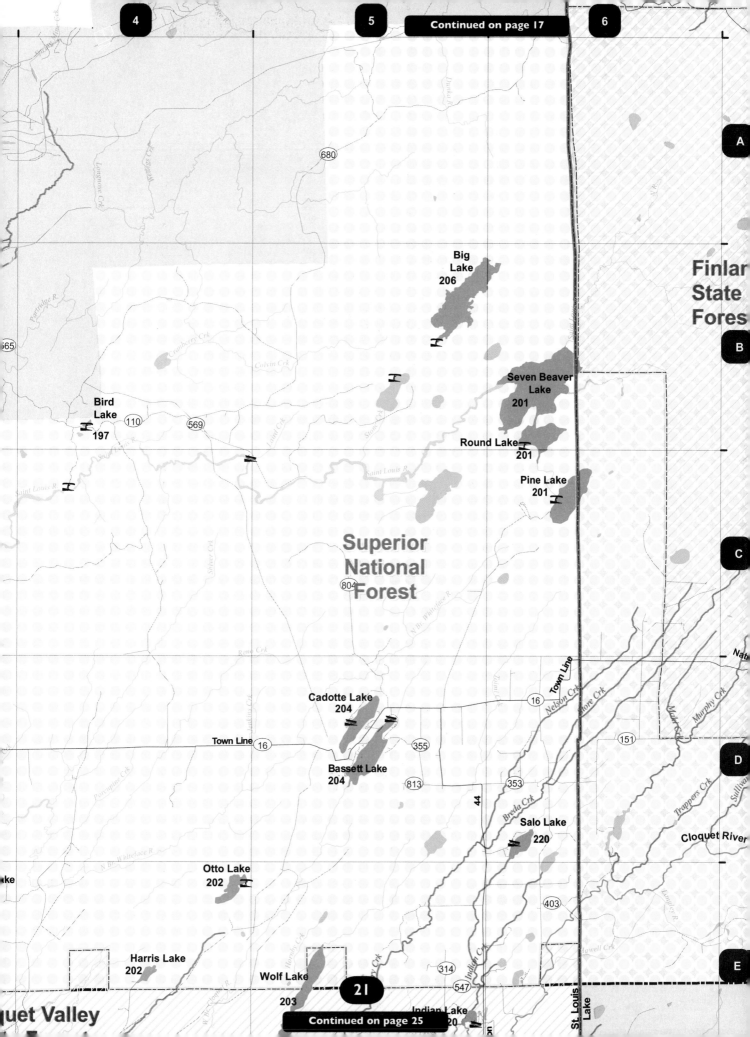

A

Finlar
State
Fores

680

Big
Lake
206

B

565

Seven Beaver
Lake
201

Bird
Lake
197

110

569

Round Lake
201

Pine Lake
201

Superior
National
Forest

804

C

Town Line

Cadotte Lake
204

16

Nelson Crk

16

151

Town Line

16

355

Bassett Lake
204

813

353

D

44

Breda Crk

Salo Lake
220

Otto Lake
202

403

Cloquet River

Harris Lake
202

E

Wolf Lake

314

547

St. Louis
Lake

203

Indian Lake

quet Valley

Continued on page 25

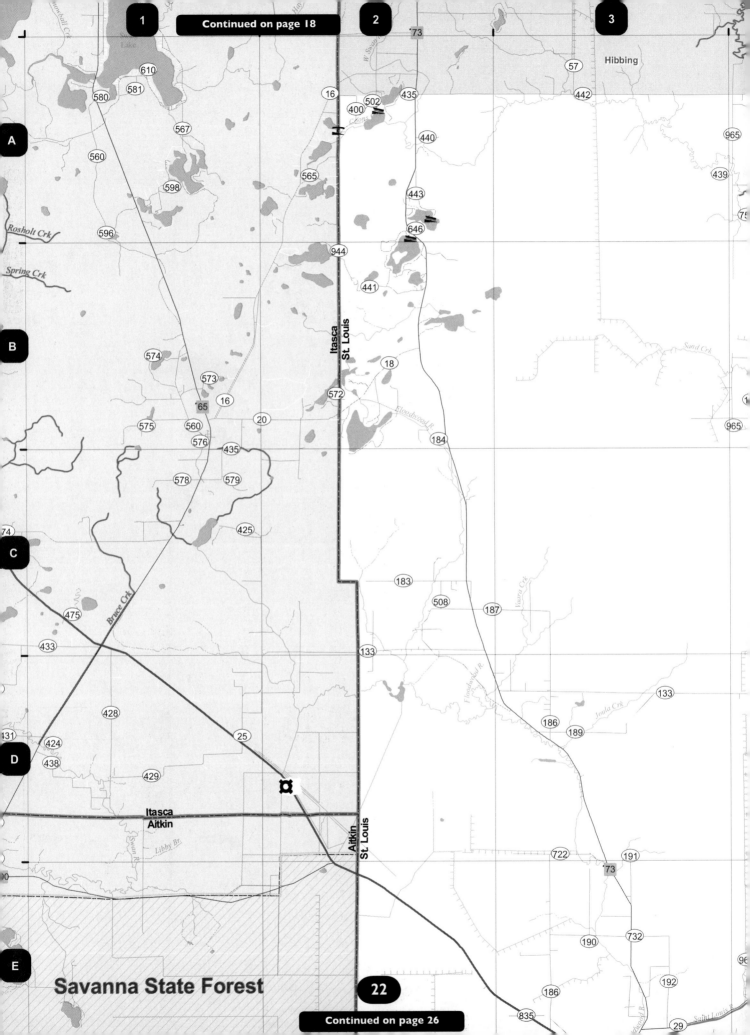

73

Hibbing

57

16   435   442

502

400

440

965

567

443

560

439

598

646

75

596

944

Rosholt Crk

441

Spring Crk

574

Itasca
St Louis

573

18

65   16

572

575   560

20

576

965

435

184

578   579

425

133

183

74

508   187

475

433

133

428

186

25

189

424

431

438

429

Itasca
Aitkin

Aitkin
St Louis

191

722   73

190   732

E

Savanna State Forest

186

835

192

29

Continued on page 26

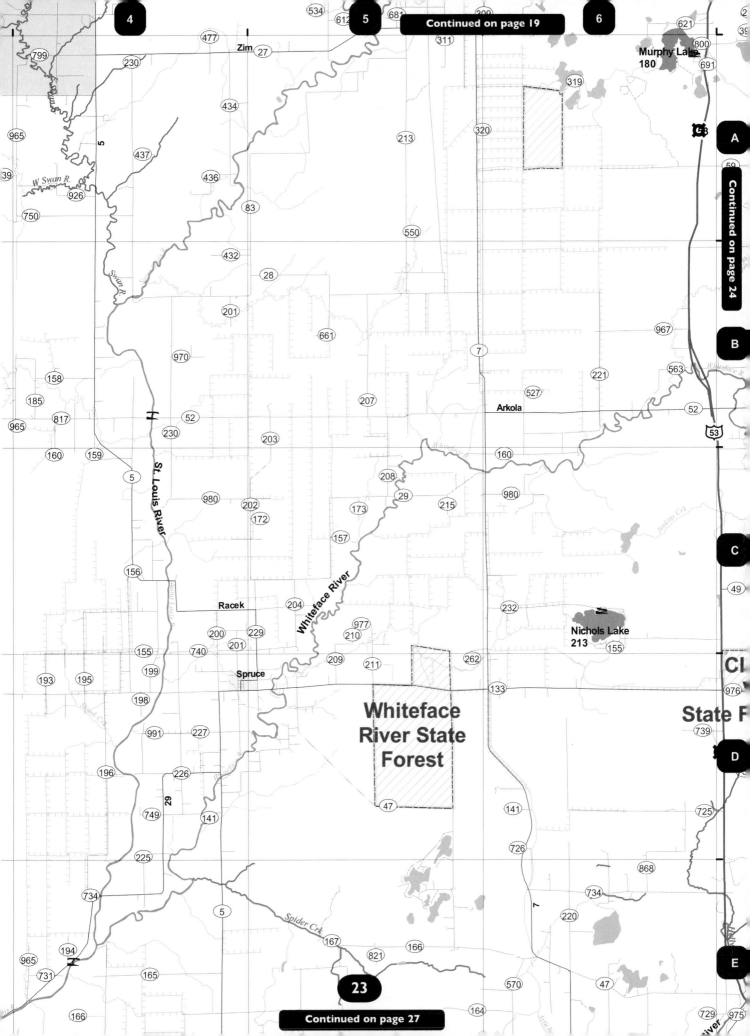

Continued on page 19

Continued on page 24

L

A

59

B

C

49

CI

976

State F

739

D

725

E

Murphy Lake
180

691

800

621

39

534
612
681
200
311

477
Zim 27

799

230

965

437

926

W Swan R.

750

39

434

436

83

432

28

201

661

970

158

185

817

965

160

159

52

230

5

St. Louis River

980

202

172

156

Racek

204

Whiteface River

200 229

201

740

155

199

198

193 195

991

227

196

226

29

749

141

225

734

194

965

731

165

5

Spider Crk.

167

166

821

166

570

47

164

Swan R.

Spruce

977
210

209 211

Whiteface
River State
Forest

47

133

262

232

Nichols Lake
213

155

141

726

868

734

220

7

729 975

213

320

550

7

213

527

Arkola 52

53

160

208

29 215

173

157

980

221

563

Whiteface R.

967

319

Jenkins Crk.

Continued on page 27

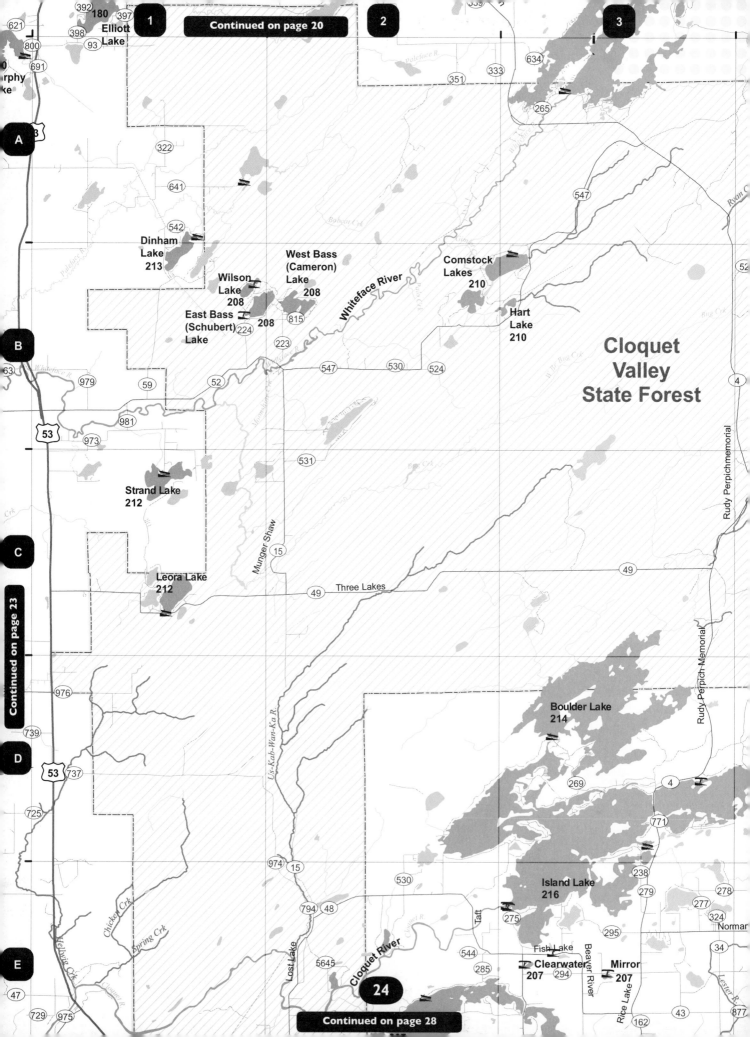

Continued on page 20

Continued on page 23

Continued on page 28

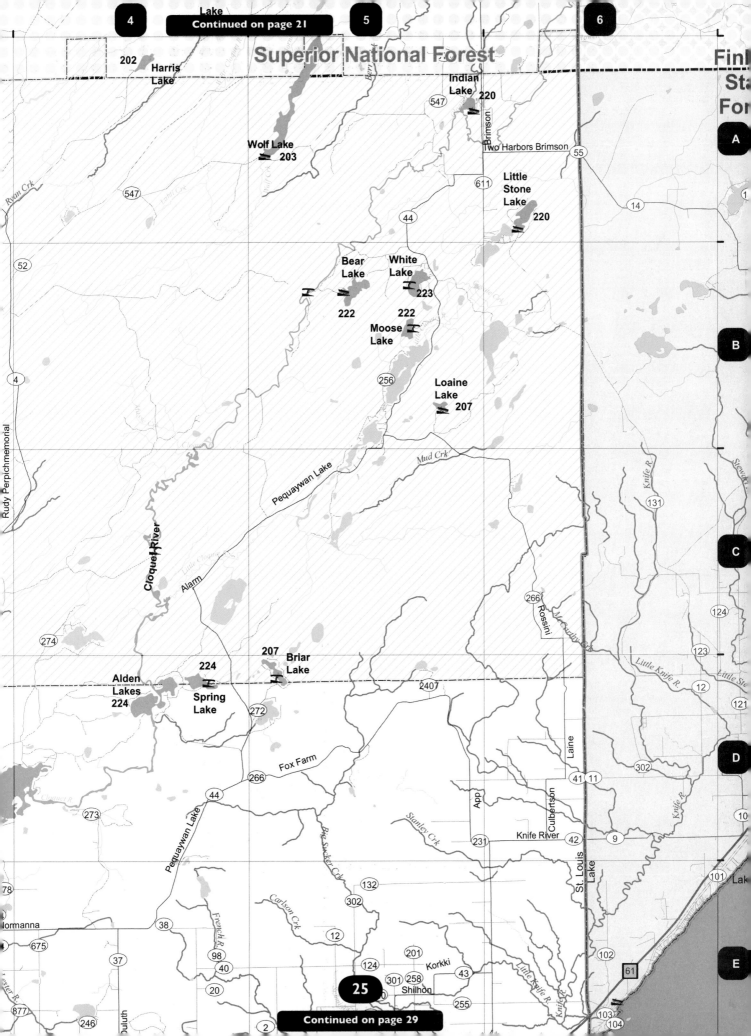

Lake
Continued on page 21

Superior National Forest

Fin
Sta
For

202 Harris
Lake

Indian
Lake 220

A

Brimson

Wolf Lake
203

Two Harbors Brimson 55

547

611

Little
Stone
Lake
220

14

52

44

4

Bear
Lake

White
Lake
223

B

222

222

Moose
Lake

256

Loaine
Lake
207

Rudy Perpichmemorial

Pequaywan Lake

Mud Crk

Knife R.

131

Cloquet River

Little Cloquet

Alarm

C

266 Rossini

McCuddy Crk

124

274

123

Little Knife R.

Little Ste

12

207 Briar
Lake

2407

121

Alden
Lakes
224

224

Spring
Lake

272

Laine

App

Knife R.

D

302

Fox Farm

266

41 11

44

273

Pequaywan Lake

Stanley Crk

Culbertson

Knife River 42

9

231

St. Louis

10

Big Sucker Crk

French R.

Carlson Crk

132

302

101

78

lormanna

38

12

102

61

E

675

37

98

201
Korkki

301 258

43

Little Knife R.

40

124

25

Shilhon

255

Duluth

20

246

2

Continued on page 29

103
104

877

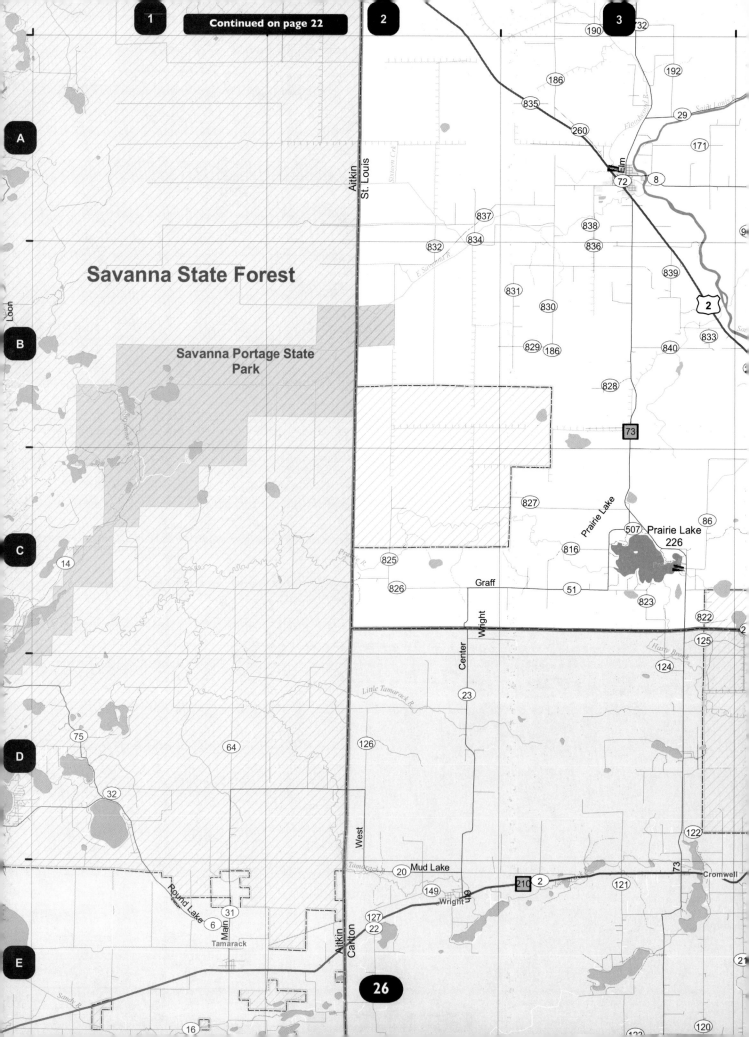

A

B

C

D

E

Savanna State Forest

Savanna Portage State Park

Loon

190
32
192
186
835
260
29
Flowback R.
St. Louis R.
171
Elm
72
8
837
838
832
834
836
E Savanna R.
839
831
830
U.S. 2
833
829
186
840
828
73
Prairie Lake
827
86
507
Prairie Lake
226
816
825
51
Graff
Prairie R.
826
823
Wright
Center
822
125
124
Hay Brook
23
Little Tamarack R.
126
75
64
122
West
32
73
Cromwell
Round Lake
122
20
Mud Lake
121
Tamarack R.
149
210
2
Wright
31
6
127
22
Main
Aitkin
Carlton
Tamarack
16
Sand R.
120
123
21

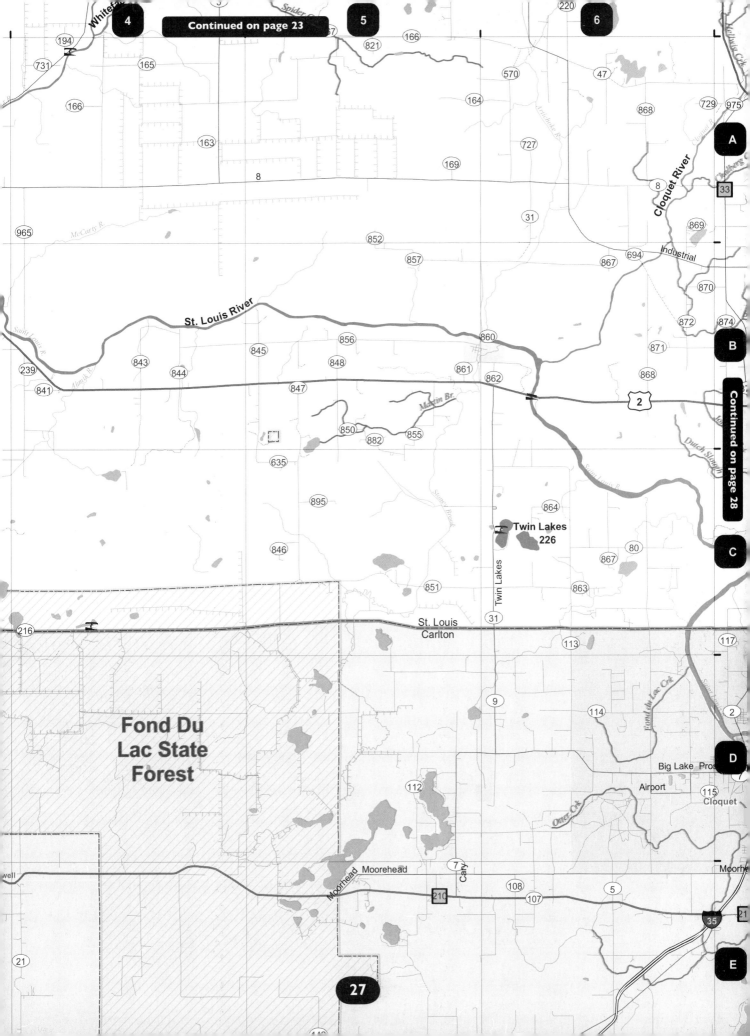

Continued on page 23

194

731

165

166

166

163

8

169

965

McCarty R.

852

857

31

Cloquet River

8

33

A

869

867

694

Industrial

870

St. Louis River

856

872

874

845

848

860

871

B

239

843

844

861

862

868

841

847

US 2

Continued on page 28

Martin Br.

850

882

855

635

895

864

Twin Lakes
226

846

80

867

C

851

Stoney Brook

Twin Lakes

863

216

St. Louis
Carlton

31

113

117

Fond Du
Lac State
Forest

9

114

Fond du Lac Crk.

2

D

Big Lake Pros

Airport

115

Cloquet

112

Otter Crk.

well

Moorhead Moorehead

7

Cary

210

108

107

5

Moor

21

35

21

E

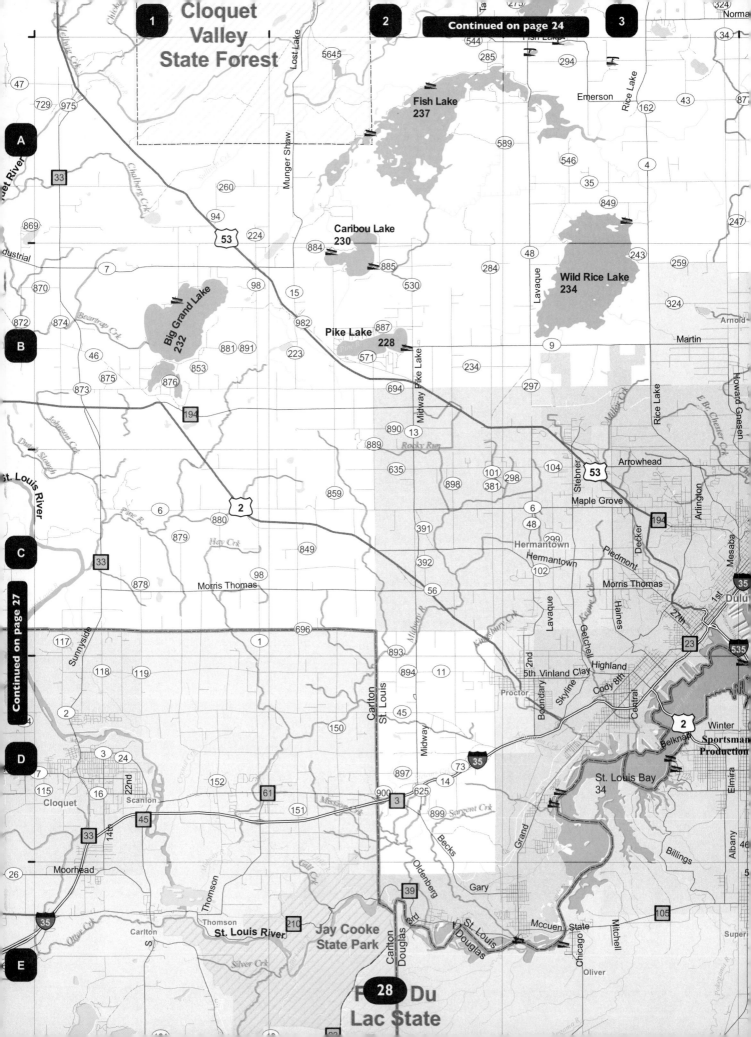

Continued on page 27

A

B

C

D

E

Fish Lake
237

Caribou Lake
230

Wild Rice Lake
234

Big Grand Lake
232

Pike Lake
228

Midway Pike Lake

Rocky Run

Arrowhead

Maple Grove

Hermantown
Hermantown

Morris Thomas

Duluth

St. Louis River

Morris Thomas

Sunnyside

Scanlon

Cloquet

Moorhead

Carlton

Thomson

St. Louis River

Jay Cooke State Park

Proctor

Midway

5th Vinland Clay
Skyline
Boundary
2nd
Lavaque

Highland
Getchell
Haines
Cody 8th
Central

1st
27th

Belknap

Winter

**Sportsman
Production**

St. Louis Bay
34

Elmira

Billings

Albany

Becks

Grand

Gary

Mitchell

McCuen State

Chicago

Oliver

Superi

St. Louis
Douglas
Carlton
Douglas

Oldenberg

28

F̶ Du
Lac State

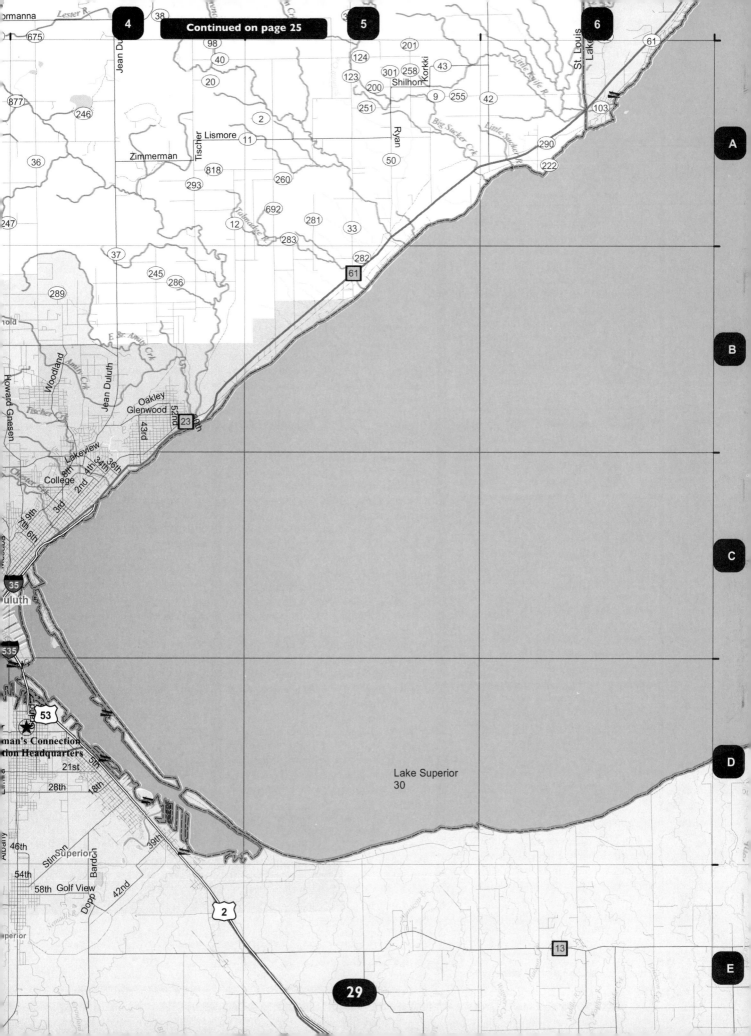

Continued on page 25

A

B

C

D

E

Lake Superior
30

WESTERN LAKE SUPERIOR

FISHING INFORMATION

The largest Great Lake has made a tremendous comeback from the days of taconite tailings and sea lampreys. The lake trout fishery has rebounded, chinook and coho salmon also roam the frigid water. Steelhead and kamloops rainbows make their spring spawning run up the streams. Controversy continues to surround this lake's evolving fishery as anglers complain of fewer salmon and steelhead. Nonetheless, this is a fascinating lake to fish.

Lake Superior is considered to be an oligotrophic lake. Oligotrophic lakes are generally clear, deep and free of weeds. This also results in a lack of nutrients and often smaller populations of fish. However, oligotrophic lakes often develop a food chain capable of sustaining a very desirable fishery of large game fish. Normally the extreme depths restrict a viable fishing resource, but this isn't the case for the western end of Lake Superior. Although for the most part this end of the lake does not have reefs and permanent structure to fish, rocky shorelines provide quality spawning habitat for lake trout. Both chinook and coho salmon also fare well in this environment.

Russ Francisco at Marine General, 1501 London Road, Duluth, MN, 218-724-8833, says each year can be a little different, but says there are general rules of thumb to follow when fishing the big lake. After ice out, the south shore's shallower waters warm first and more lake trout are caught there early in the season. Once the smelt run begins, trout are caught in good numbers along Park Point ("The Beach") and the north shore near Duluth. As water warms, lake trout move back to deeper water and salmon begin to appear along the south shore, usually around late May and early June. As summer progresses and water temperatures continue to rise, salmon will move up the north shore.

Francisco pointed out that in a typical year; anglers begin catching lake trout along the south shore and near Park Point at the beginning of May. As May comes to an end, the north shore near Duluth becomes productive. During July, anglers begin fishing near the Lester River area and, in August, move further up the shore or out to deeper water. Once fall approaches, the pattern reverses.

The baits used on the big lake also follow the season according to Francisco. "It will start with stick baits, mostly metallic colors in blues and purples, then greens and yellows and finally to pinks." This pattern reverses in fall. As temperatures warm, spoons become more productive. "The colder the water, the more silver the fish are. Anglers might be catching fish using silver spoons near Duluth when water warms and fish are more active. Meanwhile, up the shore near Two Harbors, silver Bombers will be more effective."

Winter anglers have good success on the big lake also. As a rule, most lakers are caught in 90- to 150-feet of water. One and a half to 2 ounce jigs tipped with smelt or ciscoes are used here. Francisco said that sucker minnows have also been productive lately. Kamloops rainbows ("loopers") will stage off river mouths during ice fishing season as they prepare for their spring spawning run. Small baits are the rule: 1/32 to 1/64 ounce tipped with wax worms or night crawlers. Crappie minnows have also been effective. Loopers are much easier to fish, since they are typically in 5- to 12-feet of water this time of year.

When ice goes out, anglers will cast similar small baits under a large bobber into the lake for loopers before the spawning run takes place. During autumn, when chinook salmon begin staging near the river mouths, anglers cast spoons and stick baits for them.

According to Captain Steve Johnson at Lake Superior Charter Fishing, Duluth, MN 800-531-3474, www.LakeSuperiorFishing.com, fishing for trout and salmon on Lake Superior can be divided into three separate approaches. "I'd say top water, suspended, and bottom fishing are the three basic techniques," he said. "Top water fishing is primarily a springtime technique. You troll the surface down to about fifteen feet with artificial baits that resemble smelt and herring. Rapalas, Bombers, and Challengers are just a few of the productive baits."

"For suspended fish, you need to switch to Dipsy Divers and downriggers," says Johnson. "Both will get your lures deep, but downriggers are the most precise, and you're able to get deeper with them. When the fish are suspended, we usually switch to spoons."

Bottom fishing is somewhat complicated to fish, but very productive according to Johnson. "Flies or squids, which are attached to flasher or dodgers, are what we usually use," said Johnson. "You can also tip your lures with bait like, smelt, herring, or sucker minnows. Downriggers and wire line are also used."

Most local anglers agree that Lake Superior can be a very difficult body of water to fish. It can be a tough place to consistently hook into your quarry. Johnson explains his beliefs about why this massive lake can be tough to figure out. "The reason for the tough fishing is that the fish-holding structure is continuously changing," said Johnson. "The western end of the lake doesn't have reefs or permanent bottom structure the fish like. Structure is limited to forage base and water temperatures. Water temperature and the forage are always moving, so where you catch fish today may not be where to catch them tomorrow."

Johnson says when fishing top-water; look for a change in surface temperatures. "This is where fish tend to migrate," said Johnson. "Colder water is more dense than warmer water, so you can often see these changes by the color of the water and the amount of sediment in contains. Cold water will be clearer and often calmer than warm water. Once surface water warms, you will need to seek a change in water temperature that is vertical in the water column. This change is called a thermocline. This is when you switch from top water fishing to suspended or bottom fishing."

Johnson says Lake Superior fish like water temperatures in the low forties to low fifties. This of course, isn't written in stone. If there is an opportunity for an easy meal available in warmer or cooler water, salmon and trout will often venture into these areas to feed.

Make sure to try and develop a pattern to efficiently use your time on Lake Superior. "Once you catch your first fish of the day, try to understand why you caught it," said Johnson. "Your boat speed, lure color and style, and depth of the bait are all things to consider. Make sure to note water temperature and clarity. When you catch your second fish, see what factors are common to catching both fish. Now you are on your way to developing a pattern as to what bait to use, how deep to fish it, and what temperature or water clarity to stay in."

Another factor in finding fish on Superior is to pay attention to water currents and wind direction. "Monitoring currents and winds on the lake are key tools to help you decide where you will be fishing," said Johnson. "East winds bring warm surface waters to the western end. Warmer water requires that you need to fish deeper and deeper. Off shore winds, south, north, and west, will blow the surface water away from western Lake Superior and pull the colder water from the bottom to the surface. This now becomes new structure and it takes days for the fish to realize that it exists."

"How the currents move is wind driven. Wherever the depth of the lake is less than average, typically along shorelines, current always follows the direction of the wind. Wherever the depth of the lake is greater than average, the current reverses and travels against the wind. You can visually see this on the lake during an east wind when the discolored water from the south shore is traveling easterly against the wind. Fish holding structures are now on the move with these currents."

Generally the best times to fish Lake Superior are in early spring for coho and small chinook salmon, anywhere from April to the first part of May. Starting around late May into June, walleye fishing can be very good. Lake trout fishing can be good all year, but usually the best bite is from mid-July through September.

Retired Lake Superior charter captain Bob Smith doesn't feel color has tremendous importance when searching for Superior fish. I don't think color makes a lot of difference," he said. "Finding fish can be tough, but don't keep changing lures. If you locate suspended fish, for instance, stick with a lure and change your speed, fast, slow, then zig-zag up and down, until you find what triggers strikes. It's like a smorgasbord. You want to give them a variety. In other words, if you've got 4 downriggers down, and you get a fish on one particular lure, leave the other lines alone. Leave that smorgasbord there. You can start playing with that one lure and that one lure may out-produce everything you've got on the boat. If you start changing all your lines over, you no longer have a smorgasbord. There's nothing to hold their attention. If you can hold their attention, then all you've gotta do is get them to strike. They'll go back and forth from one lure to the other. Every fifteen minutes crank it real fast. That will trigger them. Remember, they're predators. Normally when one minnow takes off, all the minnows take off. If you've got a variety of baits down there and one of them takes off real fast, they'll nail it. Flutter spoons work really well for that. Only use heavier spoons during the warmer part of the year when they start going down a little bit. In spring, I use Rapalas and Bombers and such, right on the very top." Smith suggest using thinner spoons the deeper you're fishing. Many local anglers state that green is the top color for catching salmon and trout from western Lake Superior waters due to its visibility in deeper water.

Smith says you don't have to travel too far to find fish. "If you go off the Superior entry about seven tenths of a mile, just a little off the line on the Minnesota side, there's a hump ("Rock Pile") out there and that's usually pretty good all year for lakers," said Smith. "There are dredgings and stuff out there. I've caught the biggest salmon throughout the year straight out from the Duluth entry up to the Lester River. I think the big boat action has

something to do with it. They churn up the water and the salmon seem to like that. I don't know if they're getting minnows out there or what. In morning or later when it gets a little warmer, fish will be around the Lester River, especially when they're preparing to spawn. Everybody fishes early in morning, but as the water starts to warm up a little and boat traffic gets a little heavier, fish take off. They seem to go down to the bottom and out to deeper water. When they quit biting in shore, move out 3 or 4 miles and fish the bottom and you'll start picking up chinook salmon, right on the bottom with the lakers. I know it's crazy, but that's what they seem to do. You'll want to fish either real early in morning or late in evening. It's feast or famine. I just fish for lakers and if I get a salmon, it's a bonus. If you know the salmon are there, speed up a little bit."

"The Lester and Nemadji Rivers go straight out into Lake Superior," said Smith. "When that water goes out, it has to be replaced, so it brings cold water right down the middle. When the water gets real warm on both edges, go right down the middle and you will catch fish. Most of the time, these fish are suspended. Years ago, in the 1930's to the 60's, when the old coal burners left the Duluth harbor, they'd throw out their cinders. Today, if you bottom bounce between the harbor and Lester River, you'll pull up cinders. Bait fish hang out in that stuff. Lake trout hang tight to the bottom looking for that. You can pull them up and see their red noses where they've been dive bombing on those cinders. Not many people know that those cinders are down there, but they are and there's a lot of them. From the Duluth entry out toward the middle to the 120 foot line, is usually pretty good water. There's no snags in the middle of the lake. From the 120 foot line out deeper, you start running into silt. I believe that's the backwash coming into Duluth and then being pulled back out. From the Lester River, straight across the lake toward Wisconsin, you've got rocks the same contour as the shore. The rock ledge drops all the way down until we get in what we call "the trench." You can feel it on the downrigger. It's just soupy debris that's laying in this trench. Once you get past the trench you start running into sand, gravel and clay, all the way in toward the Wisconsin side. The deepest water is right next to the Duluth side. In addition to the trench, many local anglers will fish near the pump house when salmon and trout move into deep water past the 120 foot mark. This is an excellent area to work the bottom for big summertime fish.

When trolling for trout or salmon, Smith suggests not setting the hook to improve your hookups. "Those hooks are sharp," said Smith. "Next time you get a fish, take the hook out and put it back in just exactly where you took it out, except right along side of it. See how

much pressure it takes, you can do it with the slightest pull using just two fingers. Why set the hook? All you do is pull a piece of meat out. If the hooks are sharp, they'll set themselves. Most of the salmon and other fish are lost, because people are horsing them. If you don't pull on them, they don't pull back. If you play them out and let them swim in, they'll swim right into the net, if it's done properly. Lake trout are the same way. They'll usually come up pretty easy, but when they get into the prop wash, its the same thing as reeling very fast. So when you hit that prop wash, you want to back off a lot."

When fishing flatlines in rough water, Smith suggests not letting out too much line. "Running flat lines can be a real problem in rough water," said Smith. "Some think the farther back you go off a trolling board line, the deeper the plug goes, but that's not so. It works just the opposite. Too much line will pull the plug up to the surface, because it can't pull all that line under. Don't run your lures too far behind the board lines and, in rougher water, run shorter yet. This way, the plug will dive down and the wave won't grab the line and pull the bait up to the top. You can start out with bombers and such on the surface and let them out about 30 ft. If you don't get

Cont'd on page 34

Lake Trout, like this beauty caught by Kurt Martwig of Duluth, are the exception in western Lake Superior, which is essentially a lake trout fishery.

LAKE SUPERIOR SHIPWRECKS

#	Name	Vessel	East	North
1	Thomas Wilson (stern)	steel whaleback freighter	92° 4' 9.41" W	46° 47' 0.67" N
2	Mayflower (bow)	wooden scow	92° 0' 39.78" W	46° 48' 11.70" N
3	A.C. Adams	wooden tugboat	91° 59' 18.06" W	46° 49' 10.92" N
4	Niagra	wooden logging tug	91° 46' 21.47" W	46° 56' 40.74" N
5	S.P. Ely	wooden schooner barge	91° 40' 41.05" W	47° 0' 41.94" N

N

Knife River   Knife River   Knife River   Knife Ri
App
Culbertson
St. Louis   Lake
Homestead
Knife River
Larsmor
133
247
94
375
485
Korkki
Knife River Marina
120   55   259
Shilhon   Shilhon
371
506
Ryan   Ryan
Stoney
Point   7
Lismore
Bromar
Tower
61
65   137   260
42   63   207   433
515
Bluebird
Landing
51   132   199   349   425
French
River
French
River   40   135   219   312   367   395   419   383
McQuade Rd
McQuade
Landing   71   145   258   222   347   351   338
62   147   237   226   298   302   294   292   285
Lakewood Rd
The
Pump   54   154   190   203   251   235   235
Pump
Cribbing   176   The Trench   222   214   208
Lester River   The
Culvert   63
55   Reef off
the Culvert   157   155   175   190   203   215
Arnold   136   142   160   177   182   200
Martin   Martin   137   145   160   164
Brighton Beach   125   130   143   155   176   185
Woodland   Duluth   Oakley   The
Glenwood   Ball   31   58   113   100   117   130   139   147   146   158   163   180   191   The Line
Jean Duluth   Glenwood   52nd   23   80   96   130   127   150   152   160   175
Superior   69   88   100   117   118   124   131   137   142   152   143
The
Apartments   70   81   109   114   119   137   95   154
Chester Creek   35   52   48   82   93   99   107   120   123   134   144   129
79   79   85   91   108   115   127   143   116
194   70   75   77   82   102   115   108   89   95
The
Pocket   29   77   82   91   111   115   104   103
Duluth
Entry   2   34   51   71   77   83   99   107   66   67
Harbor
Cove
Marina   Lakehead Boat
Basin, Inc.   11   64   74   81   84   98   93   81   77   69   66   57   54
535   The Beach   66   75   75   92   60   58
53   57   64   70   73   83   60   60   55   52   45   48   40   33
Winter   Grand   Winter   St Louis
Bay   56   Rock
Pile   56   62   53   67   47   47   49
21st   21st   21st   Barkers
Island
Marina   The
Corner   59   Superior
Entry   14   48   53   50   35   31   36   40   33
28th   28th   18th   13   26
35   Superior   39   41   38   21
2   Kamadji River   Dutchman
Creek
Shore   46th

Source: Minnesota Department of Natural Resources, USGS

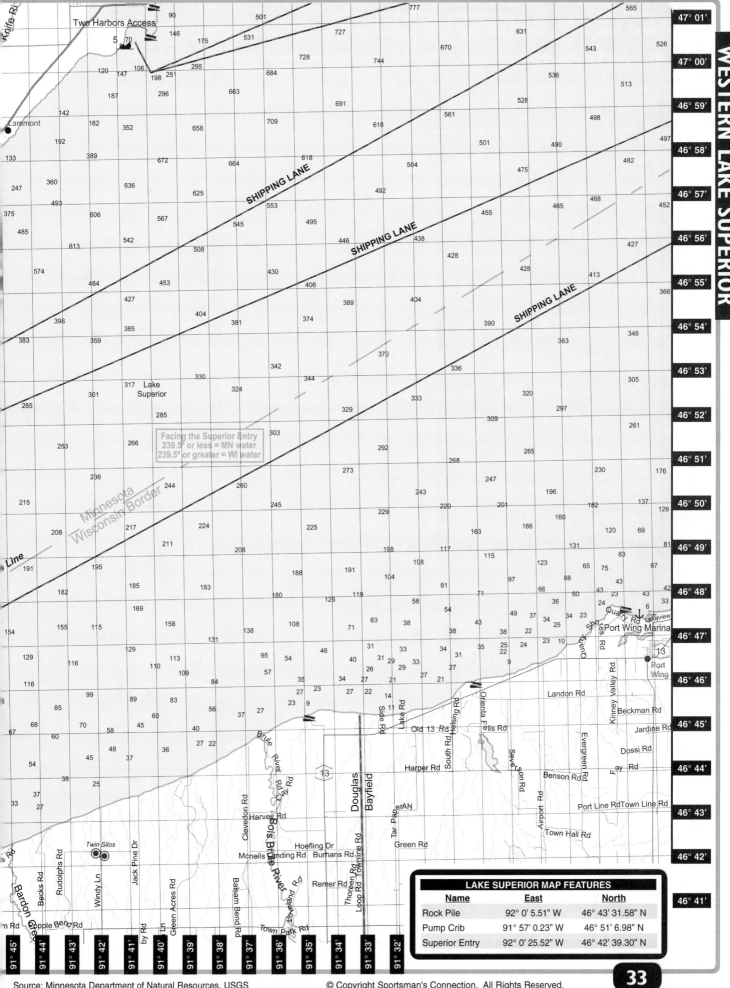

SHIPPING LANE

Facing the Superior Entry
239.5° or less = MN water
239.5° or greater = WI water

Minnesota
Wisconsin Border

Lake Superior

Two Harbors Access

Larsmont

Port Wing Marina
Port Wing

LAKE SUPERIOR MAP FEATURES		
Name	**East**	**North**
Rock Pile	92° 0' 5.51" W	46° 43' 31.58" N
Pump Crib	91° 57' 0.23" W	46° 51' 6.98" N
Superior Entry	92° 0' 25.52" W	46° 42' 39.30" N

33

Source: Minnesota Department of Natural Resources, USGS

WESTERN LAKE SUPERIOR

Cont'd from page 31

something, put out another 10 to 30 feet. Rough water will change your speed something fierce. The only thing you can do is just twist back and forth until you get something going. There'll be days out there when you drop the downrigger down to the bottom and the waves are so bad that your line just goes slack. Once the lines are out there, they shouldn't tangle. When you get a strike, bring a fish in or let lines out; you have to keep the boat straight. That's when most people get into trouble. In rough water, use a little heavier, deeper diving bait. Crocodiles and some other heavier spoons stay down real good. Sliders are super out there. A slider is nothing but a leader that's sewed to your line. When you're bouncing bottom, every time that thing bounces, the line will jerk. Sometimes that'll out-produce everything.

Buglines are definitely worth your time to explore, according to Smith. "Buglines are always good," said Smith. "The buglines or slicks can run for miles. You'll have a little trouble keeping stuff off your line, but go through them. The salmon, especially coho, love it."

Steelhead and loopers aren't on Smith's list of most commonly caught species. "I don't normally get into those, but once in a while you'll catch one," he said. "They're more of a shoreline fish and I believe that's why they were put in. You'll catch more of those when you're casting. If a person has a trolling board and runs right up next to shore, you'll probably have a better chance. Run yellowbirds, those real small trolling boards, almost right up to the shore with a short lead behind them, then run them right back out again so you're changing your depth to get it out. With a small boat, I think you could do really well on them. They seem to like the north shore, but early in the year you can catch them just about any place. Most of those are bug eaters; you have to go to small baits. They'll take bigger ones, but they like the small stuff."

Outriggers or planer boards should be part of your Lake Superior arsenal, according to Smith. "The ones that go way out on the side work real good, but I've had better luck using them with a one pound ball instead of a Dipsy Diver," said Smith. "Use the same kind of hookup you do with a Dipsy Diver, except use a three-way swivel and go 3 feet down from the 3-way swivel to the ball. I do the same thing bouncing bottom with a bottom bouncing rod: 3 feet down and then 3 feet back to the flasher, and then 3 feet from the flasher to the lure. Contrary to what many people think, a boat doesn't necessarily scare the heck out of a fish. I have brought lines in and watched fish come out from underneath my boat and hit a bait. On a real calm day, they get underneath the boat and they'll swim along in the shade. Throw a Dipsy Diver out on the shady side and drop it down until you can just still see it, no deeper. Salmon or trout in front of the boat will see the boat and swim a little off to the side and dive. They'll usually dive below the Dipsy Diver. They don't look down, they see up. So after the boat goes by, here comes the Dipsy. I like to run 7- to 10-feet of line or more behind the Dipsy Diver, so it doesn't spook them."

Smith says line weight choices can very depending on the situation. "I use 17-pound test line because we give it a lot of abuse," he said. "Ordinarily, 12-pound test is fine. Again, most fish are lost because of pulling too hard on them. With 12-pound line, you have the tendency to back off a little. That helps in bringing in a good size fish. If you bring them in faster than a pound a minute, you're going way too fast. If you've got a 25 pound fish on, it's going to take you 25 minutes. You want to play the fish out and have fun with him. If they come out of the water, that's when you're gonna lose them. If you set that drag light and just keep playing them, they'll come in."

If you're a fan of walleye fishing, don't worry, big walleyes live in western Lake Superior. Even though the majority of walleye fishing fans will head to the St. Louis River early in the spring to hook them, the walleye population isn't necessarily resident. According to Dennis Pratt, Wisconsin DNR Western Lake Superior fisheries biologist, the walleyes you'll catch in the western end of Lake Superior are lake fish. "The walleyes are truly lake fish," said Pratt. "Sure, walleyes will move into the river to spawn and forage, but they'll constantly move in and out depending on water temperatures and if forage is available." Some of the most popular fishing locations for walleyes are river mouths. Try the mouths of the Nemadji, Amnicon and occasionally the Brule when they start heading up the South Shore. Although you can drift through the shallows with live bait rigs to hook these fish, the most effective method is to troll. You can zero in on active fish using your electronics and trolling stickbaits, crankbaits and spinner rigs behind planer boards. Experiment with speed and depths until you lock into an active pod of fish. If you find a school of baitfish on your fish finder, the odds are pretty good walleyes or other gamefish will be there waiting to feed.

VISIBILITY OF COLORS UNDER WATER
Clear Water Lake with Slight Algae Bloom

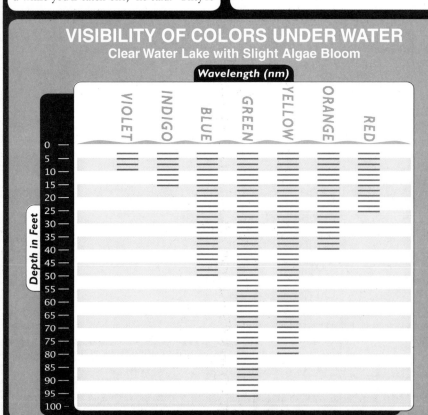

Wavelength (nm)

VIOLET · INDIGO · BLUE · GREEN · YELLOW · ORANGE · RED

Depth in Feet: 0, 5, 10, 15, 20, 25, 30, 35, 40, 45, 50, 55, 60, 65, 70, 75, 80, 85, 90, 95, 100

FISHING INFORMATION

The lower St. Louis River has undergone many changes over the years. From the early settlements around the mid-1800's when commercial fisheries netted tens of thousands of walleyes and speared huge sturgeons from their spawning grounds, through the industrial boom years when raw wastes were routinely discharged into the river, the fishery in this Lake Superior estuary has taken its licks. The latest challenge to fisheries biologists is the invasion of European ruffes and zebra mussels, brought in from the ocean by commercial ships.

Since the development of the Western Lake Superior Sanitary District (WLSSD) when industrial and domestic wastes began to be treated before being discharged, the river has rebounded in dramatic fashion. Water quality has improved and the Minnesota and Wisconsin Departments of Natural Resources have combined their efforts in revitalizing and restoring game fish populations.

The St. Louis River is now home to one of the best walleye fisheries in the state. In addition, good populations of muskies, northern pike, smallmouth bass, crappies and catfish along with some largemouth bass, bluegills and occasional brown trout inhabit these waters, making this a very rewarding place to fish.

The vast majority of the walleyes in the lower St. Louis River migrate from Lake Superior. "The walleye population is actually a Lake Superior migratory fish," Dennis Pratt, Wisconsin DNR's Western Lake Superior fisheries biologist, told us. "Walleyes spend their lives in Lake Superior and use the St. Louis River for spawning and rearing purposes, for a short period of time."

Pratt also stressed that these walleyes are very slow growing due to the fact that they spend most of their lives in Lake Superior's cold water where they only maintain themselves, growing little, if at all. While they find adequate forage in the big lake, this cool water fish requires water temperatures of at least 60 degrees to achieve significant growth. A recent Wisconsin study on tagged spawning walleyes in the Fond du Lac area showed a mean length of a 3 year old male Walleye at 15.2 inches or about 1.2 pounds. This same walleye will typically only reach about 20 inches or 3 pounds when it is 10 years old. A 10 pound female will often be 20 years old or more.

The walleye bag limit is usually set at 2, with a minimum length of 15 inches,

for this border water and western Lake Superior. "Although the bag limits here seem restrictive, they are very much needed to protect the quality of this fishery," Pratt emphasized. "Because we have such a high percentage of people who live along or near the river, if we had less restrictive regulations, the fishery quality would diminish quickly. These fish are very sensitive and slow growing; we have aged some up to 25 years old." This, and the fact that many of these bigger fish may be "hot" from years of absorbing the river system's pollutants, is a strong argument for catch and release of all but the smaller, eating-size fish. Consumption advisories remain in effect for fish caught in the St. Louis River. Check your current angling regulations and consumption advisories carefully. Special license requirements apply for some sections, and exotic species rules and special bag limits apply throughout this system.

It's the spring walleye movement that attracts anglers in droves to the St. Louis. According to Pratt, the peak of spawning usually takes place in the latter part of April, sometimes extending into early May, depending upon the weather. Walleyes will actually ascend the river system underneath the ice prior to this period. Local anglers say the Fond du Lac dam area (p. 38) has so many walleyes that time of the year, you could walk across them and not get your feet wet. The larger females are the first to leave the river following the spawn, so the trophies will often have already made their way to the big lake by the time the season opens.

Most of the spawning occurs in the first mile below the dam. Following the spawn, when the fishing season opens, anglers will crowd boat to boat in the area below Highway 23 and catch and release thousands of these fish as they migrate back toward Lake Superior. It is not unusual for a single angler to hook as many as 50 to 100 walleyes per day during this period. The angler going out to get his two fish limit will hardly have enough time to get his line wet before limiting out.

Understanding the walleyes' migration in this system is key to catching them, as they make their way downstream during late spring through summer. Pratt told us that while many of the mature fish remain in the river system through mid-June, juveniles (not yet of spawning age) enter the system in early May and remain throughout the summer to feed. As June approaches, the ratio of juvenile fish to mature fish

increases. In years when the size structure of the juveniles is greater, angling can remain good late into the summer months. Many believe mature walleyes may be spending more time in the river than in years past due to improved water quality. Walleyes that spend most of their time in Lake Superior are a washed out silver color while a "river walleyes" will be a bright green-gold. Most anglers throw the "yellow bellies" back, as they are less desirable to eat and probably more contaminated.

The lower St. Louis River's fish habitat can be broken down into four basic sections: 1) above Spirit Lake (to Fond du Lac dam) (pp. 38-39); this section is more like a typical river with its faster current and channel, 2) Spirit Lake (p. 40), which is more like a regular lake, 3) the bay area below Spirit Lake (p. 40), which is flanked by industry and doesn't receive as much attention from anglers and, 4) the harbor (from the Blatnik Bridge) (pp. 42-43), which is more influenced by lake water coming in and out of the area and has a sandy bottom.

Walleye migration can best be understood by watching the boats move down the river as the season progresses. If you were to take a time-lapse photo everyday from opener through summer, you could just follow the boats going down the river.

Many local anglers will start fishing during walleye season near the Highway 23 bridge by drifting a crawler harness in chartreuse, orange, green or pink in 8- to 10-feet of water. Use about a 1/4 ounce weight to get the rig down. Many 2- to 4-pound walleyes are caught early in the season. Around the first of June, move down to the area near Boy Scout Landing. Just up from this area is "Walleye Alley" (p. 38), where anglers will congregate to work the walleyes over pretty hard. Be prepared to play bumper boats here through the first few weeks of June. Jigs tipped with minnows are an effective offering for catching walleyes. Beginning in late June through August, head toward the Oliver bridge and into Spirit Lake for walleyes (p. 40). The area between buoys 60 and 63, just up from Spirit Lake, is another spot that is fished heavily during this period. Walleyes also stack up in a 35 foot hole near the southeast bank, just up from the Oliver bridge, in late summer. While you can still get walleyes in September, fishing tends to slow down.

Russ Francisco, at Marine General, 1501 London Road, Duluth, 218-724-8833, echoed much of the information on seasonal walleye movements, adding that the fish seem to stay in the system longer when there is more rain due to increased oxygen levels. He told us that many anglers work Spirit Lake (p. 40) with a nightcrawler under a slip bobber in deeper areas, and the same baits under a corkie in as little as 3- to 5-feet of water during June. He also pointed out that many areas of the river have up to a 4 mph current depending upon water flow, which is dramatically affected when Minnesota Power opens the Fond du Lac dam. Anglers control the speed of their drifts with a water sock or trolling motor.

Many anglers move further downstream for mature walleyes during July and August, working the shipping channels below the old Arrowhead Bridge (p. 41) into the bay and harbor. It can seem pretty strange for the first-time visitor to the area to be fishing in this industrial area with its big ships, but the fish are there. Try trolling Shad-Raps and other deep running crank baits in these areas until you locate schools, reverting to crawler harnesses or jigs and minnows as desired. The anchorage area of the harbor (pp. 42-43), by the Superior Entry, is a standby of many charter boat captains looking for walleyes when the big lake gets too rough. Anglers also work the sand flats found in the harbor along Minnesota Point and moving out into the channel depending upon whether the fish are actively feeding. The areas around the entries, especially Wisconsin's, can also be productive this time of year. Some savvy anglers will chase the big females on their way back to the big lake early in the season at these locations, trolling with planer boards and stickbaits or crankbaits.

A not so well-kept secret is the St. Louis River's rebounding muskie fishery. An indigenous species to the river, this great predator suffered a serious decline during the years when industrial and domestic wastes contaminated their habitat. Minnesota and Wisconsin have joined in helping revitalize this fishery through regular stockings of fingerlings. Combined with improved water quality, the restoration process has resulted in a burgeoning fishery.

Russ Francisco, of Marine General, said that muskie fishing has been hot over the last several years with some in the 30- to 40-pound class being caught, along with the more common 10- to 20-pounders. The presence of the larger fish would suggest that some of the native fish survived the tough years. Muskies can be found in many

of the shallow bays between Highway 23 and Grassy Point (p. 40). Also try timber and rocky shorelines around Boy Scout Landing (p. 39) and Pokegama Bay (p. 40). While crank baits generate some action, the black and dark brown bucktails seem to be the choice of most muskie hunters, according to the folks at Marine General. The pilings found along the old Piers near the Blatnik Bridge (p. 41) area also hold some big muskies.

Tom Jones, Minnesota DNR fisheries specialist, spends most of his river-fishing time chasing muskies. While he has his own "milk run" of favorite spots, there isn't really a particular pattern to locating and hooking these fish. "Some people say look for wood, others say go to the weeds, but it doesn't matter," Jones claims. "It's the same with depth. You catch them in two feet, six feet and in deeper water. Some of the bigger ones seem to be caught when trolling deep water." Jones also believes that baits are more a matter of angler preference than muskie preference. "Bucktails, jerk baits, surface baits, and crank baits all take fish. I catch more muskies on bucktails, but that's because I usually use bucktails."

Jones chases these giants from June through November. While most anglers concentrate on the upper stretches rarely venturing below Grassy Point, Jones believes that these fish are all over the river system. No one seems to fish the industrial areas for muskies, but he is sure that some lunkers are hiding out there. The bays are good, especially before they become too weedy and difficult to fish, but channels are also good. Some anglers begin pursuing muskies after the primary walleye run is over, beginning in July. Many trophy hunters will use bait to hook muskies in fall. The only drawback is the tendency for muskies to be hooked deeply, because they'll often swallow bait. To prevent this, try a quick-strike rig. This ingenious device allows you to set the hook as soon as the muskie starts to take off with your bait.

Northern Pike are also pretty common in the lower St. Louis River. Francisco told us of a time shortly after the river began to clean up when a number of 25-pound-plus pike were brought in by anglers. "I'm sure it hurt the fishery for so many big females to be taken," he said. The Minnesota DNR stocked good numbers of adult northern pike rescued from a winter kill lake in Aitkin County from 1989 to 1993. This was part of a top down predator management strategy employed in an attempt to

reduce the European ruffe population. It isn't clear as to whether this has had, or will have, its desired result. It is evident, however, that the northern pike population has increased which may result in a shift in the overall characteristic of this fishery, according to DNR fisheries specialists. They are quick to add that this system is in a constant state of flux, considering the introduction of exotics and other factors. In fact according the Dennis Pratt, almost 25% of the fish found in this system are non-native. He says DNR biologists from both Wisconsin and Minnesota find a new non-native fish on average of once every two years.

Anglers are reportedly catching larger numbers of pike, but sizes vary. Some say that the overall size structure of pike has suffered since muskie numbers have increased. This is purely speculative, though. Muskie fishermen say that they're seeing some bigger northerns following or taking their lures. Unlike muskies, northerns will seek out much cooler water, so work feeder creeks and cool springs found upstream early in the season. Later, as water warms, move out toward the big lake. Anglers have some success fishing the breakwaters near the Duluth entry, especially during fall, when northerns are laying in colder water. Trophy pike may be the exception in this system, as in most waters. The possibility of catching one is there, and some very respectable fish are often caught in the process.

Smallmouth bass angling is very good. Most smallies are caught above Boy Scout Landing using jigs tipped with twister tails or minnows. "The upper part of the river looks like it could be in Missouri with its submerged trees, stumps and other garbage," Francisco reported. "This is classic smallmouth habitat." The Wisconsin DNR gave the smallmouth population a shot in the arm in the early 1980's with some fingerling stockings. Once the river was cleaned up, this species seems to have thrived. Smallies run larger in this system than a typical river, because there is plenty of food and areas to escape the current below Fond du Lac dam. Anglers often catch these fish by accident and have reportedly hooked them throughout the lower sections of the river as well. With all of the zebra mussels in the system, the water has cleared up considerably over the last few years. This is now allowing aquatic vegetation to grown in deeper water than in years past. This development may help

improve the smallmouth bass fishery even more, along with other species which use weeds as cover and many juvenile fish which use weedbeds as a nursery of sorts.

Black crappies also received a boost from DNR stocking during the 1980's. Populations can fluctuate from year to year, but anglers catch some real slabs. Some of these big crappies are caught off piers and pilings, often accidentally by walleye fishermen, according to Francisco. "Once they catch one, anglers will throw small crank baits at them. Some crappies are big, up to 3 pounds." Francisco told us that nice crappies are also caught shore fishing in the Morgan Park and Gary areas (p. 39) where the old steel and cement plants' pipes enter the river. There are some deep water pockets in these areas that hold crappies. Pokegama Bay and Kimballs Bay (p. 40) on the Wisconsin shore are also popular crappie areas, especially with ice anglers. A minnow-tipped jig seems to be the preferred bait fished through ice.

What is a river without catfish? Most of the larger channel cats hide out in deep channels throughout the river. Drift crawlers or chicken livers for them. These fish are bottom feeders, so check the consumption advisories before eating them.

Early in the year, anglers catch some cohos and lake trout off breakwaters of the Duluth entry and in the harbor by Bayfront Park. Brown trout are also beginning to show up in anglers' creels with more frequency, mainly by accident.

The European ruffe, white perch and zebra mussel have been inadvertently introduced into the lower St. Louis River from international freighters. It is illegal to possess these species, so they must be immediately returned to the river, dead or alive. The purpose of this regulation is to reduce the possibility of these exotics being introduced into other lakes or rivers. Make sure to clean out your livewells when you return from a day on the water. Also, be sure to clean your boat to help prevent the spread of these exotics.

Boy Scout Landing (p. 39), in New Duluth, is one of the best areas to fish the river from shore, according to local experts. The DNR has put in a fishing pier and anglers have caught some very nice fish there. This area is a favorite for walleyes and bass. You can also catch catfish, muskies and northern pike from the landing. Just downstream from Fond du Lac, Perch Lake Park (p. 38) provides some good shore fishing, too. There is a path between the park and another parking area a

few hundred feet downstream where anglers fish rip rap for walleyes and northerns. As mentioned previously, shore anglers in the Gary, New Duluth and Morgan Park areas catch some nice crappies near the old steel and cement plants. You can also do a little exploring along the river where abandoned slip piers are located. Walleyes, northerns, smallmouth and muskies feed and live in the deep water and flats found here. The breakwater at the Duluth entry produces some cohos in spring and northern pike in fall. The area along Bayfront Park (p. 42) is good for northerns in summer, and some walleyes earlier in the year. Anglers also fish from the breakwater by the fishing ramp on Park Point (p. 42) for walleyes and smallmouth bass. If your legs are up to it, hike in from the end of the road at Park Point to the anchorage area of the Superior Harbor Basin for a variety of gamefish including walleyes, northerns and smallmouth bass. An old railroad pier has been converted to a fishing pier underneath the Blatnik Bridge on Rice's Point where walleyes, northerns, muskies and crappies are caught. Fish moving in and out from the bay and harbor must travel through this constricted area, so it's just a matter of getting their attention. The area near the dismantled Arrowhead Bridge (p. 41) outside of Billings Park in Wisconsin has a fishing pier where anglers do pretty well fishing the deep water found nearby. A fishing pier is also available at the Willard Munger ramp between Riverside and Morgan Park but fishing can be spotty here, as it is outside of the main river channel. Wisconsin's Kimballs Bay and Pokegama Bay (p. 40) areas also get some attention from shore fishermen. Spirit Lake (p. 36) is another area to try.

A very interesting development in the St. Louis River is the burgeoning lake sturgeon population. According the Dennis Pratt, both Minnesota and Wisconsin started to stock lake sturgeon into the system in the early 1980's. "We planted lake sturgeon in the St. Louis River from 1983 until 2003," he said. "We planted a variety of fish at different stages of their life cycle to help the population take hold. Now the lake sturgeon are not only present, they're common. You'll find them from the St. Louis River to the western Apostle Islands. Before we started stocking them, we never captured a single sturgeon in samplings."

Before everyone gets their sturgeon gear ready, Pratt says it will be at least another generation before anglers may have catch-and-keep regulations for sturgeon. "It takes about 25 years for a female to become mature enough to spawn," he said. "Then, they'll only spawn once every 4 or 6 years. We haven't seen a spawning female yet. There have been males returning to the spawning areas where we released them ready to spawn, but no females yet. It may be another 25 years or more before we see an actual season for catching and keeping lake sturgeon. The population needs to be able to be self-sustaining before we could ever consider an open season." Right now you need to immediately release any sturgeon you catch.

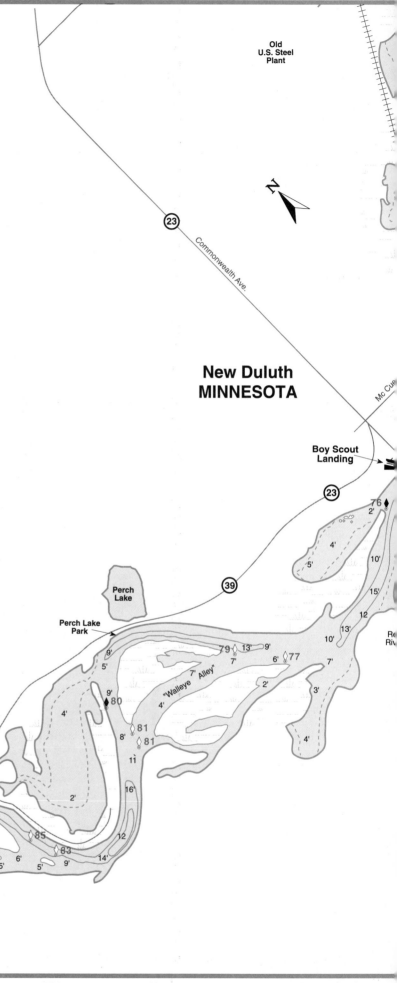

Source: Minnesota Department of Natural Resources, USGS

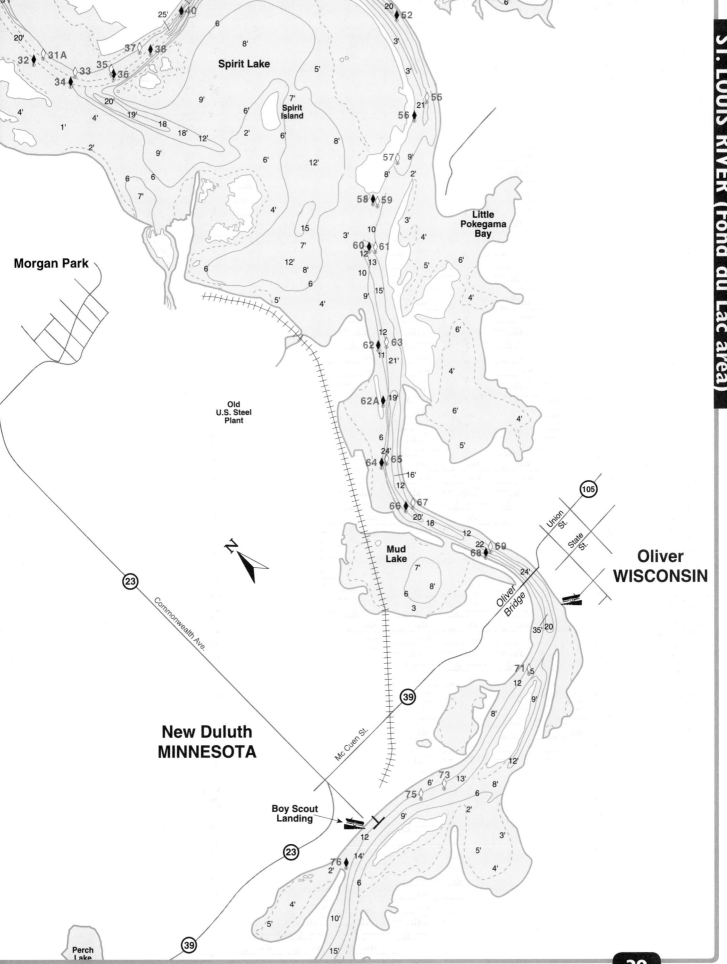

Spirit Lake

Spirit Island

Morgan Park

Little Pokegama Bay

Old U.S. Steel Plant

Mud Lake

Oliver WISCONSIN

Oliver Bridge

Union St.

State St.

New Duluth MINNESOTA

Mc Cuen St.

Commonwealth Ave.

Boy Scout Landing

Perch Lake

Source: Minnesota Department of Natural Resources, USGS

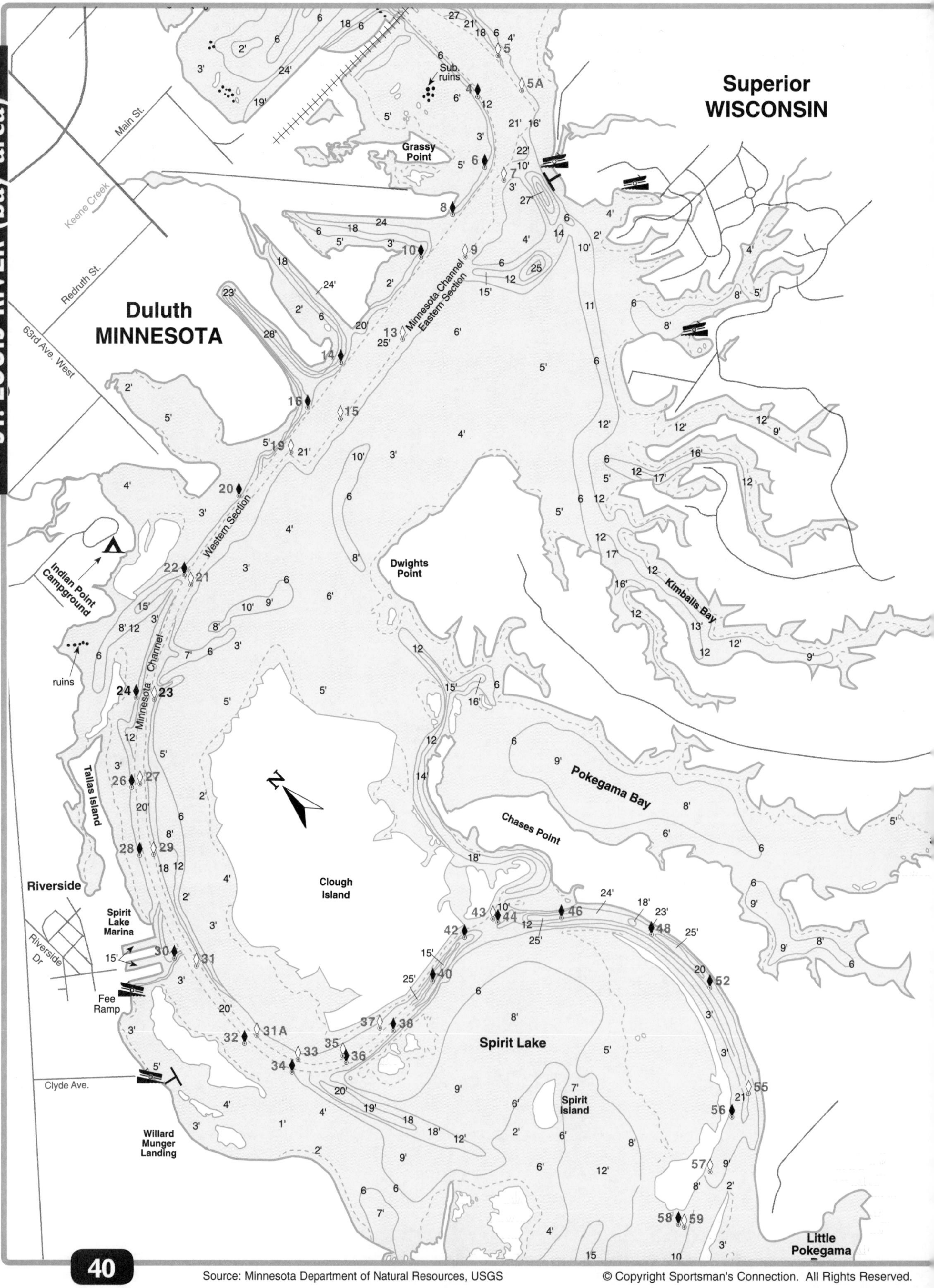

**Superior
WISCONSIN**

**Duluth
MINNESOTA**

Main St.

Keene Creek

Redruth St.

63rd Ave. West

Grassy Point

Sub.
ruins

Minnesota Channel
Eastern Section

Western Section

Minnesota Channel

Dwights
Point

Indian Point
Campground

ruins

Tallas Island

Kimballs Bay

Pokegama Bay

Chases Point

Riverside

Spirit Lake Marina

Riverside Dr

Fee
Ramp

Clough
Island

Spirit Lake

Spirit
Island

Clyde Ave.

Willard
Munger
Landing

Little
Pokegama

Source: Minnesota Department of Natural Resources, USGS

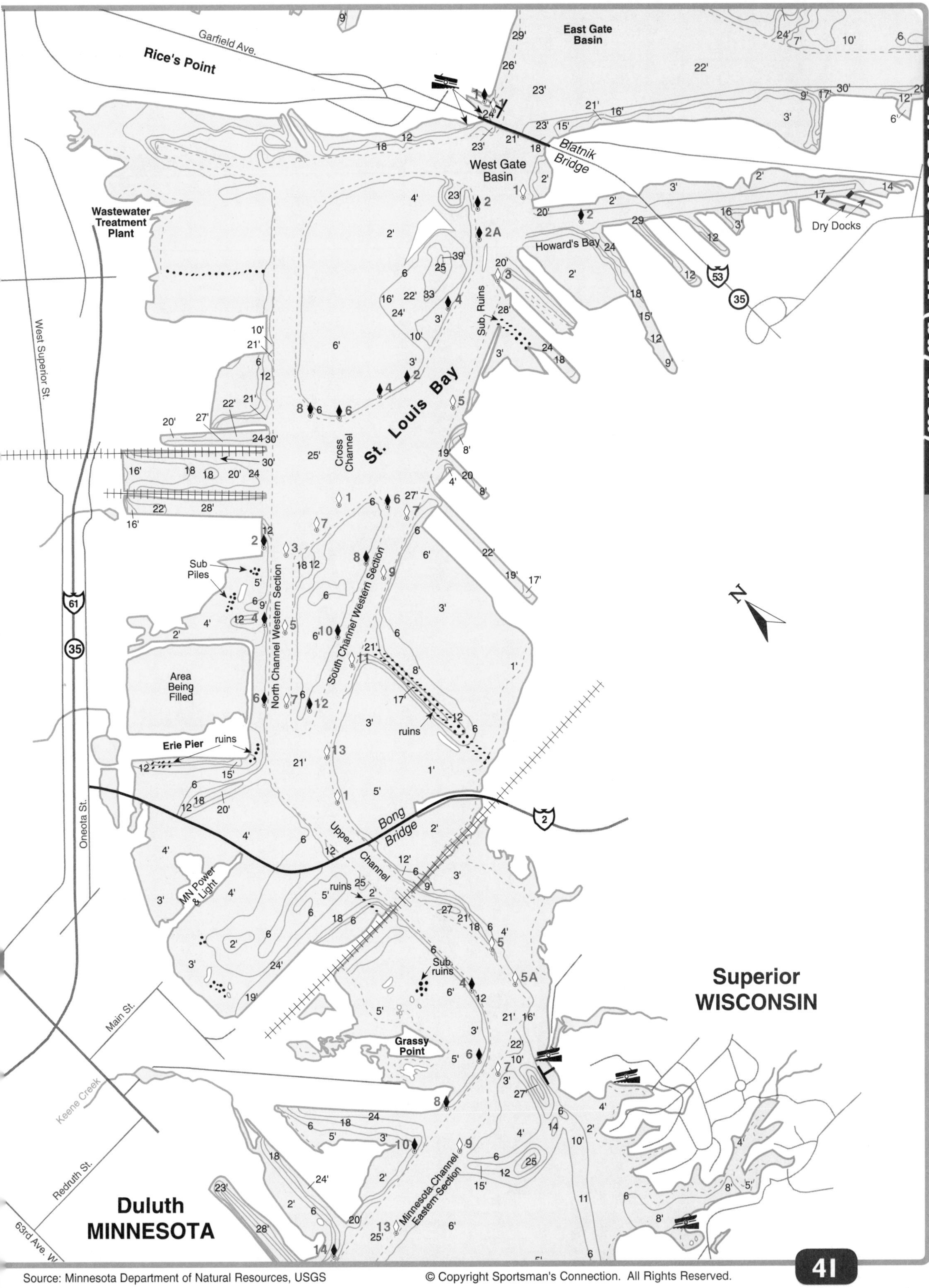

Garfield Ave.

Rice's Point

East Gate Basin

West Gate Basin

Blatnik Bridge

Howard's Bay

Dry Docks

Wastewater Treatment Plant

West Superior St.

Sub. Ruins

St. Louis Bay

Cross Channel

Sub Piles

North Channel Western Section

South Channel Western Section

Area Being Filled

Erie Pier ruins

ruins

Oneota St.

Upper Channel

Bong Bridge

MN Power & Light

Grassy Point

Sub. ruins

Superior WISCONSIN

Keene Creek

Main St.

Redruth St.

63rd Ave. W.

Minnesota Channel Eastern Section

Duluth MINNESOTA

Source: Minnesota Department of Natural Resources, USGS

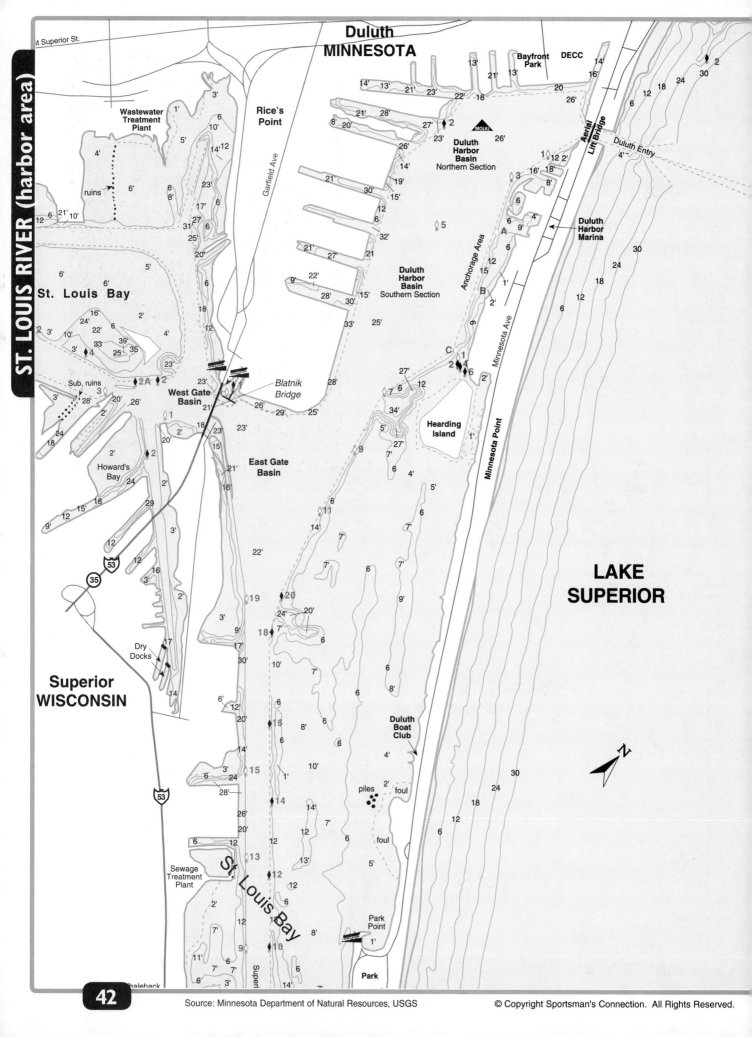

Duluth
MINNESOTA

Bayfront Park

DECC

Rice's Point

Wastewater Treatment Plant

ruins

Garfield Ave

Duluth Harbor Basin
Northern Section

Aerial Lift Bridge

Duluth Entry

Duluth Harbor Marina

St. Louis Bay

Anchorage Area

Duluth Harbor Basin
Southern Section

Sub, ruins

West Gate Basin

Blatnik Bridge

Hearding Island

Minnesota Point

Minnesota Ave

Howard's Bay

East Gate Basin

Superior
WISCONSIN

LAKE SUPERIOR

Dry Docks

Duluth Boat Club

piles

foul

foul

Sewage Treatment Plant

St. Louis Bay

Park Point

Park

Source: Minnesota Department of Natural Resources, USGS

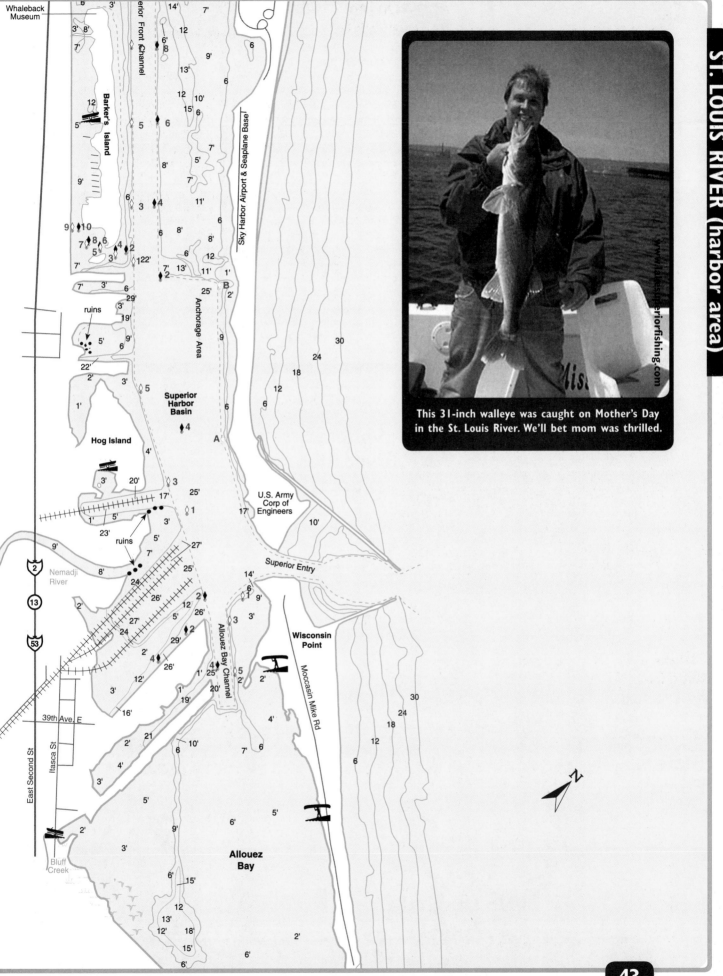

Whaleback
Museum

Barker's Island

erior Front Channel

Sky Harbor Airport & Seaplane Base

ruins

Anchorage Area

Superior Harbor Basin

Hog Island

ruins

Nemadji River

39th Ave. E

Itasca St

East Second St

Bluff Creek

Allouez Bay Channel

U.S. Army Corp of Engineers

Superior Entry

Wisconsin Point

Moccasin Mike Rd

Allouez Bay

This 31-inch walleye was caught on Mother's Day in the St. Louis River. We'll bet mom was thrilled.

www.lakesuperiorfishing.com

N

Source: Minnesota Department of Natural Resources, USGS   © Copyright Sportsman's Connection. All Rights Reserved.

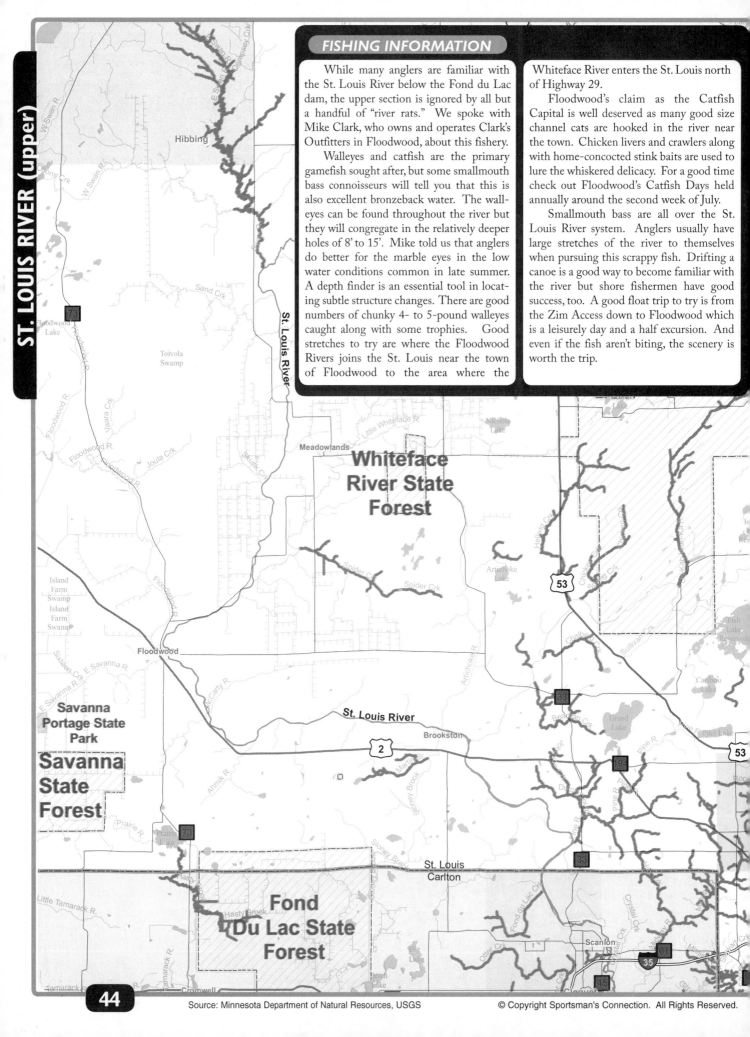

FISHING INFORMATION

While many anglers are familiar with the St. Louis River below the Fond du Lac dam, the upper section is ignored by all but a handful of "river rats." We spoke with Mike Clark, who owns and operates Clark's Outfitters in Floodwood, about this fishery.

Walleyes and catfish are the primary gamefish sought after, but some smallmouth bass connoisseurs will tell you that this is also excellent bronzeback water. The walleyes can be found throughout the river but they will congregate in the relatively deeper holes of 8' to 15'. Mike told us that anglers do better for the marble eyes in the low water conditions common in late summer. A depth finder is an essential tool in locating subtle structure changes. There are good numbers of chunky 4- to 5-pound walleyes caught along with some trophies. Good stretches to try are where the Floodwood Rivers joins the St. Louis near the town of Floodwood to the area where the Whiteface River enters the St. Louis north of Highway 29.

Floodwood's claim as the Catfish Capital is well deserved as many good size channel cats are hooked in the river near the town. Chicken livers and crawlers along with home-concocted stink baits are used to lure the whiskered delicacy. For a good time check out Floodwood's Catfish Days held annually around the second week of July.

Smallmouth bass are all over the St. Louis River system. Anglers usually have large stretches of the river to themselves when pursuing this scrappy fish. Drifting a canoe is a good way to become familiar with the river but shore fishermen have good success, too. A good float trip to try is from the Zim Access down to Floodwood which is a leisurely day and a half excursion. And even if the fish aren't biting, the scenery is worth the trip.

Source: Minnesota Department of Natural Resources, USGS

FISHING INFORMATION

The north shore of Lake Superior is famous for its beauty. The setting is equally spectacular when it comes to angling in and around the streams that flow into the big lake. Steelhead and kamloops rainbow trout ("loopers") make their spawning runs here in spring and chinook and coho salmon spawning runs are in fall. Water runs deep along shorelines where anglers can even reach lake trout.

The spring steelhead run consists mainly of loopers which have been routinely stocked to help provide more catches for anglers. Most streams have some kind of run, but the more popular rivers in the Duluth area include Lester, Sucker, Knife and French and the Stewart near Two Harbors (Lake County). Make sure to check current regulations due to various fishing restrictions in the streams. Most anglers use a stiff fly rod or long spin casting rod to throw yarn flies on a line weighted with a split shot for these fighters. Setting the hook on the snaggy bottom is a common occurrence, so be prepared to re-tie several of these rigs. Anglers also have success floating spawn bags at the mouths of the streams.

Chinook salmon begin staging off the mouths of the streams in late August when anglers have some success fishing for them in Lake Superior. Russ Francisco at Marine General, 1501 London Road, Duluth, MN, 218-724-8833, says that some anglers wait until dark to cast from shore for chinook salmon, which are more actively feeding near the surface at this time (check your regulations for time restrictions near the rivers). After rain creates enough water to flow in the streams, usually in late September, chinook salmon will come in to spawn. Francisco says the overall number for chinook salmon has been down in recent years. "Chinooks are still there, but not in the same numbers in years past," he said. "You can still catch them, just not as many. Chinook salmon, around 18 pounds or so, are the average size fish you'll catch when they make their fall run."

Coho salmon are quite abundant, but according to Francisco they are not nearly as predictable as they were in years past. "There really is no rhyme or reason for what coho salmon do anymore," he said. "They used to be very predictable in their movements. They'd show up after the chinook had made their run. Now you just can't predict when they'll be around. During most winters, fishable ice forms along the shore of Superior, but over the last few years there really hasn't been any good ice. Coho normally have a tendency to group up just under the ice where they are easy to locate and catch. Unfortunately, without good ice, the coho catch seems to be more random and spread throughout the entire year."

Stream Name	Latitude / Longitude Coordinates (river mouth)	miles above boundary	miles below boundary	Trout Species	Shoreline Status
Amity Creek	46.83947 -92.00702	8.4	1.3	B	P,G
Amity Creek, East Br.	46.85588 -92.02923	8.3	0.0	B	P,G
Captain Jacobson Creek	47.01731 -91.79715	3.9	1.0	B,R	P,G
Carlson Creek	46.97174 -91.91775	2.4	0.0	B	P
Chester Creek	46.7972 -92.07963	5.0	0.3	B,Bn	P,G
Chester Creek, E. Br.	46.8191 -92.10964	3.7	0.0	B	P
French River	46.89925 -91.89226	18.4	2.4	B,Bn,R,C	P,G,SE
Hartley Creek	46.81423 -92.05158	2.3	0.0	B,Bn	P
Keene Creek	46.72542 -92.16265	6.8	0.0	B,Bn	P
Kingsbury Creek	46.72342 -92.18634	5.4	0.0	B	P
Knife River, Little	46.94501 -91.809	0.0	7.3	B,Bn,R	P,G
Lester River	46.83616 -92.00586	30.1	4.6	B,Bn,R,C	P,G,SE
Midway River	46.68899 -92.37642	22.9	0.0	B,Bn	P,G
Miller Creek	46.76413 -92.13291	9.7	0.0	B,Bn,R	P,G
Mission Creek	46.65884 -92.2762	4.1	0.0	B	P
Rocky Run Creek	46.80672 -92.26121	7.9	0.0	B	P
Ross Creek	47.02084 -91.94039	4.9	0.0	B	P,G
Sargent Creek	46.65358 -92.22693	5.3	0.0	B,Bn	P,G
Schmidt Creek	46.90177 -91.88792	5.8	1.0	B,Bn,R	P
Stewart Creek	46.68793 -92.29086	3.1	0.0	B	P
Sucker River	46.92188 -91.84773	11.1	7.0	B,Bn,R	P,G,SE
Talmadge Creek	46.88334 -91.91409	5.6	0.5	B,Bn	P,G
Tischer Creek	46.81423 -92.05158	3.5	0.1	B,Bn	P

ST. LOUIS COUNTY TROUT STREAMS

KEY: **B** = Brook Trout / **Bn** = Brown Trout / **R** = Rainbow Trout / **C** = Chinook Salmon

P = Private land / **G** = Government land (state, federal, county) /
SE = Private lands with landowners having granted angling easement

Fishing for salmon or trout from shore is pretty basic according to Francisco. You'll only need a couple of baits and a handful of spoons. "There are really two baits of choice to fish for anything along the shoreline near the mouths of a stream," says Francisco. "You'll either want to float a wax worm under a bobber or fish nightcrawlers off the bottom. These will produce throughout the year." Francisco also suggests fishing with spoons during late fall and early spring. "One of the most common ways anglers

fish around here is to have one rod rigged with bait and use another rod to cast a spoon. To do this, you must be at least 1,000 feet away from the mouth of a river, but it can really be very productive."

Above the first barriers, brook, rainbow and brown trout inhabit many of the streams that flow into Lake Superior. Francisco says the most abundant trout specie you'll find is brook trout. See the charts on these pages for species and shoreline status of these streams.

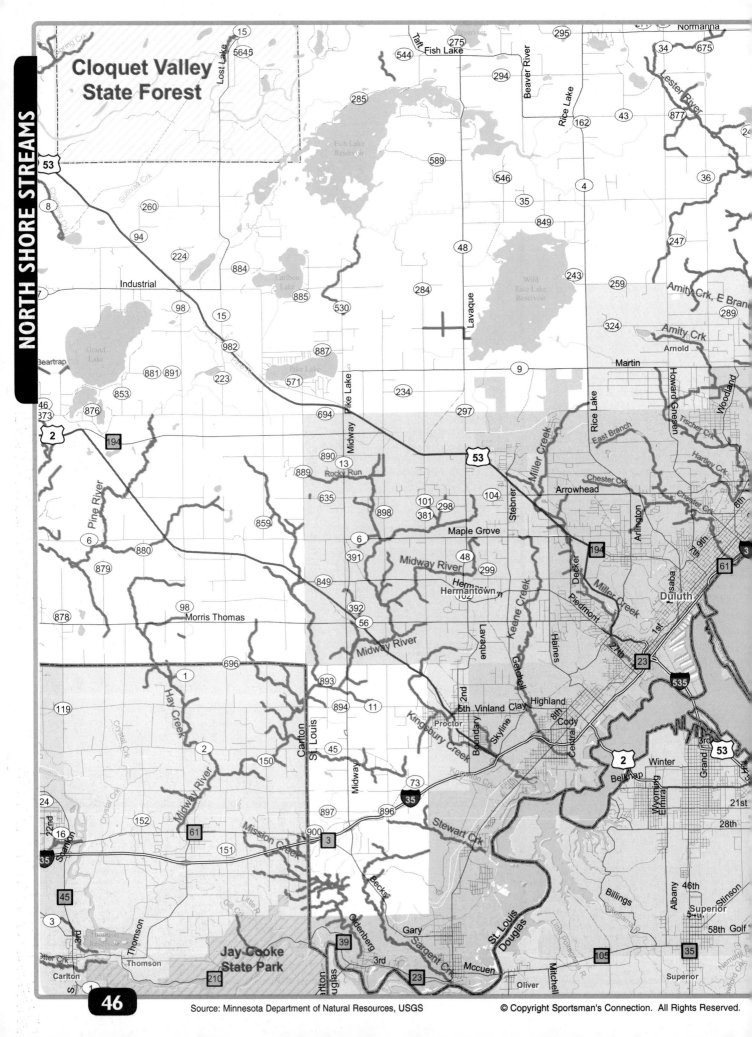

Cloquet Valley
State Forest

Source: Minnesota Department of Natural Resources, USGS

Cloquet Valley State Forest

Pequaywan Lake

256

Little Cloquet

44

Alarm

Heuna Lake

272

Fox Farm 266

273

44

Normanna 38

French River

98

40

20

246

43

Zimmerman

818

293

Lismore 11

Lester River

12

692

283

Talmadge River

282

37 259

245 286

89 Arnold

Martin

Amity Crk, E Branch

Jean Duluth

Amity Crk

Lester River

Glenwood Oakley

43rd

Duluth

Lakeview

2407

Stanley Crk

231

App

Sucker River

132

302

Little Knife River

201

124

301 258

123

200

251

2

260

281

33

50

Ryan

French River

61

Schmidt Crk

Korkki

43

Shilhon

255

Homestead

Sucker River

Little Sucker River

290

222

Knife River, West Branch

Rossini

266 267

McCarthy Crk

Laine

Knife River, West Branch

Culbertson

41 11

42

9

St. Louis Lake

Stanley Crk

Knife River

101

102

103

131 Knife River

132

124

123

Little Stewart River

12

121

Little Knife River

302

122

Knife River

10

Stewart River

LAKE SUPERIOR

Springtime brings trout (and trout fisherman) to the mouths of the North Shore rivers.

www.lakesuperiorfishing.com

47

FISHING INFORMATION

When the fishing action on the lakes and reservoirs slows down or if you want to get a break from the crowds or wind, try floating the Cloquet River for a different angling experience. Smallmouth bass, walleyes, northern pike, brown trout, brook trout and channel catfish can be caught in various sections of the river.

The upper Cloquet is defined as that area above Island Lake Reservoir and the lower Cloquet is the stretch below Island Lake to the St. Louis River. According to the Department of Natural Resources (DNR), most of the fish found in the upper section are walleyes and northerns, but some smallmouth are also present, and brook trout can be found in the far upper reaches and cold-water tributaries. The lower section, according to the DNR, is home to smallmouth bass, walleyes, northerns, channel catfish and some brown trout.

The upper Cloquet winds through wild country with undeveloped shoreline except for that of Alden and Island Lakes. The scenery is relaxing and the wildlife is abundant. The map shows the river's rapids which are categorized as Class I ("easy rapids with small waves and few obstructions") and Class II ("rapids with waves up to three feet high. Some maneuvering is required".) The area just above Island Lake includes some Class II - III rapids which most canoeists portage

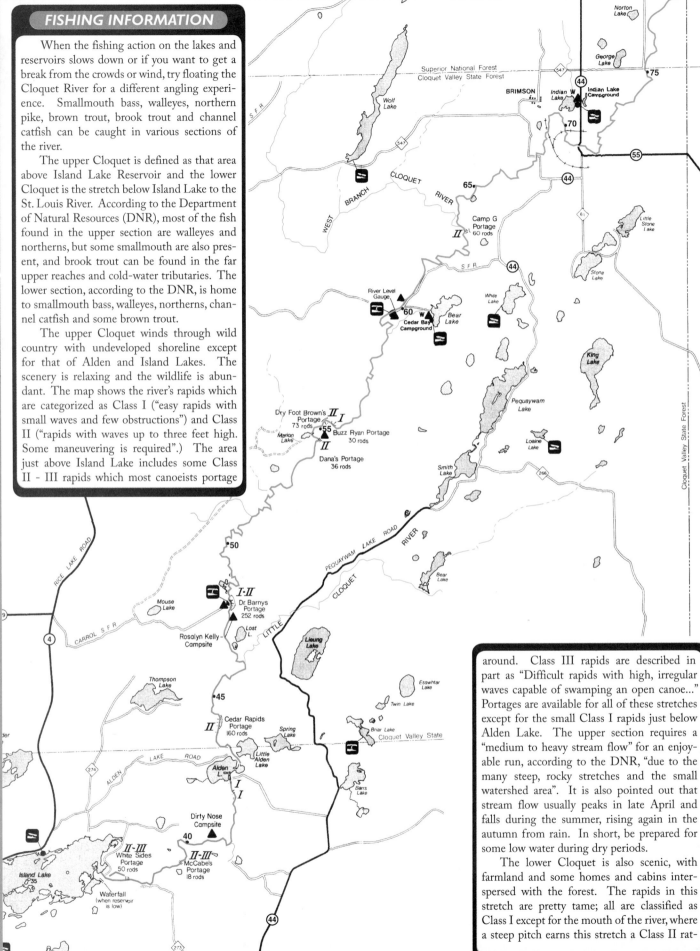

around. Class III rapids are described in part as "Difficult rapids with high, irregular waves capable of swamping an open canoe..." Portages are available for all of these stretches except for the small Class I rapids just below Alden Lake. The upper section requires a "medium to heavy stream flow" for an enjoyable run, according to the DNR, "due to the many steep, rocky stretches and the small watershed area". It is also pointed out that stream flow usually peaks in late April and falls during the summer, rising again in the autumn from rain. In short, be prepared for some low water during dry periods.

The lower Cloquet is also scenic, with farmland and some homes and cabins interspersed with the forest. The rapids in this stretch are pretty tame; all are classified as Class I except for the mouth of the river, where a steep pitch earns this stretch a Class II rat-

Source: Minnesota Department of Natural Resources, USGS

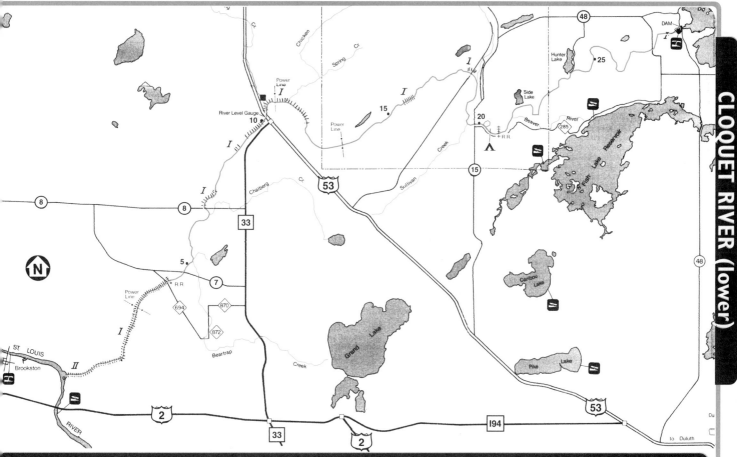

ing. The lower river is generally much wider and slower than the upper river and water levels can vary significantly depending upon releases from Minnesota Power's Island Lake Reservoir dam.

We spoke with Scott VanValkenburg, owner and operator of Fisherman's Corner in Pike Lake north of Duluth, about this oft-overlooked fishery. Smallmouth bass provide much of the action and the area just above Island Lake is one good spot to try for the bronzebacks which average about a pound along with some 3-pound class fish. Try floating leeches or crawlers in the pools below rapids or use a jig and minnow but be prepared for snags. Small Mepps-type spinner lures also work. Scott said that it seems that the smallies run a little bigger in the upper river. Both the upper and lower reaches provide some decent walleye fishing. Fish for them much the same way as you do for smallmouth by working the pools just below the rapids. The lower river has more flat water so look for the faster moving water found in the smaller channels for both walleyes and smallmouth bass. Work your bait near structure that breaks the current; this is where the game fish will lurk for forage drifting downstream.

Trout, both browns and brookies, are scattered throughout the river, according to Scott, with greater numbers of them hooked in the lower river, while the upper river seems to produce larger fish, generally. Scott said that 1 to 1-1/2 pound "specs" and 2 pound browns are typical. A 3-pound brookie can be caught but "you'll have to work for them." Both species of trout prefer colder water which can be found near feeder creeks and springs as well as below rapids in deeper pools. Mepps and Panther spinners produce as do worms and night crawlers. Use a worm blower to inflate a night crawler placed on a plain hook attached to a light line with a small split shot and drift the pools for brown trout. Remember, browns are very easily spooked so keep a low profile and don't bang around in the canoe.

The best time of the year for trout on the Cloquet tends to be early and late in the season when the water is cold. Later in the summer fly fishermen have some success by monitoring the Mayfly hatch. Timing is everything then. Scott told us that there seems to be two hatches: one of small Mayflies and another of the larger ones. While some trout are caught on flies during the hatch of small Mayflies, it's when the large Mayflies hatch that fishing heats up. Cast your Mayfly imitation lure or anything remotely resembling a Mayfly for that matter, in an area where you see trout rising and prepare for some heart-stopping action.

Channel catfish don't receive as much attention in the Northland as other game fish, and the whiskered fish isn't the prettiest sight, but they make great table fare. Catfish are a delicacy in many parts of the country and those caught from clean water are very tasty indeed. The lower Cloquet harbors a pretty good population of cats which can be found in some of the same fish-holding areas below the faster moving water in pools. Rock or gravel bottoms, anywhere where you see rippling water, will attract catfish. Bridge pilings also hold these fish. Depth isn't an issue with cats except during bright light conditions when they move deeper to avoid the light. Your standard catfish baits work here: stink baits, night crawlers, gobs of worms or minnows. catfish seek out prey by smell more so than by sight, but live bait also works. Chicken liver, dead shad or smelt lead the list of stink baits, but serious catfishermen will develop their own stink bait recipe. Get your bait near the bottom. A typical Cloquet River catfish is around 3 pounds and a 6 pounder is considered large. There are some bigger ones but this isn't trophy catfish water.

The slower water of the wider sections of the Cloquet holds some northern pike but most are of the "hammer handle" variety. There are some big ones however, and they are basically ignored by most river anglers. The key is to cover as much water as possible by casting spoons, spinner baits and crank baits while drifting these slow sections.

Take a break from the "same ol', same ol'" of lake fishing and give the Cloquet a try. As experienced river anglers know, river fish seem to be bothered less by the unstable weather patterns and "dog day" doldrums that their lake cousins use as excuses for developing lock jaw.

Source: Minnesota Department of Natural Resources, USGS

RAINY LAKE *St. Louis County*

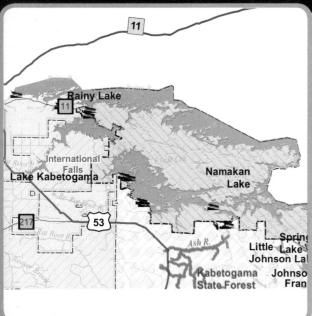

Area map page / coordinates:	8 ,9 / A,B-1,2,3,4,5
Watershed:	Rainy Lake
Surface water area / shorelength:	220,800 acres / 88.8 miles
Maximum / mean depth:	161 feet / NA
Water color / clarity:	9.2 feet (2010)
Shoreland zoning classification:	General development
Management class / Ecological type:	Centrarchid / centrarchid
Accessibility:	Refer to access table on facing page
Accommodations:	Resorts, marinas, boat rental, camping, picnicking

NO RECORD OF STOCKING

NET CATCH DATA

Date: 04/01/2010	Gill Nets		Trap Nets	
species	# per net	avg. fish weight (lbs.)	# per net	avg. fish weight (lbs.)
Black Crappie	0.29	0.56	2.10	0.93
Northern Pike	1.79	3.95	3.35	2.22
Rock Bass	0.71	0.30	-	-
Sauger	1.67	0.31	0.10	0.93
Smallmouth Bass	0.46	1.06	-	-
Walleye	6.12	1.41	3.20	3.57
White Sucker	1.54	1.64	1.70	2.78
Yellow Perch	6.29	0.32	3.05	0.15

LENGTH OF SELECTED SPECIES SAMPLED FROM ALL GEAR

Number of fish caught for the following length categories (inches):

species	0-5	6-8	9-11	12-14	15-19	20-24	25-29	>30	Total
Black Crappie	1	6	28	14	-	-	-	-	49
Burbot	-	-	1	1	-	-	-	-	2
Lake Whitefish	-	-	5	3	4	1	-	-	13
Northern Pike	-	-	11	6	26	38	16	13	110
Pumpkin. Sunfish	1	-	-	-	-	-	-	-	1
Rock Bass	1	16	-	-	-	-	-	-	17
Sauger	-	16	18	6	2	-	-	-	42
Smallmouth Bass	-	1	5	3	2	-	-	-	11
Tullibee (Cisco)	-	16	20	70	34	-	-	-	140
Walleye	2	13	38	45	41	64	8	-	211
White Sucker	-	8	1	7	41	14	-	-	71
Yellow Perch	30	130	50	2	-	-	-	-	212

FISHING INFORMATION

If you're looking for a place to get away from it all and fish your heart out, Rainy Lake should be at or near the top of your list of places to try.

There may be lakes in Minnesota which offer as good, or perhaps even better, fishing, but Rainy Lake is top-notch, regardless of comparison.

Rainy Lake covers just over 220,000 acres, 83,000 acres are within Minnesota, and 350 square miles puts it very near the top of the size chart. It's larger than Red Lake, Leech Lake, and Vermilion combined. It's almost big enough to include Winnibigoshish in that group, as well. Make no mistake, the lake is simply huge. It's 60 miles long and 12 miles wide.

If you want isolation, you've got that on Rainy. Rainy's south shoreline is developed from Ranier eastward to Black bay, a distance of some 11 miles, but at Dove Island in the middle of Black Bay Narrows, the development ends. So do the roads. There's a 30-mile stretch of wilderness eastward to the next habitation at Kettle Falls where, incidentally, you can portage into other wilderness lakes. Altogether, the lake encompasses some 2,500 miles of shoreline, and it's dotted with roughly 1,600 islands, lots of them amenable to camping. So, if getting away from your daily grind is truly a goal, Rainy Lake really is a good place to do it. If you can't get away by yourself in this lake's myriad islands, coves, bays and broad reaches, you just aren't trying.

On the other hand, if you like a little company, you can find that, too. The 11-odd miles of southern shoreline from Ranier to Black Bay Narrows are dotted with numerous resorts, private campgrounds and a couple of houseboat rental firms. Ranier and International Falls are nearby, and they offer theaters, golf, museums, and other amenities to occupy your time when you're not doing something water-oriented. Then there's Voyageur's National Park, a wilderness preserve of nearly 218,000 acres. The park includes Rainy Lake's south shore, east of its visitor center on Black Bay and offers interpretive services, parking, camping, etc. for the entire area.

If you like diverse choices in planning a fishing vacation, you can find those on Rainy Lake. Basically, there are a couple of ways to go: expensive or cheap. If you want an inexpensive week on the lake, you can put in a canoe at one of the launch sites and camp free for your entire stay at several Voyageurs National Park campsites. Your only costs will be for transportation to the area and groceries. On the other hand, you can rent a houseboat or stay at one of the American plan resorts and pay as much as you'd like. The various lodges offer plenty of accommodations and amenities. Add the cost of boat rental and guide service and you can run up quite a bill. The choice is up to you.

Rainy Lake is known far and wide for its walleye fishing. It offers good angling, as well, for northern pike, smallmouth bass and crappies. There are even a few muskies, though most of the muskie action is up in Bleak Bay, well within Canadian waters. There is, to be sure, no muskie action on the U.S. side of the International Boundary.

Jerry Snyker, owner of The Fisherman, 100 Memorial Drive, International Falls, MN, 218-283-9440, says Rainy's walleye population is benefiting from voluntary angler catch-and-release. As a result, average size has improved. There was a time when 2 1/2- to 3-pound fish were about average. Average size actually dropped below a pound several years back, but it's been on the increase since 1995. Says Snyker, average size is back to 1 1/2 to 1 3/4 pounds. Numbers of good-size fish have been rising every year. This is in part because area resort owners and guides have been actively promoting catch-and-release. Fish over 10 pounds aren't all that uncommon, and fish up to 17 pounds have been caught. Some expect the

Cont'd on page 62

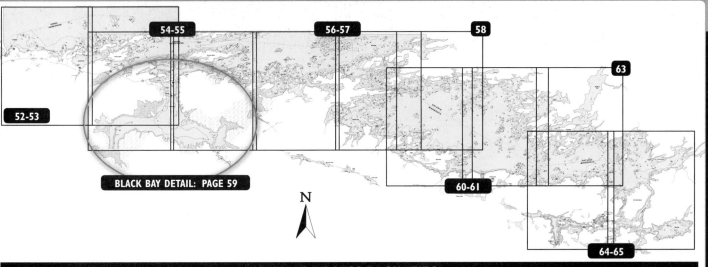

BLACK BAY DETAIL: PAGE 59

N

PUBLIC ACCESS FACILITIES

#	Site Admin	Ramp	pg #	Lat / Long	Access Description
1.	State	Concrete	52	48° 37' 2.83" N / 93° 20' 40.43" W	In the town of Ranier, north of CR-20
2.	State	Concrete	52	48° 36' 14.08" N / 93° 16' 26.71" W	On the southwest shore of Jackfish Bay, north of Hwy. 11E on Township Road 493
3.	State	Concrete	53	48° 35' 56.80" N / 93° 14' 0.59" W	On the west shore of Tilson Bay, north of Hwy. 11 on CR 136
4.	State	Concrete	53	48° 35' 35.95" N / 93° 9' 33.01" W	On Dove Island, east of Krause Bay; east on Hwy. 11
5.	National Park Service	Concrete	53	48° 35' 4.09" N / 93° 9' 40.84" W	At the Rainy Lake Visitors Center on the west shore of the Black Bay Narrows; east on Hwy. 11, south on Park Road to Township Road 342

AREA NAMES REFERENCE

pg #	Area Name	pg #	Area Name	pg #	Area Name	pg #	Area Name
53-54	Aeroplane Island	63-64	Dry Island, Little	60	Kawawia Island	52	Ranier
56	Alder Creek	55	Drywood Island	60	Kempton Bay	63	Rat River
55	American Island, Big	57	Duckfoot Island	60	Kempton Channel	63	Rat River Bay
53-54	American Island, Little	55	Dyweed Island	65	Kettle Channel	53-54	Red Pine Islands
53-54	American Narrows	53	Eight Mile Island	64	Kettle Falls	53-54	Red Sucker Islands
58,60	Anchor Islands	52	Elks Bay	65	Kettle Falls Dam	53-54	Review Islands
61	Anderson Bay	58,60	Emerald Islands	65	Knox Bay	52	Roberts Island
53,55	Angling Island	52	Enos Islands	53-54	Krause Bay	63-64	Sand Bay Island
56	Arden Island	61	Finger Bay	63-64	Lindoo Island	55	Sand Point
53-54	Bald Rock Point	57	Finlander Bay	56	Lost Bay	55	Sand Point Island
53-54	Beaver Island	57	Finlander Island	60	Lyman Island	56	Seven Sisters Islands
57,60	Big Island (by Kempton Channel)	57	Finlander Island, Little	57	MacKenzie Island	58,60	Shetland Island
63	Big Island (by Rat River Bay)	63-64	Fish Camp Island	57	Marion Bay	55	Shortys Reef
52	Birch Point	61	Fishmouth Lake	65	MacKenzie Point	63-64	Smith Island
65	Birch Point	57	Fox Island	64	Mica Island	64	Snake Island
54-55	Black Bay (detail pg. 8)	53-54	Frank Bay	61,64	Minnitaki Island	57,60	Soldier Point
53,55	Black Bay Narrows	57,60	Frank Island	61	Moose Bay	55	Springers Point
63-64	Blackpoint Island	53-54	Fransen Island	64	Namakan Narrows	65	Squirrel Falls Dam
57	Bleak Bay	53,55	Fraser Island	53-54	Neil Point	64	Squirrel Island
60	Blueberry Island	63	Friendly Passage	57,60	Nelson Island	64	Squirrel Narrows
65	Breezy Island	57,60	Gaylord Point	57,60	Norway Island	56	Steamboat Island
61	Browns Bay	53-54	Grassy Island	65	Oak Point Island	53-54	Steeprock Island
57,60	Brule Island	53-54	Grassy Narrows	52	Ogard Point	60	Stoffels Point
55	Bushyhead Island	61,64	Green Island	56	Olson Bay	65	Stokes Bay
65	Canadian Channel	53-54	Grindstone Island	56	Olsons Reef	53-54	Stop Island
55	Capstan Rock	61	Gull Rocks	63	Oscar Island	56	Stubs Shoal
57	Channel Island	61	Gunsight Island	57,60	Pater Noster Island	55	Sunrise Point
63	Cormorant Bay	65	Hale Bay	57	Payson Island	53-54	Susan Island
56	Cranberry Bay	57,58	Hallelujah Point	61	Peary Lake	55	Tango Bay
56	Cranberry Creek	56	Harbor Island	55	Perry Point	65	Three Sister Islands
56	Cranberry Island	55	Harrison Bay	58,60	Pine Islands	57,60	Three Sisters Island
56	Diamond Island	52	High Rock Point	53-54	Pine Narrows	53-54	Tilson Bay
55	Dove Bay	57,60	Hitchcock Bay	65	Pothole Island	63-64	Vague Point
53	Dove Island	53-54	Hvosief Island	65	Pound Net Bay	63-64	Virgin Island South
55	Dove Point	60	Idle Hour Islands	55	Powder Island	61	Willow Bay
63-64	Dry Island, Big	52	Jackfish Bay	53-54	Prues Island	61	Windmill Rock
		53-54	Jackfish Island	63-64	Rabbit Island		
		53-54	Jackpine Island	53-54	Rainy Lake Visitors Center		
		58,60	Junior Island				

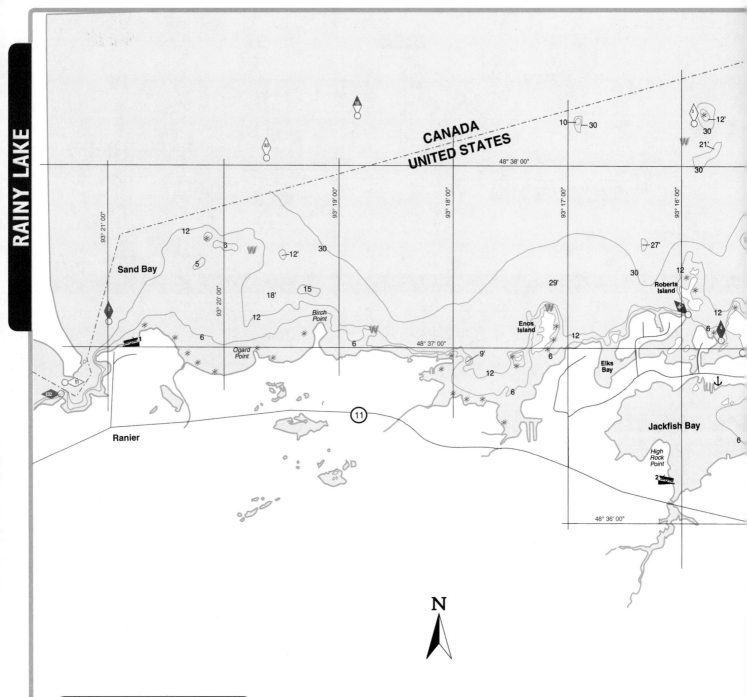

CANADA
UNITED STATES

48° 38' 00"

93° 21' 00"

93° 19' 00"

93° 18' 00"

93° 17' 00"

93° 16' 00"

Sand Bay

93° 20' 00"

12

6

5

12'

30

18'

15

12

Birch
Point

6

Ogard
Point

Ranier

48° 37' 00"

6

9'

12

6

Enos
Island

29'

30

27'

Roberts
Island

12

30

12

6

12

Elks
Bay

6

Jackfish Bay

High
Rock
Point

2

21'

30

30

30

12'

3

W

10

30

48° 36' 00"

11

N

FISHING SPOTS BY SPECIES LEGEND

W	Walleye
N	Northern Pike
B	Bass
C	Crappie

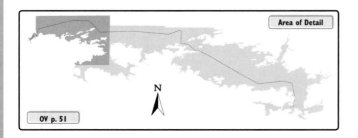

Area of Detail

N

OV p. 51

Source: Minnesota Department of Natural Resources, USGS

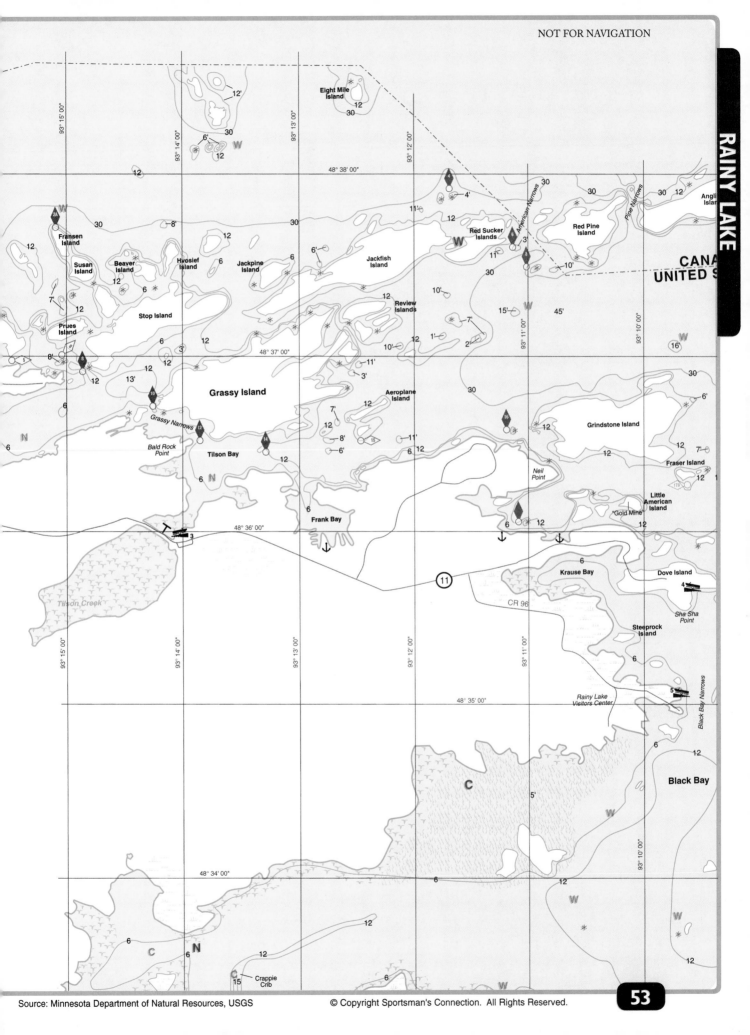

Source: Minnesota Department of Natural Resources, USGS

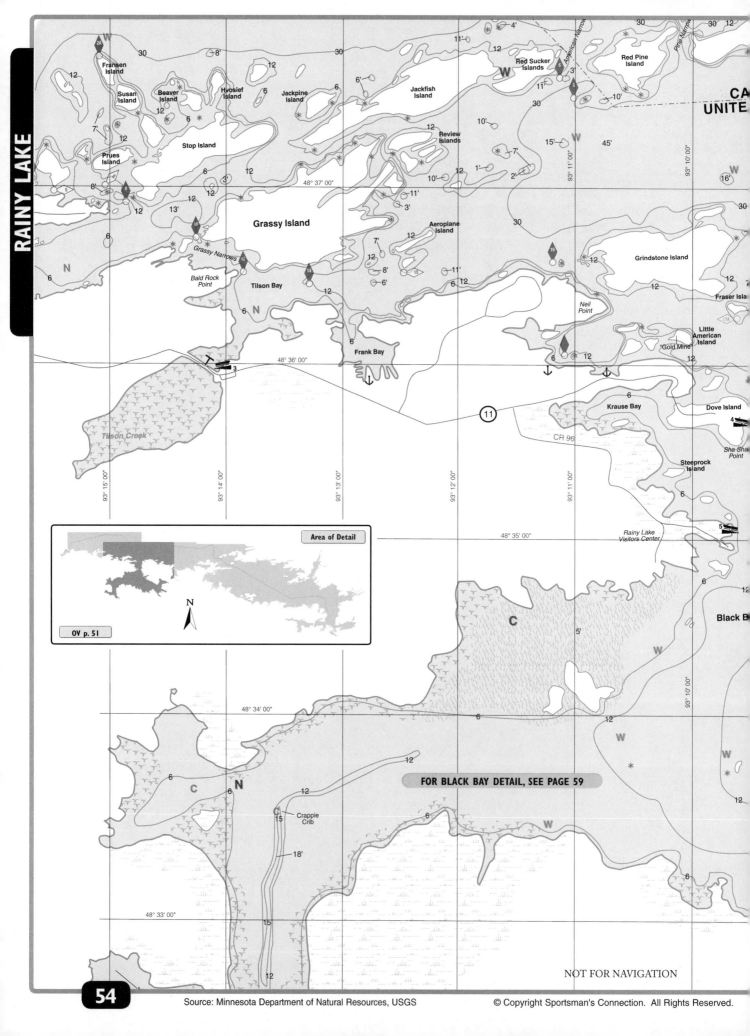

Fransen Island

Susan Island

Beaver Island

Hvosief Island

Jackpine Island

Stop Island

Prues Island

Grassy Island

Grassy Narrows

Bald Rock Point

Tilson Bay

Frank Bay

Tilson Creek

Jackfish Island

Review Islands

Aeroplane Island

Red Sucker Islands

Red Pine Island

CA
UNITE

American Narrow

Pine Narrow

Grindstone Island

Fraser Isla

Neil Point

Little American Island

"Gold Mine"

Dove Island

Sha Sha Point

Krause Bay

CR 96

Steeprock Island

Rainy Lake Visitors Center

Black B

FOR BLACK BAY DETAIL, SEE PAGE 59

Crappie Crib

48° 37' 00"

48° 36' 00"

48° 35' 00"

48° 34' 00"

48° 33' 00"

93° 15' 00"

93° 14' 00"

93° 13' 00"

93° 12' 00"

93° 11' 00"

93° 11' 00"

93° 10' 00"

93° 10' 00"

Area of Detail

OV p. 51

N

NOT FOR NAVIGATION

54

Source: Minnesota Department of Natural Resources, USGS

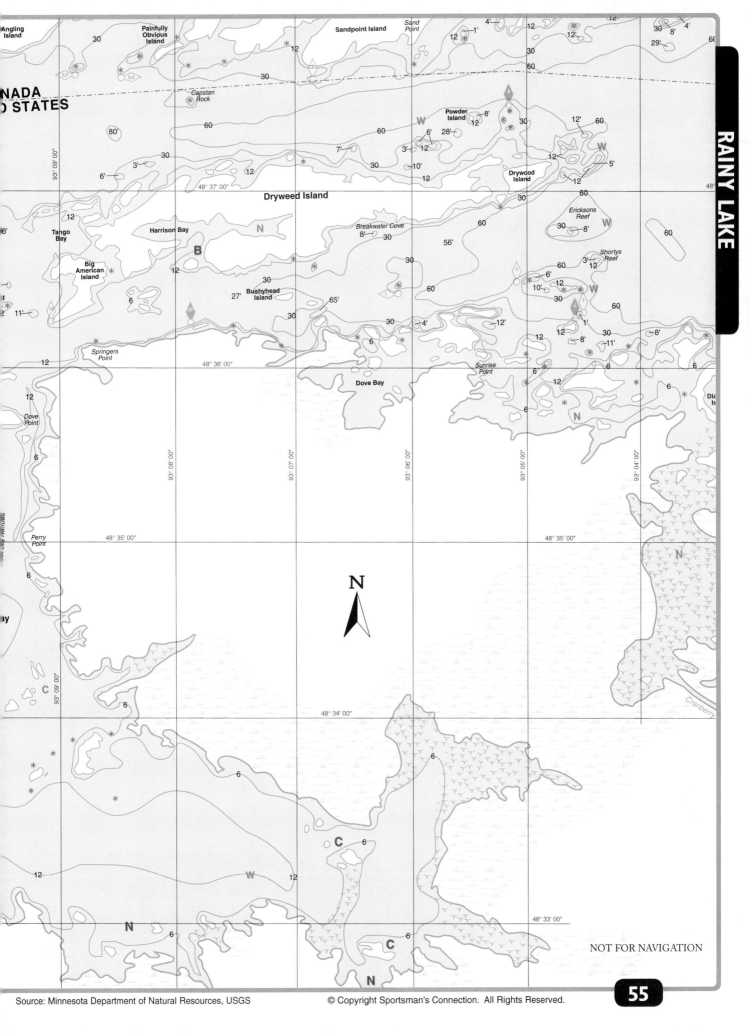

Angling
Island

30

Painfully
Obvious
Island

30

Capstan
Rock

NADA
O STATES

80'

60

3'

6'

12

Sandpoint Island

Sand
Point

12

4'

12'

30

60

Powder
Island

W

6'

7'

28'

12

3'

10'

12

30

30

12

12'

30

12'

5'

12

Drywood
Island

60

60

29'

30

8'

W

12'

4'

60

48° 37' 00"

Dryweed Island

12

Tango
Bay

Harrison Bay

N

B

Big
American
Island

12

27'

Bushyhead
Island

30

6

11'

Springers
Point

12

48° 36' 00"

12

Dove
Point

6

30

30

65'

30

Breakwater Cove

8'

30

56'

60

30

60

30

30

4'

6

Dove Bay

Ericksons
Reef

30

8'

60

3'

12

Shortys
Reef

6'

12

10'

30

W

60

12

8'

12

1'

11'

6

8'

60

W

Sunrise
Point

12

6

N

Dia
Is

12

93° 09' 00"

93° 08' 00"

48° 35' 00"

93° 07' 00"

93° 06' 00"

93° 05' 00"

93° 04' 00"

48° 35' 00"

Perry
Point

6

N

6

C

6

N

N

48° 34' 00"

6

6

93° 09' 00"

12

C

6

W

12

48° 33' 00"

N

6

C

6

Source: Minnesota Department of Natural Resources, USGS

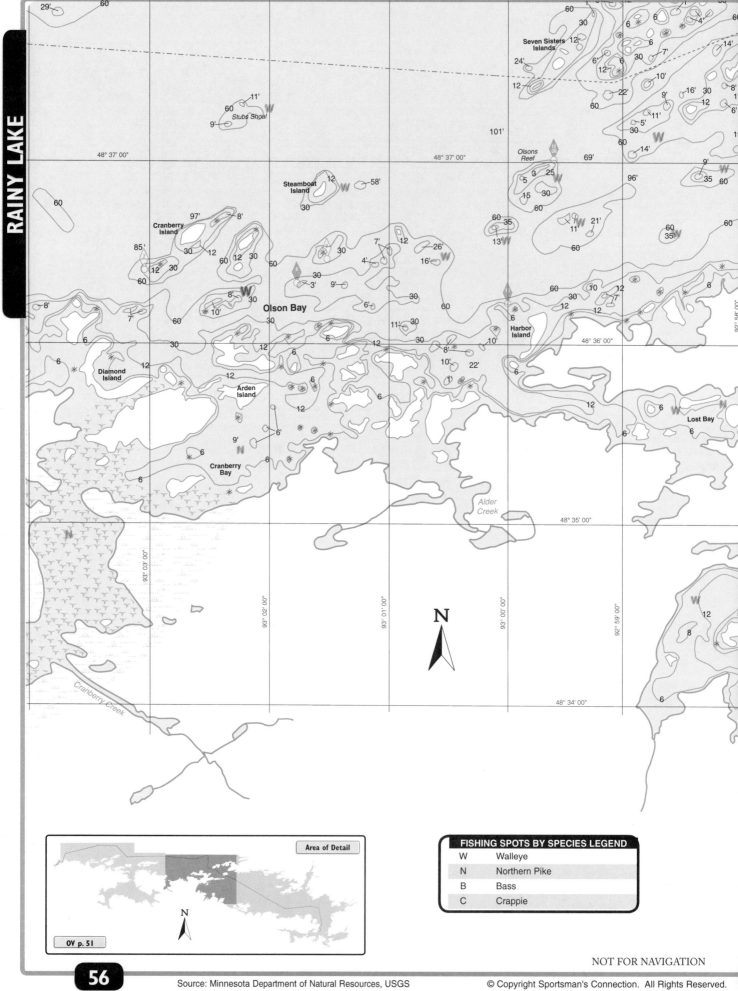

Seven Sisters Islands

Stubs Shoal

Steamboat Island

Cranberry Island

Olson Bay

Olsons Reef

Harbor Island

Diamond Island

Arden Island

Cranberry Bay

Lost Bay

Alder Creek

Cranberry Creek

48° 37' 00"

48° 36' 00"

48° 35' 00"

48° 34' 00"

93° 03' 00"

93° 02' 00"

93° 01' 00"

93° 00' 00"

92° 59' 00"

92° 58' 00"

Area of Detail

OV p. 51

FISHING SPOTS BY SPECIES LEGEND

W	Walleye
N	Northern Pike
B	Bass
C	Crappie

NOT FOR NAVIGATION

Source: Minnesota Department of Natural Resources, USGS

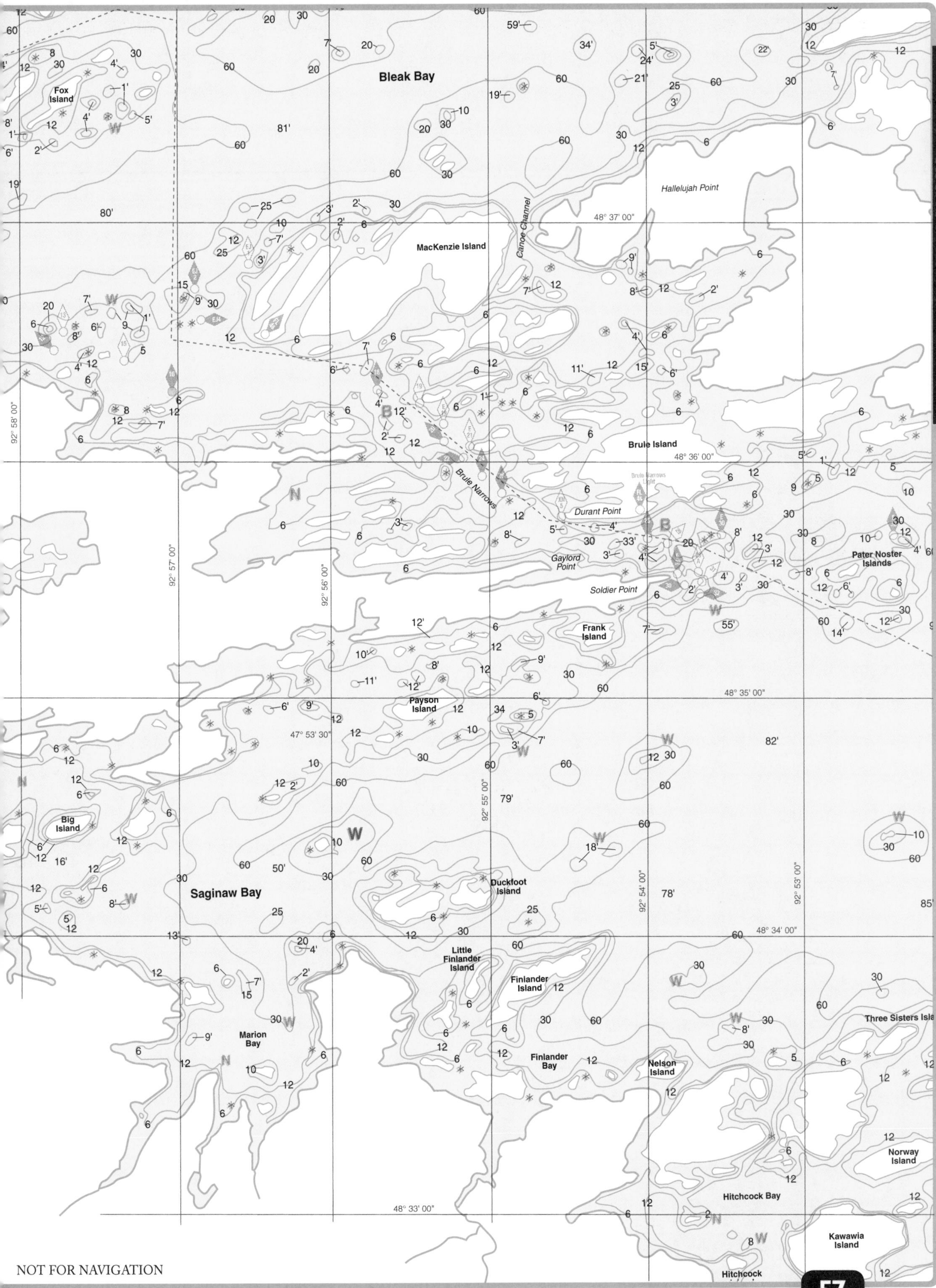

Fox Island

Bleak Bay

81'
80'

MacKenzie Island

Canoe Channel

Hallelujah Point

48° 37' 00"

Brule Island

48° 36' 00"

Brule Narrows

Durant Point

Gaylord Point

Soldier Point

Brule Narrows Light

Pater Noster Islands

Frank Island

48° 35' 00"

Payson Island

47° 53' 30"

82'
79'

Big Island

Saginaw Bay

Duckfoot Island

48° 34' 00"

Little Finlander Island

Finlander Island

Three Sisters Isla

Marion Bay

Finlander Bay

Nelson Island

85'

78'

Norway Island

Hitchcock Bay

Kawawia Island

48° 33' 00"

Hitchcock

92° 58' 00"   92° 57' 00"   92° 56' 00"   92° 55' 00"   92° 54' 00"   92° 53' 00"

NOT FOR NAVIGATION

57

Source: Minnesota Department of Natural Resources, USGS

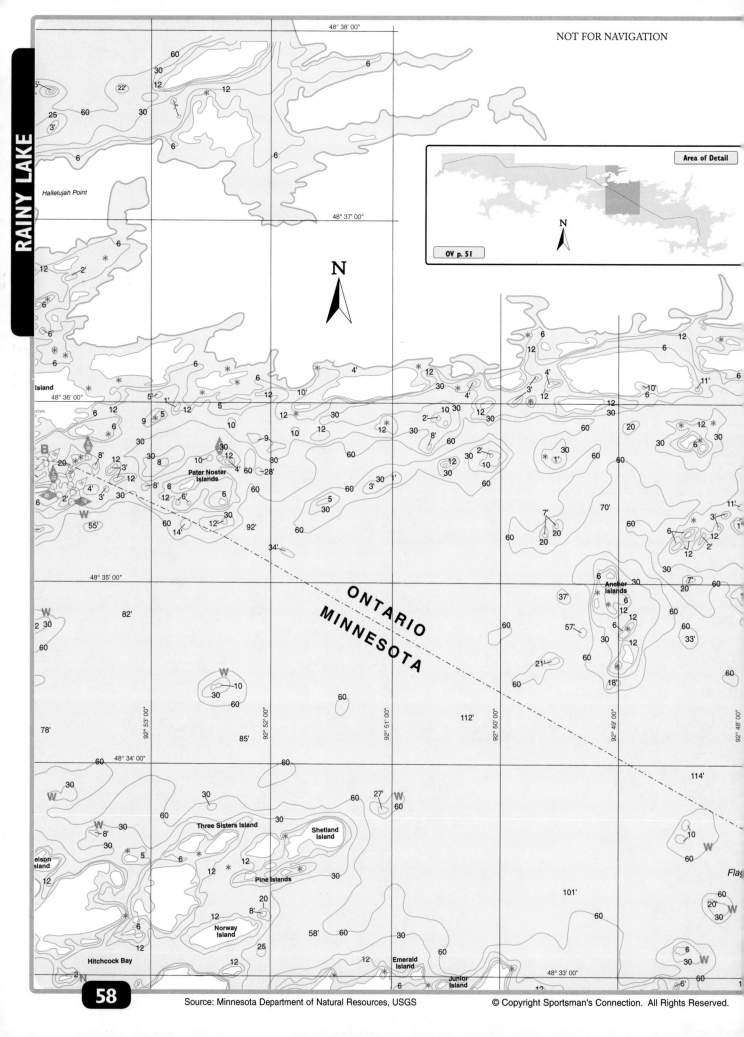

NOT FOR NAVIGATION

Source: Minnesota Department of Natural Resources, USGS

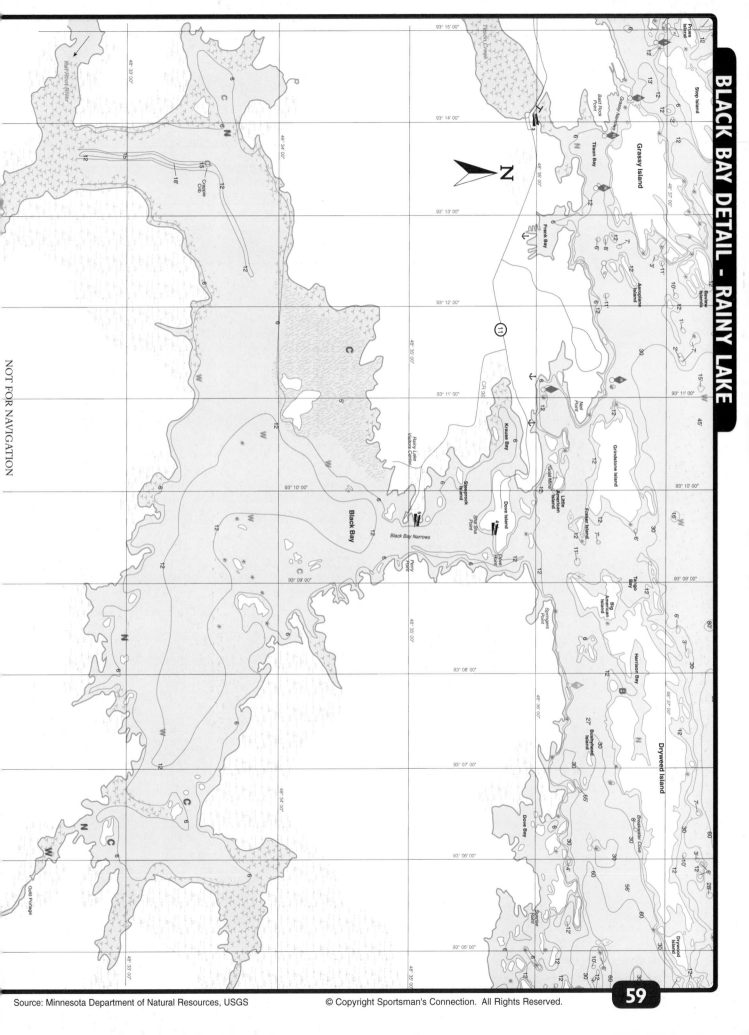

NOT FOR NAVIGATION

RAINY LAKE

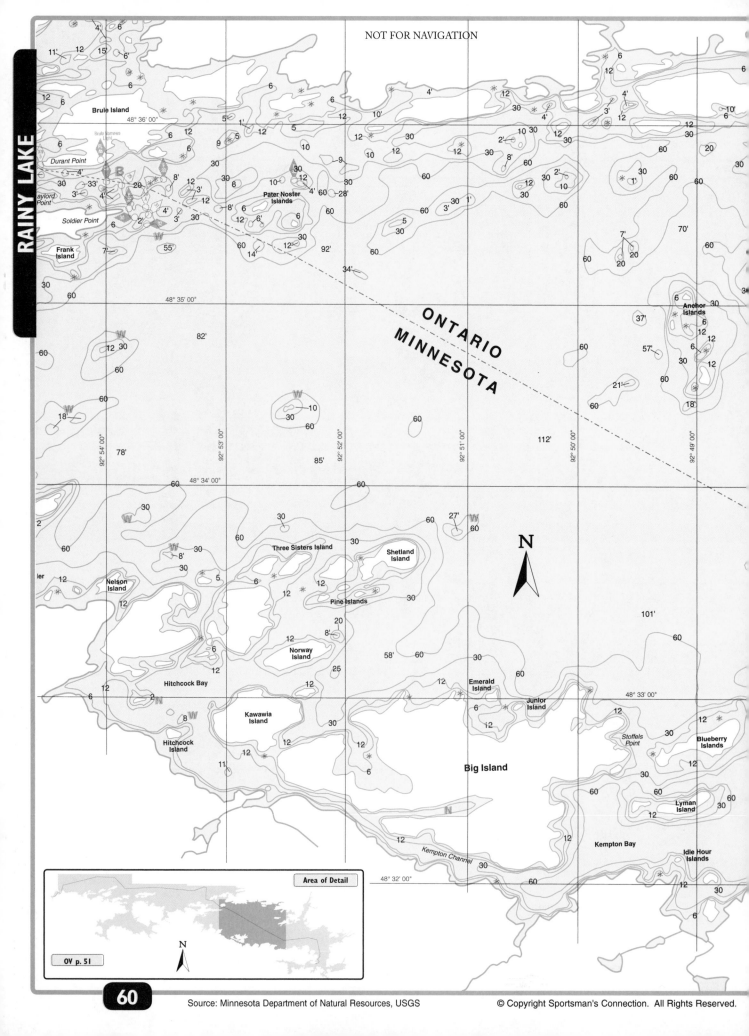

Source: Minnesota Department of Natural Resources, USGS

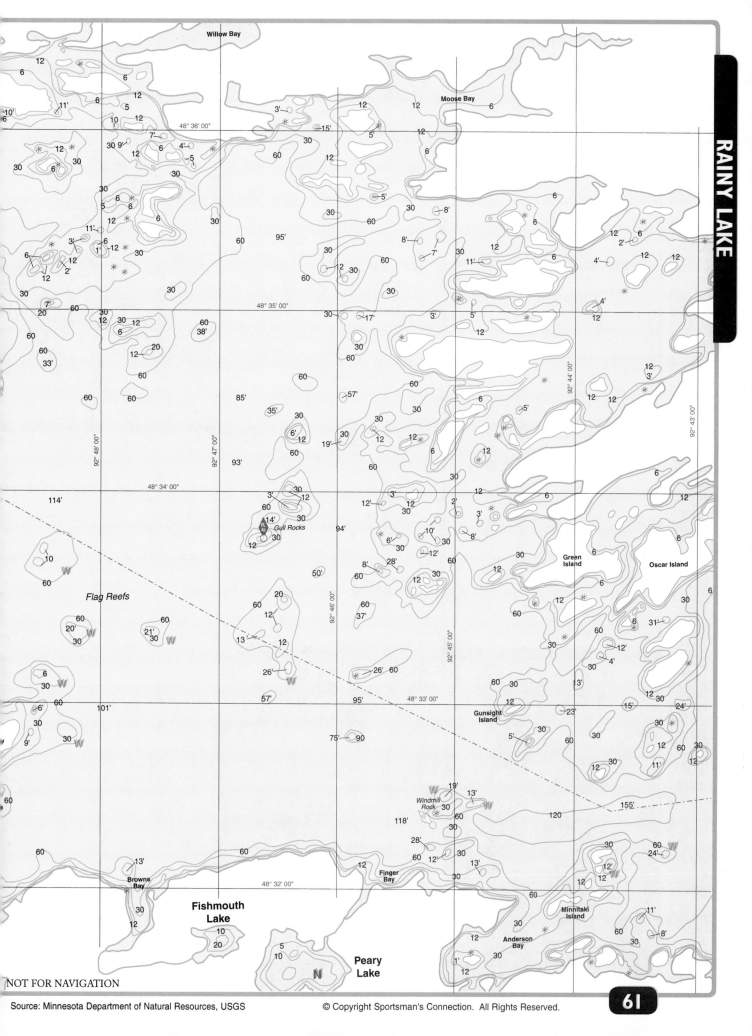

NOT FOR NAVIGATION

Cont'd from page 50

next state record walleye to come from this lake. So by all means try your luck here. "The fishing on Rainy Lake is continually getting better," says Snyker. "Things are going well for walleyes and other species in the lake. The fishing just keeps improving."

There are two main areas to chase walleyes. In the spring, you'll want to concentrate on the shallows, where the water warms quickly, helping the walleyes to overcome their post-spawn sluggishness. Black Bay is an excellent spot to do your walleye hunting at this time of year, says Snyker. In fact, it's good through June when a north wind piles feeding fish up on its south shore. Fish the edges of the emerging weedbeds between, say, 8 and 12 feet, with jig-and-minnow combinations. As the water warms shift your attention to the mid-lake islands and reefs. Try the 12-foot-deep reef north of Roberts Island and Shorty's Reef toward the lake's western end. Don't neglect similar structure around Windmill Rock and north of Rabbit Islands, down toward the lake's eastern end. Use your electronics to locate the fish around the structure, then move in with a live bait rig or jig tipped with a nightcrawler or leech. Recent DNR surveys of Rainy confirm the catch rates of walleyes have significantly increased over the last 30 years. There are various protective limits in place so make sure to check the regulations before heading out.

Rainy's abundant northern pike can be found in or around the shallow bays throughout open-water season. Although the pike aren't especially large on average at a bit over 2 pounds, there are some true monsters to be found in Rainy Lake. Fish upwards of 38 inches have been caught over the years. Black Bay, near the Rat Root River inlet is an especially good early-season location to try for them. And big Pike can similarly be found Tilson Bay, Jackfish Bay, Cranberry Bay, Marion Bay, and most of the other bays along the lake's south shore. Work the shoals early, and then head out to the deep side of the weedline as the season advances. Again, live bait

is most often used. If fishing with live bait for pike isn't your cup of tea John Janousek, National Promotions Manager of Crestliner Boats, 609 13th Ave., NE, Little Falls, MN, www.crestliner.com, has a suggestion. "I hardly ever fish with bait when I'm on Rainy fishing for pike," he says. "Locate deep humps and points on the main lake. Use your electronics and find baitfish plus gamefish. Make sure you've got a leader tied on. Use a 1-ounce bass jig. I use the Northland Jungle Jig. I dress it with a fluke. The best color is white. Just drop it to the bottom and rip it up and down off the bottom. I've caught pike up to 20 pounds with this technique."

For the lake's smallmouth bass, you'll want to check out the lake's rocky structure. Areas south of MacKenzie and Brule Islands are well-known bass producers, Snyker says, as is the reef just north of the Kettle Channel, near the lake's eastern end. There's excellent bass fishing, too, in the lake's North Arm, which is entirely in Canadian waters. Live bait techniques will work well, but just like northern pike fishing Janousek recommends hardware over live bait. "I just don't think you need to fish with live bait," he says. "Live bait will work, but I catch bigger fish using lures like spinnerbaits, jerkbaits or topwater lures like a Rapala Skitterpop. You can cover more water in less time with these lures and catch some quality fish." The DNR reports that the smallmouth bass population has grown and has been protected by the catch-and-release ethics common to most bass anglers.

In recent years, meanwhile, crappies have been getting more numerous, and Snyker says cribs placed in Black Bay have helped provide a focal point for this population. There's an especially good spot near the middle of the Rat Root River inlet. The crib is near the north end of the 12- to 18-foot-deep trench at mid-channel, right where the river bends east to enter the main bay area. Crappie minnows are a good choice, with or without a jig. Small leeches can also be productive. The most recent DNR survey showed

the crappie population to be in great shape. The catch rate was at a record high.

For the best spots to fish, see the accompanying map. Snyker and several of the guides with whom he associates marked 87 spots which are known to be among the best fish-producers. We'd like to extend our thanks to them.

All the marked areas are on the U.S. side of the lake, though; we offer no designation of fishing spots in Canadian waters. This is in response to the "Walleye wars" of recent years which have seen U.S. guides, resort owners and state agencies at odds with their Canadian counterparts over the Rainy Lake fishery. At the heart of this controversy is the belief that U.S. anglers take more fish from the lake than do Canadian anglers; in fact, Canadian authorities contend the lake is being overfished. Adding fuel to the fire here is the fact that U.S. anglers have tended to stay most often at resorts on the U.S. side of the International Border, crossing into Canadian waters only to fish. As a result, Canadians have argued, Ontario has profited little from fish that have been removed from its waters; all the benefit has gone south of the border. In response, Canadian authorities placed severe restrictions on fish harvests by U.S. anglers who don't stay at Canadian resorts. If you're going out on the big lake, learn where the International Boundary is. Stay south of it if you don't want to become involved in Canadian enforcement efforts. To avoid any confusion contact Snyker at his store prior to your departure onto Rainy Lake. He'll let you in on the latest regulations, plus give you the skinny on the hot bite.

Spiny waterfleas have been found in Rainy Lake. To help prevent the spread of this invasive species, the DNR advises anglers and boaters to drain bilges and bait buckets and let them dry between trips. Also make sure to wash your boat down, preferably with hot water such as a pressure washer available at many car wash facilities.

Rainy Lake is a great bet for big smallmouth bass.

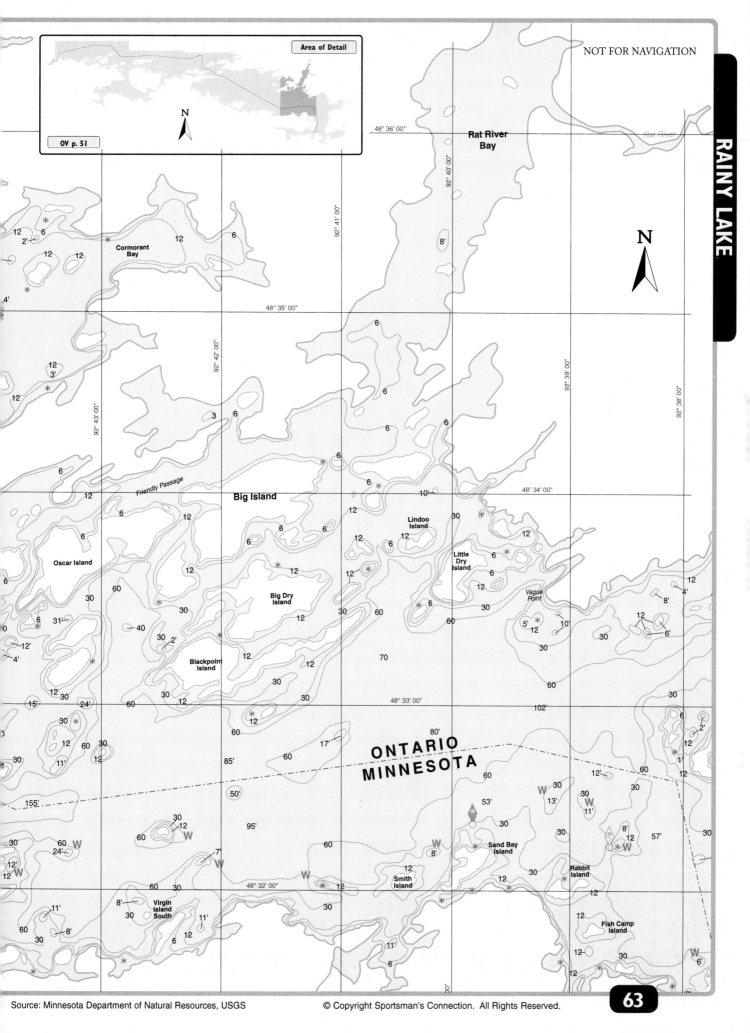

Area of Detail

N

OV p. 51

Cormorant Bay

Rat River Bay

48° 36' 00"

92° 40' 00"

92° 41' 00"

N

48° 35' 00"

92° 42' 00"

92° 43' 00"

92° 39' 00"

92° 38' 00"

Friendly Passage

Big Island

48° 34' 00"

Lindoo Island

Little Dry Island

Vague Point

Oscar Island

Big Dry Island

Blackpoint Island

70

48° 33' 00"

102'

80'

ONTARIO
MINNESOTA

155'

53'

Sand Bay Island

Rabbit Island

95'

57'

Virgin Island South

48° 32' 00"

Smith Island

Fish Camp Island

63

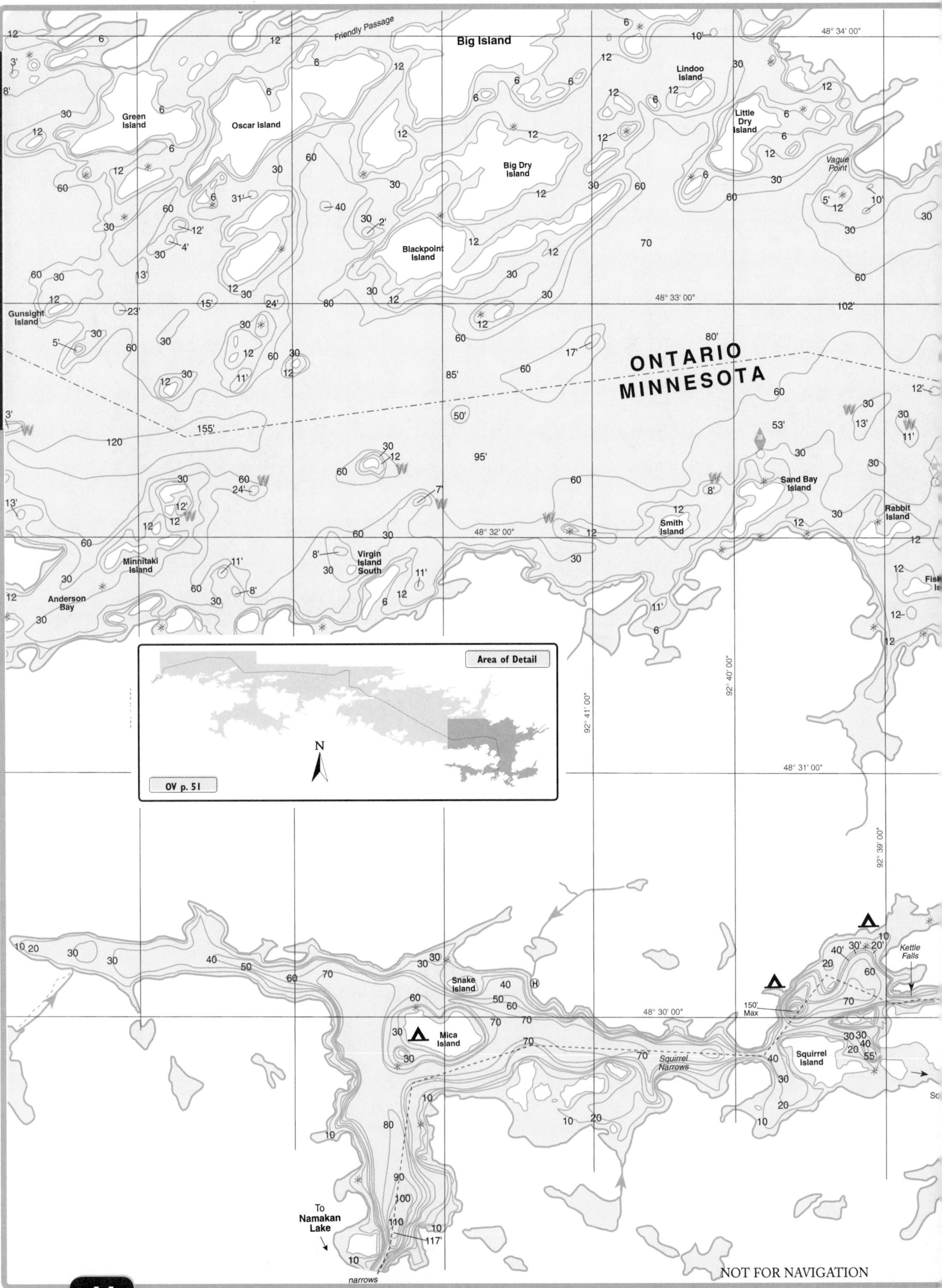

Big Island
Friendly Passage

Green Island
Oscar Island
Lindoo Island
Little Dry Island
Vague Point

Big Dry Island

Blackpoint Island

Gunsight Island

ONTARIO
MINNESOTA

Sand Bay Island

Smith Island

Rabbit Island

Minnitaki Island

Virgin Island South

Anderson Bay

Fish Is

Area of Detail

N

OV p. 51

Snake Island

Kettle Falls

Mica Island

Squirrel Narrows

Squirrel Island

To Namakan Lake

narrows

150' Max

NOT FOR NAVIGATION

Source: Minnesota Department of Natural Resources, USGS

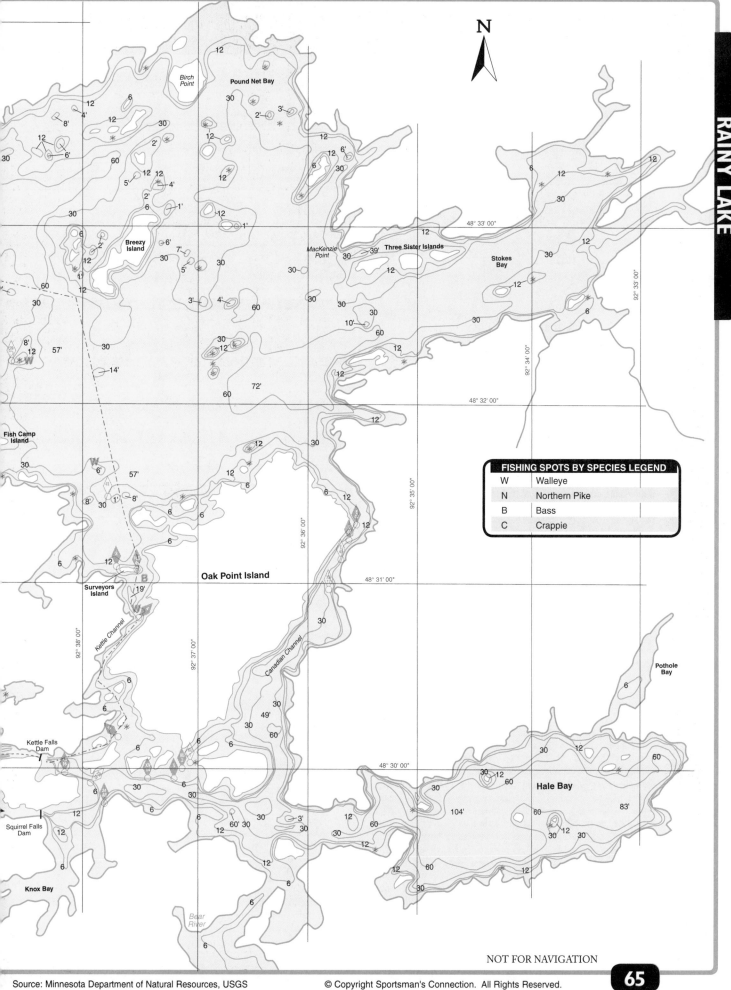

N

Birch Point

Pound Net Bay

Breezy Island

MacKenzie Point

Three Sister Islands

Stokes Bay

Fish Camp Island

FISHING SPOTS BY SPECIES LEGEND

W	Walleye
N	Northern Pike
B	Bass
C	Crappie

Oak Point Island

Surveyors Island

Kettle Channel

Canadian Channel

Pothole Bay

Kettle Falls Dam

Hale Bay

Squirrel Falls Dam

Knox Bay

Bear River

48° 33' 00"

48° 32' 00"

48° 31' 00"

48° 30' 00"

92° 33' 00"

92° 34' 00"

92° 35' 00"

92° 36' 00"

92° 37' 00"

92° 38' 00"

NOT FOR NAVIGATION

Source: Minnesota Department of Natural Resources, USGS

Area map page / coordinates:	8,9 / B,C,D-1,2,3,4
Watershed:	Rainy Lake
Surface water area / shorelength:	24,034 acres / NA
Maximum / mean depth:	80 feet / 21 feet
Water color / clarity:	Clear / 8.8 feet (2010)
Shoreland zoning classification:	General development
Management class / Ecological type:	Walleye / soft-water walleye
Accessibility:	Refer to access table on facing page
Accommodations:	Resorts, marina, boat rental, camping, picnicking, restrooms

FISH STOCKING DATA

year	species	size	# released
08	Walleye	Fry	2,035,000
09	Walleye	Fry	2,000,000
10	Walleye	Fry	2,500,000

NET CATCH DATA

Date: 06/12/2010	Gill Nets		Trap Nets	
species	# per net	avg. fish weight (lbs.)	# per net	avg. fish weight (lbs.)
Black Crappie	0.10	0.03	-	-
Northern Pike	2.40	2.61	-	-
Rock Bass	0.55	0.26	-	-
Sauger	3.05	0.52	-	-
Smallmouth Bass	0.45	1.23	-	-
Walleye	8.95	1.64	-	-

LENGTH OF SELECTED SPECIES SAMPLED FROM ALL GEAR

Number of fish caught for the following length categories (inches):

species	0-5	6-8	9-11	12-14	15-19	20-24	25-29	>30	Total
Black Crappie	2	-	-	-	-	-	-	-	2
Burbot	-	-	-	-	-	1	-	-	1
Lake Whitefish	-	-	1	-	1	-	-	-	2
Northern Pike	-	-	1	3	20	12	6	6	48
Rock Bass	3	8	-	-	-	-	-	-	11
Sauger	1	4	30	22	4	-	-	-	61
Smallmouth Bass	-	1	-	7	1	-	-	-	9
Tullibee (Cisco)	-	21	16	48	60	-	-	-	145
Walleye	1	25	21	41	53	36	2	-	179
White Sucker	-	4	4	8	17	3	-	-	36
Yellow Perch	26	76	102	1	-	-	-	-	205

FISHING INFORMATION

Lake Kabetogama is a rarity among boundary-area lakes. For starters, its waters are entirely within the bounds of the United States. In addition, it's not included in the Boundary Waters Canoe Area Wilderness. There are no motor exclusions or restrictions.

Kabetogama is a Canadian shield lake. It's 25,000-plus acres offer plenty for anglers and nature lovers alike. Shorelines generally are rocky and lined with jackpine, other evergreens and birch, and slope away fairly gradually in most cases to a depth of around 50 feet, the DNR lists max depth at 80 feet. There are plenty of reefs, rocks and humps throughout the lake. In the main part of the lake, the bottom is chiefly rock and rubble, while in the bays you'll find plenty of sand and peat muck. Water is generally the color of weak iced tea, and clarity is quite good at roughly 9 feet. This situation allows good weed growth. You'll find the outside weedline between 8 and 10 feet down and in some cases a long way from shore. This means long, healthy weedbeds, with nice, well-defined edges. There's plenty of habitat in Kabetogama. There are good spawning beds and excellent structure to attract and hold fish. It's no wonder that the lake is known for walleyes, trophy northern pike, plenty of smallmouth bass, jumbo perch and nice, but somewhat scarce, black crappies. Steve Vick at Gander Mountain, 4275 Haines Road, Hermantown, MN, 218-786-9800, says the lake is loaded with quality walleyes, smallmouth bass and northern pike.

Working windward shorelines is often the best walleye fishing strategy on this big lake, although some areas deserve special attention. One area which deserves a good look in spring is near the lake's western shore. The sand flats between Cemetery Island and the Three Sisters Islands are a walleye spawning area, and some big fish can be taken right up until June on minnows fished on live bait rigs or trolling crankbaits. While you're near the western end, don't ignore the small rocky island there. You'll find nice walleyes among the rocks and emerging weed growth. Moving east, try for spring walleyes east of Donut Island on the sandbar and around the reefs and weeds near Moxie Island. In summer, try the small reefs just off Mallard Bay on the northwest and the nearby flats around Etling Island and Sucker Creek. Moving east again, you'll encounter "the flats" around Center Reef; these are famous walleye producers in a southwest wind and should be worked with live bait. In addition, you'll want to visit the rocks off both ends of Calculus Island on the north shore and also the deep flats surrounding the island. Make sure to try the breaks and humps around Knox and Chase islands. You'll often get good action on live bait rigs fished in the 20- to 25-foot range. The last DNR survey in 2010 showed the walleye population to be within the normal range. An average walleye here weighs about 1.6 pounds.

Large northern pike inhabit the weedy bays in this lake, and there are a lot of them to choose from. The weedline in Moose Bay is a particular hotspot and should be worked with spinnerbaits during the day or topwater gear in evening. You'll also want to try Irwin Bay and Duck Bay, all around Sphunge and Moxie Islands, and the weedline south of Lone Tree Island. You'll often find the big fish down 8 to 10 feet. Like walleyes, northern pike populations were also in the normal range during the last DNR lake survey. Average weight for pike was 2.61 pounds.

If you want to catch smallmouth bass, work inline spinners close to the rocks around the School Teacher Islands on the northwest. The rocks around the Shipwreck Islands in the western end are an excellent smallie spot, as are the reefs north and east of Fin Island and the reefs around Caple Rock, toward Kabetogama's western end.

For crappies, try around Wolf Island and in the lake's far northeast arm. Eks Bay is especially well known as a crappie producer. Kabetogama is located within Voyageurs National Park, which places the campgrounds and other amenities within convenient reach. Access is easy, and resorts, houseboat and regular boat rental, plus food and groceries, etc. are all readily available.

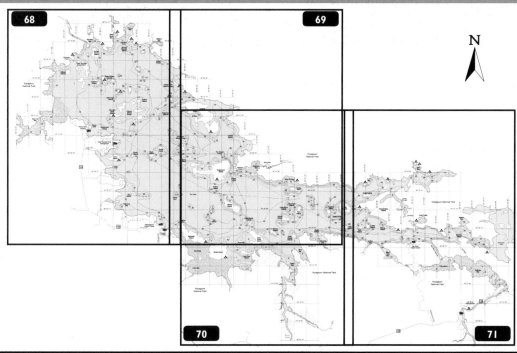

PUBLIC ACCESS FACILITIES

#	Site Admin	Ramp	pg #	Lat / Long	Access Description
1.	State	Concrete	68	48° 29' 10.92" N 93° 4' 23.49" W	South shore, western end of lake at Rocky Point Landing; Hwy. 122 north to County Road 673, east to the access located at the end of County Road 695
2.	State	Concrete	68	48° 28' 58.01" N 93° 3' 28.29" W	South shore, western end of lake adjacent to Chief Wooden Frog Campground; follow Hwy. 122 north to access
3.	National Park Service	Concrete	68	48° 26' 40.27" N 93° 1' 41.82" W	South shore at Kabetogama Visitor's Center; north off Hwy. 123
4.	State	Gravel	68	48° 26' 26.92" N 93° 1' 20.33" W	South shore at Gappas Landing; north off Hwy. 123
5.	National Park Service	Concrete	71	48° 26' 7.86" N 92° 50' 53.18" W	South shore at the Ash River Visitors Center, just west of Sullivan Bay; Ash River Recreation Trail, east on Ash River Trail, north on Meadwood Road, follow Voyageurs National Park Road north
6.	State	Concrete	71	48° 24' 19.90" N 92° 48' 32.96" W	Located on west shore of Ash River, just south of the Ash River Campground, off Hwy. 129

AREA NAMES REFERENCE

pg #	Area Name	pg #	Area Name	pg #	Area Name
71	Ash River	68	Fin Island	68	Picnic Island
71	Ash River Narrows	69 / 70	Flats, The	69 / 70	Pin Cherry Island
71	Bablore Island	69 / 70	Freedom Island	68	Pine Island
68	Bald Eagle Island	68	Gappas Landing	69 / 70	Pine Island
68	Bald Rock Bay	68	Grassy Island Group	69 / 70	Potato Island
68	Bittersweet Island	69 / 70	Grave Island	68	Ram Island
71	Blind Ash Bay	70	Green Island	69 / 70	Richie Island
69 / 70	Blue Fin Bay	68	Hacksaw Pass	69 / 70	Richie Island, Little
69 / 70	Blunt Island	69	Harris Island	68	Rotten Wood Island
69 / 70	Bowman Island	69 / 70	Headlight Island	71	Round Bear Island
70	Brook Creek	71	Indian Bay	71	Rudder Bay
69 / 70	Cable Rock	70	Irwin Bay	68	School Teacher Island
68	Camel Back Island Group	69 / 70	Jug Island	68	Sheep Island
68	Cemetery Island	68	Killiam Islands	68	Shipwreck Islands
68	Center Reef	69 / 70	Knox Island, Little	69 / 70	Slatinsky Bay
69 / 70	Chase Island	68	LaBounty Point	69	Sphunge Island
68	Chief Wooden Frog Island	71	Larkin Island	69	Stagles Point
69	Clyde Creek	70	Lone Tree Island	68	State Point
69 / 70	Cuculus Island	71	Long Slough	69	Sucker Creek
69	Cutover Island	71	Lost Bay	69 / 70	Sugarbush Island
70	Daley Bay	71	Lost Lake	71	Sullivan Bay
70	Daley Creek	68	Mallard Bay	68	Three Sisters Islands
69 / 70	Deer Creek	69 / 70	Martin Island	68	Tom Cod Bay
69 / 70	Deer Point Island	69 / 70	Martin Island, Little	71	Twin Island
69 / 70	Donut Island	68	Moose Bay	71	Wilson Island
70	Duck Bay	70	Moxie Island	70	Wolf Island
68	Echo Island	70	Mud Bay	68	Wooden Duck Island
71	Elks Bay	69 / 70	Nashata Point	68	Yewbush Island Group
68	Etling Island	69 / 70	Nebraska Bay	71	Yoder Island
71	Filla Island	68	Peterson Bay	68	Zollner Island

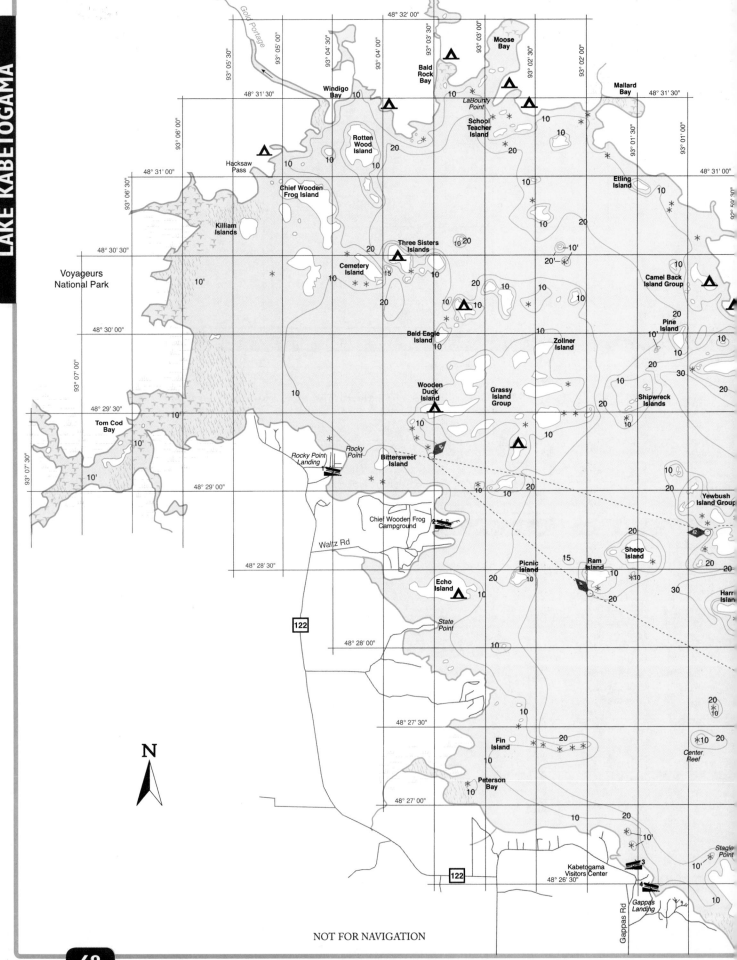

Gold Portage

48° 32' 00"

93° 05' 30"
93° 05' 00"
93° 04' 30"
93° 04' 00"
93° 03' 30"
93° 03' 00"
93° 02' 30"
93° 02' 00"

Moose Bay

Bald Rock Bay

Mallard Bay

48° 31' 30"

Windigo Bay

10

LaBounty Point

School Teacher Island

93° 06' 00"

20

10

10

10

Hacksaw Pass

10

10

10

93° 01' 30"
93° 01' 00"

48° 31' 00"

Etling Island

10

48° 31' 00"

93° 06' 30"

Chief Wooden Frog Island

Killiam Islands

10

10

10

10

20

10

48° 30' 30"

Three Sisters Islands

20

20

10 20

10'

Camel Back Island Group

10

Voyageurs National Park

Cemetery Island

20

15

10

20'

20

Pine Island

20

10'

93° 07' 00"

10'

20

10

10

10

30

48° 30' 00"

Bald Eagle Island

10

Zollner Island

20

10

48° 30' 00"

10

20

10

10

20

Shipwreck Islands

10

Wooden Duck Island

Grassy Island Group

10

10

30

20

Tom Cod Bay

10'

10

10

10

20

10'

10'

Rocky Point Landing

Rocky Point

Bittersweet Island

10

10

10

20

10'

20

Yewbush Island Group

48° 29' 00"

10'

10

93° 07' 30"

10'

Chief Wooden Frog Campground

42

Waltz Rd

20

Sheep Island

20

48° 28' 30"

15

Ram Island

30

Harri Islan

Echo Island

10

Picnic Island

20

10

10

20

122

State Point

20

20

48° 28' 00"

10

48° 27' 30"

10

Fin Island

20

20

10

10 20

Center Reef

10

Peterson Bay

10

48° 27' 00"

10

20

Stagle Point

10'

10'

20

122

Kabetogama Visitors Center

3

48° 26' 30"

4

10

Gappas Rd

Gappas Landing

N

NOT FOR NAVIGATION

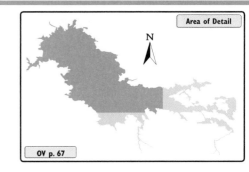

Area of Detail

N

OV p. 67

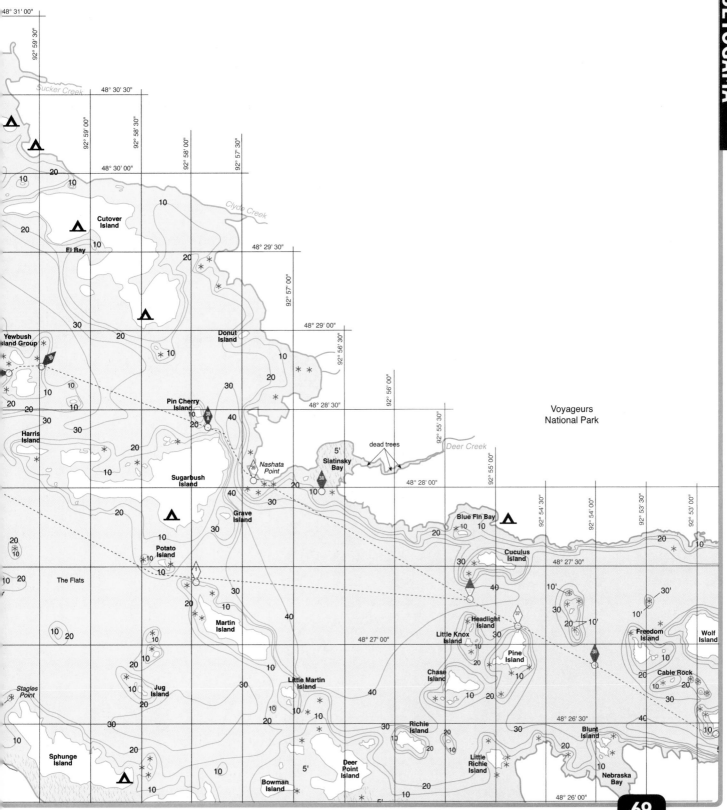

Source: Minnesota Department of Natural Resources, USGS

El Bay

20

92° 57' 00"

30

20

Donut
Island

10

48° 29' 00"

92° 56' 30"

10

30

30

20

Pin Cherry
Island

10

30

40

20

92° 56' 00"

48° 28' 30"

Voyageurs
National Park

92° 55' 30"

dead trees

Deer Creek

5'
Slatinsky
Bay

Nashata
Point

5'

38

Sugarbush
Island

40

20

10

48° 28' 00"

92° 55' 00"

20

Grave
Island

40

30

20

10

Blue Fin Bay

10   10

92° 54' 30"

92° 54' 00"

92° 53' 30"

92° 53' 00"

92° 52' 30"

30

40

Cuculus
Island

48° 27' 30"

20

Potato
Island

10

10

30

40

The Flats

10   20

Martin
Island

30

40

Headlight
Island

37

10'

30

20

10'

10'

30'

10'

Wolf
Island

10

10

30

Little Knox
Island

Freedom
Island

10

20

Jug
Island

10

20

30

Little Martin
Island

10

10

Chase
Island

Pine
Island

10

10

34

Cable Rock

20

10

30

48° 27' 00"

20

30

10

10

20

Richie
Island

30

20

10

48° 26' 30"

Blunt
Island

40

50

Green
Island

34

10

30

Sphunge
Island

20

10

5'

Bowman
Island

Deer
Point
Island

10

20

Little
Richie
Island

10

Nebraska
Bay

48° 26' 00"

Duck Bay

Moxie Island

10

Lone Tree
Island

5'

5'

Mud
Bay

5'

Daley
Bay

48° 25' 30"

Voyageurs National Park

Irwin Bay

5'

48° 25' 00"

Voyageurs
National Park

48° 24' 30"

48° 24' 00"

Daley Creek

NOT FOR NAVIGATION

53

Brook
Creek

48° 23' 30"

Source: Minnesota Department of Natural Resources, USGS

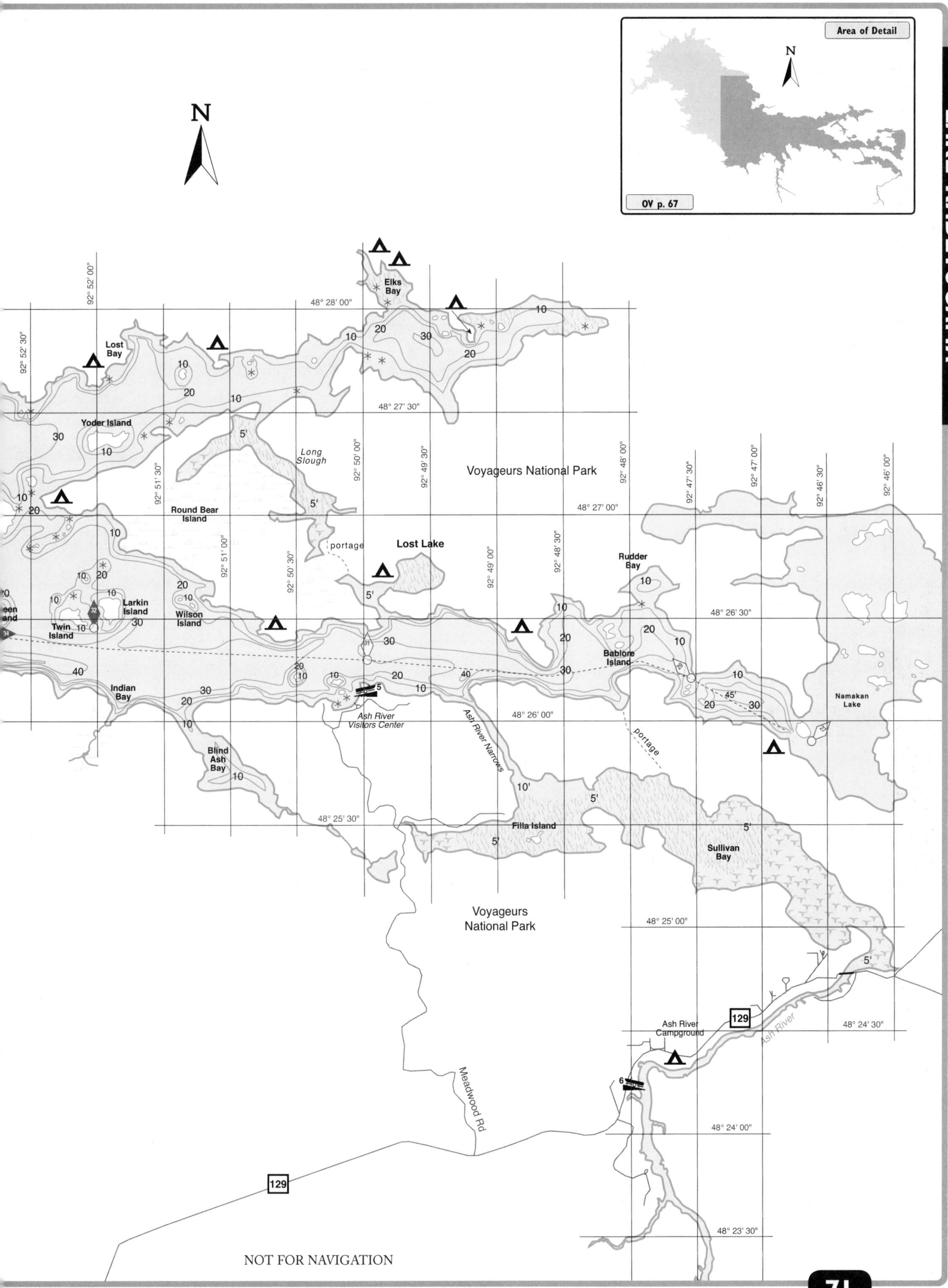

Area of Detail

N

OV p. 67

N

Elks
Bay

48° 28' 00"

10

10

20

30

10

20

20

Lost
Bay

10

10

20

10

Yoder Island

30

10

48° 27' 30"

5'

Long
Slough

Voyageurs National Park

48° 27' 00"

10

10

20

Round Bear
Island

5'

portage

Lost Lake

Rudder
Bay

10

30

20

10

48° 26' 30"

20

10

10

20

Larkin
Island

20

10

Wilson
Island

30

Bablore
Island

45'

Twin
Island

10

30

Namakan
Lake

40

10

20

30

40

20

30

20

10

Indian
Bay

30

10

5

20

10

Ash River
Visitors Center

Ash River Narrows

48° 26' 00"

portage

10

Blind
Ash
Bay

10

10'

5'

5'

Filla Island

5'

Sullivan
Bay

48° 25' 30"

5'

Voyageurs
National Park

48° 25' 00"

5'

129

Ash River

48° 24' 30"

Ash River
Campground

6

48° 24' 00"

Meadwood Rd

129

48° 23' 30"

92° 52' 00"

92° 52' 30"

92° 51' 30"

92° 51' 00"

92° 50' 30"

92° 50' 00"

92° 49' 30"

92° 49' 00"

92° 48' 30"

92° 48' 00"

92° 47' 30"

92° 47' 00"

92° 46' 30"

92° 46' 00"

NOT FOR NAVIGATION

71

NAMAKAN LAKE *St. Louis County*

Area map page / coordinates:	9 / B,C,D-4,5,6
Watershed:	Rainy Lake
Surface water area / shorelength:	24,066 acres / 14.6 miles
Maximum / mean depth:	150 feet / NA
Water color / clarity:	Clear to light green tint / 10.7 feet (2010)
Shoreland zoning classification:	Recreational development
Management class / Ecological type:	Walleye-centrarchid/centrarchid-walleye
Accessibility:	Via navigable channel from Kabetogama, Crane and Rainy Lakes
Accommodations:	Resorts, marinas, boat rental, camping, picnicking

FISHING INFORMATION

Make no mistake, Namakan Lake is impressive. At 24,000-plus acres, it's one of the larger bodies of water in a state known for big lakes. Its iced tea-color water isn't what one is programmed to expect in the "land of sky blue waters," but its scenery certainly is. You'll find about every kind of boreal vista there is on this big lake. There are broad stretches of wide-open water. In addition, there are numerous islands. Many of these are topped with stands of spruce and pine. Many of these host wilderness campsites where an angler can stop off to prepare a shore lunch or to pitch a tent after a long day on the water. Then there are those narrow, rocky channels. Their sides are so high and sheer that they remind you of the "concrete canyon" locks on the Welland Canal or St. Lawrence Seaway. The channels can become wind tunnels when a strong breeze is blowing, but they're worth a visit.

One kind of scenery you won't find an abundance of on Namakan, though, is the man-made variety. There are a few resorts which rent cabins and boats. There's also a trading post with beverages, toilets, gas, bait, etc. The country around Namakan is primarily wilderness. Namakan and its neighbor, Sand Point, are on the eastern boundary of Voyageurs National Park, and they form part of the International Border between the U.S. and Canada. This puts them a bit out of the way. In fact, no roads lead to Namakan. So if you want to fish the lake, you're forced to enter indirectly, there are several ways to do this. Namakan is accessible by water from all directions. You can launch your boat on Crane Lake and enter Namakan from the south via Sand Point Lake and Namakan Narrows. Or, you can put in at Kabetogama Narrows or Ash River and motor or paddle in from the west. You can launch on Rainy Lake and get into Namakan from the north via the Kettle Falls Flowage. There is room to get a canoe in, as well, from the Boundary Waters Canoe Area Wilderness (BWCAW) or Ontario's Quetico Provincial Park via the Namakan River, which flows into the lake's eastern end. It may be isolated, but it's accessible with a little effort.

The folks at Gander Mountain, 4275 Haines Road, Hermantown, MN, 218-786-9800, say this lake is loaded with walleyes. A good angler can always find walleyes on Namakan. Fish the Namakan River mouth and upriver a bit in spring, backtrolling a jig-and-minnow combination, live bait rig or troll a deep-running crankbait. You might also want to try the islands and humps off the mouth of Namakan Narrows during the same period. Move farther west later in the year on this big lake in search of walleyes. The reefs around Pat Smith Island are a well-known walleye hotspot from June on, and the rocks and reefs along the lake's south side, west of Pat Smith and in the area of Pike Island are good producers, as well. The north shore, too, north and west of Gull Island also offers excellent walleye

angling. Heading farther west, try the rocks off the east side of Randolph Island and off the south end of Blue Island. In high summer, the rocks and reefs south of Namakan Island and between Stevens Island and Sheen Point should be trolled in evening with live bait or stickbaits. During the 2010 DNR lake survey, the overall numbers of walleyes proved to be good, but slow growing,

Namakan Lake is also well known for its northern pike fishing. There are lots of pike in the 22- to 24-inch length range, and there are plenty of larger ones available, as well. In fact, fish in the 30-inch range are taken with some regularity. Try fishing Moose Bay, Junction Bay and other shallower areas early with sucker minnows or a #3 Mepps. Later, try the deepwater sides of the shoals. During summer, get out early and work large jerkbaits

NO RECORD OF STOCKING

NET CATCH DATA

	Gill Nets		Trap Nets	
Date: 09/27/2010		avg. fish		avg. fish
species	# per net	weight (lbs.)	# per net	weight (lbs.)
Black Crappie	0.15	0.40	-	-
Burbot	0.05	2.74	-	-
Lake Whitefish	0.10	0.61	-	-
Northern Pike	1.90	4.88	-	-
Rock Bass	0.70	0.22	-	-
Sauger	1.90	0.27	-	-
Smallmouth Bass	0.25	1.21	-	-
Tullibee (Cisco)	8.60	1.01	-	-
Walleye	6.20	0.75	-	-
White Sucker	1.30	2.07	-	-
Yellow Perch	6.45	0.20	-	-

LENGTH OF SELECTED SPECIES SAMPLED FROM ALL GEAR

Number of fish caught for the following length categories (inches):

species	0-5	6-8	9-11	12-14	15-19	20-24	25-29	>30	Total
Black Crappie	-	2	1	-	-	-	-	-	3
Burbot	-	-	-	-	-	1	-	-	1
Lake Whitefish	-	-	1	1	-	-	-	-	2
Northern Pike	-	-	-	-	8	16	6	8	38
Rock Bass	2	12	-	-	-	-	-	-	14
Sauger	-	7	28	3	-	-	-	-	38
Smallmouth Bass	-	1	1	2	1	-	-	-	5
Tullibee (Cisco)	-	32	25	48	67	-	-	-	172
Walleye	-	13	62	25	17	7	-	-	124
White Sucker	-	1	2	2	20	1	-	-	26
Yellow Perch	14	103	12	-	-	-	-	-	129

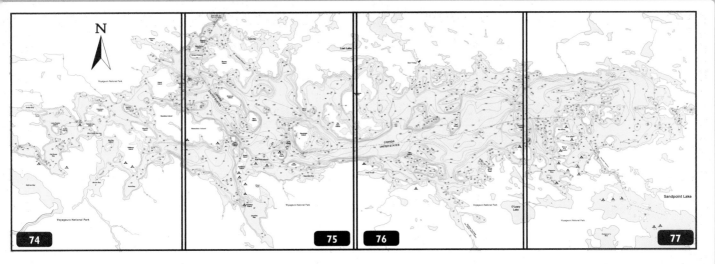

AREA NAMES REFERENCE

pg #	Area Name	pg #	Area Name	pg #	Area Name
75	Alden Island	74	Hoist Bay	76	Pike Island
76	Bear River	74	Johnson Bay	75	Randolph Bay
74	Big Sky Island	75	Jug Island	75	Randolph Island
75	Black Point	75	Junction Bay	77	Sandpoint Lake
76	Blackstone Island	74	Kohler Bay	74	Sexton Island
74	Blind Indian Narrows	74	Kohler Point	75	Sheen Island
77	Blind Pig Island	74	Kubel Island	75	Sheen Point
75	Blue Island	74	Lone Squaw Island	75	Six Deer Island
75	Blyo Island	75	McManus Island	74	Stevens Island
75	Canadian Channel	74	Moose Bay	75	Strawberry Island
74	Cemetery Island	75	Moose Island	74	Sullivan Bay
76	Deep Slough	77	My Island	77	Swanson's Bay
75	Erickson Island	74-75	Namakan Island	74	Sweetnose Island
75	Fox Island	77	Namakan Narrows	74	Tar Point
75	Gagnon Island	75	Namakan Seaplane Base	76	Three Sister Reef
74	Gehering Point	75	Narrows to Rainy Lake	75	Twin Alligator Island
75	Gold Island	74	Old Dutch Bay	74	Williams Island
76	Gull Island	76-77	O'Leary Lake	75	Wolf Pack Islands
75	Hamilton Island	75	Paddy Bay	77	Your Island
77	Hammer Bay	76	Pat Smith Island	74	Ziski Island

or buzzbaits around these same areas. Often pike will annihilate your offerings just as the sun is rising. Even though fishing shallows with fast-moving baits can be productive and quite fun, you may want to slow down your bait a bit during summer and fall. Not only should you slow down, but try fishing deep water with a large sucker minnow or a bass jig dressed with a large minnow or soft plastic bait. The jig with bait or plastic is often overlooked by anglers fishing for pike, but it can often produce some stout fish. Stick with the lighter colored bass jigs, white is a favorite color and very productive. Whatever you do, make sure and have a leader tied on. With some pike measuring over 40 inches swimming in Namakan, standard monofilament or braided line can get shredded in a hurry. DNR data indicates that overall growth for pike is outstanding and that maximum size was exceptional.

Whatever you do, though, don't ignore the smallmouth bass in Namakan. The lake has developed quite a

reputation for smallies, and it's well deserved. You'll generally find them in the same areas as walleyes early in the year. The reefs and rocks north of Gull Island are especially good producers, as is the narrow cut between Six Deer and Blackstone Islands. Use jigs or minnows early. Later, switch to small jerkbaits, inline spinners, spinnerbaits or crankbaits. If you like excitement, fish for pike using topwater baits. You'll need to make sure and bring along a good supply of topwaters, because the abundant pike population may take a few of your favorite lures home with them. To focus on smallies, use lures like a Sammy or Zara Spook. Both of these are excellent walking baits, which are particularly effective when you want to fish fast and cover a lot of open water, like over submerged humps or reefs. Poppers or chuggers like a Pop-R or a G-Splash can really be dynamite when fishing isolated rocks or shallower areas around islands or points. There's something about that plop-plop sound that drives smallies wild. Color choice for both poppers

and walking baits is fairly simple, anything with a clear or white belly seems to work just fine.

Both the black crappie and yellow perch numbers were low during the last DNR lake survey. Black crappie abundance was the lowest recorded since 1996. The mean length for crappies was just over 6 inches long. Yellow perch were below the median level for this class of lake. The mean length was 6.6 inches, which was equal to area average, but below the statewide average of 7.2 inches.

Since this lake is international water, you'll want to make sure you have a Canadian license and are up on both Minnesota and Canadian regulations before fishing. Licenses and info are readily available at the resorts, the trading post and other outlets in the area.

Source: Minnesota Department of Natural Resources, USGS

Area of Detail

OV p. 73

N

N

Johnson
Bay

48° 28' 30"

5'

48° 28' 00"

Voyageurs National Park

48° 27' 30"

Kubel
Island

Geher
Poir

Kohler Bay

Sexton
Island

Cemetery
Island

48° 27' 00"

Namakan Island

Kohler
Point

Tar
Point

Nokomis
Island

Sweetnose
Island

Stevens
Island

Ziski
Island

Blind Indian Narrows

48° 26' 30"

Big Sky
Island

Old Dutch
Bay

Williams
Island

48° 26' 00"

48° 25' 30"

Sullivan Bay

Moose Bay

Voyageurs National Park

Hoist Bay

48° 25' 00"

92° 47' 30"

92° 47' 00"

92° 46' 30"

92° 46' 00"

92° 45' 30"

92° 45' 00"

92° 44' 30"

92° 44' 00"

92° 43' 30"

Source: Minnesota Department of Natural Resources, USGS

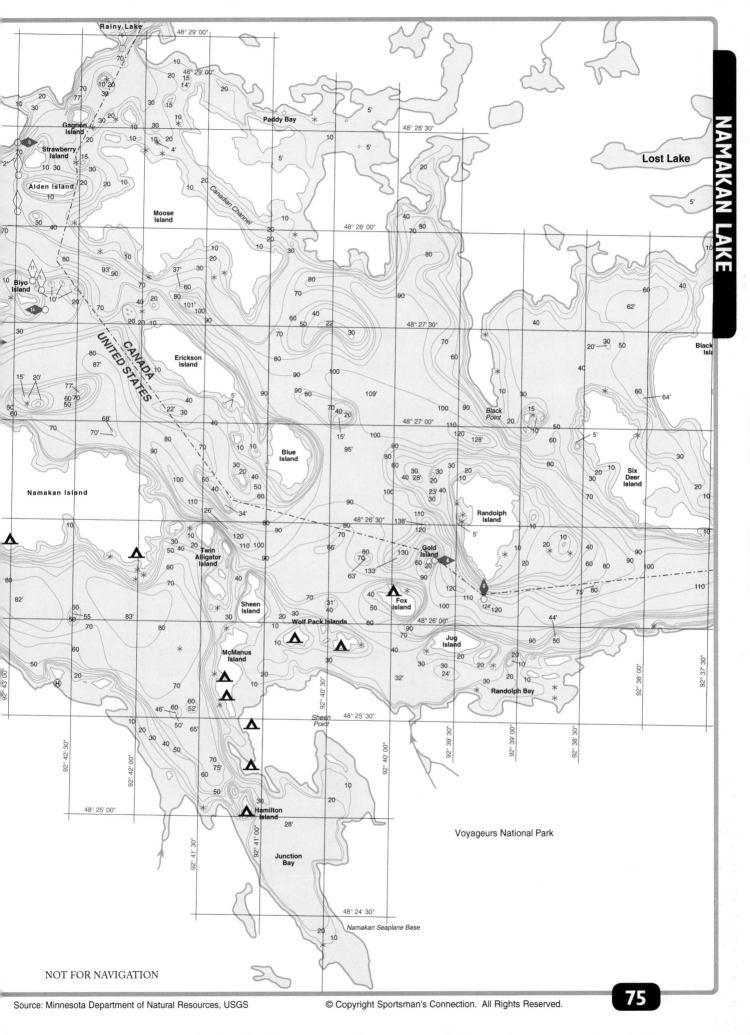

Lost Lake

Rainy Lake

Paddy Bay

Gagnon Island

Strawberry Island

Alden Island

Moose Island

Canadian Channel

Biyo Island

CANADA
UNITED STATES

Erickson Island

Blue Island

Namakan Island

Twin Alligator Island

Sheen Island

McManus Island

Wolf Pack Islands

Fox Island

Gold Island

Randolph Island

Black Point

Six Deer Island

Black Isla

Jug Island

Randolph Bay

Sheen Point

Hamilton Island

Junction Bay

Voyageurs National Park

Namakan Seaplane Base

NOT FOR NAVIGATION

Source: Minnesota Department of Natural Resources, USGS

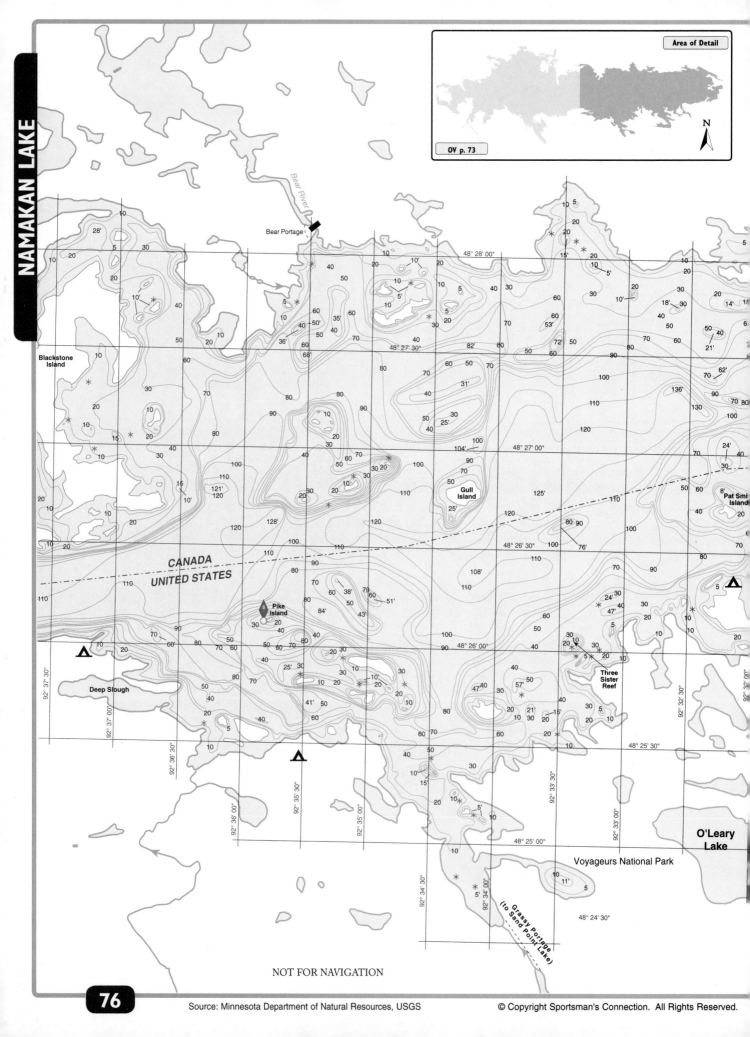

Area of Detail

OV p. 73

N

Bear River

Bear Portage

Blackstone
Island

48° 28' 00"

48° 27' 30"

CANADA

UNITED STATES

48° 27' 00"

Gull
Island

48° 26' 30"

Pat Smith
Island

Pike
Island

Deep Slough

Three
Sister
Reef

48° 26' 00"

48° 25' 30"

48° 25' 00"

O'Leary
Lake

Voyageurs National Park

(to Grassy Portage
to Sand Point Lake)

48° 24' 30"

92° 37' 30"

92° 37' 00"

92° 36' 30"

92° 36' 00"

92° 35' 30"

92° 35' 00"

92° 34' 30"

92° 34' 00"

92° 33' 30"

92° 33' 00"

92° 32' 30"

NOT FOR NAVIGATION

Source: Minnesota Department of Natural Resources, USGS

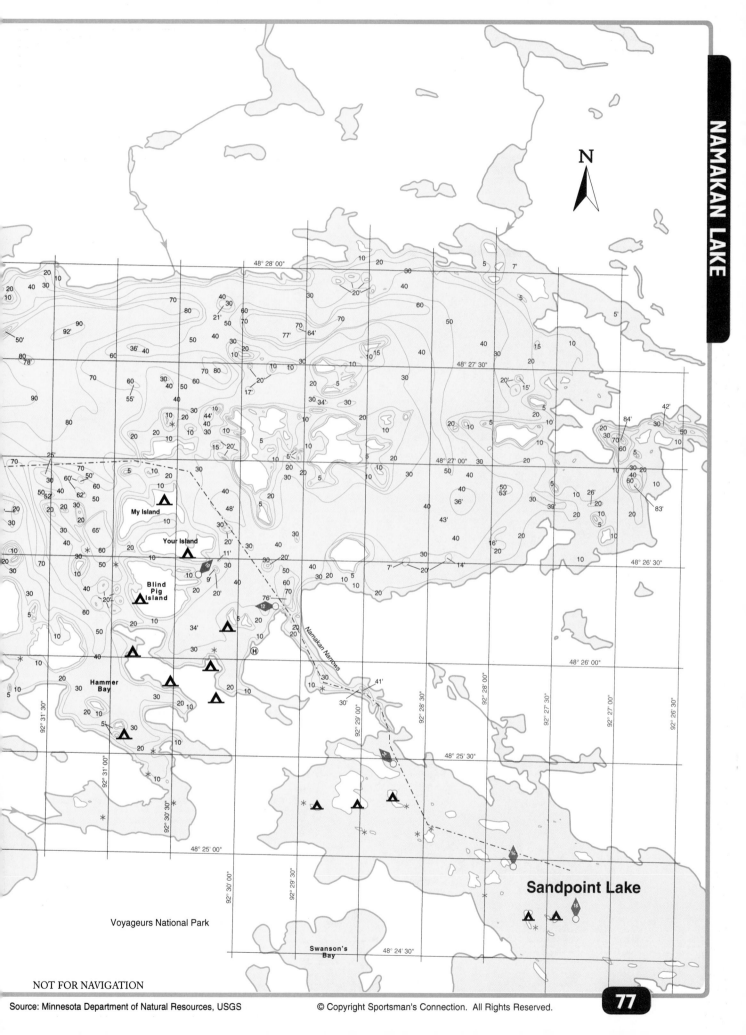

N

My Island

Your Island

Blind
Pig
Island

Hammer
Bay

Namakan Narrows

Sandpoint Lake

Voyageurs National Park

Swanson's
Bay

NOT FOR NAVIGATION

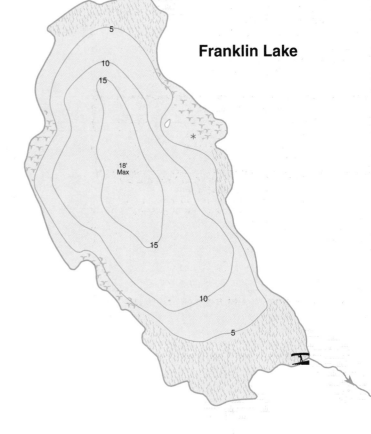

Franklin Lake

Franklin Lake, St. Louis County

Area map page / coordinates: 9 / E-5
Surface area / shorelength: 156 acres / 2.2 miles
Accessibility: Carry-down access to the southeast shore from FR 203 (0.5 mile portage)
48° 17' 40.77" N / 92° 36' 35.96" W

LENGTH OF SELECTED SPECIES SAMPLED FROM ALL GEAR
Survey Date: 07/31/2006
Number of fish caught for the following length categories (inches):

species	0-5	6-8	9-11	12-14	15-19	20-24	25-29	>30	Total
Bluegill	-	-	-	-	-	-	-	-	-
Northern Pike	-	1	1	4	29	29	3	-	67
Walleye	-	-	14	4	63	30	1	-	112
Yellow Perch	45	72	11	-	-	-	-	-	128

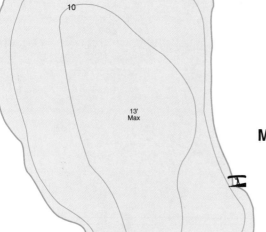

Marion Lake

N

Marion Lake, St. Louis County

Area map page / coordinates: 9 / E-5
Surface area / shorelength: 163 acres / 2.5 miles
Accessibility: Carry-down access to east shore or via Marion Creek by boat
48° 17' 6.43" N / 92° 40' 5.72" W

LENGTH OF SELECTED SPECIES SAMPLED FROM ALL GEAR
Survey Date: 08/01/2005
Number of fish caught for the following length categories (inches):

species	0-5	6-8	9-11	12-14	15-19	20-24	25-29	>30	Total
Bluegill	7	7	-	-	-	-	-	-	14
Northern Pike	-	-	1	3	10	23	4	2	43
Walleye	-	-	1	5	15	9	1	-	31
Yellow Perch	28	7	-	-	-	-	-	-	35

Marion Creek

NOT FOR NAVIGATION

Source: Minnesota Department of Natural Resources, USGS

Mukooda Lake, St. Louis County
Located in Voyageurs National Park

Area map page / coordinates: 9 / D,E-6
Surface area / shorelength: 774 acres /5.5 miles
Accessibility: Carry-down access to northeast shore from Sand Point Lake; also from King Williams Narrows
48° 19' 26.99" N / 92° 28' 49.40" W
48° 20' 51.66" N / 92° 28' 55.89" W

FISH STOCKING DATA

year	species	size	# released
06	Lake Trout	Yearling	3,810
08	Lake Trout	Yearling	3,788
10	Lake Trout	Yearling	3,881

LENGTH OF SELECTED SPECIES SAMPLED FROM ALL GEAR
Survey Date: 08/13/2007
Number of fish caught for the following length categories (inches):

species	0-5	6-8	9-11	12-14	15-19	20-24	25-29	>30	Total
Black Crappie	2	1	20	9	-	-	-	-	32
Bluegill	8	14	-	-	-	-	-	-	22
Lake Trout	-	-	-	1	3	-	-	1	5
Largemouth Bass	4	6	14	22	7	-	-	-	55
Longear Sunfish	1	34	-	-	-	-	-	-	35
Northern Pike	-	-	-	-	2	36	7	4	50
Smallmouth Bass	-	-	2	1	3	-	-	-	6
Walleye	-	-	-	-	1	7	1	-	9

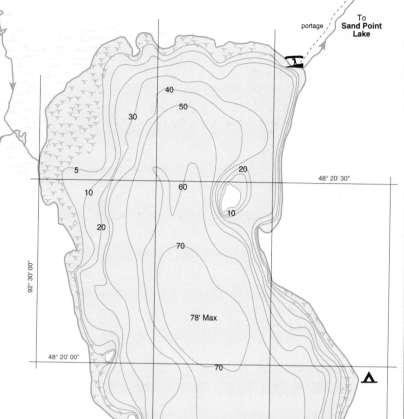

Mukooda Lake

N

Little Trout Lake

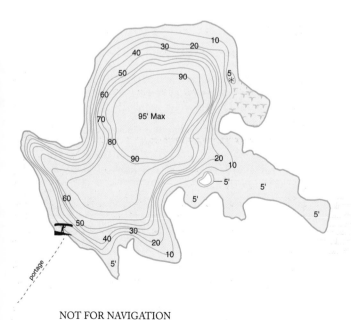

NOT FOR NAVIGATION

Little Trout Lake, St. Louis County
Located in Voyageurs National Park

Area map page / coordinates: 9 / C-6
Surface area / shorelength: 272 acres / 4.1 miles
Accessibility: Carry-down access to southwest shore from Grassy Bay on Sand Point Lake
48° 23' 32.78" N / 92° 31' 46.85" W

FISH STOCKING DATA

year	species	size	# released
02	Lake Trout	Yearling	1,249
04	Lake Trout	Yearling	1,410
06	Lake Trout	Yearling	1,212

LENGTH OF SELECTED SPECIES SAMPLED FROM ALL GEAR
Survey Date: 08/10/2009
Number of fish caught for the following length categories (inches):

species	0-5	6-8	9-11	12-14	15-19	20-24	25-29	>30	Total
Lake Trout	-	-	-	-	-	-	1	-	1
Northern Pike	-	-	-	-	4	-	6	-	10
Rock Bass	17	7	-	-	-	-	-	-	24
Smallmouth Bass	-	-	6	10	10	-	-	-	26
Tullibee (Cisco)	-	2	31	1	-	-	-	-	36
Walleye	-	-	-	-	6	9	8	-	24
White Sucker	-	-	-	-	6	-	-	-	6
Yellow Perch	-	3	-	-	-	-	-	-	3

JOHNSON LAKE
St. Louis County

Area map pg / coord: 9 / D-5,6

Watershed: Rainy Lake

Surface area: 1,674 acres

Shorelength: 19.7 miles

Max / mean depth: 88 feet / NA

Water color / clarity: Clear / 9.13 feet (2004)

Shoreland zoning class: Rec. dev.

Mgmt class / Ecological type: Centrarchid / centrarchid

Accessibility: Carry-down access to south shore of eastern main lake from FR 203
47° 48' 47.88" N / 91° 53' 46.65" W

Accommodations: Resort, boat rental, camping, picnicking

SPRING LAKE
St. Louis County

Area map pg / coord: 9 / D-5

Watershed: Rainy Lake

Surface area: 219 acres

Shorelength: 4.1 miles

Max / mean depth: 60 feet / NA

Water color / clarity: Clear / 12.5 feet (2009)

Shoreland zoning class: Nat. envt.

Mgmt class / Ecological type: Centrarchid / trout

Accessibility: Via navigable channel or portage from Johnson Lake
47° 4' 7.93" N / 91° 59' 49.52" W

Accommodations: None

NO RECORD OF STOCKING

NET CATCH DATA

Date: 06/28/2004

species	Gill Nets # per net	Gill Nets avg. fish weight (lbs.)	Trap Nets # per net	Trap Nets avg. fish weight (lbs.)
Lake White fish	7.9	2.16	-	-
Northern Pike	3.3	3.23	-	-
Rock Bass	0.5	0.17	-	-
Smallmouth Bass	1.4	0.89	-	-
Tullibee (Cisco)	7.2	0.11	-	-
Walleye	3.8	2.15	-	-
White Sucker	6.0	2.38	-	-
Yellow Perch	1.8	0.15	-	-

LENGTH OF SELECTED SPECIES SAMPLED FROM ALL GEAR
Number of fish caught for the following length categories (inches):

species	0-5	6-8	9-11	12-14	15-19	20-24	25-29	>29	Total
Lake Whitefish	-	-	4	5	65	20	-	-	94
Northern Pike	-	-	-	-	10	15	11	3	39
Rock Bass	2	4	-	-	-	-	-	-	6
Smallmouth Bass	1	3	4	7	2	-	-	-	17
Tullibee (Cisco)	-	73	3	-	-	-	-	-	76
Walleye	-	1	3	7	26	5	3	-	45
Yellow Perch	3	16	3	-	-	-	-	-	22

FISH STOCKING DATA

year	species	size	# released
05	Lake Trout	Yearling	2,094
07	Lake Trout	Yearling	1,646
09	Lake Trout	Yearling	1,902
09	Lake Trout	Adult	350

NET CATCH DATA

Date: 08/17/2009

species	Gill Nets # per net	Gill Nets avg. fish weight (lbs.)	Trap Nets # per net	Trap Nets avg. fish weight (lbs.)
Lake Trout	0.17	8.71	-	-
Lake Whitefish	12.17	2.90	-	-
Northern Pike	0.17	4.96	-	-
Smallmouth Bass	1.33	1.24	-	-
Tullibee (Cisco)	24.50	0.14	-	-

LENGTH OF SELECTED SPECIES SAMPLED FROM ALL GEAR
Number of fish caught for the following length categories (inches):

species	0-5	6-8	9-11	12-14	15-19	20-24	25-29	>29	Total
Lake Trout	-	-	-	-	-	-	1	-	1
Lake Whitefish	-	-	6	7	6	54	-	-	73
Northern Pike	-	-	-	-	-	-	1	-	1
Smallmouth Bass	-	-	4	1	3	-	-	-	8
Tullibee (Cisco)	-	137	7	-	-	-	-	-	147

FISHING INFORMATION

Johnson and Spring Lakes are well off the beaten path. They lie up near the Canadian border and are accessible via a quarter-mile portage off a forest road, which angles northeastward from Highway 53. If you're staying at the lone resort in the area, the operators will pick you up with an ATV. Otherwise, you'll have to hoof it over a trail that's nice, but only about 4 feet wide.

Johnson Lake is well worth your time and the hike to get there. This 1,674-acre lake has depths that reach 88 feet with water clarity to 9.13 feet. There are tales of 30-inch walleyes being caught, but the DNR didn't find them during their survey in 2004. Their numbers showed the average walleye being 17.5 inches and 2.15 pounds. Abundance levels are down from previous years. Toss a jig around the islands and points for walleyes, especially where the bottom drops off to the 20-foot level or deeper. Northern pike caught during the survey ranged from 16 to 34.8 inches, with an average size of 23.9 inches. Weedy bays are good spots to

try for northerns; toss spoons or spinnerbaits to weedlines or still-fish with a sucker minnow and bobber. Smallmouth bass are abundant, with sizes ranging from 5.4 to 16.1 inches. Look for rocks to find smallies. Crankbaits are excellent lures to try as are spinnerbaits and jerkbaits. Of course in a pinch its tough to beat a split-shot rig and a leech or a nightcrawler to hook a few smallmouth bass.

Spring Lake is accessible via portage from Johnson Lake. The DNR has been stocking lake trout here since 2000. Smallmouth bass averaged 12.9 inches and 1.5 pounds during the last survey and are considered the most fishable population in the lake. Fish the points toward the south end in your pursuit of smallmouth. Lake whitefish are fairly abundant. Only one northern pike was caught during the most recent survey, and it should be noted that past specimens have tested high for mercury. Check with the DNR for any current consumption warnings. Children and pregnant women should be especially careful.

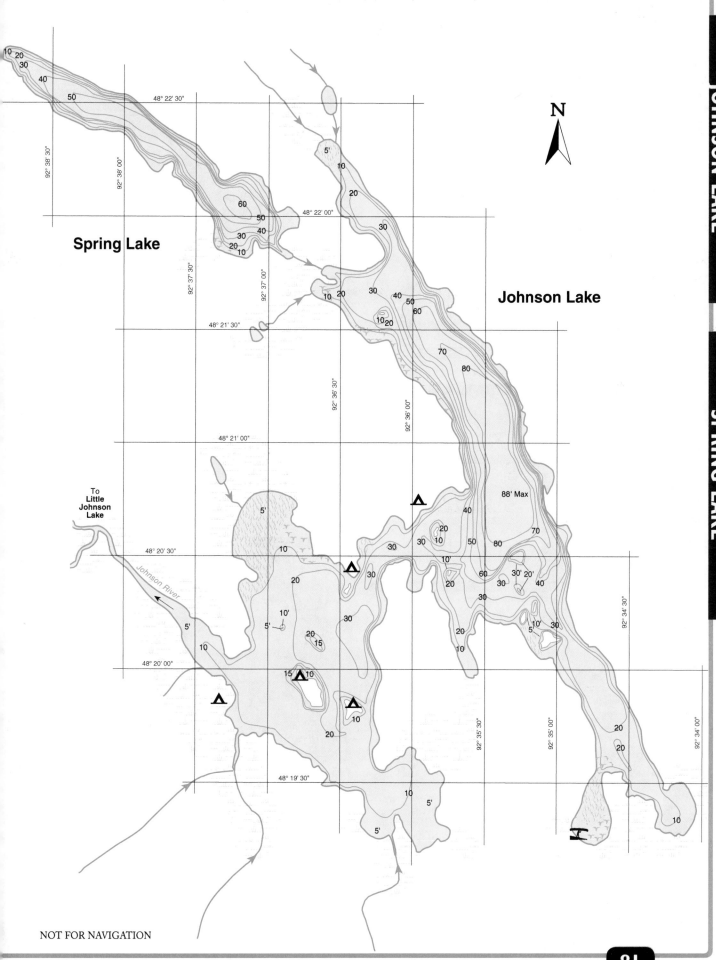

Spring Lake

Johnson Lake

To
Little
Johnson
Lake

Johnson River

88' Max

N

NOT FOR NAVIGATION

Source: Minnesota Department of Natural Resources, USGS

ASH LAKE
St. Louis County

LITTLE JOHNSON LAKE
St. Louis County

Area map pg / coord: 10 / A,B-3

Watershed: Rainy Lake

Surface area: 690 acres

Shorelength: 5.8 miles

Max / mean depth: 29 feet / NA

Water color / clarity: Brown tint / 8.0 feet (2008)

Shoreland zoning class: Rec. dev.

Mgmt class / Ecological type: Walleye-centrarchid / centrarchid-walleye

Accessibility: State-owned public access with concrete ramp on north shore, south off Co. Rd. 518
48° 13' 12.99" N / 92° 55' 42.28" W

Accommodations: Resort, camping, picnicking, restrooms

Area map pg / coord: 9 / D-5

Watershed: Rainy Lake

Surface area: 566 acres

Shorelength: NA

Max / mean depth: 28 feet / NA

Water color / clarity: Green tint / 9.5 feet (2010)

Shoreland zoning class: Nat. envt.

Mgmt class / Ecological type: Centrarchid / centrarchid

Accessibility: Via navigable channel (Johnson River) from Johnson Lake

Accommodations: None

FISH STOCKING DATA			
year	species	size	# released
05	Walleye	Fingerling	10,135
07	Walleye	Fingerling	12,927
09	Walleye	Fingerling	8,277

NET CATCH DATA
Date: 06/16/2008

	Gill Nets		Trap Nets	
species	# per net	avg. fish weight (lbs.)	# per net	avg. fish weight (lbs.)
Black Crappie	2.78	0.32	7.83	0.28
Bluegill	0.78	0.25	1.83	0.19
Northern Pike	4.33	5.90	0.42	5.38
Smallmouth Bass	0.44	1.47	0.17	0.48
Walleye	0.78	3.79	-	-
White Sucker	9.67	2.11	0.42	3.05
Yellow Perch	97.56	0.18	6.08	0.14

LENGTH OF SELECTED SPECIES SAMPLED FROM ALL GEAR
Number of fish caught for the following length categories (inches):

species	0-5	6-8	9-11	12-14	15-19	20-24	25-29	>29	Total
Black Crappie	-	100	17	1	-	-	-	-	119
Bluegill	16	12	1	-	-	-	-	-	29
Golden Shiner	20	1	-	-	-	-	-	-	21
Northern Pike	-	-	-	-	1	7	19	17	44
Smallmouth Bass	-	-	2	4	-	-	-	-	6
Walleye	-	-	2	-	1	3	1	-	7
White Sucker	-	1	4	23	53	11	-	-	92
Yellow Perch	28	903	9	-	-	-	-	-	951

NO RECORD OF STOCKING

NET CATCH DATA
Date: 08/09/2010

	Gill Nets		Trap Nets	
species	# per net	avg. fish weight (lbs.)	# per net	avg. fish weight (lbs.)
Lake Whitefish	0.22	4.33	-	-
Northern2 Pike	4.89	1.38	-	-
Rock Bass	0.11	0.17	-	-
Smallmouth Bass	2.67	1.63	-	-
Walleye	3.00	1.76	-	-
White Sucker	0.44	3.12	-	-
Yellow Perch	2.78	0.16	-	-

LENGTH OF SELECTED SPECIES SAMPLED FROM ALL GEAR
Number of fish caught for the following length categories (inches):

species	0-5	6-8	9-11	12-14	15-19	20-24	25-29	>29	Total
Lake Whitefish	-	-	-	-	2	-	-	2
Northern Pike	-	-	-	2	27	13	-	-	44
Rock Bass	1	-	-	-	-	-	-	-	1
Smallmouth Bass	-	1	4	10	8	-	-	-	24
Walleye	-	5	1	4	8	8	1	-	27
White Sucker	-	-	-	-	3	1	-	-	4
Yellow Perch	13	10	2	-	-	-	-	-	25

FISHING INFORMATION

Crappies top the list for quality gamefish on **Ash Lake** located near Orr, MN. The most recent DNR survey indicated that the black crappie population was abundant with good size due to a variety of year classes present. The folks at Anderson Sports Port, Highway 53, Orr, MN, 218-757-3411, say the lake yields some really nice crappies on occasion. Spring is the best time to look for them. Try small minnows on a jig in shallows, near the creek and river inlets. You can catch them later in the year, of course, but you'll have to work a little harder to catch them then. Fish deep weed edges to locate crappies later in summer. Stick with a small minnow or leech fished under a slip bobber or a split shot rig.

Walleyes aren't as plentiful here as they are in other area lakes. The latest

DNR survey indicated that Ash wasn't producing huge numbers of walleyes with 75% of the lakes in its class showing more abundant populations. The two prominent points which face each other in the lake's western end produce walleyes in good numbers, though. Each slopes away to a hole at least 25-feet deep, so these areas can produce fish all year long. Pike are fairly abundant in this lake, according to DNR surveys. Look for them in the wood on the lake's east end or the south end weeds. Try large minnows under a slip bobber, a flashy spinnerbait or jerkbait. Yellow perch numbers are very high on Ash. According to the last DNR survey, the overall numbers were so high they were approaching levels in the late 1970s and early 1980s, which prompted a fish removal project.

If you're not having luck catching fish in Ash Lake, head into **Little Johnson Lake**. At 566 acres, this lake is not tiny, but it is shallow with 98% of the lake being less than 15 feet deep. Smallmouth bass are your best bet here. Recent DNR surveys found average smallies measuring about 14 inches long.

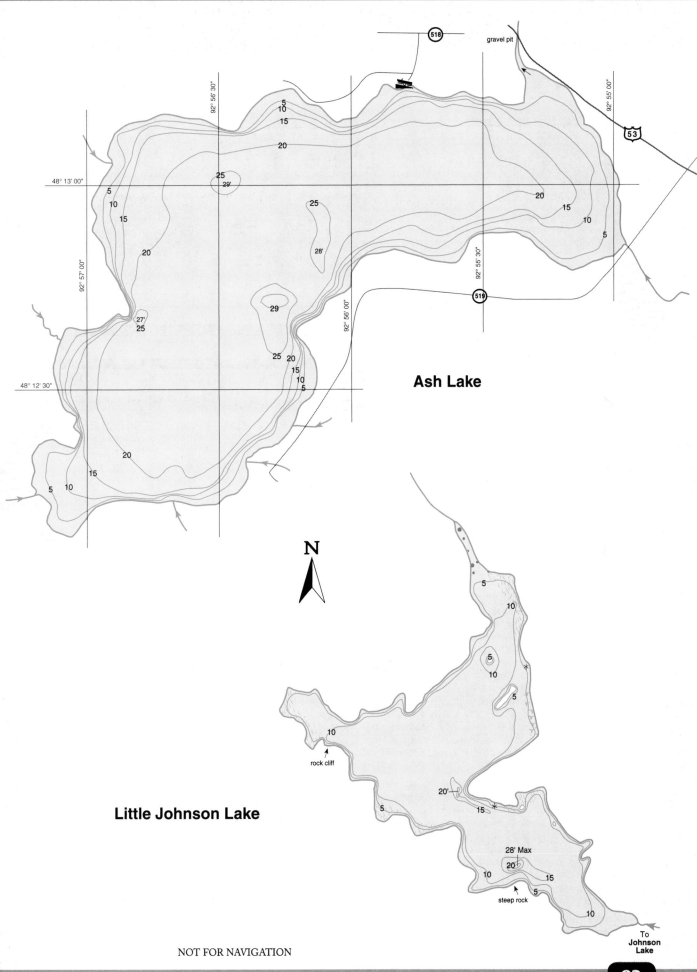

Ash Lake

Little Johnson Lake

N

rock cliff

20'

15

28' Max

20

steep rock

To
**Johnson
Lake**

NOT FOR NAVIGATION

Source: Minnesota Department of Natural Resources, USGS

SAND POINT LAKE *St. Louis County*

Area map page / coordinates:	9 / C,D,E-6
Watershed:	Rainy Lake
Surface water area / shorelength:	8,526 acres / 92.0 miles
Maximum / mean depth:	184 feet / NA
Water color / clarity:	Light green tint / 7.9 feet (2010)
Shoreland zoning classification:	Recreational development
Management class / Ecological type:	Walleye / soft-water walleye
Accessibility:	Via navigable channel from Crane Lake
	48° 19'34" N / 92° 27'55" W
Accommodations:	Resort, marina, boat rental, camping, picnicking, restrooms

FISHING INFORMATION

Sand Point Lake is smaller, 8,526 acres - 5,179 of which are in Minnesota - and more accessible than its near neighbor to the north, big old Namakan. However, there still isn't any road access on the Minnesota side. You can get there by boat from accesses on Crane and Kabetogama lakes. The easier access makes Sand Point more popular with recreational boaters and anglers. Fortunately, the fishery hasn't suffered much as a result. Sand point Lake offers good fishing for walleyes up to 8 pounds and larger, for big northern pike, as well as opportunities for smallmouth bass and crappies.

The folks at Gander Mountain, 4275 Haines Road, Hermantown, MN, 218-786-9800, say walleye fishing is what most anglers are after on Sand Point. In fact, on opening weekend, you'll find 20 to 30 boats clustered around the island on the Minnesota side of the lake's southern section, north of King Williams Narrows. Speaking of that narrows, you'll want to fish that, as well, early in the season, with jig-and-minnow combinations. In the upper section, you'll find good early walleye fishing around Swanson's Bay, and in the middle section, try Clearwater Bay. Trolling crankbaits such as Ruff Guys or Shad Raps or spinner rigs and crawlers is a good way to locate active walleyes during summer. Target the various points, shoals and drop-offs throughout the lake. Remember, walleyes will often suspend during summer to feed on tullibee so make sure to use your electronics to help locate fish over open water. You can hook walleyes throughout the day, but they usually don't like sunny days that much. Fishing is often much better during lowlight hours of early morning or evening. Walleye abundance was above what is found in most lakes of this class, according to the DNR. The average walleye was about 15 inches long, but the fish are slow-growing compared to the rest of the state.

Fish the finger bay west of King Williams Narrows with large sucker minnows or spinnerbaits for northern pike. Don't ignore Redhorse Bay on the Canadian side. If you want to catch a large pike, try fishing with an oversized lure. A large jig and sucker is a good way to start. Fish it on bass flipping gear and make sure to have a leader in place. Popping this combo off the bottom along points, humps and drop-offs can draw strikes from big pike. The pike population is doing well in Sand Point. DNR data showed their numbers to be above what is found in 75% of similar lakes. Total length of the pike sampled ranged from 17.1 to 39.2 inches. Pike growth was above the area and statewide averages.

In the lake's far-western arm, you'll find two fair-size bays separated by a broad point containing a campground. Fish the north bay during winter and summer for crappies. The south bay is a good spring crappie prospect.

NO RECORD OF STOCKING

NET CATCH DATA

Date: 10/05/2010	Gill Nets		Trap Nets	
species	# per net	avg. fish weight (lbs.)	# per net	avg. fish weight (lbs.)
Black Crappie	0.53	0.33	-	-
Lake Whtiefish	0.20	2.31	-	-
Northern Pike	3.53	3.07	-	-
Rock Bass	0.47	0.30	-	-
Sauger	0.67	0.26	-	-
Smallmouth Bass	0.13	0.86	-	-
Tullibee (Cisco)	6.20	0.46	-	-
Walleye	15.27	0.97	-	-
White Sucker	1.27	2.26	-	-
Yellow Perch	1.67	0.12	-	-

LENGTH OF SELECTED SPECIES SAMPLED FROM ALL GEAR
Number of fish caught for the following length categories (inches):

species	0-5	6-8	9-11	12-14	15-19	20-24	25-29	>30	Total
Black Crappie	3	2	3	-	-	-	-	-	8
Lake Whitefish	-	-	-	-	2	1	-	-	3
Northern Pike	-	-	-	-	13	23	11	6	53
Rock Bass	2	4	1	-	-	-	-	-	7
Sauger	-	1	9	-	-	-	-	-	10
Smallmouth Bass	-	-	1	1	-	-	-	-	2
Tullibee (Cisco)	1	20	44	23	5	-	-	-	93
Walleye	-	16	104	51	40	14	4	-	229
White Sucker	-	-	1	5	9	3	1	-	19
Yellow Perch	9	16	-	-	-	-	-	-	25

Whenever you're fishing for crappies make sure and have a few slip bobbers, small jigs, small minnows and leeches. This basic assortment of gear will catch crappies under most conditions. You may also want to bring along some small jig spinners. Lures like a Road Runner or a Beetle spin can be terrific for catching crappies when they're in the shallows. During the 2004 DNR lake survey, the black crappie population was found to be quite abundant. In fact, it was three times greater than the median for similar lakes.

If you want to catch a few yellow perch, they are in Sand Point Lake, but they're generally not too big. The DNR data from the last lake survey showed perch numbers to be the highest recorded in the last few years. The average length however was not very large at 6.2 inches and the growth rate

88

89

was lower than the area and statewide averages.

Bass busters can find both smallmouth and largemouth bass in Sand Point. If you're targeting largemouth bass, find some vegetation. Look for emergent vegetation in various shallow bays and you'll find largemouth bass. A solid battle plan is to have a rod rigged with a soft plastic or jig-and-pig combo, another with a spinnerbait or crankbait and another with a topwater presentation. Since visibility in this water is down to 10 feet or so, it's

a good idea to use either lighter line or a fluorocarbon or fluorocarbon coated line, just in case the fish are line shy. As far as color choices for lures, it's usually a good bet to stick with black and blue or green pumpkin for your jig, green pumpkin, watermelon, smoke or black fro your soft plastic, white, black or chartreuse for your spinnerbait, minnow, shad or perch colors for crankbaits and anything with a white belly for your topwater lure.

Smallmouth bass will be found almost anywhere you

find walleyes. Check out the various islands, rocky shorelines, points and drop-offs. Smallmouths can be anywhere. Use slightly lighter gear for smallies and stick with lure choices like soft plastics tubes on a jig, spinnerbaits, topwaters and crankbaits, all colors in the same hues you're using for largemouth bass. Make sure to add jerkbaits to your smallie line up, too. Smallmouth bass will often come from long distances to crush an erratically retrieved jerkbait.

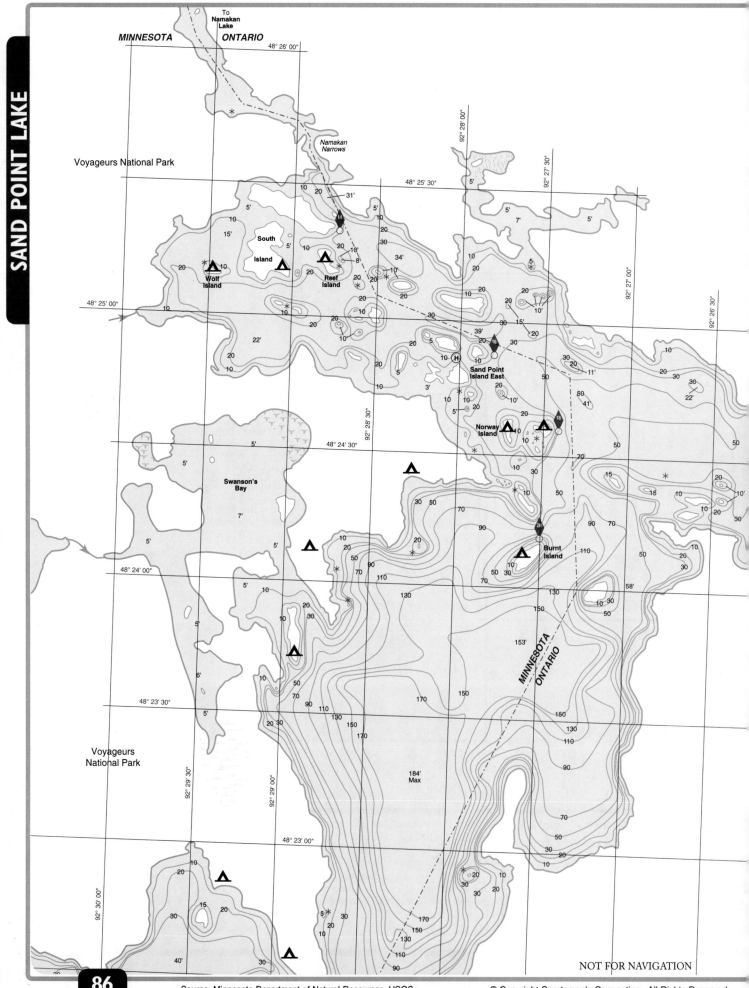

To
Namakan
Lake

MINNESOTA   ONTARIO

48° 26' 00"

Voyageurs National Park

Namakan
Narrows

48° 25' 30"

31'

South
Island

Wolf
Island

Reef
Island

48° 25' 00"

22'

Sand Point
Island East

92° 28' 30"

48° 24' 30"

Norway
Island

Swanson's
Bay

Burnt
Island

48° 24' 00"

48° 23' 30"

Voyageurs
National Park

92° 29' 30"

92° 29' 00"

48° 23' 00"

153'

184'
Max

MINNESOTA
ONTARIO

92° 30' 00"

40'

NOT FOR NAVIGATION

Source: Minnesota Department of Natural Resources, USGS

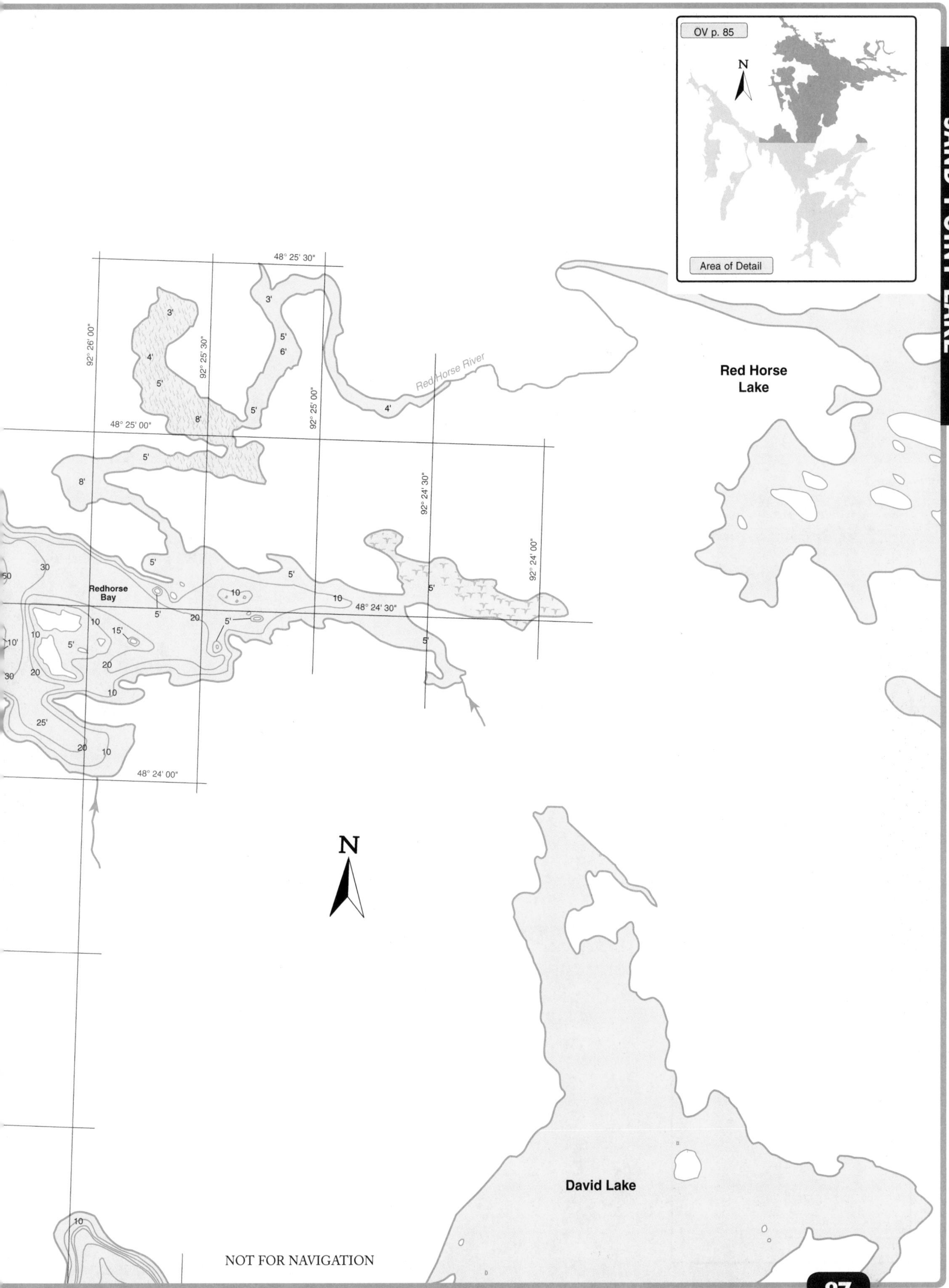

OV p. 85

N

Area of Detail

48° 25' 30"

92° 26' 00"

92° 25' 30"

92° 25' 00"

92° 24' 30"

92° 24' 00"

3'

3'

5'

6'

4'

5'

5'

8'

5'

Red Horse River

4'

Red Horse
Lake

48° 25' 00"

5'

8'

30

5'

5'

50

Redhorse
Bay

10

5'

48° 24' 30"

10

5'

10°

10

15'

5'

20

5'

5'

10

10

20

30

20

5'

25'

20

10

48° 24' 00"

N

David Lake

10

10

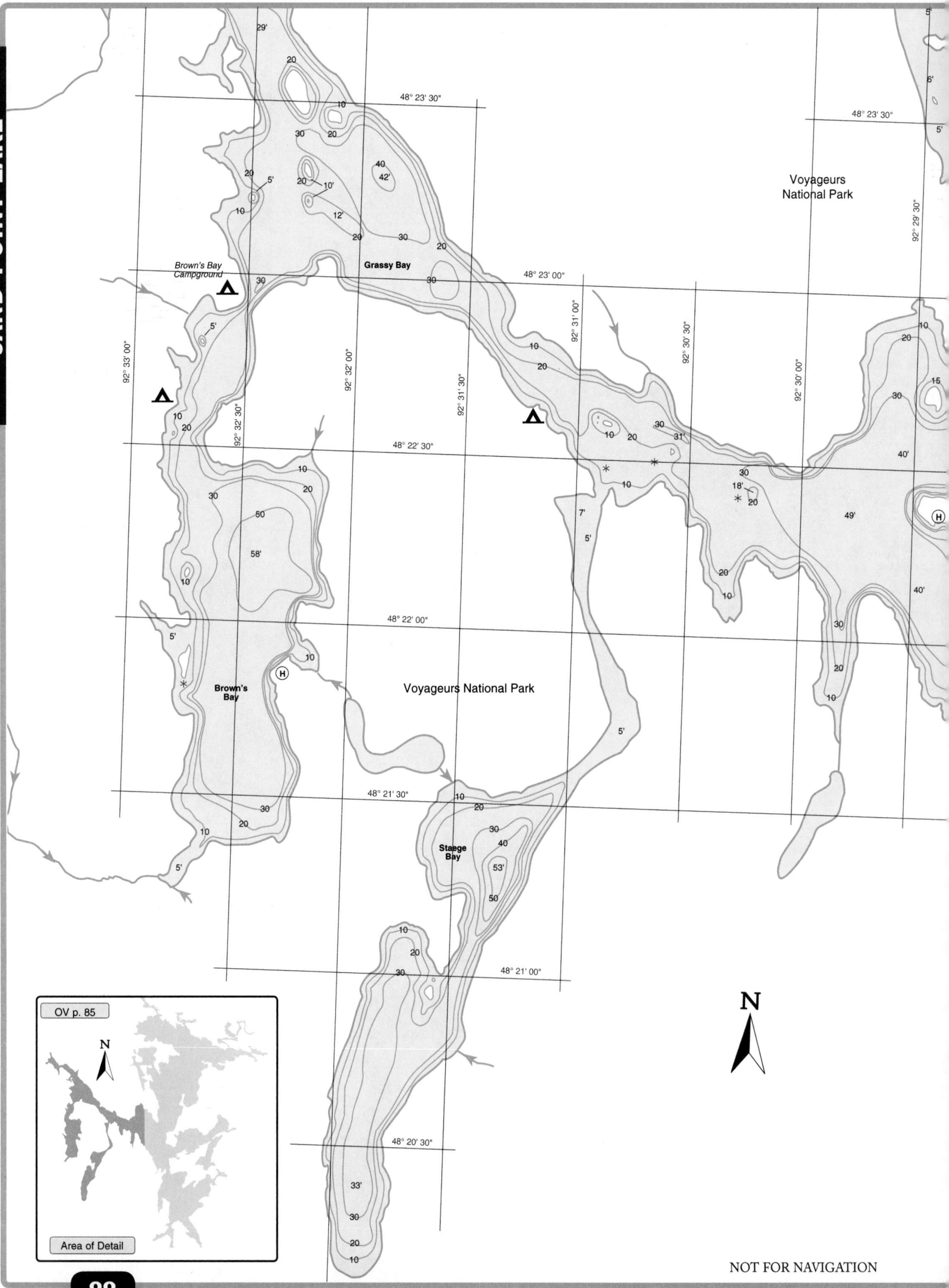

Voyageurs
National Park

29'

20

48° 23' 30"

30

20

48° 23' 30"

40
42'

20

5'

10'

20

10

12'

20

30

Brown's Bay
Campground

30

Grassy Bay

30

48° 23' 00"

10

20

30

48° 22' 30"

10

20

30

50

58'

10

10

20

48° 22' 00"

5'

10

H

*

Brown's
Bay

Voyageurs National Park

10

20

30

48° 21' 30"

5'

10

20

30
40

Staege
Bay

53'

50

10

20

30

48° 21' 00"

10

20

30

48° 20' 30"

33'

30

20

10

31'

20

30

10

20

30

18'
20

49'

H

40'

40'

20

10

30

20

10

10
20

20

10

7'

5'

*
*

5'

92° 33' 00"

92° 32' 30"

92° 32' 00"

92° 31' 30"

92° 31' 00"

92° 30' 30"

92° 30' 00"

92° 29' 30"

15

20

10

5'

N

OV p. 85

N

Area of Detail

88

Source: Minnesota Department of Natural Resources, USGS

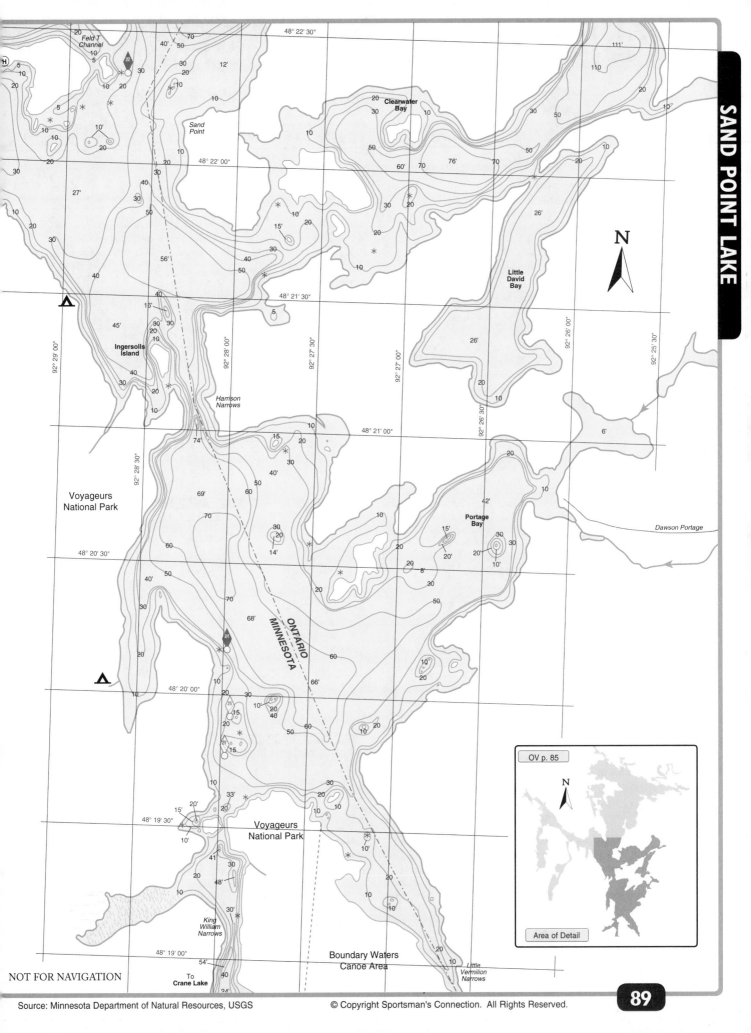

Feld T Channel

Sand Point

Clearwater Bay

Little David Bay

N

Ingersolls Island

Harrison Narrows

Voyageurs National Park

ONTARIO
MINNESOTA

Portage Bay

Dawson Portage

Voyageurs National Park

King William Narrows

Boundary Waters Canoe Area

Little Vermilion Narrows

To Crane Lake

NOT FOR NAVIGATION

OV p. 85

N

Area of Detail

89

CRANE LAKE St. Louis County

Area map page / coordinates:	9 / E-6
Watershed:	Vermilion
Surface water area / shorelength:	2,921 acres / 36.7 miles
Maximum / mean depth:	80 feet / NA
Water color / clarity:	Light brown stain / 9.5 feet (2006)
Shoreland zoning classification:	Recreational development
Management class / Ecological type:	Walleye / centrarchid

Accessibility: 1) County-owned public access with concrete ramp on west shore at Voyageurs National Park Ranger Station, north of Camp 40 Creek

48° 16' 7.59" N / 92° 29' 18.16" W

Accessibility: 2) State-owned public access on south shore off Co. Rd. 425

48° 16' 8.31" N / 92° 28' 14.79" W

Accommodations: Bordered by Voyageurs National Park and Kabetogama State Forest, fishing piers, resorts, marina, boat rental, camping, picnicking, restrooms

FISHING INFORMATION

If you're looking for a reliable fish-producer, you don't have to look any farther than Crane Lake. Year after year, it's been one of the better fishing waters south of the Canadian border. With just under 3,000 acres of water to fish, you'll find solid populations of northern pike, walleyes, crappies and smallmouth bass.

Northern pike fishing in these tea-colored waters can be very good. The latest DNR survey showed the pike abundance to exceed the lake class median. The average northern pike sampled measured 23.7 inches long and weighed 3.5 pounds. Some pike captured measured over 40 inches. Summertime fishing for pike is very popular on Crane Lake. Try trolling weedlines at 18 to 20 feet with spinners, spoons and crankbaits. A good summer spot is the weedline off the northeast shore of Bear Island toward the big lake's southern end.

Walleyes in Crane Lake are primarily targeted during spring, although you also can catch them later on with a little extra effort. Early in the season, try around the little islands, near the mouth of the lake's northwest arm. Don't miss Rollick Bay on the west shore. A warm current from Rollick Creek attracts fish and usually produces a good early walleye bite. Later in the year, fish the deeper reefs. In fall, try around Indian Island, the rocks off the island's southwest shore, and the little hump in between. Drifting weed edges with live bait will usually produce fish, but trolling open water with crankbaits or spinner rigs and nightcrawlers can produce when walleyes suspend in summer. The DNR found that during its last survey, the walleye abundance in gillnets has continued to increase since the mid-1980s.

Bear Island and around nearby Baylis Island are known as great crappie producers. You'll also find good numbers of crappies in East Bay. Small minnows, leeches, spinners and jigs are productive at fooling crappies.

Smallmouth bass numbers have continued to increase on this lake since the 1960s. During the last DNR survey, the numbers of smallies gillnetted was the fifth highest on record and the average length of smallmouth bass was the highest recorded on the lake. Rocks and smallies go together like peanut butter and jelly. You'll find no shortage of rocks on Crane Lake. So, finding good smallmouth habitat isn't very hard. Fish any of the rocky points, ledges or islands and you'll be in smallie territory. Start your search with a fast-moving lure like a jerkbait or a spinnerbait. Smallies are suckers early in the day or when the sky is overcast for an aggressively fished bait whizzing overhead. Of course, if the sun is shining and the wind isn't blowing, you may need to switch to finesse tactics. Try a jig-and-tube combo or a dropshot rigged soft plastic fished deeper on rocky points, drop-offs and ledges. If you're not a purist, use a split-shot rig and a nightcrawler or leech. You never know what you'll catch with that combo.

NO RECORD OF STOCKING

NET CATCH DATA

Date: 08/28/2006	Gill Nets		Trap Nets	
species	# per net	avg. fish weight (lbs.)	# per net	avg. fish weight (lbs.)
Black Crappie	0.14	0.55	-	-
Burbot	0.07	1.02	-	-
Lake Whtiefish	0.07	2.00	-	-
Northern Pike	2.29	3.41	-	-
Rock Bass	0.57	0.29	-	-
Sauger	2.07	0.48	-	-
Smallmouth Bass	0.43	0.83	-	-
Tullibee (Cisco)	0.36	0.56	-	-
Walleye	10.00	0.68	-	-
White Sucker	4.93	1.96	-	-
Yellow Perch	7.43	0.13	-	-

LENGTH OF SELECTED SPECIES SAMPLED FROM ALL GEAR

Number of fish caught for the following length categories (inches):

species	0-5	6-8	9-11	12-14	15-19	20-24	25-29	>30	Total
Black Bullhead	-	-	-	-	-	-	-	-	-
Black Crappie	-	-	2	-	-	-	-	-	2
Bluegill	-	-	-	-	-	-	-	-	-
Brown Bullhead	-	-	-	-	-	-	-	-	-
Muskellunge	-	-	-	-	-	-	-	-	-
Northern Pike	-	-	-	-	7	15	5	5	32
Rock Bass	3	5	-	-	-	-	-	-	8
Sauger	-	1	15	11	-	-	-	-	27
Smallmouth Bass	1	3	-	-	1	-	-	-	5
Tullibee (Cisco)	-	2	1	2	-	-	-	-	5
Walleye	-	18	61	42	10	4	1	-	136
Yellow Perch	19	82	3	-	-	-	-	-	104

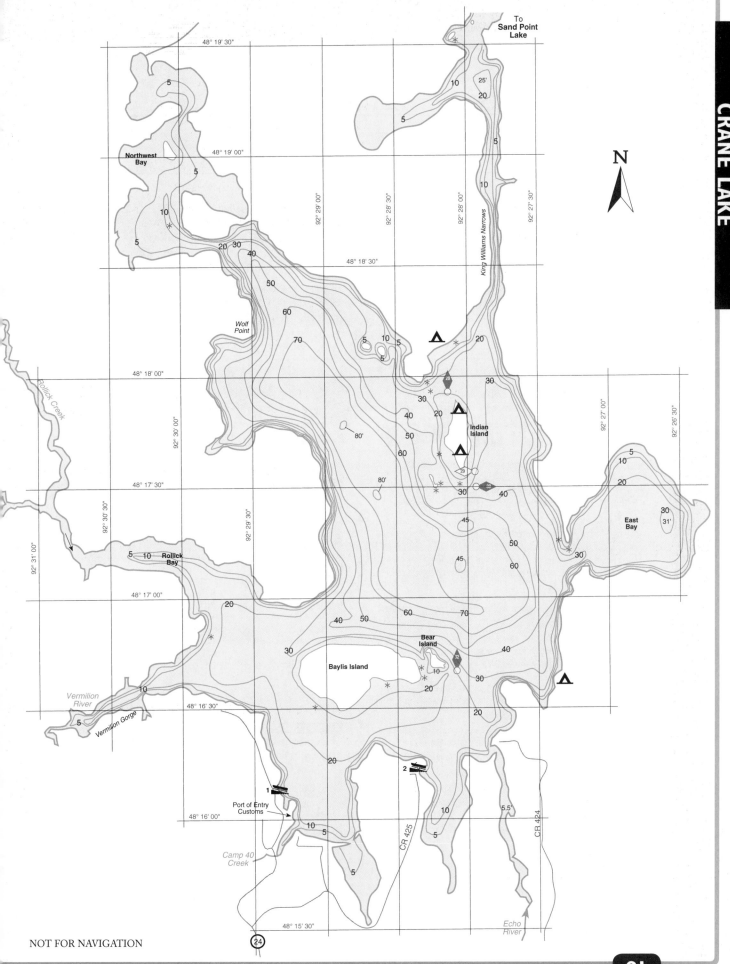

N

Northwest
Bay

Wolf
Point

Indian
Island

King Williams Narrows

To
Sand Point
Lake

East
Bay

Rollick Creek

Rollick
Bay

Baylis Island

Bear
Island

Vermilion
River

Vermilion Gorge

Port of Entry
Customs

Camp 40
Creek

Echo
River

CR 425

CR 424

NOT FOR NAVIGATION

24

Source: Minnesota Department of Natural Resources, USGS

PELICAN LAKE *St. Louis County*

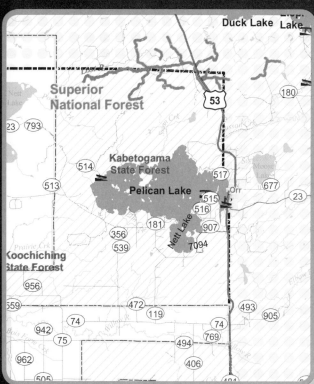

Area map page / coordinates:	10,11 / C,D-2,3,4
Watershed:	Vermilion
Surface water area / shorelength:	11,546 acres / 49.4 miles
Maximum / mean depth:	38 feet / 12 feet
Water color / clarity:	Light green / 6.0 feet (2007)
Mgmt class / Ecological type:	Walleye-centrarchid / northern pike-sucker

Accessibility: 1) County-owned public access with gravel ramp on northwest shore, at the end of County Road 514 — 48° 4' 26.25" N / 92° 58' 41.94" W

Accessibility: 2) State-owned public access with concrete ramp on southeast shore, just north of Haslam Point, off County Road 516 — 48° 3' 2.68" N / 92° 51' 42.50" W

Accessibility: 3) County-owned public access with concrete ramp on southeast shore adjacent to campground, at the end of County Road 515 — 48° 3' 41.92" N / 92° 51' 27.95" W

Accessibility: 4) County-owned public access with gravel ramp on northeast shore, at the end of County Road 517 — 48° 4' 31.55" N / 92° 50' 22.18" W

Accessibility: 5) City-owned public access with concrete ramp on east shore of Orr Bay in the City of Orr — 48° 3' 13.80" N / 92° 49' 59.88" W

Accommodations: Resorts, boat rental, camping, picnicking

FISHING INFORMATION

Pelican Lake provides plenty of water for an angler to explore. At 11,546 acres, this lake located at Orr provides fishing enthusiasts a chance to bag largemouth and smallmouth bass, black crappies, northern pike and walleyes. In fact, if you're willing to target multiple fish species on your fishing trip, your odds of getting skunked are pretty low.

Both largemouth and smallmouth bass are abundant on Pelican Lake. Locating largemouth bass habitat on Pelican is fairly easy. Find submerged weeds and you'll find largemouth. You can find largemouth in any of the bays throughout the warm weather months. A basic, but effective, approach is to fish shallow cover early with topwater lures, spinnerbaits or soft plastics. As the day progresses, move to deeper weed edges. Fish crankbaits, Carolina-rigged plastics or jigs through these areas. Smallmouth bass numbers were also solid. Smallmouth bass love points and islands; fortunately Pelican Lake has plenty of both. Whatever you do, don't miss the topwater fishing opportunities for smallies. Cast a chugger or walking bait near a point or island early in morning and be prepared for some action. Don't forget get to bring a supply of tubes and jig heads. The tube is one of the most effective lures anywhere smallies live. Choose the 3- to 4-inch variety in colors such as smoke, green pumpkin, watermelon or pumpkinseed. You can work tubes in shallows or along deeper breaks.

Crappie numbers are quite solid on Pelican. DNR data showed black crappie abundance to exceed the average for most lakes in Minnesota. Although the crappie growth rate was considered slow, the DNR expects the crappie fishing to be good for several years. The west end of the lake is a productive area to fish for them.

Like their largemouth bass buddies, northern pike hang out in weeds. Sure, you'll find some of the bigger pike using deeper drop-offs in summer months, but the majority of these toothy fish hang out in weeds looking to ambush a meal. Any of the lakes weedbeds can produce pike. Drift deeper weed edges with a live bait rig and a large minnow. Walleye numbers were below average during the last DNR survey, but the growth rate is high. Good areas to fish for them are reefs, drop-offs and rocks around Bald, Bern and Backus Islands near the lake's eastern end. Actually, any of the islands or points can hold walleyes.

NO RECORD OF STOCKING

NET CATCH DATA

Date: 07/23/2007	Gill Nets		Trap Nets	
		avg. fish		avg. fish
species	# per net	weight (lbs.)	# per net	weight (lbs.)
Black Bullhead	0.5	0.72	0.2	0.52
Black Crappie	8.1	0.2	8.1	0.21
Bluegill	13.5	0.18	7.9	0.21
Brown Bullhead	4.1	0.81	2.91	1.02
Golden Shiner	0.3	0.1	0.1	0.07
Largemouth Bass	1.5	1.51	0.7	0.25
Northern Pike	22.2	2.44	1.3	2.0
Pumpkin. Sunfish	4.6	0.16	6.1	0.22
Rock Bass	0.2	0.68	0.7	0.29
Smallmouth Bass	1.3	2.42	0.1	2.57
Walleye	2.1	2.95	0.1	3.34
White Sucker	1.1	2.48	-	-
Yellow Perch	44.3	0.14	0.8	0.14

LENGTH OF SELECTED SPECIES SAMPLED FROM ALL GEAR

Number of fish caught for the following length categories (inches):

species	0-5	6-8	9-11	12-14	15-19	20-24	25-29	>30	Total
Black Bullhead	-	-	13	-	-	-	-	-	13
Black Crappie	132	133	30	1	-	-	-	-	296
Bluegill	150	225	-	-	-	-	-	-	375
Brown Bullhead	2	9	56	57	1	-	-	-	125
Largemouth Bass	4	16	4	5	5	-	-	-	34
Northern Pike	-	-	12	24	90	143	77	13	361
Pumpkin. Sunfish	83	121	-	-	-	-	-	-	204
Rock Bass	3	12	3	-	-	-	-	-	18
Smallmouth Bass	-	-	2	6	12	-	-	-	20
Walleye	-	-	1	2	17	13	2	-	35
Yellow Perch	204	458	16	-	-	-	-	-	678

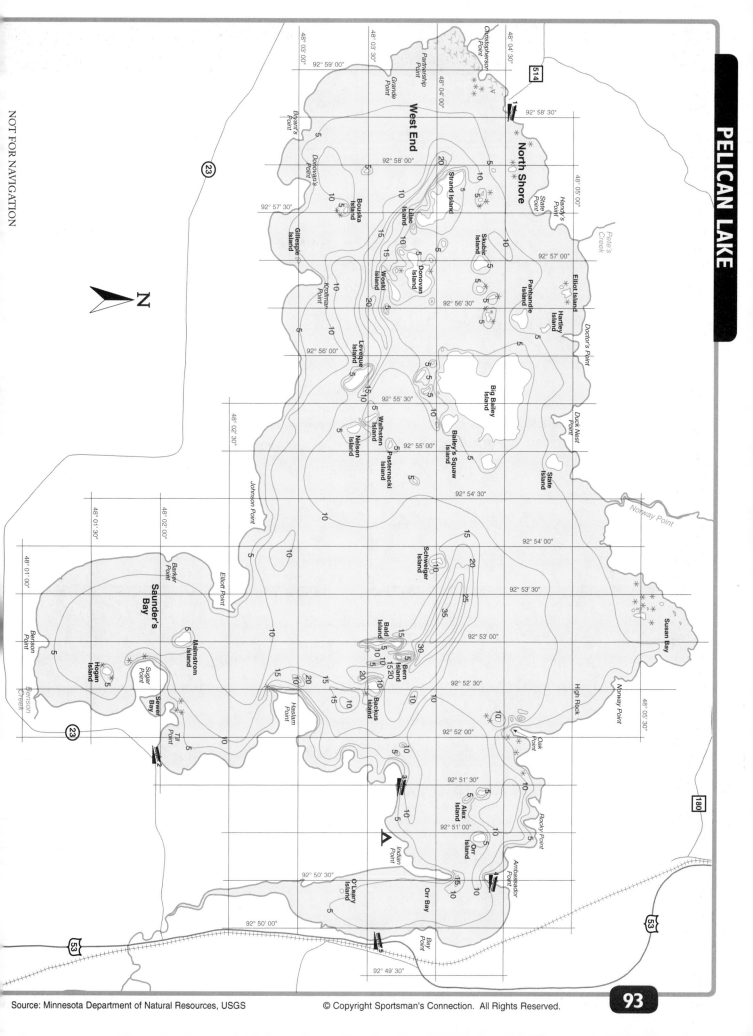

NOT FOR NAVIGATION

N

North Shore

West End

Saunder's Bay

Christopherson Point
Partnership Point
Grande Point
Bryant's Point
Donovan's Point
Strand Island
Bouska Island
Gillespie Island
Lilac Island
Skubic Island
Donovan Island
Woski Island
Krollman Point
Leveque Island
Walhsten Island
Nelson Island
Pasternacki Island
Bailey's Squaw Island
Big Bailey Island
Panhandle Island
Hartley Island
Elliot Island
Handy's Point
State Point
Pete's Creek
Doctor's Point
Duck Nest Point
State Island
Norway Point
Johnson Point
Barker Point
Benson Point
Benson Creek
Elliott Point
Hogan Island
Sugar Point
Malmstrom Island
Sewer Bay
Till Point
Haslam Point
Schweiger Island
Bald Island
Bern Island
Backus Island
Indian Point
O'Leary Island
Alex Island
Orr Island
Orr Bay
Bay Point
Ambassador Point
Rocky Point
Oak Point
High Rock
Susan Bay
Norway Point

48° 04' 30"
48° 04' 00"
48° 03' 30"
48° 03' 00"
48° 02' 30"
48° 02' 00"
48° 01' 30"
48° 01' 00"

92° 59' 00"
92° 58' 30"
92° 58' 00"
92° 57' 30"
92° 57' 00"
92° 56' 30"
92° 56' 00"
92° 55' 30"
92° 55' 00"
92° 54' 30"
92° 54' 00"
92° 53' 30"
92° 53' 00"
92° 52' 30"
92° 52' 00"
92° 51' 30"
92° 51' 00"
92° 50' 30"
92° 50' 00"
92° 49' 30"

48° 05' 00"
48° 05' 30"

514
23
180
53
23
53

Source: Minnesota Department of Natural Resources, USGS

© Copyright Sportsman's Connection. All Rights Reserved.

BLACK DUCK LAKE
St. Louis County

Area map pg / coord: 11 / A,B-4

Watershed: Rainy Lake

Surface area: 1,250 acres

Shorelength: 12.1 miles

Max / mean depth: 30 feet / 17 feet

Water color / clarity: Clear / 14.0 feet (2007)

Shoreland zoning class: Rec. dev.

Mgmt class / Ecological type: Walleye-centrarchid / centrarchid-walleye

Accessibility: State-owned public access with concrete ramp on north shore, near the Duck River outlet 48° 12' 31.33" N / 92° 48' 33.72" W

Accommodations: None

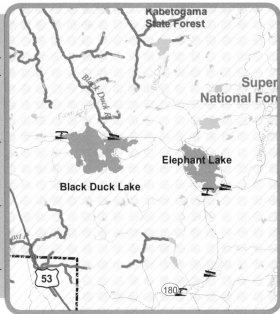

ELEPHANT LAKE
St. Louis County

Area map pg / coord: 11 / B-4

Watershed: Vermilion

Surface area: 724 acres

Shorelength: 7.5 miles

Max / mean depth: 30 feet / 16 feet

Water color / clarity: Light stain / 8.3 feet (2009)

Shoreland zoning class: Rec. dev.

Mgmt class / Ecological type: Walleye-centrarchid / centrarchid-walleye

Accessibility: State-owned public access with concrete ramp on southeast shore, by outlet; carry-down access to south shore 48° 11' 5.67" N / 92° 43' 43.26" W

Accommodations: Resorts, boat rental

NO RECORD OF STOCKING

NET CATCH DATA

Date: 06/25/2007

species	Gill Nets # per net	Gill Nets avg. fish weight (lbs.)	Trap Nets # per net	Trap Nets avg. fish weight (lbs.)
Black Crappie	3.2	0.42	6.1	0.24
Bluegill	14.4	0.19	8.3	0.13
Common Shiner	-	-	-	-
Golden Shiner	0.1	0.09	0.3	0.07
Northern Pike	5.8	3.64	0.2	4.97
Pumpkin. Sunfish	0.3	0.14	0.6	0.15
Smallmouth Bass	0.8	1.27	0.1	0.78
Walleye	7.1	1.85	0.3	6.34
Yellow Perch	41.2	0.21	1.8	0.12

LENGTH OF SELECTED SPECIES SAMPLED FROM ALL GEAR

Number of fish caught for the following length categories (inches):

species	0-5	6-8	9-11	12-14	15-19	20-24	25-29	>29	Total
Black Crappie	11	72	24	4	-	-	-	-	111
Bluegill	157	102	9	-	-	-	-	-	268
Northern Pike	-	-	-	-	4	35	28	5	72
Pumpkin. Sunfish	7	3	-	-	-	-	-	-	10
Smallmouth Bass	-	-	1	9	-	-	-	-	10
Walleye	-	12	8	14	31	18	6	-	89
Yellow Perch	162	246	100	-	-	-	-	-	508

NO RECORD OF STOCKING

NET CATCH DATA

Date: 08/03/2009

species	Gill Nets # per net	Gill Nets avg. fish weight (lbs.)	Trap Nets # per net	Trap Nets avg. fish weight (lbs.)
Black Crappie	0.22	0.58	2.92	0.33
Bluegill	0.78	0.19	4.50	0.12
Northern Pike	1.33	4.63	0.25	4.82
Pumpkin. Sunfish	-	-	0.67	0.13
Smallmouth Bass	0.22	1.89	0.08	0.10
Walleye	6.11	1.04	0.08	3.33
White Sucker	2.33	2.64	0.67	3.06
Yellow Perch	7.78	0.13	2.83	0.14

LENGTH OF SELECTED SPECIES SAMPLED FROM ALL GEAR

Number of fish caught for the following length categories (inches):

species	0-5	6-8	9-11	12-14	15-19	20-24	25-29	>29	Total
Black Crappie	9	9	19	-	-	-	-	-	37
Bluegill	47	14	-	-	-	-	-	-	61
Northern Pike	-	-	-	1	3	6	5	-	15
Pumpkin. Sunfish	7	1	-	-	-	-	-	-	8
Smallmouth Bass	-	1	-	1	1	-	-	-	3
Walleye	-	2	4	35	10	5	-	-	56
Yellow Perch	16	87	1	-	-	-	-	-	104

FISHING INFORMATION

Black Duck's clear water makes it visually appealing, but also tough to fish when the sun is shining. You'll want to get out early or late in day, or when skies are cloudy to take a swing at northern pike, walleyes and smallmouth bass. Pike anglers can hook them along any of the submerged weedlines using large sucker minnows or a variety of lures such as spinnerbaits, jerkbaits and crankbaits. The most recent DNR lake survey indicated pike abundance was slightly below average for a lake of this type, but the growth rates have been some of the highest in the International Falls management area. Walleye abundance is average for a lake of this type according to DNR data. The average walleye in Black Duck weighs just less than 2 pounds. In spring, fish around the point on the lake's southwest end. Later in the season, backtroll around the two small islands in the lake's western lobe. Black Duck also contains a smallmouth bass fishery. Try the bay on the northwest end or the big island, as the lake turns over in fall. There is nice crappie action in spring, too, at the 10- to 15-foot level in the lake's eastern-most bay.

Elephant Lake has a solid smallmouth bass and black crappie population. Walleyes are also common with a smaller population of northern pike. Fish the rocks along the shore forming the "elephant's ear," to locate smallmouth bass. Leeches are the preferred live bait, but anglers using tubes, spinnerbaits or Senkos will also whack plenty of bass. Walleyes are of average abundance according to DNR data. Average length for an Elephant Lake walleye is just under 15 inches. Early in the season, fish for them off the broad point west of big, old Buzzard Island. Later in the season, fish for both walleyes and jumbo perch in rocks along the shoreline directly north of the island. In fall, there's walleye action off the point between the "elephant's" two "front legs." Look for crappies off the same points and along weed edges. During the last DNR survey, the average crappie here was 9.5 inches long with several measuring longer than 10 inches. Pike aren't numerous, but they average just over 27 inches in length.

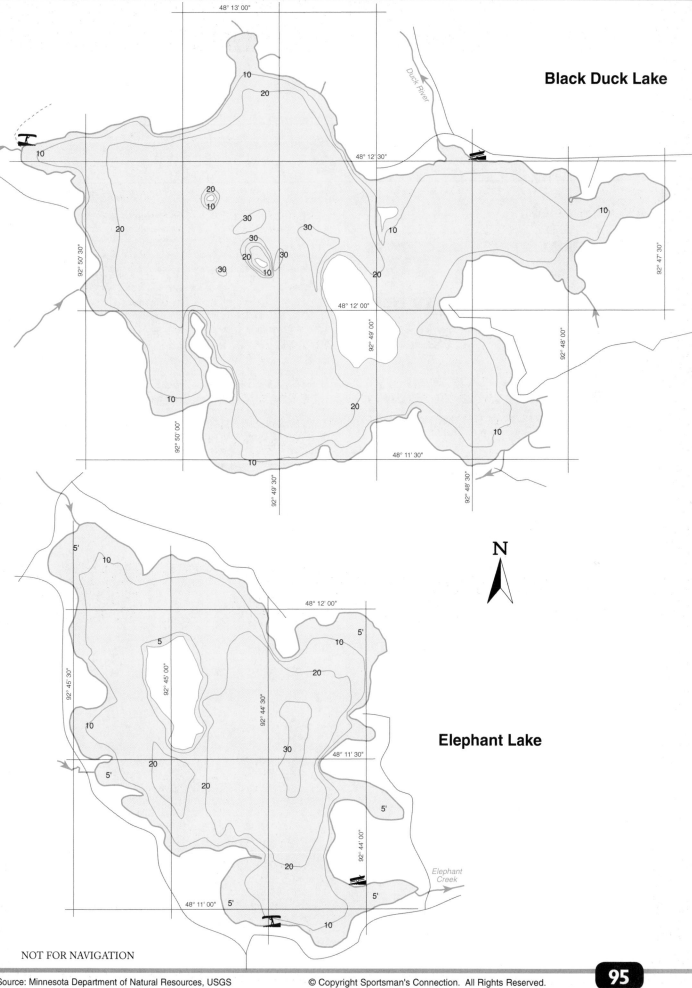

Black Duck Lake

Elephant Lake

N

NOT FOR NAVIGATION

MYRTLE LAKE
St. Louis County

Area map page / coordinates: 11 / C-5

Watershed: Vermilion

Surface water area / shorelength: 876 acres / 7.8 miles

Maximum / mean depth: 21 feet / 11 feet

Water color / clarity: Clear / 8.25 feet (2007)

Accessibility: State-owned public access with concrete ramp on south shore of eastern lake, off County Road 23

48° 4' 40.78" N / 92° 39' 10.52" W

Accommodations: Resort

FISH STOCKING DATA

year	species	size	# released
07	Walleye	Fingerling	43,075
09	Walleye	Fingerling	31,345

LENGTH OF SELECTED SPECIES SAMPLED FROM ALL GEAR

Survey Date: 06/18/2007

Number of fish caught for the following length categories (inches):

species	0-5	6-8	9-11	12-14	15-19	20-24	25-29	>30	Total
Black Crappie	8	209	34	1	-	-	-	-	252
Bluegill	11	23	2	-	-	-	-	-	36
Largemouth Bass	1	5	-	-	1	-	-	-	7
Northern Pike	-	-	4	3	27	61	18	2	115
Pumpkin. Sunfish	-	15	-	-	-	-	-	-	15
Rock Bass	-	5	-	-	-	-	-	-	5
Smallmouth Bass	-	1	-	-	3	-	-	-	4
Walleye	-	22	29	-	7	9	3	-	70
Yellow Perch	82	233	6	-	-	-	-	-	321

FISHING INFORMATION

The folks at Meyer's Minnows Gas and More, 3302 Highway 53, Orr, MN 218-757-3411, say you'll find good numbers of northern pike in Myrtle Lake, along with some nice walleyes, smallish crappies and the ever-present small bluegills.

The lake's southwest end is a great place to catch northern pike. Put down a 5-inch sucker minnow under a slip-bobber for good action. Cast spinnerbaits or jerkbaits along submerged weed edges to draw strikes from pike. For walleyes, try the 5-foot-deep bar off the north shore, which is nearly opposite the big point on the south side. Live bait such as minnows, nightcrawlers or leeches fished on a jig, split shot rig or a slip bobber work well. In summer, try the 15-foot hole off the short, broad point on the north shore. Another walleye spot is the 20-foot hole located about 100 feet off the big point on the south side. According to the latest DNR survey, walleyes aren't overly abundant, but their mean weight was large at 4.27 pounds.

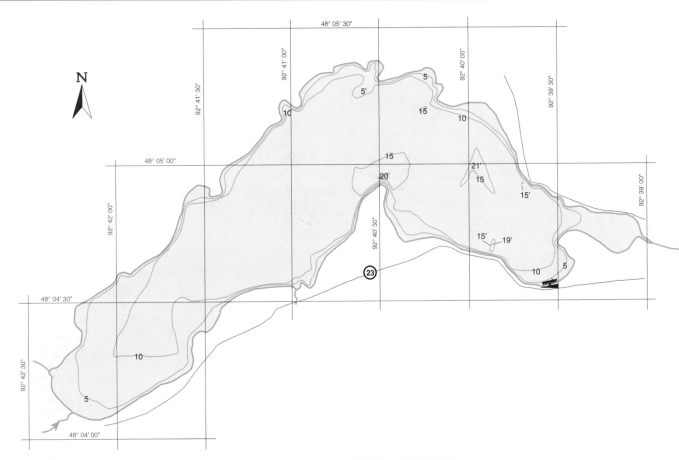

NOT FOR NAVIGATION

Source: Minnesota Department of Natural Resources, USGS

KJOSTAD LAKE
St. Louis County

Area map page / coordinates:	11 / C-5,6
Watershed:	Vermilion
Surface water area / shorelength:	437 acres / 5.7 miles
Maximum / mean depth:	50 feet / NA
Water color / clarity:	Brown stain / 8.0 feet (2007)
Accessibility:	Carry-down access to northeast shore
	48° 6' 52.90" N / 92° 35' 17.55" W
Accommodations:	None

FISHING INFORMATION

Kjostad Lake, (pronounced CHO-stad) offers anglers a shot at northern pike, walleyes, smallmouth bass, along with black crappies and bluegills. Much of this lake is private, with most of its shoreline being tied up by two large landowners. However, the DNR maintains there's public access at the end of a dirt road, roughly two miles past the Elbow Lake Road, on the left on the northeast shore of the lake. The launch is county owned.

Try fishing the steeply dropping west shore for walleyes and smallmouth bass. Fish submerged weed edges for pike. Live bait is a good bet for walleyes. Try a live bait rig or slip bobber dressed with a jumbo leech or nightcrawler to get plenty of attention. Smallies will take live bait, but don't pass up on the topwater bite during summer months. A popper or walking bait fished close to shore near deeper water will draw some ferocious strikes.

FISH STOCKING DATA

year	species	size	# released
05	Walleye	Fingerling	7,355
07	Walleye	Fingerling	12,069
09	Walleye	Fingerling	9,494

LENGTH OF SELECTED SPECIES SAMPLED FROM ALL GEAR
Survey Date: 07/09/2007
Number of fish caught for the following length categories (inches):

species	0-5	6-8	9-11	12-14	15-19	20-24	25-29	>30	Total
Black Crappie	3	2	3	2	-	-	-	-	10
Bluegill	7	5	-	-	-	-	-	-	12
Largemouth Bass	-	2	1	1	1	-	-	-	5
Northern Pike	-	-	-	-	3	5	6	4	18
Rock Bass	2	-	-	-	-	-	-	-	2
Smallmouth Bass	-	-	3	1	-	-	-	-	4
Walleye	-	-	4	3	15	2	-	-	24
Yellow Perch	2	29	-	-	-	-	-	-	31

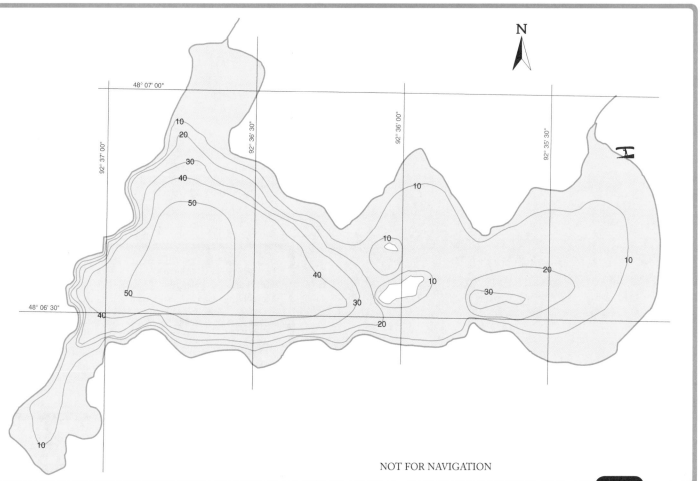

NOT FOR NAVIGATION

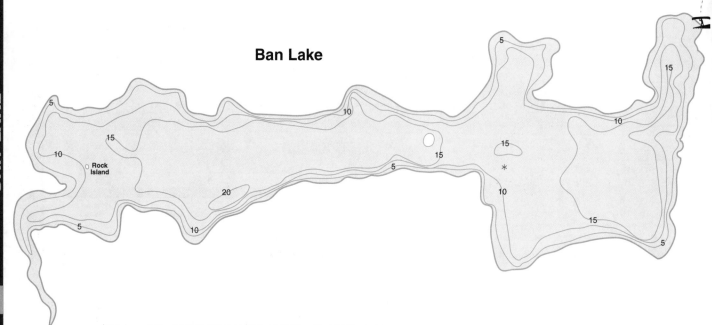

Ban Lake

Rock Island

Ban (Bass) Lake, St. Louis County

Area map page / coordinates: 11 / D-5
Surface area / shorelength: 380 acres / NA
Accessibility: Carry-down access from logging road bordering northeast shore (boat ramp currently under construction)
48° 2' 50.20" N / 92° 38' 13.26" W

LENGTH OF SELECTED SPECIES SAMPLED FROM ALL GEAR
Survey Date: 08/08/2005
Number of fish caught for the following length categories (inches):

species	0-5	6-8	9-11	12-14	15-19	20-24	25-29	>30	Total
Black Crappie	1	3	8	-	-	-	-	-	12
Bluegill	8	19	2	-	-	-	-	-	29
Largemouth Bass	5	14	18	23	1	-	-	-	61
Northern Pike	-	-	-	1	6	11	1	2	21
Pumpkin. Sunfish	-	3	-	-	-	-	-	-	3
Rock Bass	-	2	-	-	-	-	-	-	2
Smallmouth Bass	-	1	2	7	2	-	-	-	12
Walleye	-	-	-	-	2	6	1	-	9
Yellow Perch	8	20	1	-	-	-	-	-	29

N

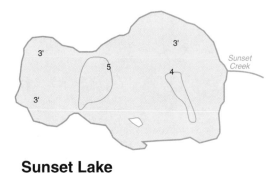

Sunset Lake

Sunset
Creek

Sunset Lake, St. Louis County

Area map page / coordinates: 11 / E-5 & 15 / A-5
Surface area / shorelength: 305 acres / NA
Accessibility: Carry-down access to south shore
47° 57' 3.06" N / 92° 40' 5.73" W

LENGTH OF SELECTED SPECIES SAMPLED FROM ALL GEAR
Survey Date: 07/22/1996
Number of fish caught for the following length categories (inches):

species	0-5	6-8	9-11	12-14	15-19	20-24	25-29	>30	Total
Black Crappie	55	2	26	9	-	-	-	-	92
Northern Pike	-	-	-	-	3	22	17	1	43
Pumpkin. Sunfish	25	2	1	-	-	-	-	-	28
Yellow Perch	164	115	16	-	-	-	-	-	295

NOT FOR NAVIGATION

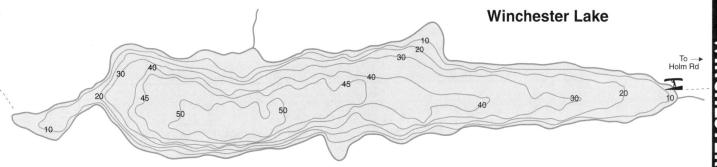

Winchester Lake

To →
Holm Rd

N

Winchester Lake, St. Louis County
Area map page / coordinates: 11 / D-6
Surface area / shorelength: 319 acres / NA
Accessibility: Carry-down access to east shore (200-foot portage across sometimes very swampy terrain)
48° 2' 13.21" N / 92° 32' 4.91" W

FISH STOCKING DATA

year	species	size	# released
08	Lake Trout	Yearling	3,747
09	Lake Trout	Yearling	3,688

LENGTH OF SELECTED SPECIES SAMPLED FROM ALL GEAR
Survey Date: 08/24/2009
Number of fish caught for the following length categories (inches):

species	0-5	6-8	9-11	12-14	15-19	20-24	25-29	>30	Total
Bluegill	19	114	-	-	-	-	-	-	133
Hybrid Sunfish	1	-	-	-	-	-	-	-	1
Lake Trout	-	6	4	12	16	2	-	-	40
Northern Pike	-	-	-	-	-	-	1	-	1
Rock Bass	2	7	-	-	-	-	-	-	9
Smallmouth Bass	-	-	1	1	-	-	-	-	2
Tullibee (Cisco)	-	125	-	-	-	-	-	-	168
White Sucker	-	2	4	9	5	-	-	-	20
Yellow Perch	-	6	5	-	-	-	-	-	11

Susan Lake, St. Louis County
Area map page / coordinates: 11 / E-5
Surface area / shorelength: 300 acres / NA
Accessibility: Carry-down access to south shore from County Road 24 (25 yard portage)
47° 58' 34.46" N / 92° 39' 36.79" W

LENGTH OF SELECTED SPECIES SAMPLED FROM ALL GEAR
Survey Date: 08/15/2005
Number of fish caught for the following length categories (inches):

species	0-5	6-8	9-11	12-14	15-19	20-24	25-29	>30	Total
Black Crappie	-	1	7	-	-	-	-	-	8
Northern Pike	-	-	1	3	9	3	1	-	17
Pumpkin. Sunfish	5	8	-	-	-	-	-	-	13
Walleye	-	2	6	15	23	5	-	-	51
Yellow Perch	3	54	77	19	-	-	-	-	153

Susan Lake

24

99

ELBOW LAKE St. Louis County

Area map page / coordinates:	11 / D-5
Watershed:	Vermilion
Surface water area / shorelength:	1,695 acres / 28.5 miles
Maximum / mean depth:	60 feet / 23 feet
Water color / clarity:	Brown tint / 6.5 feet (2008)
Shoreland zoning classification:	Recreational development
Management class / Ecological type:	Walleye / centrarchid

Accessibility: 1) County-owned public access with concrete ramp on southwest shore, off County Road 426; limited parking available

47° 59' 37.41" N / 92° 39' 41.24" W

Accessibility: 2) State-owned public access with gravel ramp on west shore of north arm at the end of the Elbow Lake State Forest Road; limited parking

48° 1' 55.86" N / 92° 36' 30.11" W

Accommodations: Bordered by Elbow Lake State Forest, resort, boat rental

FISHING INFORMATION

Aptly named for its slightly bent-arm appearance, Elbow Lake is often overlooked in favor of the Cook/Orr-area's star attraction, big Lake Vermilion. Recreational boating pressure is relatively light on Elbow, and fishing pressure is minimal, as well. In fact, you'll have the lake mostly to yourself, if you decide to pay a visit. It's considered one of the most beautiful lakes in a region where beauty is common, and it contains plenty of fish, walleyes, a few nice northern pike, a solid smallmouth bass population, a bonus largemouth or two and both crappies and bluegills.

Chris Ashbach at the Elbow Lake Lodge, 3975 Kennedy Road, Cook, MN, 218-666-2631, says Elbow Lake is certainly one of the best lakes you can visit, if you want good fishing along with plenty of calm and quiet. "We're the only lodge on the lake," he said. "We have a few cabins, a nice beach and a sheltered marina. The rest of the lake has large land owners surrounding it and overall all, everyone here does a very good job keeping the area quiet. Plus, the fishing is pretty good for walleyes, smallmouth bass and northern pike."

Walleye anglers can do pretty well on the lake's shallower north side where there is good habitat, including sand and rock points and several islands. When the lake warms, you'll get the best action around reefs and bars off the south shore and near the mouth of the east arm. Ashbach says the walleye fishing is pretty consistent with a lot of legal fish being caught regularly. The latest DNR survey showed the average walleye in Elbow Lake to measure around 16 inches, and the fish are stocked every even-numbered year to complement natural reproduction. Trolling crankbaits along deep weed edges is a productive method for locating walleyes. Fishing points, islands and drop-offs with live bait rigs or jig-and-bait combos is productive throughout the open water season.

According to Ashbach, there are tons of smallmouth bass on Elbow Lake. "Most of the smallmouth bass aren't giants, but there are a good number of fish in the 2-to 3-pound range," he said. You'll find smallies in the same areas you'll locate walleyes: points, drop-offs and weed edges. Work jerkbaits, spinnerbaits and lipless crankbaits with a fast and erratic retrieve to trigger smallie strikes. If bass are in an uncooperative mood, try fishing with a soft plastic tube or possibly a weightless Senko. Pike fishing is good along the south shore, just west of the lodge. The pike aren't huge for the most part, 3 or 4 pounds, but fish over 30 inches are taken from time to time.

FISH STOCKING DATA

year	species	size	# released
06	Walleye	Fingerling	26,960
08	Walleye	Fingerling	34,857
10	Walleye	Fingerling	15,723

NET CATCH DATA

Date: 08/11/2008

	Gill Nets		Trap Nets	
species	# per net	avg. fish weight (lbs.)	# per net	avg. fish weight (lbs.)
Black Crappie	-	-	0.87	0.51
Bluegill	-	-	9.67	0.26
Lake Whitefish	3.73	3.73	-	-
Northern Pike	0.53	2.80	0.47	1.79
Pumpkin. Sunfish	-	-	0.93	0.26
Rock Bass	-	-	0.20	0.43
Smallmouth Bass	0.33	0.25	0.07	0.27
Tullibee (Cisco)	1.07	0.14	-	-
Walleye	2.53	0.93	0.67	3.51
White Sucker	1.47	2.45	0.13	3.20
Yellow Perch	2.67	0.15	-	-

LENGTH OF SELECTED SPECIES SAMPLED FROM ALL GEAR

Number of fish caught for the following length categories (inches):

species	0-5	6-8	9-11	12-14	15-19	20-24	25-29	>30	Total
Black Crappie	-	4	8	1	-	-	-	-	13
Bluegill	16	129	-	-	-	-	-	-	145
Lake Whitefish	-	-	1	2	9	44	-	-	56
Northern Pike	-	-	1	1	5	4	4	-	15
Pumpkin. Sunfish	3	11	-	-	-	-	-	-	14
Rock Bass	-	3	-	-	-	-	-	-	3
Smallmouth Bass	2	3	1	-	-	-	-	-	6
Tullibee (Cisco)	-	16	-	-	-	-	-	-	16
Walleye	-	6	21	-	14	3	4	-	48
White Sucker	-	-	2	2	19	1	-	-	24
Yellow Perch	12	25	3	-	-	-	-	-	40

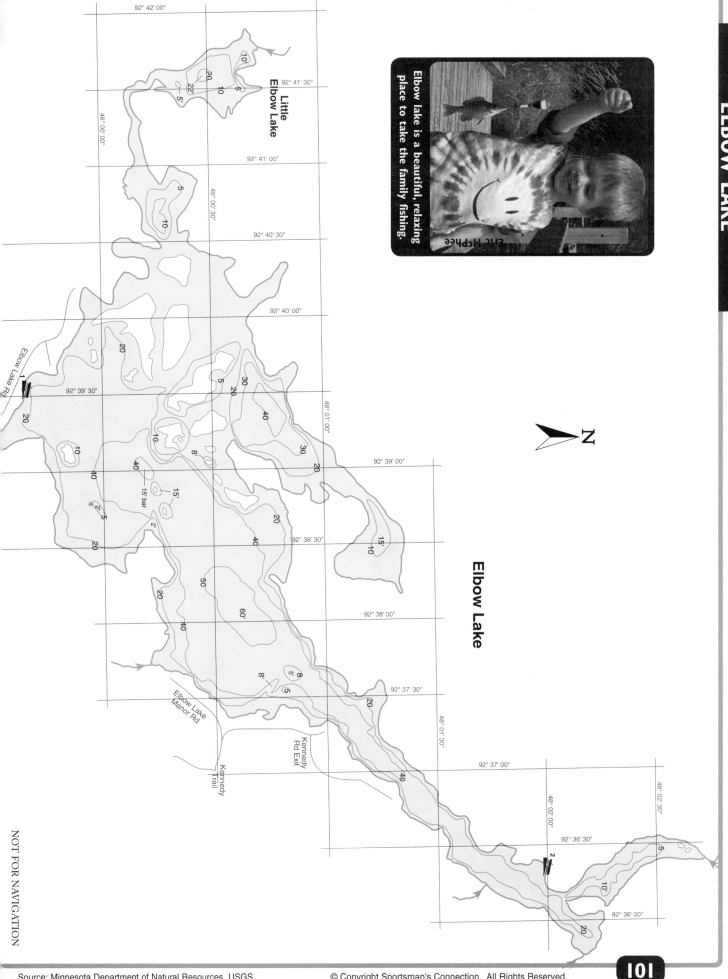

Little
Elbow Lake

Elbow Lake

Elbow lake is a beautiful, relaxing
place to take the family fishing.

Eric McPhee

N

Elbow Lake Rd

Elbow Lake Manor Rd

Kennedy Rd Exit

Kennedy Trail

15' bar

50'

60'

Source: Minnesota Department of Natural Resources, USGS

ECHO LAKE
St. Louis County

Area map page / coordinates: 11 / B-6 & 12 / B-1

Watershed: Vermilion

Surface water area / shorelength: 1,139 acres / 10.0 miles

Maximum / mean depth: 10 feet / 6 feet

Water color / clarity: Brown stain / 3.3 feet (2009)

Accessibility: USFS-owned public access with gravel ramp on south shore, adjacent to the campground; 48° 10' 17.57" N / 92° 29' 47.52" W

Accommodations: Resort, boat rental, camping, picnicking

Kabetogama State Forest

Echo Lake

Superior National Forest

Crane Lake

Echo

Vermilion River

NO RECORD OF STOCKING

LENGTH OF SELECTED SPECIES SAMPLED FROM ALL GEAR
Survey Date: 06/01/2009

Number of fish caught for the following length categories (inches):

species	0-5	6-8	9-11	12-14	15-19	20-24	25-29	>30	Total
Black Crappie	9	59	36	1	-	-	-	-	105
Bluegill	-	3	-	-	-	-	-	-	3
Northern Pike	-	-	1	1	9	21	11	3	46
Rock Bass	-	1	-	-	-	-	-	-	1
Walleye	3	38	34	31	25	14	3	-	148
White Sucker	-	-	6	20	56	4	-	-	86
Yellow Perch	17	45	4	-	-	-	-	-	66

FISHING INFORMATION

Unlike the situation in some nearby lakes which are within the BWCAW, the fish in Echo Lake are relatively easy to get to. That's because the boat-size and motor exclusions found in the Canoe Area simply don't apply. You can get a decent-size fishing rig into the lake. The folks at Anderson Sports Port, Highway 53, Orr, MN, 218-757-3291, say Echo's tea-color waters contain decent numbers of 17-inch walleyes and some even larger. In addition, there are northern pike from "snake" size on up to 10 or 12 pounds. There are nice black crappies with some measuring in excess of 12 inches long. The panfish population, aside from crappies, is not very impressive with most of the species present in small size and low numbers. The lake is shallow and doesn't contain much structure, other than relatively steep drops off points on the north side. You'll want to focus your fishing along weedlines in Echo. Live bait is a good bet for all species. There's good ice fishing action for both walleyes and northern pike.

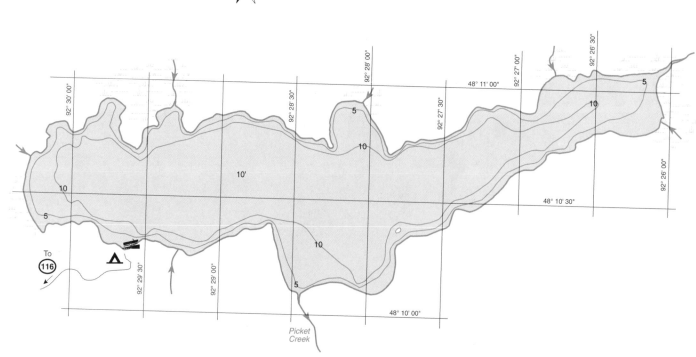

NOT FOR NAVIGATION

Source: Minnesota Department of Natural Resources, USGS

LAKE JEANETTE
St. Louis County

Area map page / coordinates:	12 / B,C-2
Watershed:	Rainy headwaters
Surface water area / shorelength:	612 acres / 6.7 miles
Maximum / mean depth:	15 feet / NA
Water color / clarity:	Light brown stain / 5.0 feet (2009)

Accessibility: USFS-owned public access with concrete ramp west of the Lake Jeanette campground, north off the Echo Trail

48° 7' 51.03" N / 92° 17' 48.84" W

Accommodations: None

FISHING INFORMATION

Lake Jeanette covers 612 acres and offers plenty of structure. You'll find a couple of deep holes off the entrances to the bays on the south side and both of these hold walleyes in summer. There are a number of submerged rocks toward the center of the lake, in the 10- to 15-foot depth range. You'll find walleyes and yellow perch around these. The 10-foot trench in the lake's northwest arm also offers angling opportunities. Work the sloping weedline for northern pike and other species. The most recent DNR survey showed walleyes averaging about 14 inches long and weighing just over 1 pound, while northern pike measured 20.6 inches in length on average weighing about 2 pounds. Matt Glowaski at Anderson Sports Port, Highway 53, Orr, MN, 218-757-3411, says walleyes will take spinner rigs tipped with leeches or crawlers. Yellow perch weren't giants in the DNR survey, but their growth rates were good. An average Jeanette perch is 8.2 inches long. Live bait is a good bet for all of these species. Leeches will work during summer months for walleyes and perch while minnows will take all three species.

FISH STOCKING DATA

year	species	size	# released
06	Walleye	Fry	600,000
08	Walleye	Fry	600,000

LENGTH OF SELECTED SPECIES SAMPLED FROM ALL GEAR

Survey Date: 07/06/2009

Number of fish caught for the following length categories (inches):

species	0-5	6-8	9-11	12-14	15-19	20-24	25-29	>30	Total
Northern Pike	-	-	-	-	19	22	5	1	47
Walleye	-	4	25	23	31	16	4	-	103
White Sucker	-	1	-	4	62	6	-	-	73
Yellow Perch	11	44	48	4	-	-	-	-	107

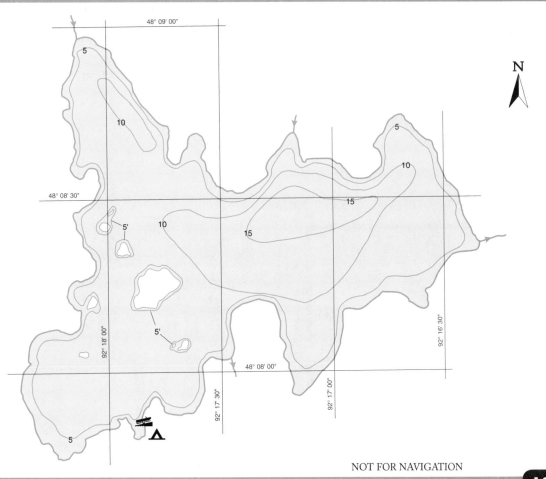

NOT FOR NAVIGATION

103

Meander Lake, St. Louis County

Area map page / coordinates: 12 / B,C-3
Surface area / shorelength: 139 acres / 3.1 miles
Accessibility: Carry-down access to south shore from FR 679; picnic area also at access site
48° 8' 4.68" N / 92° 8' 44.34" W

LENGTH OF SELECTED SPECIES SAMPLED FROM ALL GEAR
Survey Date: 08/04/1981
Number of fish caught for the following length categories (inches):

species	0-5	6-8	9-11	12-14	15-19	20-24	25-29	>30	Total
Bluegill	-	1	-	-	-	-	-	-	1
Smallmouth Bass	5	6	5	3	-	-	-	-	19
Yellow Perch	-	-	1	-	-	-	-	-	1

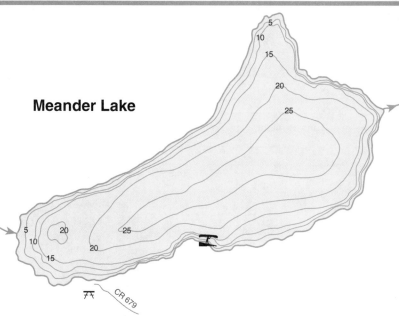

Meander Lake

CR 679

N

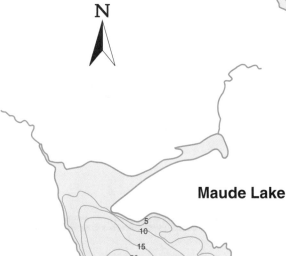

Maude Lake

Maude Lake, St. Louis County

Area map page / coordinates: 12 / C-1
Surface area / shorelength: 95 acres / 2.9 miles
Accessibility: Carry-down access to southeast shore from USFS Road 200 (160 rod portage)
48° 6' 23.01" N / 92° 20' 47.90" W

FISH STOCKING DATA

year	species	size	# released
04	Walleye	Fry	70,000
06	Walleye	Fry	70,000
08	Walleye	Fry	70,000

LENGTH OF SELECTED SPECIES SAMPLED FROM ALL GEAR
Survey Date: 06/18/2007
Number of fish caught for the following length categories (inches):

species	0-5	6-8	9-11	12-14	15-19	20-24	25-29	>30	Total
Northern Pike	-	-	-	-	3	1	2	-	6
Walleye	-	-	2	5	4	-	1	-	12
Yellow Perch	3	5	19	1	-	-	-	-	28

Crellin Lake, St. Louis County

Area map page / coordinates: 12 / C-2
Surface area / shorelength: NA / NA
Accessibility: Carry-down access from Astrid Lake to west shore (0.25 mile portage on maintained trail)
48° 6' 31" N / 92° 18' 54" W

FISH STOCKING DATA

year	species	size	# released
99	Walleye	Fry	90,000
02	Walleye	Fry	90,000

LENGTH OF SELECTED SPECIES SAMPLED FROM ALL GEAR
Survey Date: 08/13/2003
Number of fish caught for the following length categories (inches):

species	0-5	6-8	9-11	12-14	15-19	20-24	25-29	>30	Total
Yellow Perch	3	5	6	1	-	-	-	-	15

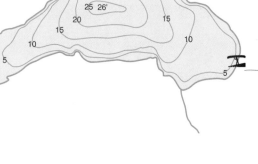

Crellin Lake

NOT FOR NAVIGATION

Source: Minnesota Department of Natural Resources, USGS

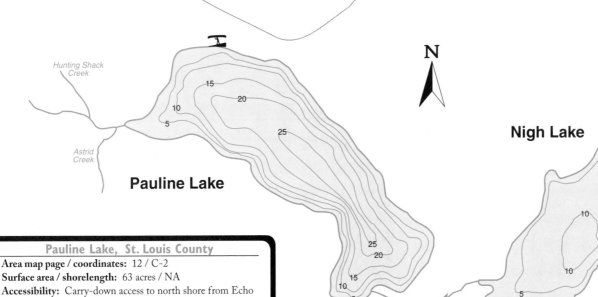

Nigh Lake

Pauline Lake

Pauline Lake, St. Louis County

Area map page / coordinates: 12 / C-2
Surface area / shorelength: 63 acres / NA
Accessibility: Carry-down access to north shore from Echo Trail (110 yard portage); carry-down access to east shore from Nigh Lake (110 yard portage)

48° 7' 37.98" N / 92° 20' 1.12" W

FISH STOCKING DATA

year	species	size	# released
06	Walleye	Fry	50,000
08	Walleye	Fry	50,000
10	Walleye	Fry	60,000

LENGTH OF SELECTED SPECIES SAMPLED FROM ALL GEAR
Survey Date: 06/21/2010
Number of fish caught for the following length categories (inches):

species	0-5	6-8	9-11	12-14	15-19	20-24	25-29	>30	Total
Northern Pike	-	-	-	1	4	1	-	1	7
Walleye	-	-	-	2	3	-	-	-	5
White Sucker	-	1	-	2	9	-	-	-	12
Yellow Perch	-	2	4	-	-	-	-	-	6

Nigh Lake, St. Louis County

Area map page / coordinates: 12 / C-2
Surface area / shorelength: 41 acres / NA
Accessibility: Carry-down access to west shore from Pauline Lake (110 yard portage); carry-down access to northeast shore from Jeanette Lake Campground (5/8 mile portage)

48° 7' 36.23" N / 92° 18' 55.96" W

FISH STOCKING DATA

year	species	size	# released
06	Walleye	Fry	40,000
08	Walleye	Fry	40,000
10	Walleye	Fry	50,000

LENGTH OF SELECTED SPECIES SAMPLED FROM ALL GEAR
Survey Date: 06/21/2010
Number of fish caught for the following length categories (inches):

species	0-5	6-8	9-11	12-14	15-19	20-24	25-29	>30	Total
Northern Pike	-	-	-	2	8	1	-	11
Walleye	-	-	1	1	1	-	-	3
Yellow Perch	4	3	-	-	-	-	-	7

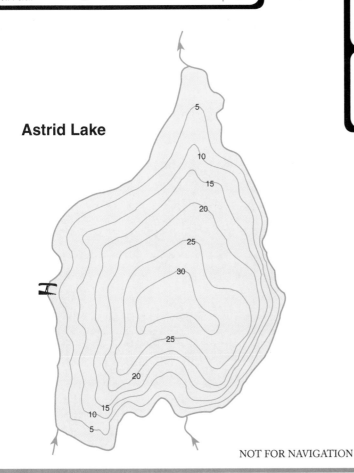

Astrid Lake

Astrid Lake, St. Louis County

Area map page / coordinates: 12 / C-2
Surface area / shorelength: 120 acres / 1.8 miles
Accessibility: Carry-down access to west shore from USFS Road 200 (0.25 mile portage); navigable channel to south lake via Hunting Shack River from Echo Trail (2 miles upstream to lake)

48° 3' 30.31" N / 91° 56' 38.53" W

FISH STOCKING DATA

year	species	size	# released
06	Walleye	Fry	100,000
08	Walleye	Fry	100,000
10	Walleye	Fry	120,000

LENGTH OF SELECTED SPECIES SAMPLED FROM ALL GEAR
Survey Date: 07/24/2006
Number of fish caught for the following length categories (inches):

species	0-5	6-8	9-11	12-14	15-19	20-24	25-29	>30	Total
Northern Pike	-	-	-	3	15	3	2	-	23
Pumpkin. Sunfish	-	1	-	-	-	-	-	-	1
Rock Bass	2	-	-	-	-	-	-	-	2
Walleye	-	4	4	1	7	-	-	-	16
Yellow Perch	1	-	1	-	-	-	-	-	2

NOT FOR NAVIGATION

Source: Minnesota Department of Natural Resources, USGS

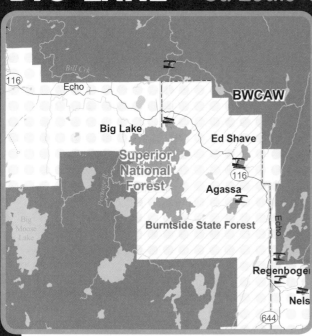

Area map page / coordinates: 13 / C,D-4

Watershed: Rainy headwaters

Surface water area / shorelength: 1,904 acres / 16.9 miles

Maximum / mean depth: 22 feet / 9 feet

Water color / clarity: Brown stain / 6.0 feet (2009)

Shoreland zoning classification: Recreational development

Management class / Ecological type: Walleye / centrarchid-walleye

Accessibility: USFS-owned public access with concrete ramp on north shore, 0.3 mile off Echo Trail

48° 5' 30.40" N / 91° 59' 26.18" W

Accommodations: Resorts, boat rental, camping, picnicking

FISHING INFORMATION

Big Lake doesn't get a lot of angling pressure, despite its promise of good fishing. The reason is its location, 25 miles northwest of Ely on County Road 116 (Echo Trail). It's a long way out for an angler who's surrounded by good fishing lakes all along the way. The dominant specie in this lake is walleye, but there are also good numbers of northern pike and perch. Clifford Noble, owner of Skube's Bait & Tackle, 1810 E. Sheridan St., Ely, MN, 218-365-5358, says you'll also find some nice smallmouth bass, although their numbers aren't very high. There is some natural reproduction of walleyes, but the DNR regularly supplements the native population with stocked fry. Somewhat shallow for northern waters, Big Lake nevertheless offers good fishing opportunities.

Noble says walleye anglers have their best success fishing the windward shorelines in a breeze. In fact, this is one of the most important angling techniques on this lake. Of course, structure is important, too, and Big Lake has more than it's share of it. A point off the north side is a reliable producer, as are the points and islands on the west side. The bigger island (which has two campsites) is also a winner, especially the rocks off its north shore. A long point in the middle of the east shore is another good spot. Most anglers have luck on Lindy rigs or spinners tipped with live bait. Big Lake has been receiving periodic supplemental walleye stockings since 1941. During the last DNR survey in 2009, the average walleye captured in DNR gillnets was slightly over 14 inches long with a weight of 1.06 pounds. Walleyes caught in DNR trapnets averaged nearly 15 inches long weighing 1.25 pounds. Both samplings were near the median for a lake of this class and size. The largest walleye captured measured 25.3 inches long.

Smallmouth bass are taken in the same locations as walleyes. You can use live bait methods or try to get them to strike fast-moving lures like jerkbaits or spinnerbaits. Smallmouth bass were once very abundant on this lake, but their numbers started to decline in the 1980s and 1990s.

Northern Pike aren't abundant on Big Lake, but you can find some if you try. The drainage area off the small southwest bay is a good spot to find northern pike, as are most of the weedbed areas at the lake's south end. Fish the margins with a flashy spoon, spinnerbait or try live bait.

Yellow perch are also available here. Their numbers are solid with an average size of 8 inches long with decent numbers of fish in the 9- to 11-inch range. Target the same spots you're fishing for walleyes and you'll find a few perch. Downsize your bait offerings slightly and you'll catch a few

of these tasty fish. Small leeches, minnows or pieces of nightcrawler will fool most perch into biting.

By far, the most abundant fish species in Big Lake is the lowly white sucker, with the majority of the population in the 2-pound class. If you'd like to catch a few of these fish, it's tough to beat a nightcrawler fished on the bottom. Target the areas close to the inlet and outlet on the lake.

There is public access with a new concrete ramp at the northeast corner of the lake, off County Road 161.

FISH STOCKING DATA			
year	species	size	# released
07	Walleye	Fry	1,500,000
10	Walleye	Fry	1,800,000

NET CATCH DATA

Date: 08/17/2009

	Gill Nets		Trap Nets	
		avg. fish		avg. fish
species	# per net	weight (lbs.)	# per net	weight (lbs.)
Black Crappie	0.07	0.22	0.08	0.17
Bluegill	-	-	0.08	1.02
Northern Pike	1.00	1.52	0.75	0.92
Rock Bass	2.40	0.34	1.08	0.30
Smallmouth Bass	0.27	1.58	-	-
Walleye	5.07	1.06	8.50	1.25

LENGTH OF SELECTED SPECIES SAMPLED FROM ALL GEAR

Number of fish caught for the following length categories (inches):

species	0-5	6-8	9-11	12-14	15-19	20-24	25-29	>30	Total
Black Crappie	-	2	-	-	-	-	-	-	2
Bluegill	-	-	1	-	-	-	-	-	1
Northern Pike	-	-	-	6	7	10	-	-	24
Rock Bass	1	43	5	-	-	-	-	-	49
Smallmouth Bass	-	-	-	4	-	-	-	-	4
Walleye	-	5	30	62	72	6	3	-	178
Yellow Perch	-	45	28	-	-	-	-	-	73

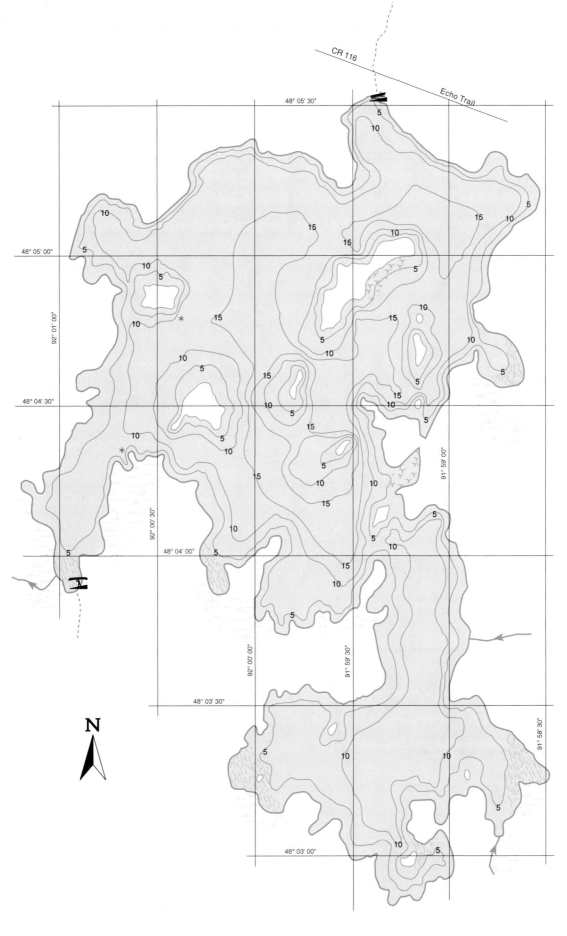

NOT FOR NAVIGATION

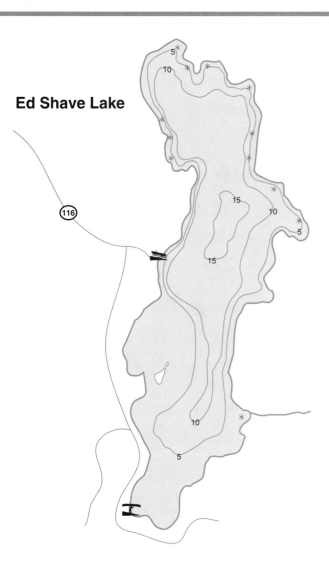

Ed Shave Lake

Ed Shave (Second) Lake, St. Louis County

Area map page / coordinates: 13 / C-5
Surface area / shorelength: 90 acres / 2.3 miles
Accessibility: State-owned public access with concrete ramp on west shore, off Co. Rd. 116 (Echo Trail)
48° 4' 26.06" N / 91° 56' 44.78" W

FISH STOCKING DATA

year	species	size	# released
08	Walleye	Fingerling	361

LENGTH OF SELECTED SPECIES SAMPLED FROM ALL GEAR
Survey Date: 07/06/2010
Number of fish caught for the following length categories (inches):

species	0-5	6-8	9-11	12-14	15-19	20-24	25-29	>30	Total
Smallmouth Bass	-	3	2	13	1	-	-	-	19
Walleye	-	8	11	16	46	-	-	-	81
White Sucker	-	-	-	-	1	-	-	-	1
Yellow Perch	9	9	-	3	-	-	-	-	21

N

Agassa Lake

Regenbogen Lake, St. Louis County

Area map page / coordinates: 13 / D-5
Surface area / shorelength: 10 acres / 0.5 miles
Accessibility: Carry-down access to south shore from the Echo Trail (0.25 mile portage)
48° 1' 27.97" N / 91° 55' 11.41" W

FISH STOCKING DATA

year	species	size	# released
06	Brook Trout	Fingerling	761
07	Brook Trout	Fingerling	974
08	Brook Trout	Fingerling	858
09	Brook Trout	Fingerling	750
10	Brook Trout	Fingerling	756

Agassa Lake, St. Louis County

Area map page / coordinates: 13 / C,D-4,5
Surface area / shorelength: 72 acres / NA
Accessibility: Carry-down access from the Echo Trail to the north shore (1.0 mile portage)
48° 3' 30.31" N / 91° 56' 38.52" W

FISH STOCKING DATA

year	species	size	# released
07	Walleye	Fry	55,000
07	Splake	Fingerling	4,107
09	Walleye	Fry	55,000

LENGTH OF SELECTED SPECIES SAMPLED FROM ALL GEAR
Survey Date: 08/06/2009
Number of fish caught for the following length categories (inches):

species	0-5	6-8	9-11	12-14	15-19	20-24	25-29	>30	Total
Walleye	-	-	3	5	3	-	-	-	11
Yellow Perch	-	5	8	-	-	-	-	-	13

Regenbogen Lake

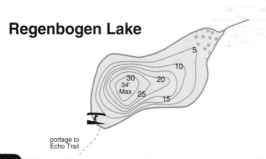

portage to
Echo Trail

NOT FOR NAVIGATION

Source: Minnesota Department of Natural Resources, USGS

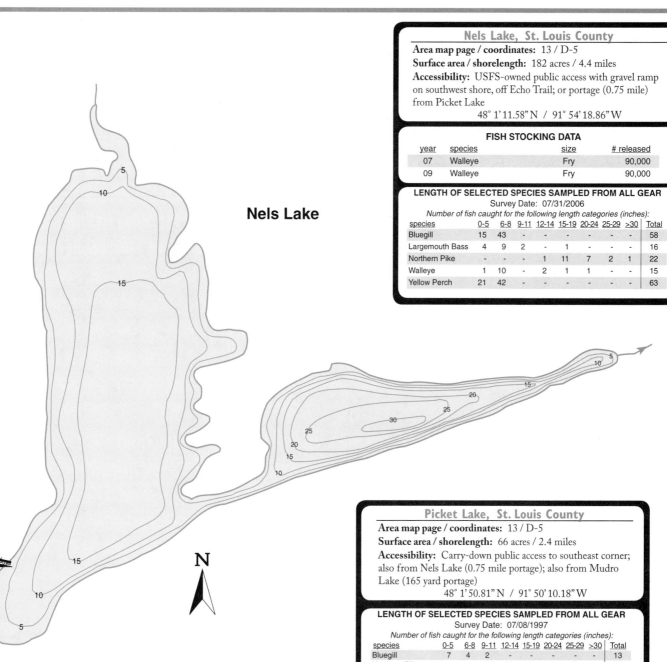

Nels Lake

Nels Lake, St. Louis County

Area map page / coordinates: 13 / D-5
Surface area / shorelength: 182 acres / 4.4 miles
Accessibility: USFS-owned public access with gravel ramp on southwest shore, off Echo Trail; or portage (0.75 mile) from Picket Lake

48° 1' 11.58" N / 91° 54' 18.86" W

FISH STOCKING DATA

year	species	size	# released
07	Walleye	Fry	90,000
09	Walleye	Fry	90,000

LENGTH OF SELECTED SPECIES SAMPLED FROM ALL GEAR
Survey Date: 07/31/2006
Number of fish caught for the following length categories (inches):

species	0-5	6-8	9-11	12-14	15-19	20-24	25-29	>30	Total
Bluegill	15	43	-	-	-	-	-	-	58
Largemouth Bass	4	9	2	-	1	-	-	-	16
Northern Pike	-	-	-	1	11	7	2	1	22
Walleye	1	10	-	2	1	1	-	-	15
Yellow Perch	21	42	-	-	-	-	-	-	63

N

Picket Lake, St. Louis County

Area map page / coordinates: 13 / D-5
Surface area / shorelength: 66 acres / 2.4 miles
Accessibility: Carry-down public access to southeast corner; also from Nels Lake (0.75 mile portage); also from Mudro Lake (165 yard portage)

48° 1' 50.81" N / 91° 50' 10.18" W

LENGTH OF SELECTED SPECIES SAMPLED FROM ALL GEAR
Survey Date: 07/08/1997
Number of fish caught for the following length categories (inches):

species	0-5	6-8	9-11	12-14	15-19	20-24	25-29	>30	Total
Bluegill	7	4	2	-	-	-	-	-	13
Northern Pike	-	-	5	2	7	1	3	-	18
Rock Bass	2	-	-	-	-	-	-	-	2
Smallmouth Bass	-	-	-	1	-	-	-	-	1
Walleye	-	7	6	1	1	1	-	-	16
Yellow Perch	7	16	2	-	-	-	-	-	25

Picket Lake

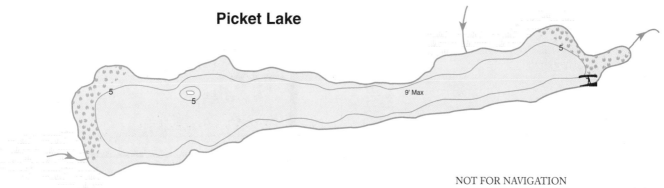

NOT FOR NAVIGATION

Everett Lake, St. Louis County

Area map page / coordinates: 13 / E-5
Surface area / shorelength: 113 acres / 3.5 miles
Accessibility: Carry-down access from Twin Lakes (50 yard portage) or from the Echo Trail (200 yard portage)
47° 59' 18.32" N / 91° 54' 50.42" W

FISH STOCKING DATA

year	species	size	# released
08	Walleye	Fry	220,000
10	Walleye	Fry	260,000

LENGTH OF SELECTED SPECIES SAMPLED FROM ALL GEAR
Survey Date: 07/09/2007
Number of fish caught for the following length categories (inches):

species	0-5	6-8	9-11	12-14	15-19	20-24	25-29	>30	Total
Black Crappie	7	4	5	7	-	-	-	-	23
Bluegill	91	39	-	-	-	-	-	-	130
Northern Pike	-	-	-	-	16	24	3	1	44
Smallmouth Bass	-	-	-	1	-	-	-	-	1
Walleye	-	2	-	-	5	1	-	-	8
Yellow Perch	23	16	-	-	-	-	-	-	39

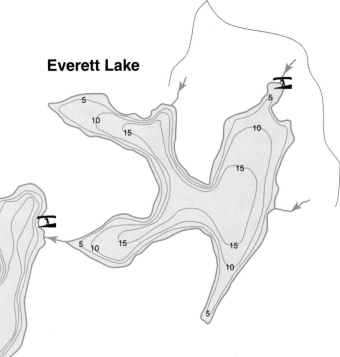

Everett Lake

East Twin Lake

West Twin Lake

N

Dead River

East Twin Lake, St. Louis County

Area map page / coordinates: 13 / E-5
Surface area / shorelength: 121 acres / NA
Accessibility: Carry-down access from Everett Lake (50 yd portage) 47° 58' 48.66" N / 91° 55' 37.43" W; also from north arm of Burntside Lake (0.75 mile portage)

FISH STOCKING DATA

year	species	size	# released
08	Walleye	Fingerling	3,000
10	Walleye	Fingerling	1,710

LENGTH OF SELECTED SPECIES SAMPLED FROM ALL GEAR
Survey Date: 06/25/2007
Number of fish caught for the following length categories (inches):

species	0-5	6-8	9-11	12-14	15-19	20-24	25-29	>30	Total
Black Crappie	14	18	10	-	-	-	-	-	42
Bluegill	102	42	-	-	-	-	-	-	144
Largemouth Bass	1	-	-	-	-	-	-	-	1
Northern Pike	-	-	1	-	20	6	3	6	36
Pumpkin. Sunfish	-	-	-	-	-	-	-	-	-
Rock Bass	-	1	-	-	-	-	-	-	1
Smallmouth Bass	-	-	-	-	-	-	-	-	-
Walleye	-	-	-	1	2	-	1	-	4
Yellow Perch	12	33	-	-	-	-	-	-	45

NOT FOR NAVIGATION

Fenske Lake

Girl Scout Camp

Resort

Echo Trail

Fenske Lake Campground

5
10
15
20
25
30
35
40
43' Max
40
35
30
25
20
15
10
5

N

portage

To Little Sletten Lake

To Everett Lake

Fenske Lake, St. Louis County

Area map page / coordinates: 13 / D-5
Surface area / shorelength: 108 acres / 4.1 miles
Accessibility: USFS-owned public access with gravel ramp on northwest corner; carry-down access from Everett Lake (660 yard portage) and Little Sletten Lake (55 yard portage)
47° 59' 51.08" N / 91° 54' 59.89" W

LENGTH OF SELECTED SPECIES SAMPLED FROM ALL GEAR
Survey Date: 06/07/2007
Number of fish caught for the following length categories (inches):

species	0-5	6-8	9-11	12-14	15-19	20-24	25-29	>30	Total
Black Crappie	1	6	6	-	-	-	-	-	13
Bluegill	55	108	-	-	-	-	-	-	163
Largemouth Bass	2	5	-	-	-	-	-	-	7
Northern Pike	-	-	-	-	15	13	7	1	36
Smallmouth Bass	-	-	3	-	-	-	-	-	3
Tullibee (Cisco)	-	-	1	-	-	-	-	-	1
Walleye	-	-	-	-	-	-	-	-	-
Yellow Perch	3	3	-	-	-	-	-	-	6

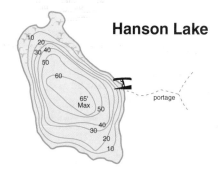

Hanson Lake

10
20
30
40
50
60
65' Max
50
40
30
20
10

portage

Hanson Lake, St. Louis County

Area map page / coordinates: 13 / E-4
Surface area / shorelength: 19 acres / 0.7 miles
Accessibility: Carry-down access from parking area off FR 450, 1.9 miles off Echo Trail (100 yard portage); also from Burntside Lake (3/8 mile portage on unmaintained trail)
47° 58' 51.13" N / 91° 56' 31.30" W

FISH STOCKING DATA

year	species	size	# released
07	Splake	Fingerling	1,060
08	Splake	Fingerling	1,008
09	Splake	Fingerling	1,000
10	Splake	Fingerling	1,051

LENGTH OF SELECTED SPECIES SAMPLED FROM ALL GEAR
Survey Date: 05/30/2006
Number of fish caught for the following length categories (inches):

species	0-5	6-8	9-11	12-14	15-19	20-24	25-29	>30	Total
Golden Shiner	-	2	-	-	-	-	-	-	2
Rainbow Smelt	1	-	-	-	-	-	-	-	1
Splake	-	-	5	2	-	1	-	-	8
White Sucker	-	-	-	-	1	-	-	-	1

NOT FOR NAVIGATION

Low Lake, St. Louis County

Area map page / coordinates: 13 / D,E-5,6
Surface area / shorelength: 316 acres / 7.9 miles
Accessibility: State-owned public access with concrete ramp on east shore, off FR 1036
47° 58' 43.92" N / 91° 48' 55.51" W

FISH STOCKING DATA

year	species	size	# released
07	Walleye	Fry	300,000
09	Walleye	Fry	300,000

LENGTH OF SELECTED SPECIES SAMPLED FROM ALL GEAR
Survey Date: 07/08/2010
Number of fish caught for the following length categories (inches):

species	0-5	6-8	9-11	12-14	15-19	20-24	25-29	>30	Total
Black Crappie	12	23	29	1	-	-	-	-	67
Bluegill	66	88	2	-	-	-	-	-	156
Largemouth Bass	-	-	1	-	-	-	-	-	1
Northern Pike	-	-	-	3	15	2	7	8	35
Rock Bass	5	1	-	-	-	-	-	-	6
Smallmouth Bass	1	4	8	4	3	-	-	-	21
Walleye	-	2	1	6	19	2	-	-	31
Yellow Perch	1	7	1	-	-	-	-	-	9

Bass Lake, St. Louis County

Area map page / coordinates: 13 / E-5
Surface area / shorelength: 174 acres / 2.8 miles
Accessibility: Carry-down access (7/8 mile portage) from Echo Trail (Cty Rd 116); also portage from Dry Lake
47° 57' 19.44" N 91° 51' 57.05" W
47° 57' 27.54" N 91° 51' 50.29" W

LENGTH OF SELECTED SPECIES SAMPLED FROM ALL GEAR
Survey Date: 07/07/1997
Number of fish caught for the following length categories (inches):

species	0-5	6-8	9-11	12-14	15-19	20-24	25-29	>30	Total
Black Crappie	31	157	20	-	-	-	-	-	208
Bluegill	55	99	4	-	-	-	-	-	158
Largemouth Bass	-	-	-	1	2	-	-	-	3
Northern Pike	-	-	5	7	36	19	5	2	74
Smallmouth Bass	-	-	-	6	-	-	-	-	6
Walleye	-	-	-	2	1	2	-	-	5
Yellow Perch	13	21	-	-	-	-	-	-	34

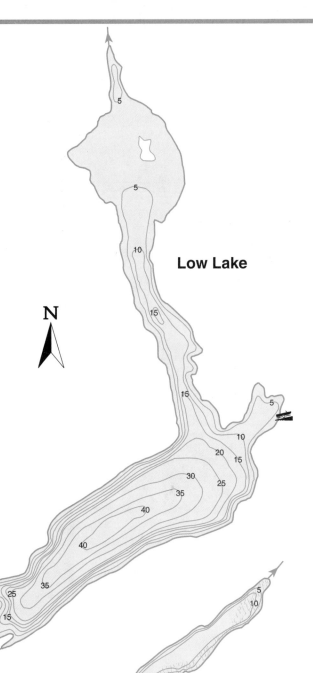

Low Lake

N

Hobo Lake

Bass Lake

Hobo Lake, St. Louis County

Area map page / coordinates: 13 / E-5,6
Surface area / shorelength: 74 acres / NA
Accessibility: Carry-down access (410 rods) from Echo Trail to southwest shore
47° 57' 27.25" N / 91° 50' 18.40" W

LENGTH OF SELECTED SPECIES SAMPLED FROM ALL GEAR
Survey Date: 07/30/2001
Number of fish caught for the following length categories (inches):

species	0-5	6-8	9-11	12-14	15-19	20-24	25-29	>30	Total
Black Crappie	1	13	4	-	-	-	-	-	18
Bluegill	2	3	-	-	-	-	-	-	5
Largemouth Bass	-	-	-	1	-	-	-	-	1
Northern Pike	-	-	-	-	-	2	5	1	8
Walleye	-	-	-	-	-	1	-	-	1
Yellow Perch	6	15	-	-	-	-	-	-	21

NOT FOR NAVIGATION

Source: Minnesota Department of Natural Resources, USGS

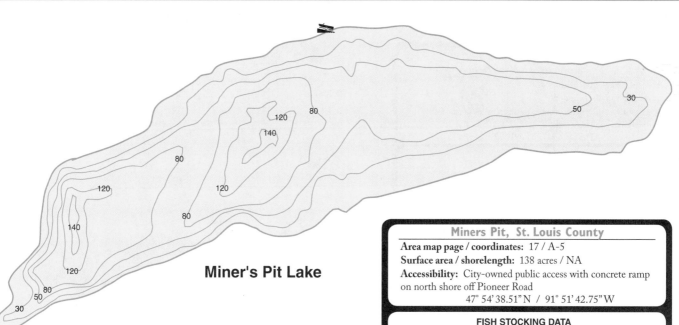

Miner's Pit Lake

Miners Pit, St. Louis County

Area map page / coordinates: 17 / A-5
Surface area / shorelength: 138 acres / NA
Accessibility: City-owned public access with concrete ramp on north shore off Pioneer Road

47° 54' 38.51" N / 91° 51' 42.75" W

FISH STOCKING DATA

year	species	size	# released
08	Rainbow Trout	Yearling	3,550
08	Brook Trout	Yearling	1,400
09	Brook Trout	Yearling	2,800
09	Rainbow Trout	Yearling	1,400
10	Brook Trout	Yearling	1,418
10	Rainbow Trout	Yearling	2,800

N

Chant Lake, St. Louis County

Area map page / coordinates: 13 / E-4
Surface area / shorelength: 16 acres / NA
Accessibility: Carry-down access (0.25 mile portage) from Burntside Lake to west shore

47° 57' 10.64" N / 91° 58' 27.12" W

FISH STOCKING DATA

year	species	size	# released
08	Brook Trout	Fingerling	1,287
09	Rainbow Trout	Fingerling	1,100
10	Brook Trout	Fingerling	1,172

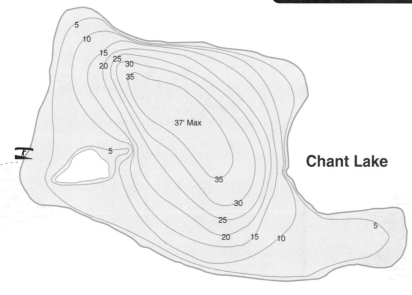

portage

Chant Lake

NOT FOR NAVIGATION

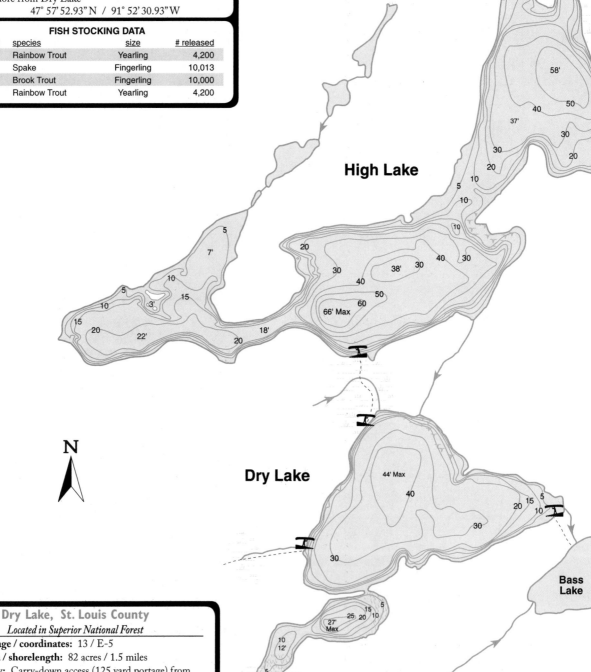

High Lake, St. Louis County
Located in Superior National Forest

Area map page / coordinates: 13 / E-5
Surface area / shorelength: 277 acres / 5.7 miles
Accessibility: Carry-down access (0.25 miles portage) to south shore from Dry Lake

47° 57' 52.93" N / 91° 52' 30.93" W

FISH STOCKING DATA

year	species	size	# released
07	Rainbow Trout	Yearling	4,200
08	Spake	Fingerling	10,013
09	Brook Trout	Fingerling	10,000
10	Rainbow Trout	Yearling	4,200

High Lake

Dry Lake

Bass Lake

N

Dry Lake, St. Louis County
Located in Superior National Forest

Area map page / coordinates: 13 / E-5
Surface area / shorelength: 82 acres / 1.5 miles
Accessibility: Carry-down access (125 yard portage) from Bass Lake (47° 57' 30.64" N / 91° 51' 51.94" W); carry-down access (0.25 mile portage) from High Lake to north shore (47° 57' 43.64" N / 91° 52' 24.08" W)

FISH STOCKING DATA

year	species	size	# released
06	Brown Trout	Yearling	2,050
08	Splake	Fingerling	4,099
09	Brown Trout	Yearling	2,050
10	Splake	Fingerling	4,310

NOT FOR NAVIGATION

Source: Minnesota Department of Natural Resources, USGS

BURNTSIDE LAKE

Area map page / coordinates: 13 / E-4,5 & 17 / A-4,5

Watershed: Rainy headwaters

Surface water area / shorelength: 7,314 acres / 74.0 miles

Maximum / mean depth: 160 feet / 50 feet

Water color / clarity: Clear / 22.2 feet (2007)

Management class / Ecological type: Lake trout / trout

Accessibility: 1) County-owned public access with gravel ramp on south shore, off County Road 404 (Wolf Lake Road) — 47° 53' 39.82" N / 92° 1' 52.87" W

Accessibility: 2) State-owned public access (fee) with concrete ramp on south shore, off County Road 404 (Van Vac Road) — 47° 55' 13.47" N / 91° 58' 28.20" W

Accessibility: 3) County-owned public access (fee) with concrete ramp adjacent to Burntside Lodge on south shore, off County Road 88 — 47° 55' 25.21" N / 91° 57' 8.58" W

Accessibility: 4) State-owned public access with concrete ramp on north shore by Dead River inlet off County Road 803 (Passi Road) — 47° 56' 58.66" N / 91° 56' 15.21" W

Accessibility: 5) USFS-owned public access with concrete ramp on west shore of north arm, off County Road 644 (North Arm Road) — 47° 59' 39.98" N / 91° 57' 25.25" W

Accommodations: Bordered by Burntside State Forest, lodge, camping, picnicking, restrooms

FISHING INFORMATION

FISH STOCKING DATA

year	species	size	# released
06	Lake Trout	Yearling	70,626
06	Walleye	Fingerling	28,947
08	Lake Trout	Yearling	61,407
08	Walleye	Fingerling	55,941
09	Lake Trout	Fingerling	1,098
09	Lake Trout	Adult	956
10	Lake Trout	Yearling	71,153
10	Walleye	Fingerling	22,200

NET CATCH DATA

Date: 07/16/2007

	Gill Nets		Trap Nets	
species	# per net	avg. fish weight (lbs.)	# per net	avg. fish weight (lbs.)
Bluegill	0.1	0.12	-	-
Lake Trout	1.1	1.05	-	-
Lake Whitefish	0.6	5.35	-	-
Northern Pike	1.4	3.69	-	-
Rainbow Smelt	1.1	0.02	-	-
Rock Bass	5.2	0.18	-	-
Smallmouth Bass	0.9	1.25	-	-
Walleye	2.1	2.86	-	-
Yellow Perch	0.6	0.28	-	-

LENGTH OF SELECTED SPECIES SAMPLED FROM ALL GEAR

Number of fish caught for the following length categories (inches):

species	0-5	6-8	9-11	12-14	15-19	20-24	25-29	>30	Total
Black Crappie	1	2	-	-	-	-	-	-	3
Bluegill	1	1	-	-	-	-	-	-	2
Lake Trout	-	4	7	6	5	2	-	-	24
Lake Whitefish	-	-	-	-	-	7	7	-	14
Northern Pike	-	-	-	-	7	8	13	3	31
Rainbow Smelt	23	-	-	-	-	-	-	-	23
Smallmouth Bass	1	4	3	5	6	-	-	-	19
Walleye	-	6	1	3	18	13	5	-	46
Yellow Perch	-	10	2	1	-	-	-	-	13

Burntside Lake is known far and wide as one of the premier lakes of northern Minnesota. The lake boasts 7,314 acres, 160-foot maximum depths, water clarity to 22.2 feet and around 150 islands, ranging in size from something barely large enough to stand on with dry feet to chunks of land a half-mile or so across. Most of the islands are pine-forested, too, making for some pretty scenery and filling the clean air with a great scent.

Clifford Noble, owner of Skube's Bait & Tackle, 1810 E. Sheridan St., Ely, MN, 218-365-5358, says you'll find big lake trout inhabiting the deeps of this big lake. There's great January lake trout fishing, says Noble; a plowed road guides anglers out onto the ice, and many take advantage of it. There are often 50 ice houses out on the lake most winters, Noble says. During open-water months, the trout head deep, and you'll take them in around 65 feet of water by vertical jigging or on downriggers and Doctor spoons or Cleos. Areas east of Dollar Island, west of Waters Island and south of Oliver Island are well known trout trolling grounds.

Smelt are affecting the walleye population on this lake. It appears that the smelt population is preventing walleyes from reproducing naturally. Good thing the DNR has been stocking walleye fingerlings for a number of years. Walleye and smelt are having a love-hate relationship here, but with the DNR serving as mediator, the walleye seem to be winning, and so are the anglers. According to the 2007 DNR survey, average walleye sizes were 16.3 inches and one measured a hefty 27 inches. You'll find walleyes around the reefs, and they're best fished at night or on overcast days because of the water clarity. Look for them in 12 to 20 feet of water. Leeches or crawlers are favorite baits. Crankbaits will work too, though Noble says live bait is most often used in this lake. The west end of Burntside, amongst the islands near the Tamarack River mouth, is one good place to try. Others are the rocks, turns, drops and bars around Long Island, Snellman Island, and Dollar Island in the lake's west arm and around Lost Girl, Ripple and Snake Islands toward the lake's center.

Northern pike and smallmouth bass are available too. Pike run large here, too. In fact, the DNR says they average around 26 inches with one big 'un sampled at 35.4 inches. A few of the pike examined had smelt for lunch. Smelt may be the reason for the Burntside northerns' decent size. Sucker minnows fished under a slip bobber will work in shallower water of the bays. You might also try trolling spoons or spinnerbaits at weedlines. Smallmouth bass are abundant on this lake, according to the DNR's creel survey. Look for bass near rocks off points and the ends of the numerous islands.

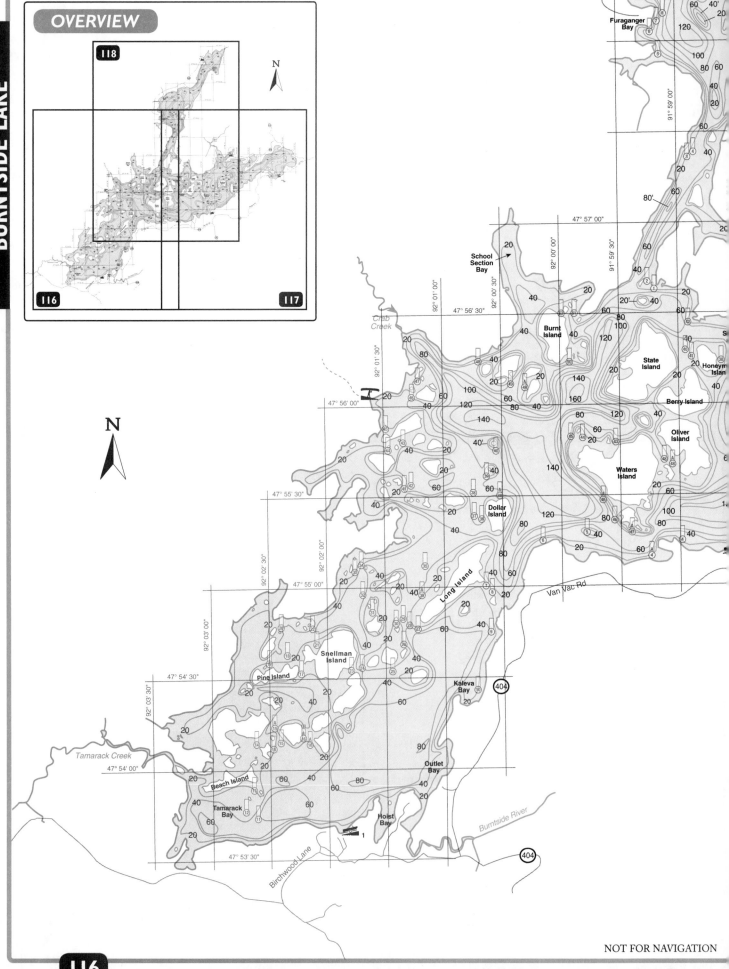

OVERVIEW

118

116   117

N

Furaganger
Bay

School
Section
Bay

Crab
Creek

N

Burnt
Island

State
Island

Honeym
Islan

Berry Island

Oliver
Island

Waters
Island

Dollar
Island

Long Island

Van Vac Rd

Snellman
Island

Kaleva
Bay

404

Pine Island

Tamarack Creek

Outlet
Bay

Beach Island

Tamarack
Bay

Hoist
Bay

Burntside River

Birchwood Lane

404

NOT FOR NAVIGATION

Source: Minnesota Department of Natural Resources, USGS

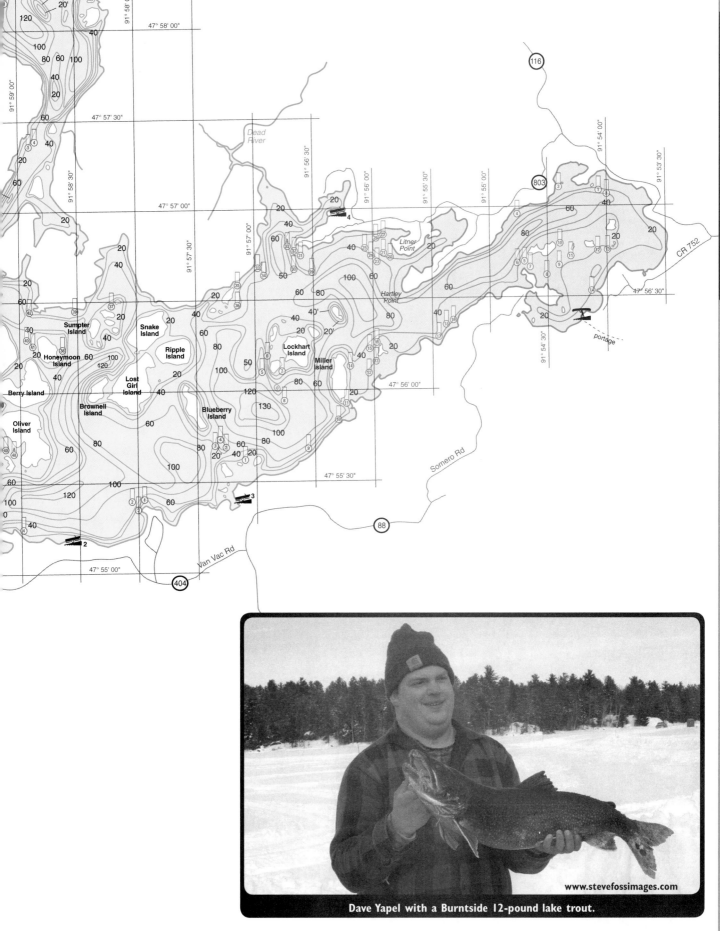

Dead River

Litner Point

Hartley Point

Sumpter Island

Snake Island

Ripple Island

Honeymoon Island

Lost Girl Island

Lockhart Island

Miller Island

Berry Island

Brownell Island

Blueberry Island

Oliver Island

Somero Rd

CR 752

portage

Van Vac Rd

www.stevefossimages.com

Dave Yapel with a Burntside 12-pound lake trout.

NOT FOR NAVIGATION

Source: Minnesota Department of Natural Resources, USGS

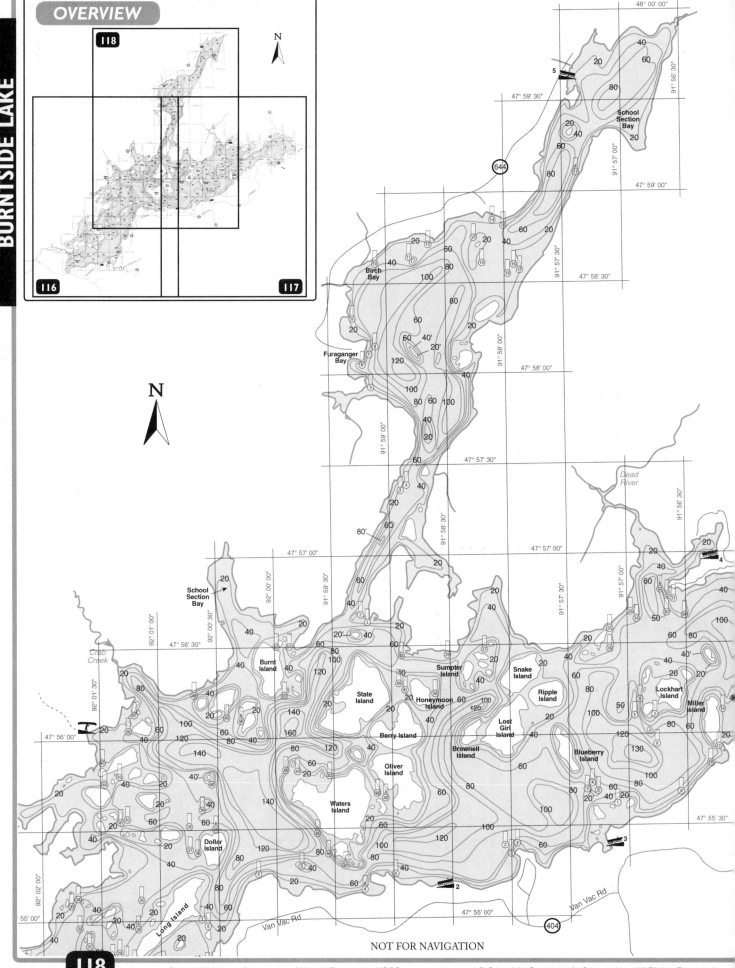

OVERVIEW

118

116   117

N

N

School Section Bay

Birch Bay

Furaganger Bay

Dead River

School Section Bay

Crab Creek

Burnt Island

Sumpter Island

Snake Island

Lockhart Island

State Island

Honeymoon Island

Ripple Island

Miller Island

Berry Island

Lost Girl Island

Blueberry Island

Oliver Island

Brownell Island

Waters Island

Dollar Island

Long Island

Van Vac Rd

Van Vac Rd

NOT FOR NAVIGATION

Source: Minnesota Department of Natural Resources, USGS

Lost Lake

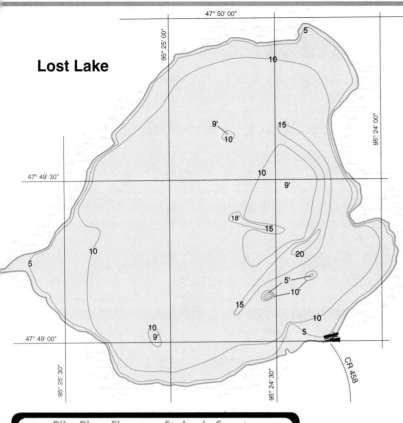

Lost Lake, St. Louis County
Area map page / coordinates: 16 / B,C-1
Surface area / shorelength: 768 acres / 4.7 miles
Accessibility: County-owned public access with ramp on southeast shore
47° 49' 0.49" N / 92° 24' 13.51" W

LENGTH OF SELECTED SPECIES SAMPLED FROM ALL GEAR
Survey Date: 08/13/1974
Number of fish caught for the following length categories (inches):

species	0-5	6-8	9-11	12-14	15-19	20-24	25-29	>30	Total
Black Crappie	-	-	2	-	-	-	-	-	2
Bluegill	-	1	-	-	-	-	-	-	1
Pumpkin. Sunfish	2	-	-	-	-	-	-	-	2
Walleye	-	5	29	69	14	4	-	1	122
Yellow Perch	2	28	30	-	-	-	-	-	60

CR 458

N

Pike River Flowage, St. Louis County
Area map page / coordinates: 16 / C-1
Surface area / shorelength: 254 acres / 5.7 miles
Accessibility: State-owned public access with gravel ramp on east shore, south of Hwy. 1 bridge overpass; also carry-down access above Pike River Dam off Co. Rd. 77
47° 40' 34.84" N / 92° 16' 52.97" W

FISH STOCKING DATA

year	species	size	# released
02	Walleye	Fry	250,000

LENGTH OF SELECTED SPECIES SAMPLED FROM ALL GEAR
Survey Date: 07/26/2004
Number of fish caught for the following length categories (inches):

species	0-5	6-8	9-11	12-14	15-19	20-24	25-29	>30	Total
Black Crappie	-	20	11	-	-	-	-	-	31
Bluegill	14	51	1	-	-	-	-	-	66
Hybrid Sunfish	5	-	-	-	-	-	-	-	5
Northern Pike	-	-	1	1	11	7	7	1	28
Pumpkin. Sunfish	11	-	-	-	-	-	-	-	11
Rock Bass	3	8	-	-	-	-	-	-	11
Walleye	-	1	-	1	4	-	-	-	6
Yellow Perch	18	21	-	-	-	-	-	-	39

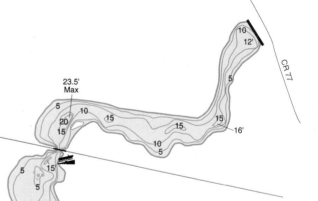

CR 77

23.5' Max

Pike River Flowage

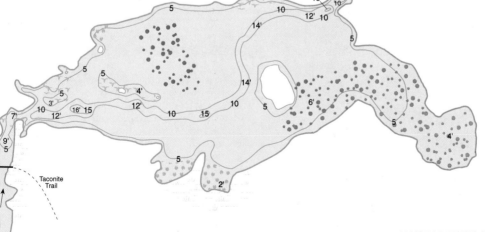

Pike River

Taconite Trail

NOT FOR NAVIGATION

Source: Minnesota Department of Natural Resources, USGS

STURGEON LAKE St. Louis County

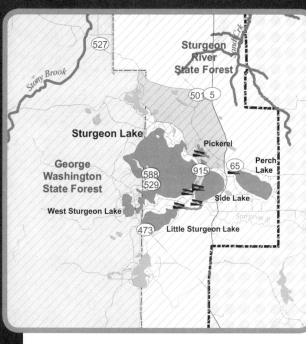

| Area map page / coordinates: | 14 / D,E-2 |

Area map page / coordinates: 14 / D,E-2

Watershed: Little Fork

Surface water area / shorelength: 1,585 acres / 18.6 miles

Maximum / mean depth: 80 feet / NA

Water color / clarity: Clear / 11.5 feet (2009)

Shoreland zoning classification: General development

Management class / Ecological type: Walleye / soft-water walleye

Accessibility: State-owned public access on east shore in park

47° 40' 11.47" N / 93° 2' 4.03" W

Accommodations: McCarthy Beach State Park, resorts, boat rental, camping

FISH STOCKING DATA

year	species	size	# released
05	Walleye	Fingerling	8,060

NET CATCH DATA

Date: 07/27/2009

	Gill Nets		Trap Nets	
		avg. fish		avg. fish
species	# per net	weight (lbs.)	# per net	weight (lbs.)
Black Crappie	0.73	0.44	1.50	0.32
Bluegill	0.73	0.09	11.64	0.19
Hybrid Sunfish	-	-	0.14	0.24
Largemouth Bass	0.07	0.77	-	-
Northern Pike	4.27	2.25	1.29	1.60
Pumpkin. Sunfish	-	-	1.21	0.16
Rock Bass	0.07	0.32	0.57	0.19
Walleye	1.33	1.53	0.07	3.75
White Sucker	0.40	2.56	-	-
Yellow Perch	0.13	0.09	0.07	0.13

LENGTH OF SELECTED SPECIES SAMPLED FROM ALL GEAR

Number of fish caught for the following length categories (inches):

species	0-5	6-8	9-11	12-14	15-19	20-24	25-29	>30	Total
Black Crappie	4	17	9	2	-	-	-	-	32
Bluegill	66	108	-	-	-	-	-	-	174
Hybrid Sunfish	-	2	-	-	-	-	-	-	2
Largemouth Bass	-	-	1	-	-	-	-	-	1
Northern Pike	-	-	1	4	38	25	9	5	82
Pumpkin. Sunfish	13	4	-	-	-	-	-	-	17
Rock Bass	7	1	1	-	-	-	-	-	9
Tullibee (Cisco)	-	1	9	3	5	-	-	-	18
Walleye	-	5	5	4	3	2	2	-	21
White Sucker	-	-	-	-	6	-	-	-	6
Yellow Perch	1	2	-	-	-	-	-	-	3

FISHING INFORMATION

Sturgeon Lake comes by its name honestly. At one time, it was full of sturgeon. These primitive-looking fish are currently listed with the Minnesota DNR as a species of concern. Overfishing, habitat loss and pollution all contributed to its dwindling population. With better management, the surgeon population is making a comeback. Rivers and lakes have been cleaned up and the DNR instituted a ban on fishing for sturgeon, except for on a few rivers bordering Canada and Wisconsin. According to George Pernat, owner of Bimbo's Octagon Restaurant and Motel, Box 397, Side Lake, MN, 218-254-2576, there are still a few 60- and 70-pounders out there. Even though you can't fish for them now, there are plenty of other species to keep an angler busy and satisfied.

Walleyes aren't tremendously numerous, says Pernat, but they average 18.8 inches and 2.4 pounds, which will certainly make a nice meal, come shore-lunch or dinner time. The DNR most recently stocked 8,060 walleye fingerlings here in 2005, which should serve to make this an even better walleye fishery in years to come. Northerns are well-worth catching, averaging 21.1 inches and over 2.2 pounds. While the numbers exceeded the averages found in other lakes, they still fell into the normal range for this lake. For both walleyes and northern pike, try floating minnows under a slip bobber. If you're targeting walleyes troll stickbaits or spinner rigs along the various drop-offs. Cast spinnerbaits, jerkbaits or topwater lures to draw strikes from pike.

Pernat says the crappie population, which had crashed at one time, has rebounded and there are now plenty of "slabs" present. Crappies caught during the most recent DNR surveys were mainly in the 6- to 8-inch range, though. Sturgeon Lake's bluegills exhibit slow growth rates. Yellow perch numbers have been low, which is considered normal for this lake. Average perch sizes are 6.3 inches and 1.1 pounds. Crappies are suckers for small minnows or leeches presented vertically under a slip bobber.

"Most of the lake is good" fishing, says Pernat. Areas showing special promise are the mid-lake humps and especially the bar and turns north and east of Barrett Island and around Hayes Island. The bridges in the channels heading to West Sturgeon, Little Sturgeon, and Side Lake are good spots, too. You'll probably want to avoid fishing in other areas of the channels, though, for there's a lot of boat traffic. The channels themselves are no-wake zones, says Pernat, and the patrolling is downright ruthless; open it up through there, and you're likely to be staring at a big, fat ticket. There's good access to this lake, both public and private. Boats of most any trailerable size can be launched.

While the fishery itself is currently in good shape, the DNR warns of potential problems with development on the lake. The DNR says, "The impact of land use decisions on one lake lot may seem relatively small, yet the combined effects of many lakeshore owners fixing up their property can result in a significant decline in water quality and habitat." To prevent a loss in water quality, the DNR recommends keeping all natural shorelines and vegetation intact, not using fertilizer on lawns, controlling runoff and maintaining septic systems. Each property owner can make a huge difference to maintain and improve the health of this fishery in years to come.

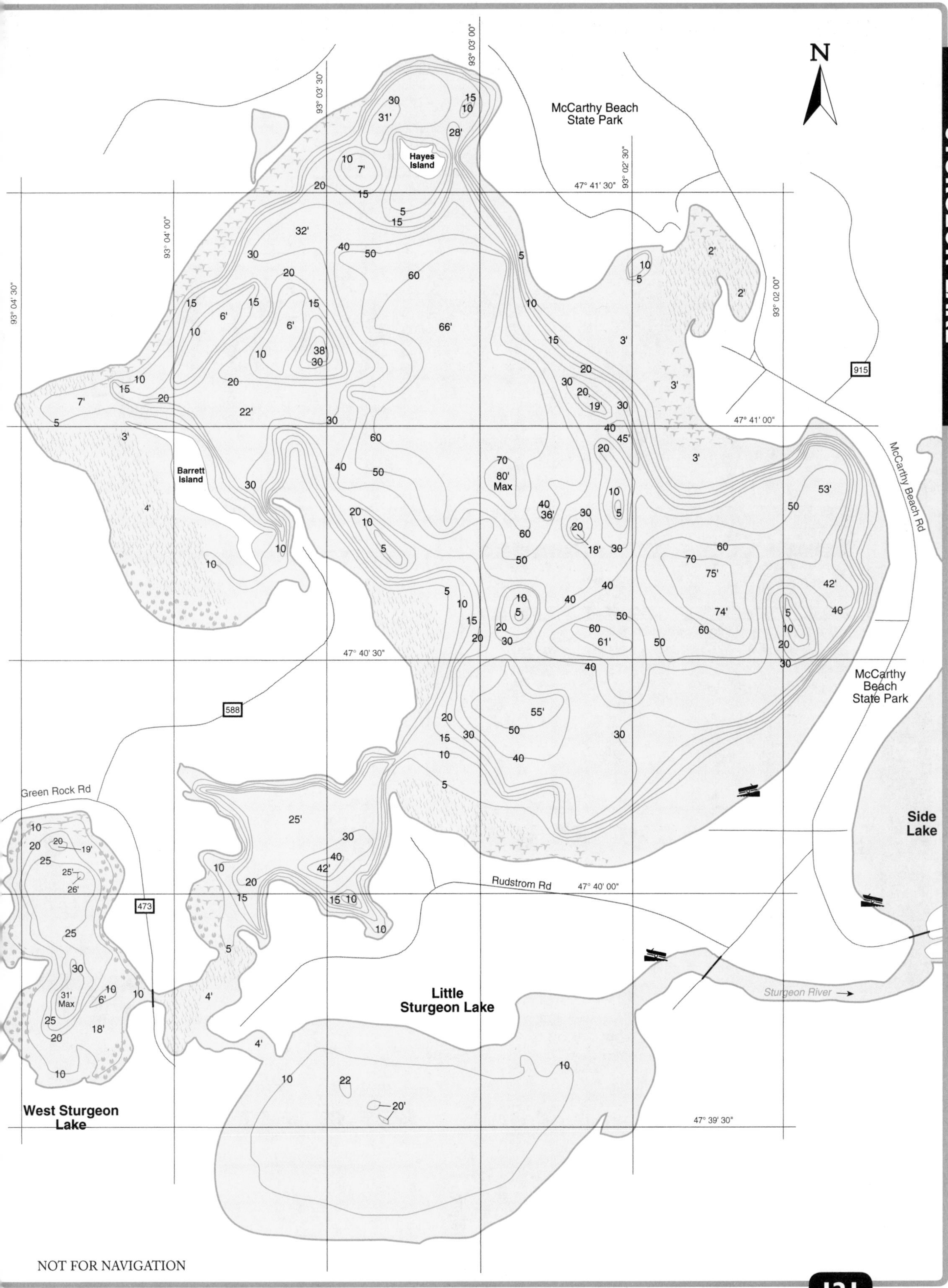

N

McCarthy Beach
State Park

47° 41' 30"

93° 03' 30"
93° 03' 00"
93° 04' 00"
93° 04' 30"
93° 02' 30"
93° 02' 00"

915

47° 41' 00"

30
15
10
31'
28'
Hayes
Island
10
7'
20
15
5
15
32'
40
50
30
60
20
10
5
15
66'
15
3'
15
6'
15
6'
10
20
5
38'
30
3'
10
20
3'
7'
22'
30
15
20
30
60
40
20
19'
45'
40
3'
5
3'
Barrett
Island
30
40
50
70
80'
Max
40
36'
60
10
5
53'
50
20
10
60
30
20
18'
42'
40
5
4'
10
20
10
5
60
40
70
75'
74'
50
60
5
10
20
40
30
60
61'
50
60
40
42'
40
10
5
15
20
30
50
30
5
55'
50

47° 40' 30"

588

McCarthy
Beach
State Park

Green Rock Rd

10
20
20
19'
25
25'
26'
25
30
31'
Max
25
18'
20
10
6'
10
10
473
5
4'
15
10
5
25'
30
40
42'
10
20
15
15
10
10

Side
Lake

Rudstrom Rd   47° 40' 00"

Sturgeon River →

4'
4'

Little
Sturgeon Lake

West Sturgeon
Lake

10
22
20'
10

47° 39' 30"

NOT FOR NAVIGATION

PICKEREL LAKE
St. Louis County

SIDE LAKE
St. Louis County

PERCH LAKE
St. Louis County

PERCH LAKE
St. Louis County

SIDE LAKE
St. Louis County

PICKEREL LAKE
St. Louis County

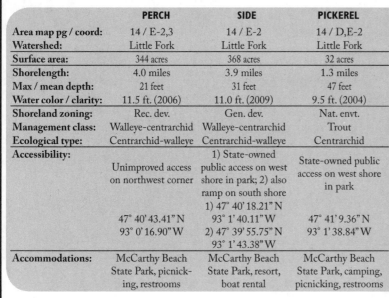

	PERCH	SIDE	PICKEREL
Area map pg / coord:	14 / E-2,3	14 / E-2	14 / D,E-2
Watershed:	Little Fork	Little Fork	Little Fork
Surface area:	344 acres	368 acres	32 acres
Shorelength:	4.0 miles	3.9 miles	1.3 miles
Max / mean depth:	21 feet	31 feet	47 feet
Water color / clarity:	11.5 ft. (2006)	11.0 ft. (2009)	9.5 ft. (2004)
Shoreland zoning:	Rec. dev.	Gen. dev.	Nat. envt.
Management class:	Walleye-centrarchid	Walleye-centrarchid	Trout
Ecological type:	Centrarchid-walleye	Centrarchid-walleye	Centrarchid
Accessibility:	Unimproved access on northwest corner	1) State-owned public access on west shore in park; 2) also ramp on south shore	State-owned public access on west shore in park
	47° 40' 43.41" N 93° 0' 16.90" W	1) 47° 40' 18.21" N 93° 1' 40.11" W 2) 47° 39' 55.75" N 93° 1' 43.38" W	47° 41' 9.36" N 93° 1' 38.84" W
Accommodations:	McCarthy Beach State Park, picnicking, restrooms	McCarthy Beach State Park, resort, boat rental	McCarthy Beach State Park, camping, picnicking, restrooms

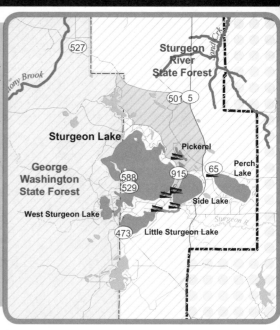

Perch Lake

FISH STOCKING DATA

year	species	size	# released
08	Walleye	Fingerling	3,434

LENGTH OF SELECTED SPECIES SAMPLED FROM ALL GEAR
Survey Date: 07/17/2006

Number of fish caught for the following length categories (inches):

species	0-5	6-8	9-11	12-14	15-19	20-24	25-29	>30	Total
Black Crappie	22	86	8	2	-	-	-	-	118
Northern Pike	-	-	-	-	3	37	25	-	65
Pumpkin. Sunfish	46	1	-	-	-	-	-	-	47
Smallmouth Bass	-	-	-	2	28	-	-	-	30
Walleye	-	9	2	-	18	9	-	-	38
Yellow Perch	2	11	1	-	-	-	-	-	14

Side Lake

FISH STOCKING DATA

year	species	size	# released
06	Walleye	Fingerling	2,749
07	Walleye	Fingerling	3,559
08	Walleye	Fingerling	2,362
09	Walleye	Fingerling	4,590
10	Walleye	Fingerling	2,700

LENGTH OF SELECTED SPECIES SAMPLED FROM ALL GEAR
Survey Date: 07/13/2009

Number of fish caught for the following length categories (inches):

species	0-5	6-8	9-11	12-14	15-19	20-24	25-29	>30	Total
Black Crappie	9	8	2	-	-	-	-	-	19
Bluegill	404	111	6	-	-	-	-	-	526
Northern Pike	-	-	-	-	24	57	7	2	90
Pumpkin. Sunfish	9	-	-	-	-	-	-	-	9
Rock Bass	1	1	-	-	-	-	-	-	2
Tullibee (Cisco)	-	1	10	25	4	-	-	-	41
Walleye	-	3	2	3	8	6	4	-	26
White Sucker	-	-	-	3	52	6	-	-	63
Yellow Perch	24	5	1	-	-	-	-	-	30

FISHING INFORMATION

George Pernat, owner of Bimbo's Octagon Restaurant and Motel, Box 397, Side Lake, MN, 218-254-2576, says **Side Lake** is a "nice all-around recreation and fishing lake" Where you'll find northern pike, walleyes, largemouth bass and panfish. The lake has a good weedline, says Pernat, which should be fished for all species. He says most locals use Daredevils for pike and live bait for walleyes. There's some decent action in winter, as well.

Perch Lake is loaded with pike and walleye of decent size, structure and abundance. Weedline-fishing is the ticket. Troll your spoon or spinnerbait just off the outside edge of weeds at the 7- to 9-foot level in summer for pike. In evening, cast the shores with topwater gear. Walleyes will be found outside weeds, as well. A minnow or leech, depending on season, should work well on the 'eyes. Smallmouth bass were introduced in this lake by an unknown source and there are now good numbser of good-sized smallies here. The most recent DNR survey, conducted in 2008, yielded 28 out of 30 fish in the 15- to 19-inch class. There are an average number of perch in Perch Lake, though their numbers are up from previous assessments.

Pickerel Lake has been stocked with rainbow and brook trout since 1999. According to the DNR survey in 2004, planted brook trout grew at a rate of 244% over a period of 5 months. Rainbow trout were notably absent from the survey, however locals say rainbows are in there. Fishing is good from shore or a car-top-size boat. Locals use worms and flies to catch trout.

Pickerel Lake

FISH STOCKING DATA

year	species	size	# released
06	Brook Trout	Yearling	718
07	Rainbow Trout	Yearling	1,400
08	Brook Trout	Yearling	1,049
09	Rainbow Trout	Yearling	1,400
10	Brook Trout	Yearling	1,058

LENGTH OF SELECTED SPECIES SAMPLED FROM ALL GEAR
Not Available; No Fish Collected (2009)

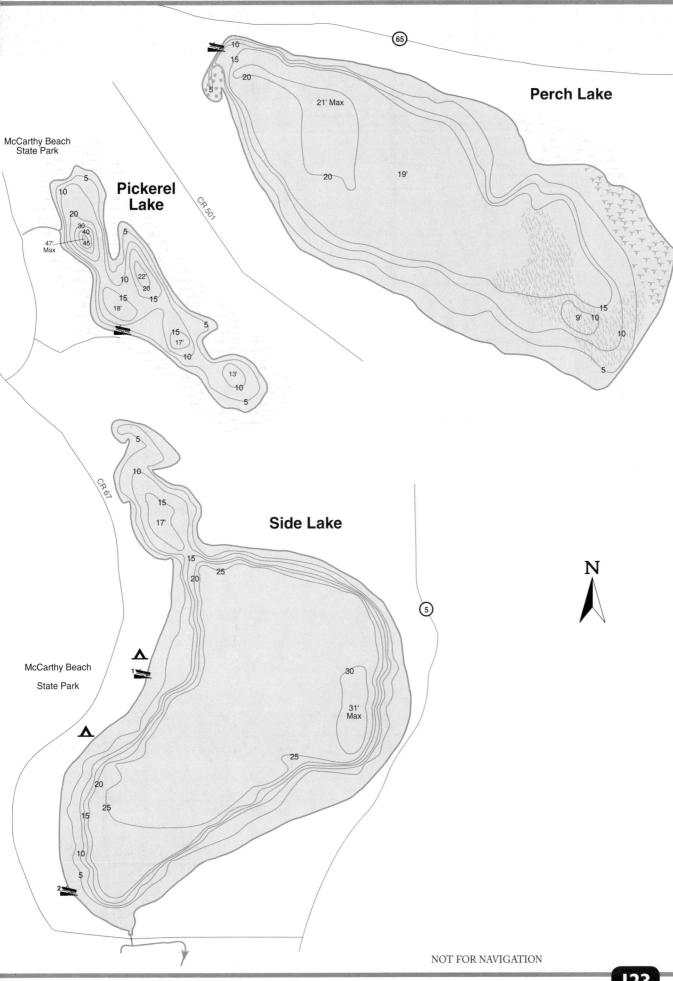

Perch Lake

65

10
15
20
5

21' Max

20
19'

20

15
9' 10
10
5

McCarthy Beach
State Park

Pickerel Lake

CR 501

5
10
20
30
40
47' 45
Max
5

10
22'
20
15 15
18'
5
15
17'
10
13'
10
5

Side Lake

CR 67

5
10
15
17'

15
25
20

5

30

31'
Max

25

McCarthy Beach
State Park

20
25
15

10
5
2

N

NOT FOR NAVIGATION

123

Auto (Arrowhead) Lake, St. Louis County

Area map page / coordinates: 15 / D-5
Surface area / shorelength: 97 acres / NA
Accessibility: State-owned public access with concrete ramp on west shore, one mile east of Hwy. 53 on Peppard Road
47° 40' 39.04" N / 92° 38' 9.46" W

FISH STOCKING DATA

year	species	size	# released
07	Walleye	Fingerling	908
09	Walleye	Fingerling	859

LENGTH OF SELECTED SPECIES SAMPLED FROM ALL GEAR
Survey Date: 08/08/2006
Number of fish caught for the following length categories (inches):

species	0-5	6-8	9-11	12-14	15-19	20-24	25-29	>30	Total
Black Crappie	-	-	-	-	-	-	-	-	-
Bluegill	57	216	-	-	-	-	-	-	273
Largemouth Bass	15	21	2	-	-	-	-	-	38
Northern Pike	-	-	-	-	1	-	-	1	2
Walleye	-	-	8	14	25	6	-	-	53
Yellow Perch	2	24	1	-	-	-	-	-	27

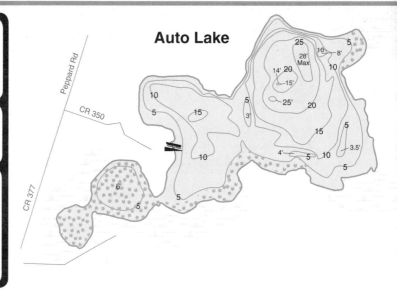

Auto Lake

James (Jammer) Lake, St. Louis County

Area map page / coordinates: 15 / E-5
Surface area / shorelength: 18 acres / NA
Accessibility: State-owned public access with concrete ramp on north shore
47° 39' 22.23" N / 92° 36' 30.60" W

FISH STOCKING DATA

year	species	size	# released
annual	Rainbow Trout	Fingerling	~ 1,500

LENGTH OF SELECTED SPECIES SAMPLED FROM ALL GEAR
Survey Date: 05/22/2007
Number of fish caught for the following length categories (inches):

species	0-5	6-8	9-11	12-14	15-19	20-24	25-29	>30	Total
Largemouth Bass	-	1	6	3	-	-	-	-	10
Rainbow Trout	-	-	-	-	2	-	-	-	2

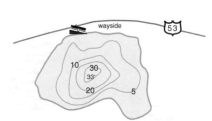

James Lake

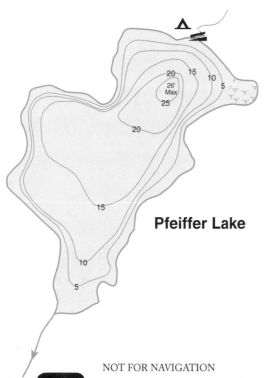

Pfeiffer Lake

N

Pfeiffer Lake, St. Louis County

Area map page / coordinates: 15 / C-6
Surface area / shorelength: 58 acres / NA
Accessibility: USFS-owned public access with concrete ramp on north shore in campground
47° 45' 0.93" N / 92° 28' 25.10" W

FISH STOCKING DATA

year	species	size	# released
06	Walleye	Fingerling	360
09	Walleye	Fingerling	417

LENGTH OF SELECTED SPECIES SAMPLED FROM ALL GEAR
Survey Date: 07/30/2007
Number of fish caught for the following length categories (inches):

species	0-5	6-8	9-11	12-14	15-19	20-24	25-29	>30	Total
Black Crappie	-	2	-	-	-	-	-	-	2
Bluegill	144	609	-	-	-	-	-	-	753
Largemouth Bass	1	3	8	1	-	-	-	-	13
Walleye	-	-	2	-	9	8	-	-	19
Yellow Perch	-	17	27	-	-	-	-	-	44

NOT FOR NAVIGATION

Source: Minnesota Department of Natural Resources, USGS

St. Louis County · LAKE VERMILION

Area map page / coordinates: 11/E-5,6 & 12/E-1 / 15/A-5,6 & 16/A-C,1-3

Watershed: Vermilion

Surface water area / shorelength: 39,272 acres / 99.9 miles

Maximum / mean depth: 76 feet / 25 feet

Water color / clarity: Light stain / 8.0 feet (2010)

Shoreland zoning classification: General development

Management class / Ecological type: Walleye / soft-water walleye

Accessibility: Refer to access table

Accommodations: Bordered by Kabetogama State Forest, Sturgeon River State Forest and Pine Island Wildlife Mgmt. Area, camping, picnicking, restrooms

FISH STOCKING DATA

year	species	size	# released
06	Walleye	Fry	16,905,000
06	Muskellunge	Fingerling	1,268
07	Muskellunge	Fingerling	1,962
07	Walleye	Fry	16,600,000
08	Muskellunge	Fingerling	1,292
08	Walleye	Fry	10,800,000
09	Muskellunge	Fingerling	2,706
09	Walleye	Fry	11,600,000
10	Muskellunge	Fingerling	4,828
10	Walleye	Fry	6,000,000

NET CATCH DATA

Date: 06/01/2010

	Gill Nets		Trap Nets	
species	# per net	avg. fish weight (lbs.)	# per net	avg. fish weight (lbs.)
Black Crappie	0.15	0.45	0.96	0.57
Bluegill	0.45	0.18	21.56	0.14
Lake Whitefish	0.10	3.63	-	-
Largemouth Bass	-	-	0.22	0.83
Northern Pike	0.70	6.28	1.15	2.60
Pumpkin. Sunfish	-	-	0.44	0.09
Rock Bass	0.15	0.53	1.04	0.27
Smallmouth Bass	0.65	1.40	0.04	0.26
Tullibee (Cisco)	14.75	0.64	-	-
Walleye	12.15	1.03	1.67	1.81
White Sucker	1.55	1.92	0.19	1.92
Yellow Perch	19.30	0.20	6.19	0.15

LENGTH OF SELECTED SPECIES SAMPLED FROM ALL GEAR

Number of fish caught for the following length categories (inches):

species	0-5	6-8	9-11	12-14	15-19	20-24	25-29	>30	Total
Black Crappie	3	6	20	-	-	-	-	-	29
Bluegill	416	170	-	-	-	-	-	-	591
Lake Whitefish	-	-	-	-	1	1	-	-	2
Largemouth Bass	3	1	-	1	1	-	-	-	6
Northern Pike	-	-	-	-	9	17	10	9	45
Pumpkin. Sunfish	12	-	-	-	-	-	-	-	12
Rock Bass	8	21	2	-	-	-	-	-	31
Smallmouth Bass	-	2	3	7	2	-	-	-	14
Tullibee (Cisco)	1	32	111	148	3	-	-	-	295
Walleye	-	17	54	126	61	28	2	-	288
White Sucker	-	-	3	9	22	2	-	-	36
Yellow Perch	219	260	66	2	-	-	-	-	553

FISHING INFORMATION

A number of years back, one of the best-known magazines in North America, perhaps the world, listed Lake Vermilion as one of the 10 most-scenic lakes in the U.S. This big, sprawling water has something like 1,200 miles of shoreline lined with multitudes of weeded bays, and even rocky cliffs along shorelines. There are so many islands located in Vermilion's 39,272 acres of water, that it would take you a full year to visit all of them at a rate of one per day. That's right, there are 365 islands, and they range in size from outcrops barely large enough to eat shore lunch on up to big chunks of land holding several resorts and cabins. The Superior National Forest and the Boundary Waters Canoe Area Wilderness (BWCAW) abut this 27-mile-long lake, and the natural scenery is simply breathtaking. That's especially true in fall, when maples, birches and aspens don their bright-hued finery.

Lake Vermilion is known for more than its scenic beauty. It's a recreational lake second to none. It's a destination for hordes of vacationers from all over the country. They fill the gaming tables and take over the slots at the nearby casino. They pile into boats, pontoons and jet skis and head out onto the water. Many locals have built summer cabins or year-around homes on this lake. Not surprisingly, property values are on the rise, along with taxes. Locals place their own demands on the lake. They also have runabouts, big pontoons, canoes, and fishing boats.

Given the numbers of people who visit Lake Vermilion in summer, you'd think there'd barely be room enough for the jet skiers and ski boats, not to mention wind-surfing rigs and the pontoons which cruise the shorelines. That's not the case. This is a big lake. It is 27 miles long and covers 76 square miles. It's divided into a number of bays, which are distinctly separate from each other. Consequently, this lake can handle several hundred recreational boats on a summer afternoon and still have room for a fishing rig or two. Don't worry, you shouldn't get run over on this lake.

The big lake built its reputation on walleyes. It's known as perhaps the "Walleye Capital of St. Louis County," and for good reason. Anglers have taken scads of these great-eating fish out of the lake, and lots more remain. As well, several million walleye fry are poured into Vermilion annually. In 2006, new regulations were adopted to help preserve this fantastic walleye fishery. All walleyes caught in the 17-to 26-inch range must be immediately released. The new possession limit was changed to 4, allowing one fish over 26 inches to be kept.

Walleyes aren't the only species in this lake. There are good-size northern pike, nice numbers of bluegills and crappies, and solid numbers of smallmouth bass. However, the biggest story at Lake Vermilion is the success of the muskie management program.

The DNR began stocking muskies back in 1985, and it seems their efforts are paying off. The most recent muskie survey shows that the program has been very successful. In fact, Vermilion is considered by many to be one of the top muskie fisheries in Minnesota, if not all of North America.

Doug Ellis, owner of Virginia Surplus Store, 105 N. 3rd Avenue, Virginia, MN, 218-741-0331, says he sells a lot of tackle to Vermilion-bound anglers, and he uses a good deal of it himself on the big lake. He says the muskie population has been coming on real strong; in fact, it's just about exploded in the last few years. "The muskie fishing on Vermilion is just phenomenal," he said. "You now have a real chance at catching a 50-inch muskie. Heck, nobody takes photos of the 45-inch muskies anymore. Recently there was a 53-inch muskie caught. That fish had a 28-inch girth."

Ellis' observations are born out by the experience of Guide Dave Swenson of Swenson's Guide Service, www.muskieguide.homestead.com, 7105 Comstock Lake Road, Cotton, MN, 218-482-5217. He says he knows of several 50-inch-plus fish which were taken from Vermilion over the last several years.

"Lake Vermilion is just awesome right now," notes Swenson. "There are lots of tourists and lots of jet skis in the summer, but there are also lots of big muskies. The DNR made a wise choice in beginning its stocking program. The fish are out there. They're thriving; they're healthy and they're growing."

Early in the season, look for muskies in a huge weedbed which virtually fills Van Ryper Bay, toward the northwest end of the big lake. Van Ryper is filled with cabbage, which gets thicker as the season progresses. You'll want to work the outside edge early with bucktails, says Swenson. From mid-July on, try weed pockets with topwater gear. You might also try Fox Bay early in the season. Work weed edges with bucktails early, using a fast retrieve with a subtle pumping motion to flare the bucktail out a bit. As the season advances, fish weed pockets with surface lures.

In summer, starting around early July, the muskie action switches to the reefs and bars. One nice spot to try then is the shallow reef off the southern tip of Knotts Island in Wolf Bay. This spot is marked by a hazard buoy and can be fished successfully with a Bobbie, a Suick, or any of your favorite jerkbaits. Position your boat in 15-to 25-feet of water, and cast your lure on top of the rocks, working it back toward the drop-off. This area is known for producing big fish and is worth a couple of passes.

Also good from early July until fall is a series of rock humps off the north branch of the Y-shaped Fectos Point, near the entrance to Greenwood Bay. Several hazard buoys mark this popular big-fish spot. Start deep and cast to the shallows, right to the buoy markers, in fact. "Don't be afraid to get your bait in shallow; you'll lose fish if you don't," says Swenson.

Similarly, Merry-Go-Round Reef, located off Norwegian point in Wakemup Bay is a great mid- to late-season spot. It's a long reef, well known to muskie anglers, and it should be worked all around, keeping

Cont'd on page 135

AREA NAMES REFERENCE

pg #	Area Name	pg #	Area Name
129,130	Ackleys Point	138	McKinley Park
133	Alpeo Island	134	Mead Island
139	Armstrong Bay	128	Merry Go Round Reef
133,136	Arrowhead Point	133	Moccasin Point
136	Banana Island	137	Moose Island
135,139	Bass Bay	139	Mud Creek Bay
135	Bear Creek	130	Murphy Point
137,141	Big Bay	129,130	Muskego Bay
137-138	Birch Island	129,130	Muskego Point
131,132	Birch Narrows	132	Muskrat Channel
137	Birch Point	130	Niles Bay
129	Black Bay	129	Norwegian Bay
133	Black Duck Bay	129,130	Norwegian Point
133	Black Duck Island	138	Nyberg Island
133,136	Black Duck Point	131,132	Oak Island
128	Boys Camp Reef	131,132	Oak Narrows
132	Breezy Point	128	Ormonds Island
134	Buzzard Island	128	Piccard Island
133	Bystrom Bay	137,141	Pike Bay
139	Cable Bay	140	Pike River
134,137-138	Canfield Portage	134-135, 137-138	Pine Island
134,137-138	Canfield Portage Bay		
128	Cemetery Point	137	Potato Island
128	Center Island	137-138	Puncher Point
137	Cherry Island	139	Raspberry Island
134,137	Comet Island	135	Rice Bay
131	Dago Bay	128	Richie Bay
136	Daisy Bay	131	Sandy Beach Point
136	Daisy Island	128	Schmidts Island
139	Dog Island	129	Second Island
131	Eagle Point	138	Seven Sisters Islands
137-138	Echo Point	132	Smarts Bay
138	Ely Island	138	Spider Island
137,141	Everetts Bay	128	Spring Bay
137,141	Everetts Point	129	Square Rock Island
133	Fectos Point	133	St. Marys Island
129	Fire Island	133	St. Paul Island
129	First Island	128	Staley Island
131	Fox Bay	137-138	Stonich Island
132	Frazer Bay	128	Stove Top Reef
137,141	Goat Island	136	Strawberry Island
132	Gold Island	138	Stuntz Bay
129	Goodwill Island	128	Sunset Bay
132	Grassy Point	134	Sunset Island
133,136	Greenwood Bay	133	Swanson Island
131	Gull Island	138	Swedetown Bay
128	Head of the Lakes Bay	128	Taylors Island
139	Hendrickson Island	132	Thirty-six Island
128	Hibbing Point	139	Timber Island
131,132	Hinsdale Island	141	Tower
141	Hoodoo Point	129	Treasure Island
129	Hoover Island	129	Turtle Island
131,132	Hoyt Island	141	Two River, East
130	Indian Bay	141	Two River, West
130	Indian Island (Indian Bay)	131	Van Ryper Bay
137,141	Indian Island (Pike Bay)	131	Vermilion Dam
135,138	Indian Point	130	Waconda Bay
134,136-137	Isle of Pines	129,130	Wakemup Narrows
138	J.B. Island	129	Wash, The
137,141	Jackrabbit Island	141	Whiskey Island
128	Jacobsons Point	129	Whitefish Island
131	Knotts Island	129,130	Windstock Island
129,130	Larson Bay	135,138	Windy Island
138	Long Island	131	Wolf Bay
135	Mattson Island	129	Woodys Cover
139	Mattson Bay	131,132	Zups Point

Source: Minnesota Department of Natural Resources, USGS

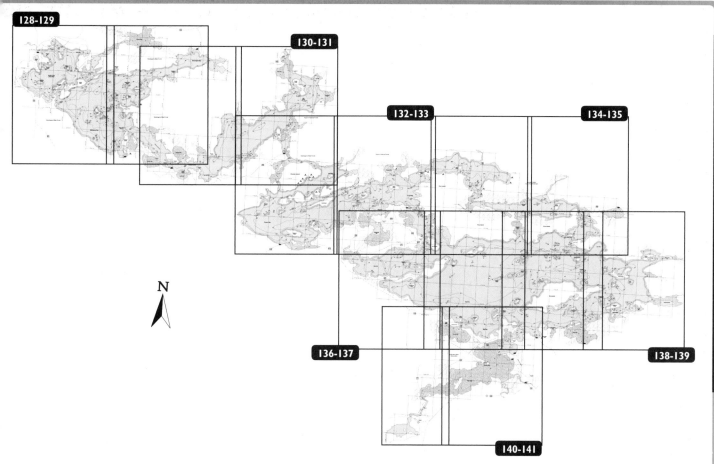

N

PUBLIC ACCESS FACILITIES

#	Site Admin	Ramp	pg #	Lat / Long	Access Description
1.	State	Concrete	128	47° 56' 50.11" N / 92° 39' 43.65" W	On the west shore of Head of the Lakes Bay, 8 miles northeast of Tower off Co. Rd. 408
2.	State	Concrete	129	47° 54' 9.27" N / 92° 35' 15.41" W	On the southeast shore of Wakemup Bay, 6 miles northeast of Cook at end of Co. Rd. 478
3.	State	Concrete	129	47° 57' 29.42" N / 92° 32' 32.09" W	On the north shore of Norwegian Bay, 10 miles northeast of Cook at the end of Co. Rd. 596
4.	State	Concrete	131	47° 54' 37.21" N / 92° 28' 24.20" W	On southwest shore of Oak Narrows, 12 miles northeast of Cook at the end of Co. Rd. 540
5.	State	(2) Concrete	132	47° 52' 1.06" N / 92° 28' 11.14" W	On the south shore of Frazer Bay, 10 miles east of Cook off Co. Rd. 418
6.	County	Concrete	133	47° 53' 22.32" N / 92° 22' 49.67" W	On Moccasin Point, 7 miles northwest of Tower at the end of Co. Rd. 929 (fee parking)
7.	County	Concrete	137	47° 49' 59.35" N / 92° 20' 55.18" W	On the north shore of Everett Bay, 3 miles northwest of Tower at the end of Co. Rd. 414
8.	City	Concrete	141	47° 49' 10.56" N / 92° 17' 40.23" W	On the north side of Hoodoo Point, 1 mile north of Tower
9.	City	Concrete	141	47° 49' 0.43" N / 92° 17' 43.68" W	On the south side of Hoodoo Point, 1 mile north of Tower
10.	City	Concrete	141	47° 48' 13.95" N / 92° 16' 57.30" W	On the East Two River, off U.S. 169 in Tower
11.	City (fee)	Concrete	138	47° 49' 41.58" N / 92° 16' 26.56" W	On south shore of McKinley Bay, 2 miles north of Tower in McKinley Park (fee parking)
12.	State (fee)	Earthen	138	47° 49' 35.08" N / 92° 14' 17.78" W	On the south shore of Stuntz Bay, 2.5 miles northeast of Tower
13.	USFS	Concrete	140	47° 53' 37.94" N / 92° 13' 2.65" W	On the north shore of Rice Bay, 8 miles northeast of Tower off Co. Rd. 408

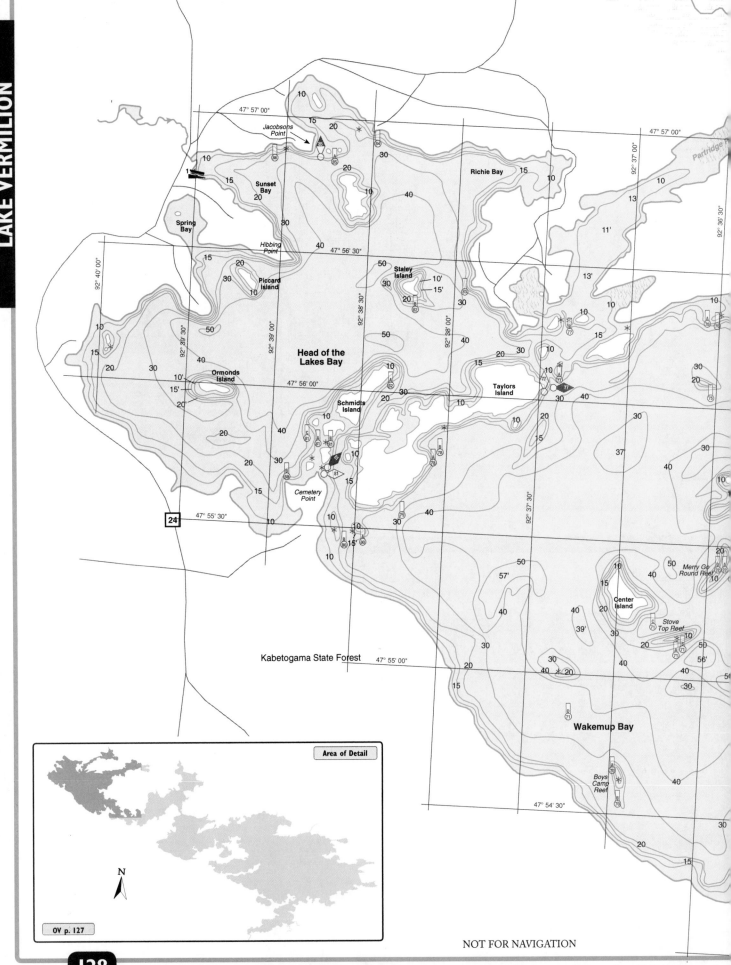

47° 57' 00"
47° 57' 00"

Jacobsons Point

Richie Bay

Partridge

Sunset Bay

Spring Bay

Hibbing Point

Piccard Island

Staley Island

47° 56' 30"

Head of the Lakes Bay

Ormonds Island

47° 56' 00"

Schmidts Island

Taylors Island

Cemetery Point

24

47° 55' 30"

Center Island

Merry Go Round Reef

Stove Top Reef

Kabetogama State Forest   47° 55' 00"

Wakemup Bay

Boys Camp Reef

47° 54' 30"

Area of Detail

N

OV p. 127

NOT FOR NAVIGATION

Source: Minnesota Department of Natural Resources, USGS

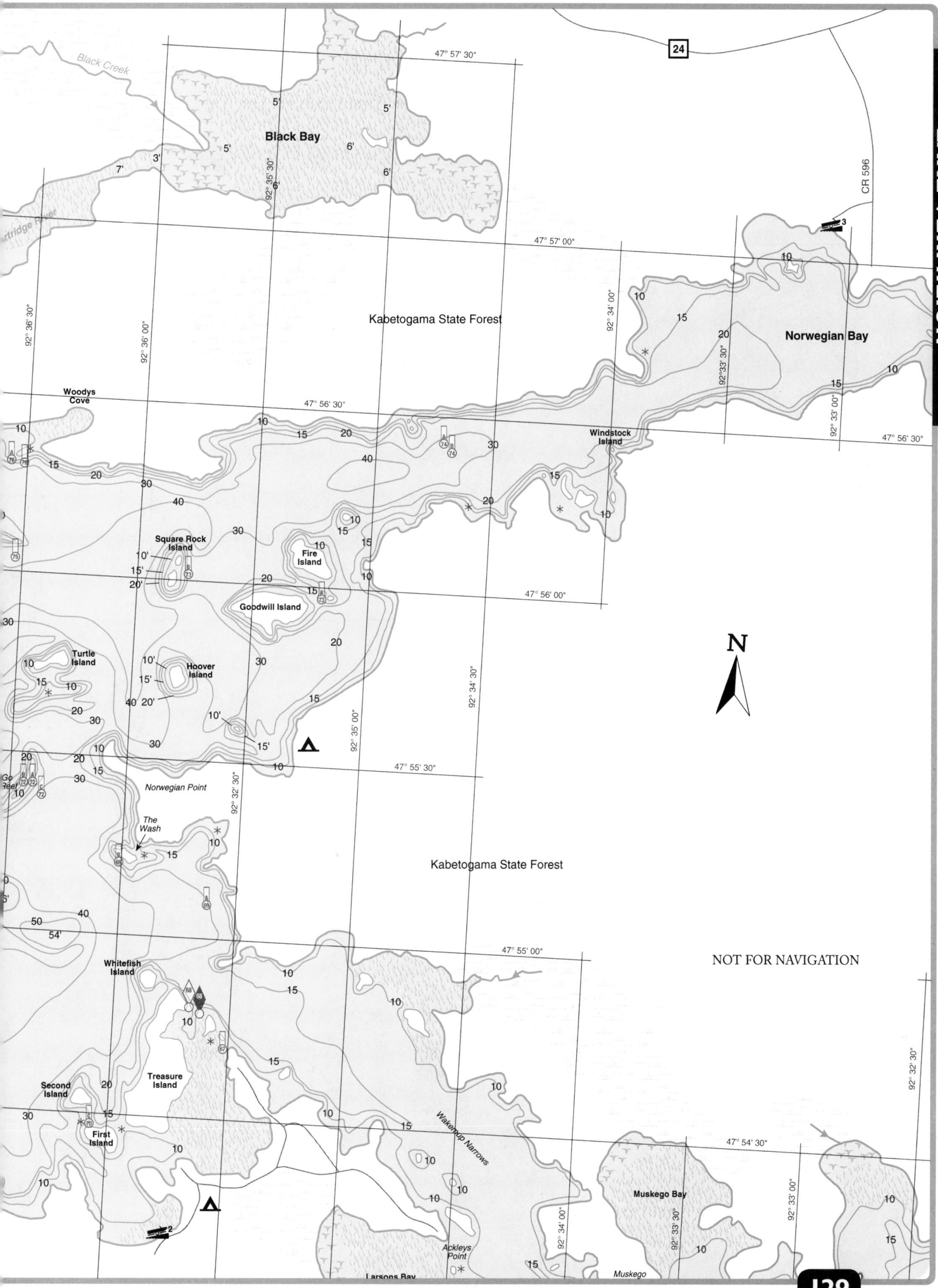

Black Creek

47° 57' 30"

5'

Black Bay

5'

5'

6'

3'

7'

6'

92° 35' 30"

92° 36'

Partridge River

47° 57' 00"

92° 34' 00"

92° 36' 30"

92° 36' 00"

Kabetogama State Forest

92° 34' 30"

10

10

15

20

Norwegian Bay

15

10

CR 596

3

10

Woodys Cove

47° 56' 30"

10

15

20

30

40

30

15

Windstock Island

47° 56' 30"

92° 33' 30"

92° 33' 00"

10

15

20

30

40

15

20

10

A
74

10

A
76

15

40

30

10

15

Square Rock Island

30

Fire Island

10

10'

15'

20'

B
73

20

15

A
73

47° 56' 00"

A
75

Goodwill Island

20

N

30

10

Turtle Island

10'

Hoover Island

30

92° 34' 30"

10

15'

15

10

40

20'

10

20

15

30

10'

30

10

92° 35' 00"

A

47° 55' 30"

20

20

30

10

15

10

Go Reef

B
72

A
72

C
72

10

92° 32' 30"

Norwegian Point

NOT FOR NAVIGATION

The Wash

15

10

B
69

Kabetogama State Forest

A
69

50

40

54'

Whitefish Island

47° 55' 00"

10

15

68

A
68

10

15

10

A
67

15

Second Island

20

Treasure Island

10

10

30

15

15

B
70

First Island

10

Wakemup Narrows

10

10

15

10

47° 54' 30"

A

10

10

10

10

Muskego Bay

92° 33' 30"

92° 33' 00"

10

2

Ackleys Point

Larsons Bay

Muskego

92° 34' 00"

15

15

10

Source: Minnesota Department of Natural Resources, USGS

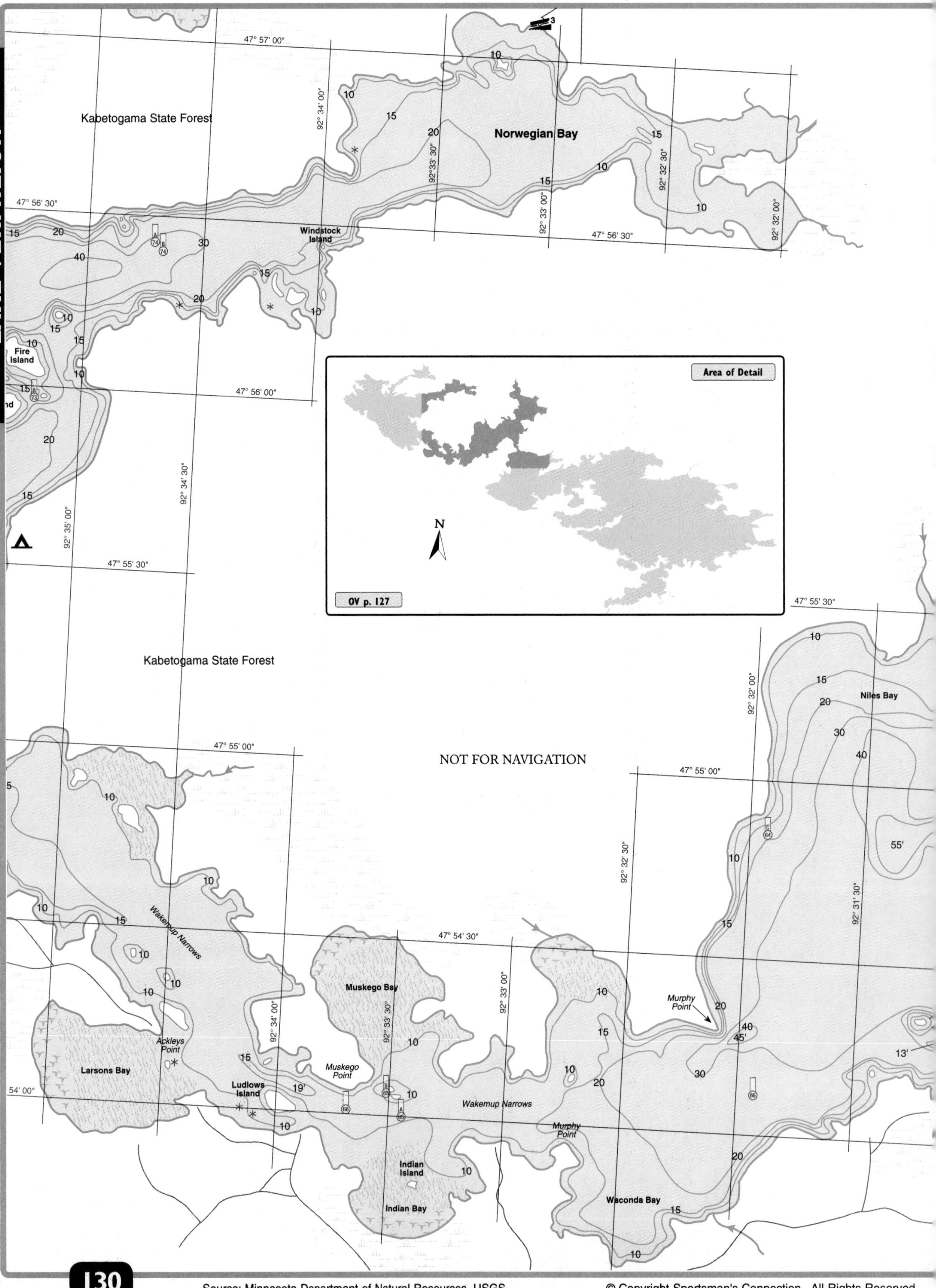

Kabetogama State Forest
Norwegian Bay
Windstock Island
Fire Island
47° 57' 00"
47° 56' 30"
47° 56' 00"
47° 55' 30"
47° 55' 00"
47° 54' 30"
54' 00"
92° 35' 00"
92° 34' 30"
92° 34' 00"
92°33' 30"
92° 33' 00"
92° 32' 30"
92° 32' 00"
92° 31' 30"
Area of Detail
OV p. 127
N
Kabetogama State Forest
NOT FOR NAVIGATION
Niles Bay
55'
Wakemup Narrows
Muskego Bay
Murphy Point
45'
13'
Ackleys Point
Larsons Bay
Ludlows Island
19'
Muskego Point
Wakemup Narrows
Murphy Point
Indian Island
Indian Bay
Waconda Bay

Source: Minnesota Department of Natural Resources, USGS

Vermilion Dam

667

N

Dago Bay

47° 57' 00"

92° 29' 00"

92° 28' 30"

Sandy Beach
Point

47° 56' 30"

Fox Bay

Knotts
Island

92° 29' 30"

92° 28' 00"

92° 27' 30"

47° 56' 00"

Van Ryper
Bay

Gull
Island

Eagle
Point

Wolf Bay

30

40

92° 30' 00"

50

10

Dago Bay

47° 55' 30"

92° 31' 00"

92° 30' 30"

47° 55' 30"

Superior National Forest

Zups Point

40

47'

40

50

40

Oak
Island

57-4

57-3

57-2

57-1

56-1

56-2

56-1

47° 54' 30"

92° 29' 30"

NOT FOR NAVIGATION

Kabetogama State Forest

92° 28' 00"

Oak
Narrows

540

92° 29' 00"

92° 28' 30"

47° 54' 00"

Hinsdale Island

Hoyt Island

19'

92° 30' 00"

Birch
Narrows

131

Superior National Forest

Zups Point

Oak
Island

Kabetogama State Forest

Oak
Narrows

540

Hinsdale Island

Hoyt Island

Birch
Narrows

Smarts Bay

Grassy
Point

Muskrat Channel

Gold Island

Frazer Bay

W

Breezy
Point

Thirty-six
Island

NOT FOR NAVIGATION

418

674

Source: Minnesota Department of Natural Resources, USGS

92° 31' 00"
92° 30' 30"
92° 30' 00"
92° 29' 30"
92° 29' 00"
92° 28' 30"
92° 28' 00"
92° 27' 30"

47° 55' 00"
47° 54' 30"
47° 54' 00"
47° 53' 30"
47° 53' 00"
47° 52' 30"

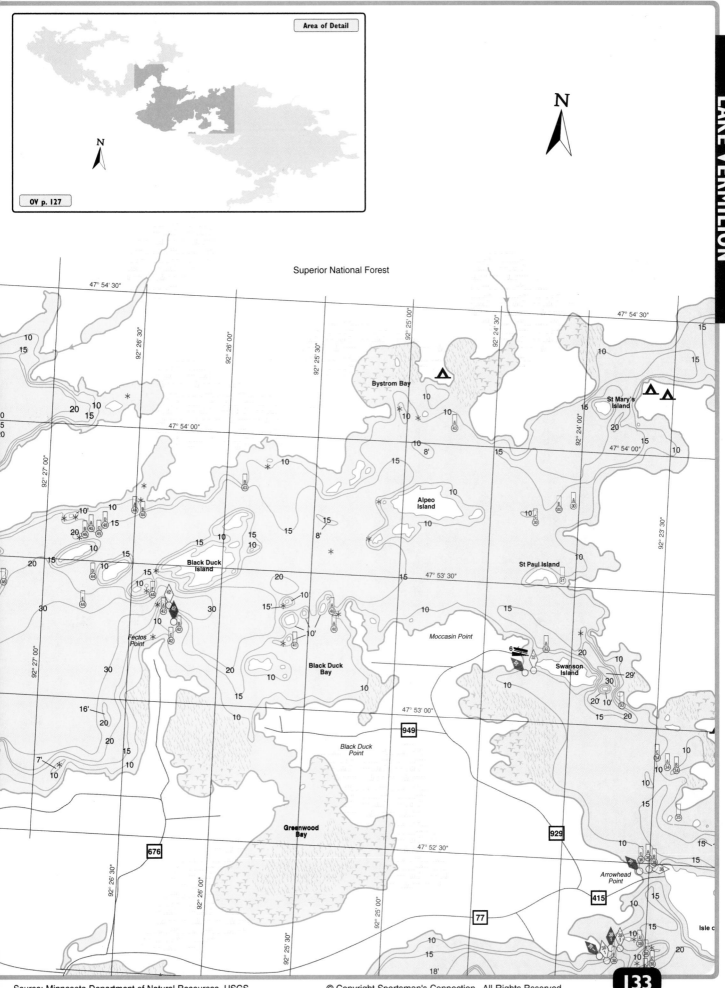

Area of Detail

N

OV p. 127

N

Superior National Forest

Bystrom Bay

St Mary's Island

Alpeo Island

St Paul Island

Black Duck Island

Fectos Point

Black Duck Bay

Moccasin Point

Swanson Island

Black Duck Point

949

Greenwood Bay

929

676

Arrowhead Point

415

77

Isle o

Source: Minnesota Department of Natural Resources, USGS   © Copyright Sportsman's Connection. All Rights Reserved.

NOT FOR NAVIGATION

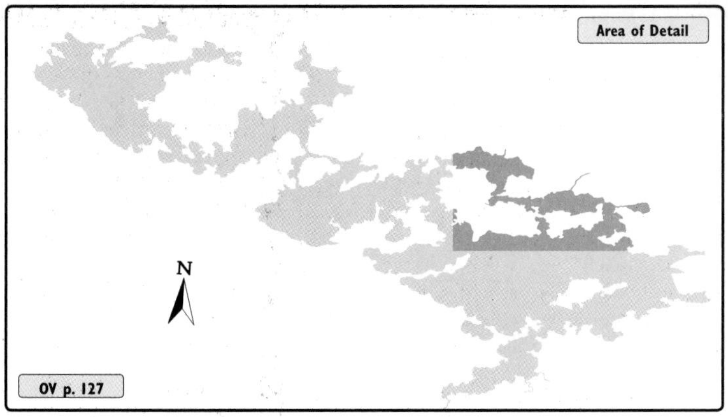
Area of Detail
N
OV p. 127

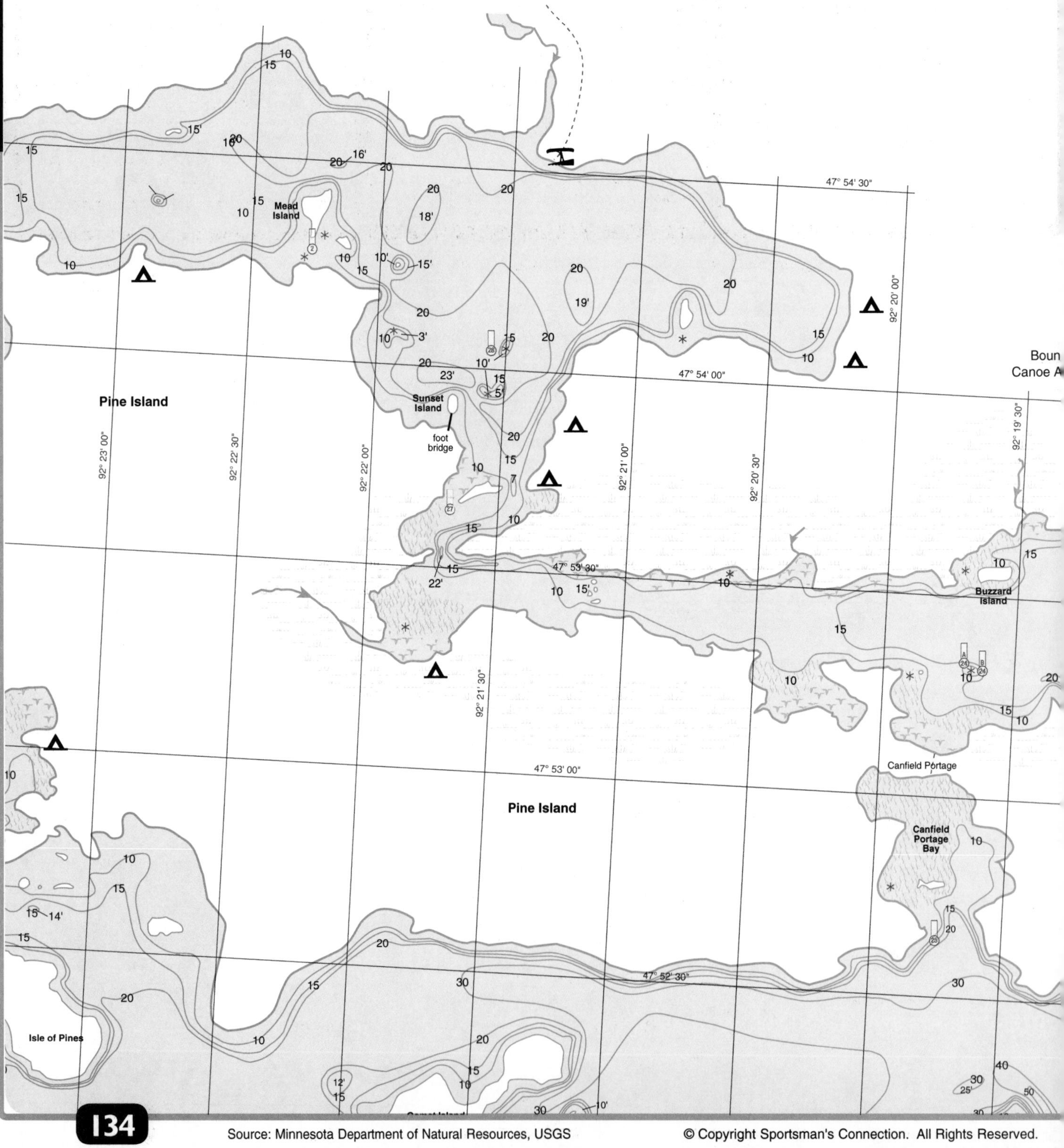
Mead Island
Pine Island
Sunset Island
foot bridge
Buzzard Island
Canfield Portage
Canfield Portage Bay
Pine Island
Isle of Pines
Boun
Canoe A
47° 54' 30"
47° 54' 00"
47° 53' 30"
47° 53' 00"
47° 52' 30"
92° 23' 00"
92° 22' 30"
92° 22' 00"
92° 21' 30"
92° 21' 00"
92° 20' 30"
92° 20' 00"
92° 19' 30"

Source: Minnesota Department of Natural Resources, USGS

Cont'd from page 126

your boat in deeper water. If you don't raise a fish move in and fish over the top. You can profitably spend an hour or two on this reef. If you aren't having much fishing success, head over to Stove Top Reef. This mid-lake rise is located south and a little west of Merry-Go-Round, off the eastern end of Center Island. Two hazard buoys mark the site. Use the same presentations and techniques as on Merry-Go-Round. If you don't raise fish there, work the shorelines of the island. Sooner or later, you're bound to tie into a muskie big enough to make your Lake Vermilion visit unforgettable.

Ellis says the walleye fishing is as good now as it's ever been, and that's especially true in winter, when action can be hot and heavy for the larger fish, those measuring 20 inches and up. Winter is a nice time to catch yellow perch in Lake Vermilion and there's good fishing as well for panfish, particularly crappies.

According to Ellis, the walleye fishing is "awesome" from ice-up to around mid December, when it begins to tail off. It remains at least adequate, though, right up to the end of the season. Right after the lake freezes, Ellis says head to the area near McKinley Park, just north of the City of Tower. Head right out onto the lake from the

public landing and fish in 8- to 10-feet of water with live bait. Be careful of the ice, especially early and late in the season. Another good early-ice spot is Everett's Bay, especially near the mouth, where the water begins to deepen. A jig-and-minnow combo here should produce good action. As the winter deepens, you'll want to work farther out on Big Bay, fishing around reefs and islands in 20 feet of water or more. Especially good, this time of year, are the breaks off Ely and Birch Island, toward the eastern end of Big Bay. Don't ignore the mouth of Stuntz Bay, off the eastern point of Long Island; this, too, is a good spot for walleye fishing with live bait.

Crappie fishing can be good during winter months, especially shortly after the lake freezes. A small jig-and-minnow combination makes a good presentation, but finding a place to offer it can be tricky. The best spots, says Ellis, are around Oak Narrows, but there's a current in this area, making the ice chancy at best. So Ellis advises extreme caution. "You can lose your life in this area," Ellis says. He advises checking locally on ice conditions before venturing out.

Open water time, of course, is when the big lake gets the most use and the most fishing pressure. Fortunately, it's also when the fish are biting best. In spring, fishing

comes to life first in the sheltered bays. Black Bay, especially, is a focus of walleye activity early on, as its dark waters warm early, helping fish to be more active. Jig-and-minnow combinations are effective in this shallow area. Work developing weeds, using a light jig on a low-stretch line to help your feel. Be sure to vary your retrieve until you discover the action fish prefer on any given day; then you can get down to serious fish-catching. Other good, early-season spots include Pike Bay, around Duffy Island, Stuntz Bay and Cable Bay. Ellis says you don't want to ignore the area below the Vermilion Dam on the north end of Wolf Bay. The bay's entire northern arm offers phenomenal spring action all the way down to Knotts Island. Similarly, you'll find good spring fishing through Oak Narrows, and in much of Norwegian Bay. Probably the best spring walleye spot on the entire lake, says Ellis, is Armstrong Bay on the lake's far-eastern end. He advises trolling with Rapalas or spinner rigs, casting a jig-and-minnow combination or bobber-fishing with minnows at emerging weedlines. As the season advances, you can stay in the same area, but move out to the surrounding reefs.

Speaking of reefs, there's an abundance of them in Lake Vermilion. That's where you'll find walleyes

Cont'd on page 140

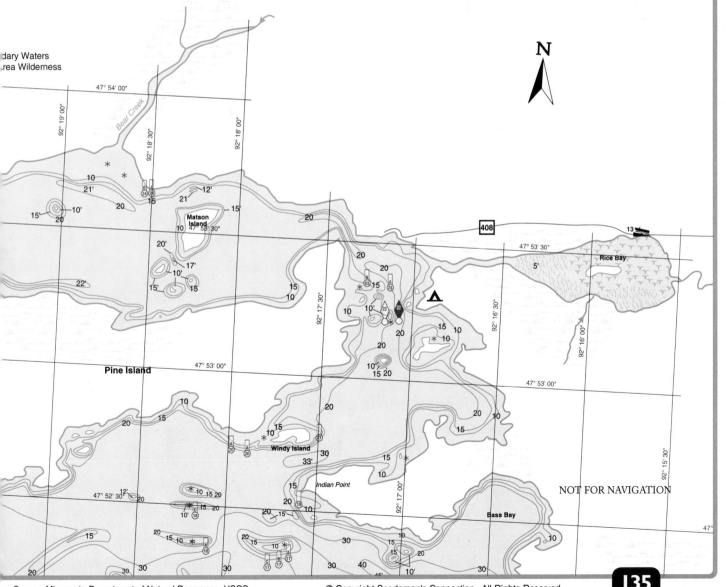

NOT FOR NAVIGATION

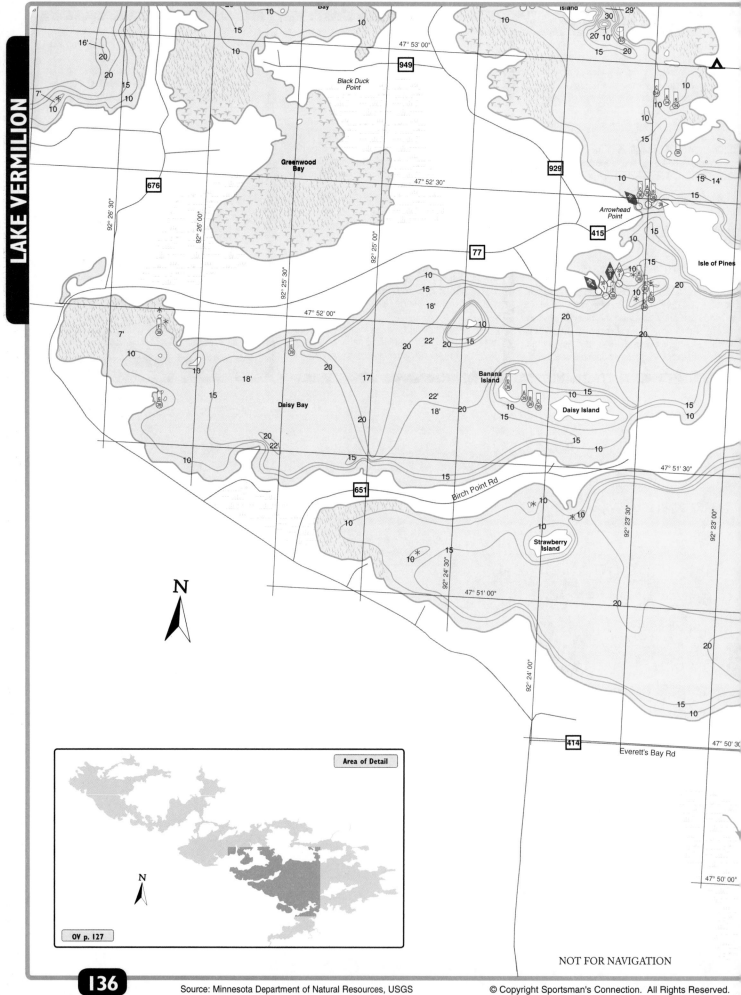

Bay

10

15

10

16'
20

20
15

10

7'
10

Island

29'
30

20 10'
43

15 20

10
10
34

10

Black Duck
Point

47° 53' 00"

949

929

10

Greenwood
Bay

47° 52' 30"

676

415

10

15

15

15

14'

15

Arrowhead
Point

36

36

10

15

Isle of Pines

77

47° 52' 00"

10

10
A
B
37

10
38

20

7'
39

10

10

18'

15

18'

10

20

22'
20

15

20

Banana
Island
39

10 15

Daisy Island

15

39

E
39

20

15

18'

17'

22'

Daisy Bay

39

20

18'
20

10

15
38

38

38

20
22'

15

15

20

15

15

47° 51' 30"

10

651

15

47° 52' 30"

Birch Point Rd

10

10

10

10

Strawberry
Island

10

15

10

47° 51' 00"

20

20

N

414

Everett's Bay Rd

47° 50' 30"

15

10

20

47° 50' 00"

Area of Detail

N

OV p. 127

NOT FOR NAVIGATION

136

Source: Minnesota Department of Natural Resources, USGS

© Copyright Sportsman's Connection. All Rights Reserved.

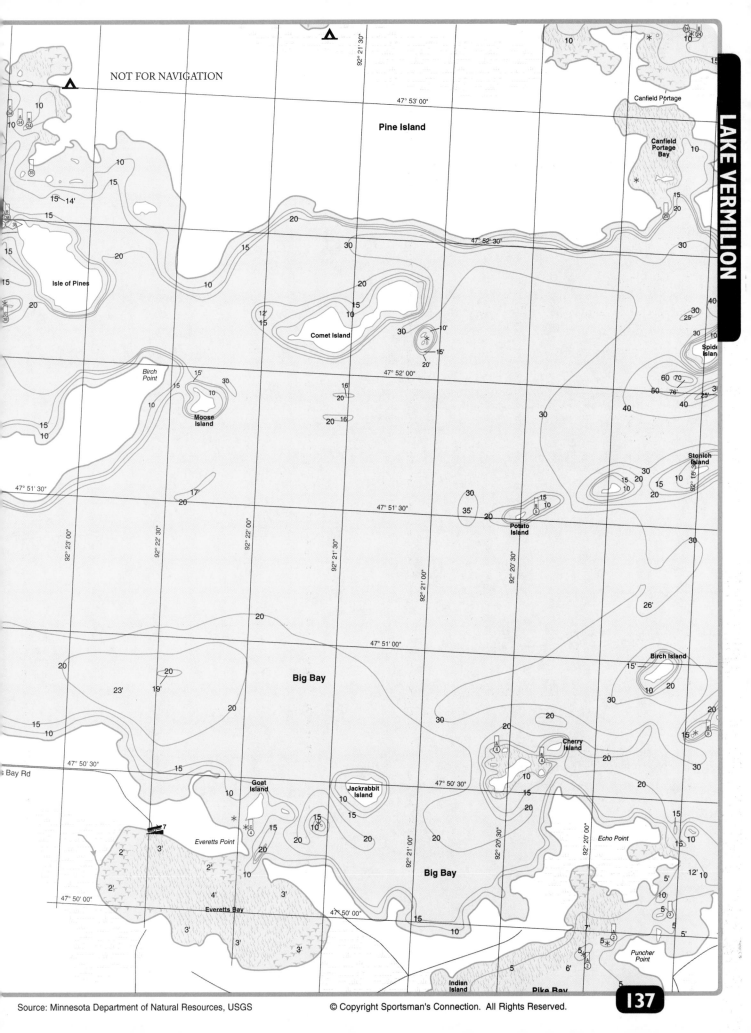

NOT FOR NAVIGATION

Pine Island

Canfield Portage

Canfield Portage Bay

Isle of Pines

Comet Island

Spider Island

Birch Point

Moose Island

Stonich Island

Potato Island

Big Bay

Birch Island

Cherry Island

Goat Island

Jackrabbit Island

Everetts Point

Echo Point

Big Bay

Everetts Bay

Puncher Point

Indian Island

Pike Bay

s Bay Rd

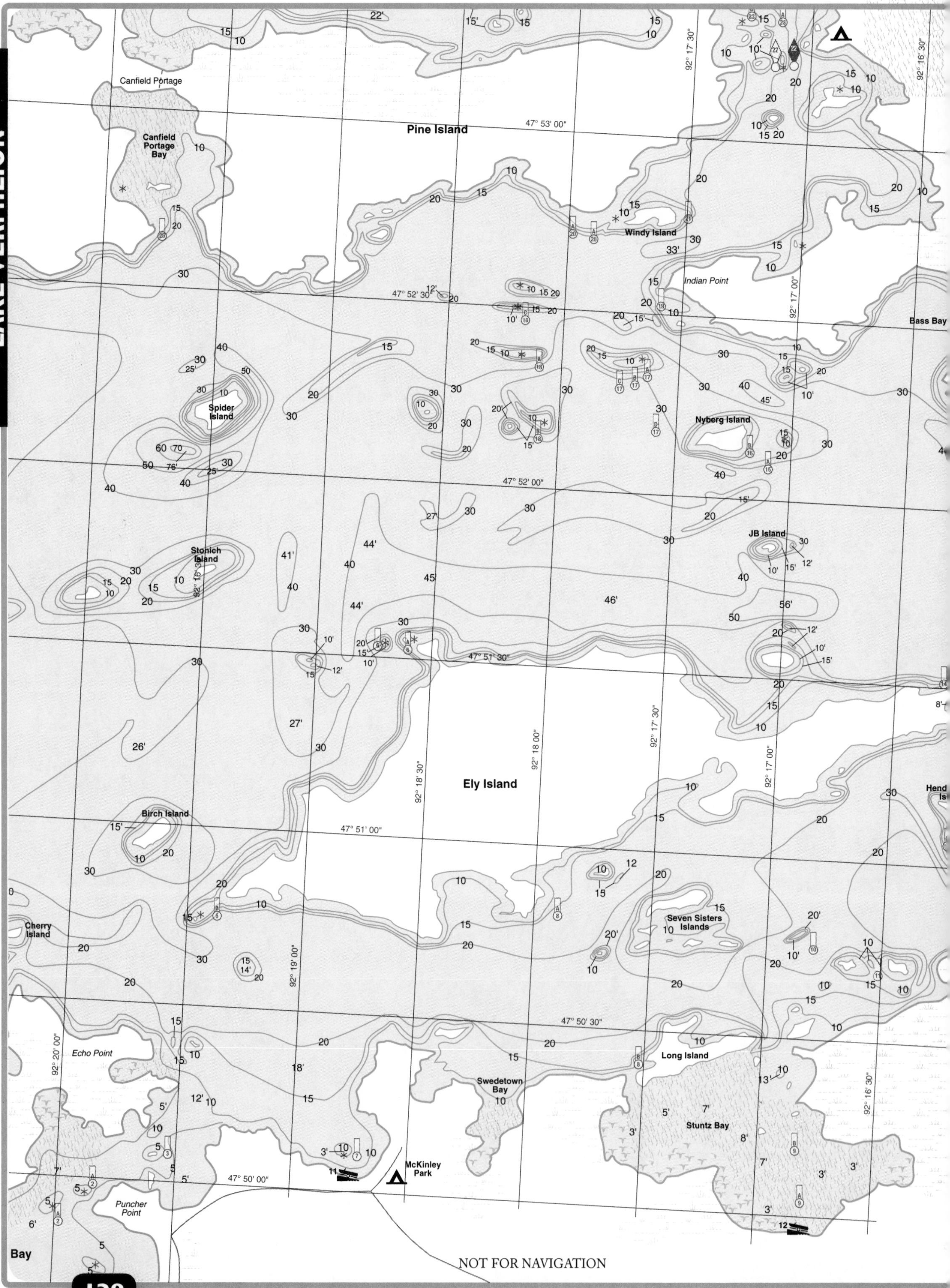

Canfield Portage

Pine Island

47° 53' 00"

Canfield
Portage
Bay

Windy Island

Indian Point

Bass Bay

Spider
Island

47° 52' 30"

Nyberg Island

47° 52' 00"

Stonich
Island

JB Island

Ely Island

Birch Island

47° 51' 30"

47° 51' 00"

Cherry
Island

Seven Sisters
Islands

Echo Point

47° 50' 30"

Long Island

Swedetown
Bay

Stuntz Bay

McKinley
Park

Puncher
Point

47° 50' 00"

Bay

Hend
Is

NOT FOR NAVIGATION

138

Source: Minnesota Department of Natural Resources, USGS

Area of Detail

N

OV p. 127

Bass Bay

Timber Island

Mud Creek Bay

Mud Creek

Birch Island

Dog Island

Hendrickson Island

Raspberry Island

Cable Bay

Armstrong Bay

Mattson Bay

N

NOT FOR NAVIGATION

Source: Minnesota Department of Natural Resources, USGS

Cont'd from page 135

during summer. The walleyes begin moving out of shallow bays to deeper areas in June, and they use the reefs, in addition to the nearby islands, as feeding grounds right into fall. That means that in the lake's eastern section, you'll want to head out into Wakemup bay, looking for deepwater structure. You'll find it between Center Island and Norwegian point. Two of the lake's more famous reefs, Merry-Go-Round and Stove Top are located there. These top out around 10 feet or less, and they attract walleyes like magnets. Jig-and-bait combinations worked around the 20-foot level are good producers, and, as noted earlier, you might even tie into a muskie in these locations. While you're in this area, don't neglect the entire shoreline of Center Island, just to the west of Stove Top. You'll also want to head straight south of Stove Top to Boys Camp Reef, which lies just off the southern shore of Wakemup Bay. All these spots are top walleye producers. If you're looking for a bonus, or are just tiring of walleye fishing, head on over to The Wash, which lies between the southern prominence of Norwegian Point and the tiny island off its tip. This reef is covered with 4- to 6-inch rocks and is home to nice-size smallmouth bass. Toss spinnerbaits or small crankbaits into the shallows. Vary your retrieve until you find the right combination. If the smallies aren't biting there, try your luck at Treasure Island. Large smallies inhabit the area between the island's east shore and the white hazard buoy to the east. Spinnerbaits and small cranks will work in this area, too.

The reefs thin out as you head through Oak Narrows into the lake's eastern portion, but that doesn't mean the walleyes do. You'll find them off the west shore of Fectos Point, nearly out to Duck Island, and the rocks off the point's tip hold both northern pike and smallies. If you fish the windward shore of Fectos, you should have some luck catching smallies. The next area to try as you head east is Banana Island and Daisy Island, off the north shore of long, narrow Birch Point. The southern portion of this area holds trophy walleyes, and occasionally a muskie, which typically hold in 8-to 18-foot depths. As your eastward journey continues, drop a jig-and-leech combo or crankbait into the water off the north sides of Potato, Taylor and Stonich Islands near the center of Big Bay. You'll find not only walleyes in the scattered boulders around these islands, but nice perch as well. If the fish aren't hitting in this area, try the reefs straight out from the channel between Pine Island and Indian Point where smallies and walleyes both roam. The southern shore of Raspberry Island is a good summer producer of walleyes, too.

For northern pike, you'll want to try Sunset Bay in spring. Pike utilize Sunset Creek as a spawning area, and, by mid- or late-May, they're heading out into deeper water to feed. A similar area can be found farther east, in the farthest reaches of Daisy Bay, just off County Road 77. Red and white spoons or larger spinnerbaits can get good action. In summer, try the deep cabbage in Van Ryper Bay, off the end of Wolf bay, above Oak Narrows. Largemouth bass inhabit many of the weedy areas of this lake. Look for them in the back bays, casting topwater, shallow-running crankbaits or spinnerbaits to the slop.

Don't neglect Lake Vermilion's crappies. Though they're a cyclical resource, they can run pretty nice. In summer, look for them at the sharp break off the south shore of Wolf Bay. A jig and small minnow or leech is a good bet for catching crappies.

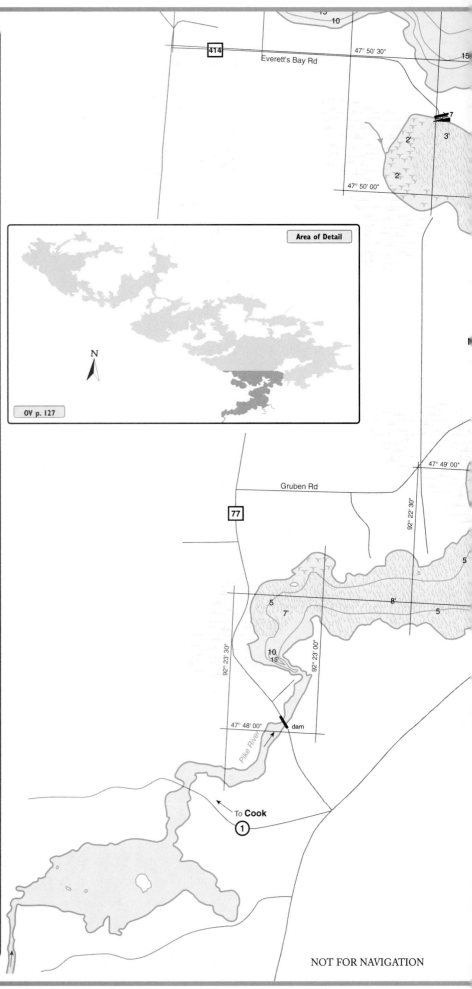

NOT FOR NAVIGATION

Source: Minnesota Department of Natural Resources, USGS

30

15

Goat
Island

10

Jackrabbit
Island

47° 50' 30"

Cherry
Island

20

30

15
14'

20

Everetts Point

15

10
15

15

20

20

20

Echo Point

15

18'

20

15

12'

Everetts Bay

47° 50' 00"

15

10

Big Bay

5'

10

47° 50' 00"

11

Indian
Island

7'

5'

Puncher
Point

Pike Bay

Nett Lake Indian
Reservation

413

Hoodoo
Point

8'

47° 49' 30"

Tower Park Airport

9

5

Whiskey Island

5

5

7'

47° 49' 00"

8'

47° 49' 00"

East Two River

Tower

Pike Bay

5

8'

7'

8'

5

West Two River

10

135

5

47° 48' 30"

N

1   169

NOT FOR NAVIGATION

Jim Roerig caught this 52-1/2-inch muskie trolling on Vermilion in November.

DARK LAKE
St. Louis County

Area map pg / coord: 15 / E-4

Watershed: NA

Surface area: 230 acres

Shorelength: 4.3 miles

Max / mean depth: 31 feet / NA

Water color / clarity: 11.5 ft. (2006)

Shoreland zoning class: NA

Mgmt class / Ecological type:
Walleye-centrarchid

Accessibility: USFS-owned public access with concrete ramp on northwest shore, off Cty. Road 663
47° 38' 19.74" N / 92° 46' 41.41" W

Accommodations: None

LEANDER LAKE
St. Louis County

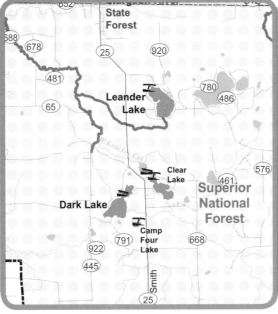

Area map pg / coord: 15 / E-4

Watershed: NA

Surface area: 247 acres

Shorelength: 3.6 miles

Max / mean depth: 45 feet / NA

Water color / clarity: Clear / 16.0 ft. (1991)

Shoreland zoning class: NA

Mgmt class / Ecological type:
Walleye-centrarchid

Accessibility: Carry-down access to northwest shore; carry-down access through USFS beach and picnic area on south shore
47° 40' 57.21" N / 92° 45' 40.97" W

Accommodations: Picnicking

FISH STOCKING DATA

year	species	size	# released
06	Walleye	Fingerling	3,666
08	Walleye	Fingerling	1,142
10	Walleye	Fingerling	2,250

NET CATCH DATA
Date: 08/07/2006

	Gill Nets		Trap Nets	
species	# per net	avg. fish weight (lbs.)	# per net	avg. fish weight (lbs.)
Black Crappie	4.0	0.04	1.2	0.21
Bluegill	0.3	0.2	5.9	0.14
Northern Pike	3.0	3.53	1.1	1.54
Pumpkin. Sunfish	-	-	0.2	0.15
Rock Bass	0.3	0.1	0.3	0.18
Walleye	1.0	2.34	-	-
White Sucker	4.2	1.81	0.8	2.10
Yellow Perch	2.3	0.08	0.2	0.09

LENGTH OF SELECTED SPECIES SAMPLED FROM ALL GEAR
Number of fish caught for the following length categories (inches):

species	0-5	6-8	9-11	12-14	15-19	20-24	25-29	>29	Total
Black Crappie	29	3	3	-	-	-	-	-	35
Bluegill	32	23	-	-	-	-	-	-	55
Northern Pike	-	-	-	2	8	12	3	3	28
Pumpkin. Sunfish	1	1	-	-	-	-	-	-	2
Walleye	-	-	-	-	5	1	-	-	6
Yellow Perch	10	6	-	-	-	-	-	-	16

FISH STOCKING DATA

year	species	size	# released
05	Walleye	Fry	59,000
07	Walleye	Fry	59,000
07	Walleye	Yearling	1,300

NET CATCH DATA
Date: 06/14/1999

	Gill Nets		Trap Nets	
species	# per net	avg. fish weight (lbs.)	# per net	avg. fish weight (lbs.)
Black Crappie	0.5	0.05	3.2	0.10
Bluegill	0.2	0.34	9.4	0.25
Northern Pike	4.5	3.80	0.7	1.66
Pumpkin. Sunfish	-	-	1.7	0.20
Rock Bass	0.2	0.10	-	-
Walleye	0.5	2.62	-	-
White Sucker	3.3	1.82	0.1	2.65
Yellow Perch	13.8	0.08	1.3	0.10

LENGTH OF SELECTED SPECIES SAMPLED FROM ALL GEAR
Number of fish caught for the following length categories (inches):

species	0-5	6-8	9-11	12-14	15-19	20-24	25-29	>29	Total
Black Crappie	26	6	-	-	-	-	-	-	32
Bluegill	35	46	5	-	-	-	-	-	86
Northern Pike	-	-	-	2	9	16	2	3	32
Pumpkin. Sunfish	7	8	-	-	-	-	-	-	15
Rock Bass	1	-	-	-	-	-	-	-	1
Walleye	-	-	-	-	2	1	-	-	3
Yellow Perch	70	25	-	-	-	-	-	-	95

FISHING INFORMATION

Dark Lake has a formidable name, which may be for a good reason. This bog stained lake is not very fertile and has low productivity. Walleye have been stocked regularly, but numbers will never be really high here as there is little natural reproduction. Northern pike are here in decent numbers. During the last survey, the DNR measured pike ranging from 17.9 to 40.2 inches. As with any decent pike waters, over-harvesting can occur. Anglers are requested to harvest a few of the smaller fish and release the larger ones. The black crappie and bluegill populations are steady, with averages at 5.4 and 6.3 inches respectively.

Dark Lake's water quality could be adversely affected by lakeshore development. Homeowners and builders should prevent run off and protect the shoreline's natural state.

Leander is a 247-acre lake. It has depths reaching to 45 feet and excellent water clarity to 16 feet. The main predator species on the lake are northern pike, walleye and largemouth bass. The pike population seems to be on the rise and assessment show that their population may even be above the norm when compared to other lakes in this class. While the population seems to be increasing, the mean length has remained fairly stagnant. The walleye population was low on this lake according to the last DNR survey. Stocking of fry has since occurred. Bluegills are another aging population in this lake. Their abundance numbers are normal and there seems to be a shift towards larger sizes. Numerous largemouth bass were observed by crews and lakeside homeowners report more frequent catch rates than in the past. Largemouth bass deserve a mention here, as they seem to be the only specie to reproduce in decent numbers.

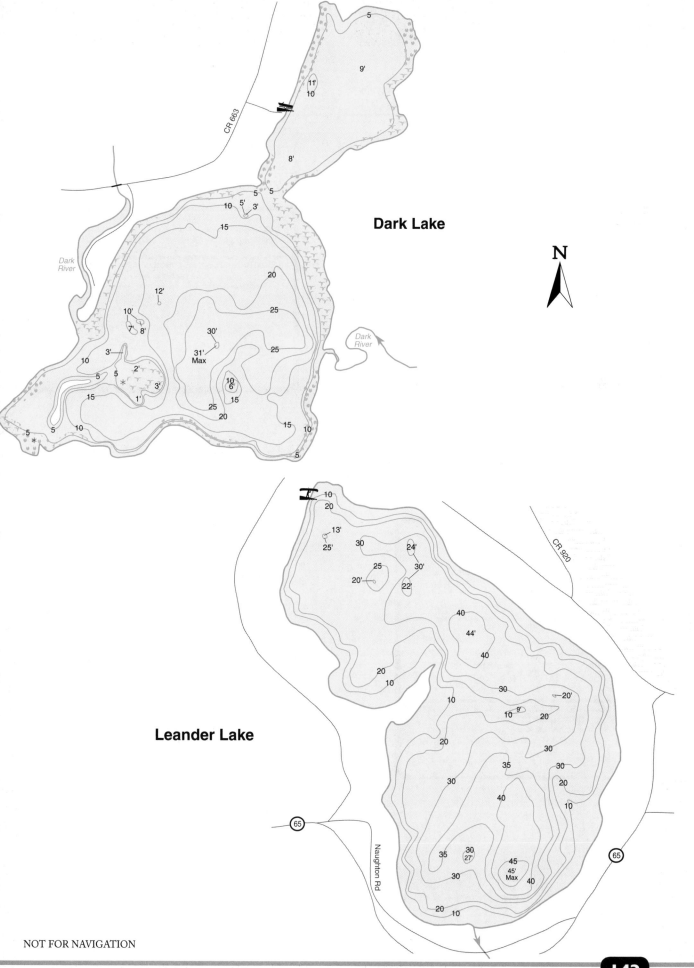

Dark Lake

Leander Lake

N

NOT FOR NAVIGATION

Source: Minnesota Department of Natural Resources, USGS

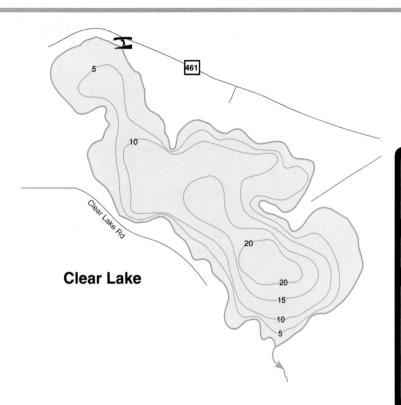

Clear Lake

Clear Lake, St. Louis County

Area map page / coordinates: 15 / E-4
Surface area / shorelength: 119 acres / 2.7 miles
Accessibility: Carry-down access to north shore off County Road 461; 47° 38' 44.93" N / 92° 45' 30.43" W

FISH STOCKING DATA

year	species	size	# released
06	Walleye	Fingerling	3,600

LENGTH OF SELECTED SPECIES SAMPLED FROM ALL GEAR
Survey Date: 06/24/2002
Number of fish caught for the following length categories (inches):

species	0-5	6-8	9-11	12-14	15-19	20-24	25-29	>30	Total
Black Crappie	32	27	1	-	-	-	-	-	60
Bluegill	132	95	1	-	-	-	-	-	228
Largemouth Bass	-	5	-	1	-	-	-	-	6
Northern Pike	-	-	-	4	3	12	16	3	38
Rock Bass	17	2	-	-	-	-	-	-	19
Smallmouth Bass	-	2	-	1	3	-	-	-	6
Walleye	-	-	-	-	7	11	1	-	19
Yellow Perch	1	1	-	-	-	-	-	-	2

N

Camp Four (Camp A) Lake, St. Louis County

Area map page / coordinates: 15 / E-4
Surface area / shorelength: 18 acres / 0.6 miles
Accessibility: Carry-down access to east shore off Hwy. 25; 2.3 miles north of Buhl on County Road 125, 7.9 miles north on County Road 25, 0.3 miles west
47° 37' 36.80" N / 92° 46' 5.63" W

FISH STOCKING DATA

year	species	size	# released
07	Rainbow Trout	Fingerling	1,512
08	Brook Trout	Yearling	375
09	Rainbow Trout	Fingerling	1,504
10	Brook Trout	Yearling	372

LENGTH OF SELECTED SPECIES SAMPLED FROM ALL GEAR
Survey Date: 10/11/2010
Number of fish caught for the following length categories (inches):

species	0-5	6-8	9-11	12-14	15-19	20-24	25-29	>30	Total
Brook Trout	-	-	2	-	-	-	-	-	2
Northern Pike	-	-	-	-	-	3	3	-	6
White Sucker	-	-	-	-	-	1	-	-	1

Camp Four Lake

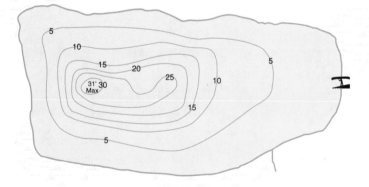

NOT FOR NAVIGATION

Source: Minnesota Department of Natural Resources, USGS

Needle Boy Lake

Needle Boy Lake, St. Louis County
Area map page / coordinates: 16 / B-3
Surface area / shorelength: 44 acres / NA
Accessibility: Carry-down access to south shore, 1.5 miles west of County Road 599; 47° 50' 10.51" N / 92° 7' 50.04" W

Six Mile Lake, St. Louis County
Area map page / coordinates: 16 / B-3
Surface area / shorelength: 104 acres / NA
Accessibility: Carry-down access to north shore (0.25 mile portage) from Six Mile Lake Rd, 1 mile west of Co. Rd. 599
47° 50' 20.14" N / 92° 8' 4.45" W

LENGTH OF SELECTED SPECIES SAMPLED FROM ALL GEAR
Survey Date: 07/06/1990
Number of fish caught for the following length categories (inches):

species	0-5	6-8	9-11	12-14	15-19	20-24	25-29	>30	Total
Bluegill	73	43	-	-	-	-	-	-	116
Hybrid Sunfish	14	11	-	-	-	-	-	-	25
Largemouth Bass	1	-	1	-	-	-	-	-	2
Northern Pike	-	-	-	1	-	1	-	-	2

Armstrong Lake, St. Louis County
Area map page / coordinates: 16 / B-3 & 17 / B-4
Surface area / shorelength: 382 acres / 3.9 miles
Accessibility: State-owned public access with concrete ramp on west shore, just north of outlet, off Hwy. 169
47° 50' 54.18" N / 92° 5' 40.64" W

FISH STOCKING DATA

year	species	size	# released
08	Walleye	Fry	200,000
10	Walleye	Fry	240,000

LENGTH OF SELECTED SPECIES SAMPLED FROM ALL GEAR
Survey Date: 07/02/2007
Number of fish caught for the following length categories (inches):

species	0-5	6-8	9-11	12-14	15-19	20-24	25-29	>30	Total
Black Crappie	5	16	4	1	-	-	-	-	26
Bluegill	160	169	1	-	-	-	-	-	330
Largemouth Bass	2	2	4	3	-	-	-	-	11
Northern Pike	-	-	-	-	5	24	11	3	43
Pumpkin. Sunfish	15	2	-	-	-	-	-	-	17
Rock Bass	27	21	1	-	-	-	-	-	49
Smallmouth Bass	-	-	4	4	4	-	-	-	12
Walleye	-	-	-	-	10	6	2	-	18
Yellow Perch	4	49	-	-	-	-	-	-	53

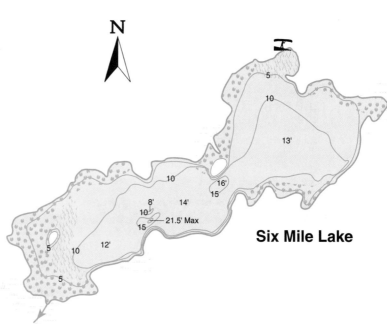

Six Mile Lake

Armstrong Lake

NOT FOR NAVIGATION

Missabe & Iron Range Railway

BEAR HEAD LAKE St. Louis County

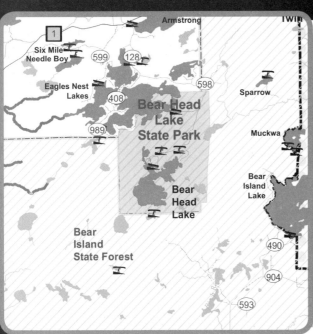

Area map page / coordinates: 16 / C-3 & 17 / C-4

Watershed: Rainy headwaters

Surface water area / shorelength: 674 acres / 11.7 miles

Maximum / mean depth: 46 feet / 12 feet

Water color / clarity: Light green tint / 9.0 feet (2004)

Shoreland zoning classification: Natural environment

Management class / Ecological type: Walleye / soft-water walleye

Accessibility: State-owned public access with concrete ramp in state park on northwest bay (park permit is required)

47° 47' 19.48" N / 92° 4' 56.51" W

Accommodations: Bear Head Lake State Park (218-365-7229), boat and canoe rental, camping, picnicking, restrooms

FISHING INFORMATION

Bear Head Lake is a 674-acre lake with a maximum depth of 46 feet. It has an irregular shoreline shape and unmineralized (soft) water. The lake was thermally stratified in 2004. It has adequate oxygen levels down to 33 feet. Lake bottom substrates along the shoreline consists of mostly rubble and gravel. An old lumber mill still has remnants of its former existence in the form of old slab wood found on the bottom of the lake. Aquatic plants are found down to 12 feet, but are fairly sparse.

The Minnesota DNR maintains access through the Bear Head Lake State Park on the northwest bay of the lake. The state park features camping, picnic facilities, toilets, and of course, the launch. A park permit is required for launching. The landing is good and can handle most trailerable boats. There are some rocks in this lake, so be careful and keep your eyes on your electronics until you find out exactly where they are. Doing so just may save you a trip to the prop shop.

"This is a great family lake," said Doug Ellis, owner of the Virginia Surplus Store, 105 3rd Avenue, Virginia, 218-741-0331. "The fish typically bite between 9 a.m. and 4 p.m., making this a great place to take the kids for some daylight action."

The DNR last surveyed the lake in 2004 and found the dominant species to be walleye, white sucker, northern pike and bluegill. The crappie and perch numbers were down from the previous assessments. Largemouth bass are hard to survey and they don't tend to be caught with a gill net or trap net. Their abundance is considered much higher than the survey indicates.

Walleyes averaged 16.3 inches and 1.8 pounds. This is larger than the 15 inch average found in other lakes of this type. The largest walleye caught in the survey was a whopping 31 inches and weighed 12 pounds. With such a big walleye lurking in this water, anglers can have a lot of fun hunting for Walter. "Walleyes hit very well on gold spinner/leech combinations near the public landing in August," says Ellis. "At other times, you can take them on jig/leech combos off reefs, particularly those in the east end." Walleye fry are stocked on this lake bi-annually at a rate of 350,000 per stocking.

Northern pike were caught at a rate of 3.3 per gillnet, which is higher than the median catch rates in previous investigations of this lake. Pike measured 20.9 inches on average and weighed over 2 pounds.

The bluegill population has grown steadily since 1969. Although the growth rates were slower than normal, the average bluegill caught was in the 6-8 inch range. While these may not be monsters, they will make for a fun family outing.

FISH STOCKING DATA			
year	species	size	# released
03	Walleye	Fry	350,000
05	Walleye	Fry	350,000
07	Walleye	Fry	350,000

NET CATCH DATA				
Date: 06/07/2004	Gill Nets		Trap Nets	
species	# per net	avg. fish weight (lbs.)	# per net	avg. fish weight (lbs.)
Black Crappie	0.8	0.29	2.3	0.52
Bluegill	1.5	0.12	11.6	0.19
Largemouth Bass	0.3	1.55	0.3	0.73
Northern Pike	3.3	2.06	2.3	2.27
Walleye	4.8	1.80	1.3	3.62
White Sucker	5.3	1.95	1.9	2.39
Yellow Perch	4.0	0.10	-	-

LENGTH OF SELECTED SPECIES SAMPLED FROM ALL GEAR
Number of fish caught for the following length categories (inches):

species	0-5	6-8	9-11	12-14	15-19	20-24	25-29	>30	Total
Black Crappie	1	19	13	3	-	-	-	-	36
Bluegill	61	82	2	-	-	-	-	-	145
Largemouth Bass	-	2	1	3	-	-	-	-	6
Northern Pike	-	-	1	-	26	31	6	2	66
Walleye	-	1	9	19	24	15	4	1	73
Yellow Perch	8	40	-	-	-	-	-	-	48

Black crappie abundance seems to be on the decline. Their numbers peaked in 1995 and have since been found in smaller quantities. On average, the crappies here are just shy of .3 pounds and the majority are in the 6-8 and 9-11 inch ranges, with a few reaching 14 inches.

According to the DNR, many of the game fish examined in the 2004 survey were infected with neascus (black spot). This is a common parasite, which has no effect on humans. Filleting the fish and cooking temperatures kill the parasite.

Less
Than
10'

47° 47' 30"

92° 05' 00"

128

15

10

20

30

30

10

15

15

20

30

30

15

10

10

15

15

40

10

10

15

10

15

30
25'

30

30
22'

30

Bear Head Lake
State Park

10

15

10

20

30

40

46' Max

92° 05' 30"

30

10

20

15

30

92° 04' 00"

47° 47' 00"

20

15

92° 04' 30"

30

20

15

10

47° 46' 30"

20

15

10

N

Source: Minnesota Department of Natural Resources, USGS

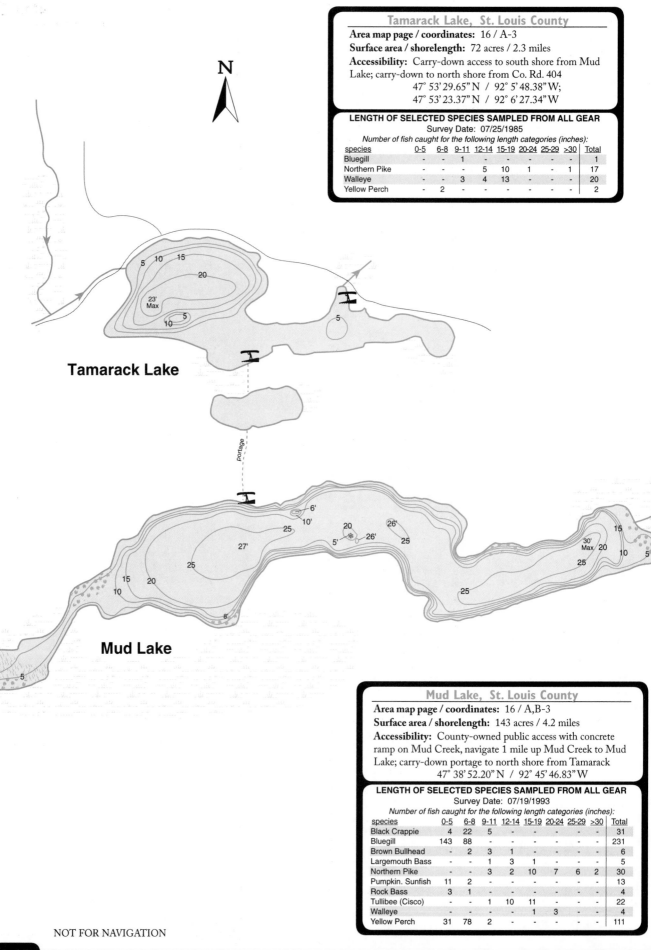

N

Tamarack Lake, St. Louis County
Area map page / coordinates: 16 / A-3
Surface area / shorelength: 72 acres / 2.3 miles
Accessibility: Carry-down access to south shore from Mud Lake; carry-down to north shore from Co. Rd. 404
47° 53' 29.65" N / 92° 5' 48.38" W;
47° 53' 23.37" N / 92° 6' 27.34" W

LENGTH OF SELECTED SPECIES SAMPLED FROM ALL GEAR
Survey Date: 07/25/1985
Number of fish caught for the following length categories (inches):

species	0-5	6-8	9-11	12-14	15-19	20-24	25-29	>30	Total
Bluegill	-	-	1	-	-	-	-	-	1
Northern Pike	-	-	-	5	10	1	-	1	17
Walleye	-	-	3	4	13	-	-	-	20
Yellow Perch	-	2	-	-	-	-	-	-	2

Tamarack Lake

Mud Lake

To

Mud Lake, St. Louis County
Area map page / coordinates: 16 / A,B-3
Surface area / shorelength: 143 acres / 4.2 miles
Accessibility: County-owned public access with concrete ramp on Mud Creek, navigate 1 mile up Mud Creek to Mud Lake; carry-down portage to north shore from Tamarack
47° 38' 52.20" N / 92° 45' 46.83" W

LENGTH OF SELECTED SPECIES SAMPLED FROM ALL GEAR
Survey Date: 07/19/1993
Number of fish caught for the following length categories (inches):

species	0-5	6-8	9-11	12-14	15-19	20-24	25-29	>30	Total
Black Crappie	4	22	5	-	-	-	-	-	31
Bluegill	143	88	-	-	-	-	-	-	231
Brown Bullhead	-	2	3	1	-	-	-	-	6
Largemouth Bass	-	-	1	3	1	-	-	-	5
Northern Pike	-	-	3	2	10	7	6	2	30
Pumpkin. Sunfish	11	2	-	-	-	-	-	-	13
Rock Bass	3	1	-	-	-	-	-	-	4
Tullibee (Cisco)	-	-	1	10	11	-	-	-	22
Walleye	-	-	-	-	1	3	-	-	4
Yellow Perch	31	78	2	-	-	-	-	-	111

NOT FOR NAVIGATION

Source: Minnesota Department of Natural Resources, USGS

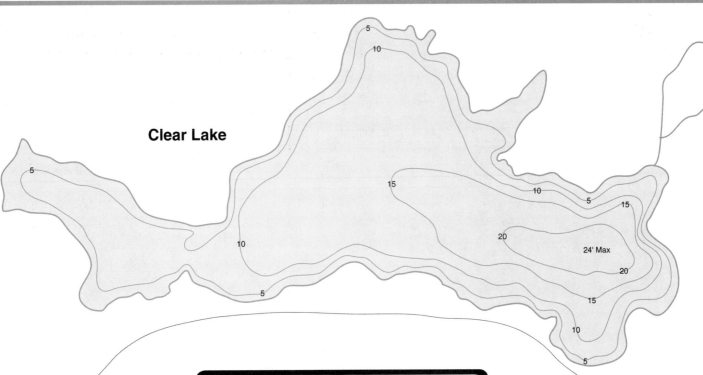

Clear Lake

Clear Lake, St. Louis County

Area map page / coordinates: 17 / B-4
Surface area / shorelength: 112 acres / NA
Accessibility: Access to east shore currently under negotiation by DNR Trails and Waterways.
47° 38' 44.93" N / 92° 45' 30.43" W

LENGTH OF SELECTED SPECIES SAMPLED FROM ALL GEAR
Survey Date: 06/24/2002
Number of fish caught for the following length categories (inches):

species	0-5	6-8	9-11	12-14	15-19	20-24	25-29	>30	Total
Black Crappie	32	27	1	-	-	-	-	-	60
Bluegill	132	9	1	-	-	-	-	-	228
Largemouth Bass	-	5	-	1	-	-	-	-	6
Northern Pike	-	-	-	4	3	12	16	3	38
Rock Bass	17	2	-	-	-	-	-	-	19
Smallmouth Bass	-	2	-	1	3	-	-	-	6
Walleye	-	-	-	-	7	11	1	-	19
Yellow Perch	1	1	-	-	-	-	-	-	2

N

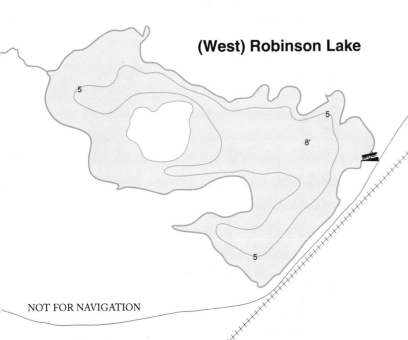

(West) Robinson Lake

(West) Robinson Lake, St. Louis County

Area map page / coordinates: 17 / B-4
Surface area / shorelength: 135 acres / NA
Accessibility: State-owned access with gravel ramp on east shore- Hwy. 169 right-of-way pull-off; parking for one vehicle; 47° 51' 31.59" N / 92° 2' 33.73" W

LENGTH OF SELECTED SPECIES SAMPLED FROM ALL GEAR
Survey Date: 06/28/2004
Number of fish caught for the following length categories (inches):

species	0-5	6-8	9-11	12-14	15-19	20-24	25-29	>30	Total
Black Crappie	3	7	1	-	-	-	-	-	11
Bluegill	5	2	-	-	-	-	-	-	7
Northern Pike	-	-	1	5	38	26	10	6	86
Pumpkin. Sunfish	42	1	-	-	-	-	-	-	43
Yellow Perch	11	17	4	-	-	-	-	-	32

NOT FOR NAVIGATION

CLEAR LAKE

ROBINSON LAKE

149

Source: Minnesota Department of Natural Resources, USGS

EAGLES NEST LAKES St. Louis County

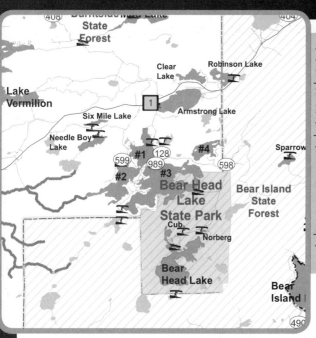

	#1	#2	#3	#4
Area map pg / coord:	16 / B-3	16 / B,C-3	17 / B,C-4	17 / B-4
Watershed:	Vermilion	Vermilion	Vermilion	Vermilion
Surface area:	324 acres	388 acres	1,028 acres	177 acres
Max depth:	76 feet	39 feet	49 feet	49 feet
Water clarity:	14 ft (2010)	11 ft (2010)	9.2 ft (2010)	18 ft (2000)
Accessibility:	State-owned public access with concrete ramp on northwest shore of #2, on Cty. Rd. 599 off Hwy. 169, 10 miles east of Tower		State-owned public access with concrete ramp in park on east shore; 10 miles east of Tower on Hwy. 169, then 5 miles south on Co. Rd. 128, then 1 mile north on park road (park sticker required)	
	47° 49' 26.03" N / 92° 6' 59.96" W		47° 48' 41.94" N / 92° 4' 2.39" W	

Accommodations: Bordered by Bear Head Lake State Park, resorts, boat rental, camping picnicking, restrooms

FISHING INFORMATION

This quartet of lake basins grouped under one name, Eagles Nest Lake, is well worth a visit. Each lake is distinguished with numbers 1, 2, 3 and 4. You can hit one lake, or hit them all, depending on what you are hunting for. All four lakes boast some similarities and differences, which anglers need to embrace to find their fishing zen.

Eagles Nest Lake 1 has been growing over the years. In the years since the DNR has been surveying this lake, the area grew from 2 resorts and 24 homes in 1955 to 72 homes in 1980 to 88 homes in 2000. With all this growth comes a few added problems for this lake. The phosphorous levels are on the high side, which most likely can be attributed to lawn fertilizers and septic system leaching. Homeowners and builders must take care to maintain their systems and cease using fertilizers to protect the watershed in years to come. Eagles Nest Lake 2 exhibited similar riparian development over the years as well.

Clifford Noble, owner of Skube's Bait & Tackle, 1810 E. Sheridan St., Ely, MN, 218-365-5358, says fishing is very good. "Eagles Nest is a very popular area for locals to fish," he said. "I get reports in particular about the walleye, bass and northern pike fishing being very good."

The DNR survey in 2009 found the fish populations on Lake 1 to be dominated by bluegills, walleyes and rock bass. Bluegill numbers have increased over time, while the other species have either remained stable or dropped in abundance. Lake 2's fish population is also dominated by walleyes, bluegills and rock bass. On Lake 3, the dominant species are wall-

Eagles Nest Lake #1

FISH STOCKING DATA

year	species	size	# released
09	Walleye	Fingerling	4,763

LENGTH OF SELECTED SPECIES SAMPLED FROM ALL GEAR

Survey Date: 07/06/2010

Number of fish caught for the following length categories (inches):

species	0-5	6-8	9-11	12-14	15-19	20-24	25-29	>30	Total
Black Crappie	7	2	25	3	-	-	-	-	37
Bluegill	271	215	2	-	-	-	-	-	494
Northern Pike	-	-	1	2	4	1	1	2	11
Pumpkin. Sunfish	4	-	-	-	-	-	-	-	4
Rainbow Smelt	2	-	-	-	-	-	-	-	2
Rock Bass	27	20	-	-	-	-	-	-	48
Smallmouth Bass	3	4	1	8	2	-	-	-	18
Walleye	-	3	10	6	40	19	3	-	82
Yellow Perch	-	4	-	-	-	-	-	-	4

Eagles Nest Lake #2

FISH STOCKING DATA

year	species	size	# released
09	Walleye	Fingerling	4,753

LENGTH OF SELECTED SPECIES SAMPLED FROM ALL GEAR

Survey Date: 07/06/2010

Number of fish caught for the following length categories (inches):

species	0-5	6-8	9-11	12-14	15-19	20-24	25-29	>30	Total
Bluegill	33	182	12	-	-	-	-	-	227
Largemouth Bass	2	-	-	-	-	-	-	-	2
Northern Pike	-	-	1	4	-	-	2	3	10
Pumpkin. Sunfish	2	1	-	-	-	-	-	-	3
Rock Bass	42	9	-	-	-	-	-	-	51
Smallmouth Bass	6	6	2	6	5	-	-	-	25
Walleye	-	2	6	4	40	15	2	-	70
White Sucker	-	-	1	8	8	-	-	-	18
Yellow Perch	1	13	1	-	-	-	-	-	16

Eagles Nest Lake #3

NO RECORD OF STOCKING

LENGTH OF SELECTED SPECIES SAMPLED FROM ALL GEAR

Survey Date: 05/27/2010

Number of fish caught for the following length categories (inches):

species	0-5	6-8	9-11	12-14	15-19	20-24	25-29	>30	Total
Bluegill	2	2	-	-	-	-	-	-	4
Largemouth Bass	-	-	-	1	-	-	-	-	1
Northern Pike	-	-	2	1	3	4	1		11
Rock Bass	29	33	1	-	-	-	-	-	63
Smallmouth Bass	-	-	2	9	2	-	-	-	13
Walleye	-	10	42	58	32	9	1	-	152
White Sucker	-	-	1	5	37	31	-	-	74
Yellow Perch	9	22	-	-	-	-	-	-	31

Eagles Nest Lake #4

NO RECORD OF STOCKING

LENGTH OF SELECTED SPECIES SAMPLED FROM ALL GEAR

Survey Date: 07/19/1995

Number of fish caught for the following length categories (inches):

species	0-5	6-8	9-11	12-14	15-19	20-24	25-29	>30	Total
Black Crappie	32	53	4	4	-	-	-	-	93
Bluegill	16	47	-	-	-	-	-	-	63
Largemouth Bass	2	2	-	1	-	-	-	-	5
Northern Pike	-	-	1	9	4	-	1	2	17
Rock Bass	60	19	-	-	-	-	-	-	79
Smallmouth Bass	-	1	-	7	4	-	-	-	12
Walleye	-	5	4	11	6	1	-	-	27
Yellow Perch	-	7	-	-	-	-	-	-	7

eyes, white suckers and bluegills. Lake 4 separates itself from the fray a bit, as its dominant species are black crappies and bluegills with increasing numbers of rock bass.

Bluegill numbers were in the fourth quartile for lakes of this class. Trapnet catches have been sky-rocketing: 2.5 were caught per hour in 1955, 13.4 in 1980, 93.8 in 1990 and 143.2 in 1995. Sizes were only average, though, measuring 5.3 inches and .12 pounds. Even with a large 10.8 incher in the mix, bluegill sizes were only in the first quartile. With quantities like this, Eagles Nest Lake 4 will provide good action for those who are just learning to fish and should keep them busy with baiting their hooks and bobber-watching. Faster action will hook kids a whole lot more than one whopper fish after a whole day's effort. Eagles Nest Lake 2 saw similar growth in abundance rates over the years, but recently, a decline. In 1955, only two bluegills were caught in trapnets compared to 227 in 2010. Lake 3's bluegill population is dropping, however, with only 4 fish captured during the 2010 survey. This was the lowest number ever recorded. The DNR suggests this "downward trend in abundance appears to be connected to reductions in plant biomass by rusty crayfish." Lake 4 had average abundance when compared to other lakes in its class, with sizes in the 6- to 7-inch range. Look for bluegills to hold in shallow submerged weeds for much of the year. Small leeches or pieces of nightcrawler fished with or without a bobber will catch them.

Lake 1 walleye numbers are on the rise here as well. Sizes average 17.1 inches and 2.2 pounds. There are some big guys in these waters, too. The DNR sampled fish from seven different year classes. With abundant rainbow smelt as forage and regular DNR stocking, basin 1 walleyes are sure to provide anglers with a lot of action on the end of their lines. Lake 2 walleyes provide a ton of fun, too. Big walleyes, averaging 17.3 inches and 2.2 pounds lurk in these waters. While this number is high compared to other lakes in this class, it is considered average compared to the past assessments on this lake. There are some big guys out there, which add to the thrill of the hunt. Lake 3's walleye numbers were up, too, but the average size was smaller than Lake 1 and 2's walleyes. Most of Lake 3's walleyes are from 13 to 15 inches. This is pretty close to Lake 4's walleye population, which is closer to 14 inches. Jigs and live bait are preferred by many anglers. You can also try trolling stickbaits or crankbaits along deeper weed edges or in the open water when they are feeding on smelt.

Northern pike numbers of quality size varies. Lake 1 pike ran up to 37 inches during the survey, but overall numbers are low. Size growth fell into the normal range. The pike on Lake 2 were slightly smaller at 20 inches and 2 pounds. The pike population density is low on Lake 3, due to scarce spawning habitat, yet the DNR did capture one lunker measuring 37.4 inches. The abundance numbers are below average on Lake 4, but the DNR pulled out a couple of whoppers: a 41 incher weighing 14.5 pounds and a 39.8 inch one weighing 15.5 pounds. If you are patient and present the right bait, you too can have a notable northern for your fishing storybook. Big pike

like big meals. Use a large sucker minnow fished along deep weed edges or drop-offs during summer months. You can also use spinnerbaits and crankbaits fished along the weed edges early and late in the day to fool a few of these toothy fish.

Bass anglers will find a good number of smallmouths and largemouths in Lake 1. Survey numbers were up for both species, despite the fact that bass generally tend to be "net shy." Bass were caught in gillnets, trapnets and electrofishing, all of which found varying sizes and averages. The largest largemouth was 16.3 inches, with the majority of those caught not exceeding 8 inches. Their sizes fell into the below average category. Smallmouths, on the other hand, were mostly in the 12- to 19-inch range, with the largest smallie caught measuring in at 19.2 inches. Lake 2 boasts a decent smallmouth fishery, with individuals across nine different year classes represented in the most recent survey. Still, it takes three years for a smallmouth to grow 7 inches in Lake 2. The largest Lake 2 smallie caught was 18 inches. Lake 3 had better numbers of smallmouths, with the abundance numbers and sizes being higher than average when compared to other lakes in this class. Smallies here ranged from 4.3 to 18.9 inches, with nearly half of the fish being 5 years old. Lake 4 also has smallmouth bass, which were measured up to 17 inches long and had fast growth rates. Look for these numbers to increase in future years. Rock bass are also present and are in found in average numbers. The best all around approach for hooking bass in these lakes is to use soft plastics. Whether you fish them weightless, Texas or Carolina rigged, you'll catch a few bass. Stick with basic colors like green pumpkin, watermelon, black or pumpkinseed. Fish for largemouth in thicker weeds and look for smallies to hold on various rocky shorelines, points, humps and drop-offs. Like bass everywhere, early and late in the day tend to be the best fishing times during warmer months, as do overcast days.

There were 16 yellow perch sampled on Lake 2 by the DNR. By comparison, Lake 1 had just 4, Lake 3 had 34 and Lake 4 had 7. Not only does Lake 2 have quantity, it also has decent sizes. On average, they were 7.3 inches and .17 pounds, which is better than most lakes in this class.

White sucker numbers were high for Lake 3 and decent for Lake 2. Fortunately, they provide excellent forage for northern pike and walleye so their presence is not only expected in these types of lakes but also desirable.

Lake 4's black crappie population is its claim to fame among the 4 Eagles Nest Lakes. The black crappie numbers were well above average for this lake and were higher than in all the past surveys and assessments done by the DNR. Most crappies were small, only about 6 inches, but the growth rates are pretty fast here. One big pig was caught measuring 13 inches and 1.4 pounds. There are several more big crappies in this lake to give that 13 incher a run for his money, with several measuring over 12 inches. Crappies love to eat small minnows and leeches. Fish either of these baits under a slip bobber on drop-offs of submerged weedlines. Small marabou or tube jigs with or without bait will also produce crappies.

Rusty crayfish were found in Lakes 1, 2 and 3. These nasty little guys are aggressive, tend to displace native crayfish and destroy aquatic vegetation. It is thought the species was accidentally introduced by anglers using it as bait. Note, that is illegal to harvest and transport crayfish in Minnesota.

Also note: Lakes 1 & 2 both have fish consumption advisories for walleye and northern pike because of elevated mercury levels.

Another beautiful Eagles Nest smallie.

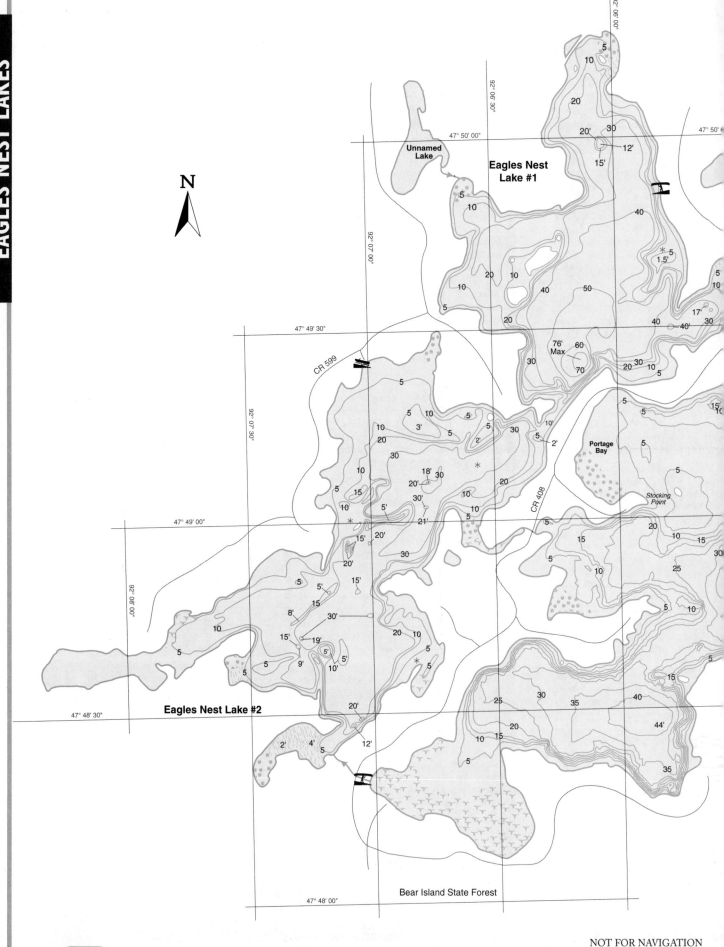

N

92° 06' 00"

47° 50' 00"

92° 06' 30"

47° 50'

Unnamed Lake

Eagles Nest Lake #1

5
10
20
30
20'
12'
15'
40

92° 07' 00"

5
10
5
1.5'
5
10

47° 49' 30"

20
10
20
40
50
10
5

CR 599

76' Max
60
70
30
20 30 10
40 40'
17'
30

92° 07' 30"

5
10
5
5
30
5
2'
5
5
10'
2'
5
5

Portage Bay

Stocking Point

5
10
20
30
18'
20'
30'
20
10
5
5
15
30'
21'
5
10

92° 08' 00"

5
15
10'
15'
20'
15'
20'
5
30

47° 49' 00"

15
10
25
20
10
15

CR 408

5
5
5
5
15'
8'
30'
15'
19'
9'
5'
10'
10
20
10
5
5
5
10
15
35

Eagles Nest Lake #2

47° 48' 30"

20'
2'
4'
5
12'

25
30
35
40
44'
35

10
15
20
5

47° 48' 00"

Bear Island State Forest

Source: Minnesota Department of Natural Resources, USGS

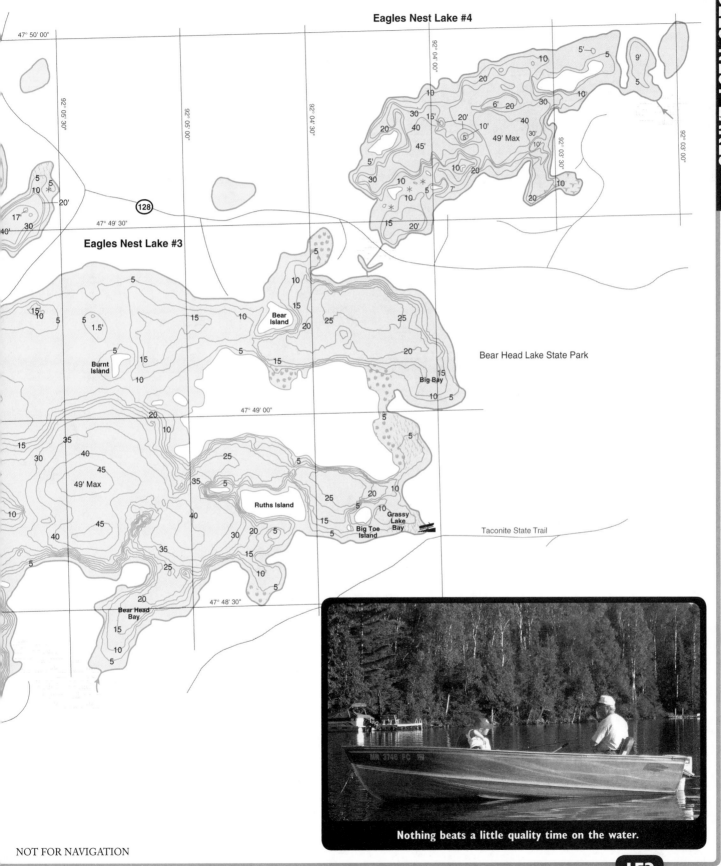

Eagles Nest Lake #4

47° 50' 00"

92° 05' 30"

92° 05' 00"

92° 04' 30"

92° 04' 00"

92° 03' 30"

92° 03' 00"

5'
5
9'
5
10
20
10
30
15'
6'
20
30
20
30
40
20
40
10'
49' Max
30'
10'
45'
5'
5'
20
5'
30
10
20
10
10
5
7
10
10
15
20'

128

47° 49' 30"

Eagles Nest Lake #3

5
10

15'
10
5
1.5'
5
15
10
15
20
25
20
Bear Island
Bear Head Lake State Park
20
15
Big Bay
15
10
5
Burnt Island
5
15
10
47° 49' 00"
5
20
10
25
5
35
40
30
45
10
49' Max
35
5
35
40
25
Ruths Island
25
20
10
10
45
40
15
30
20
5
15
5
Big Toe Island
Grassy Lake Bay
Taconite State Trail
35
25
15
5
10
20
Bear Head Bay
15
10
5

47° 48' 30"

Nothing beats a little quality time on the water.

NOT FOR NAVIGATION

LITTLE LONG LAKE
St. Louis County

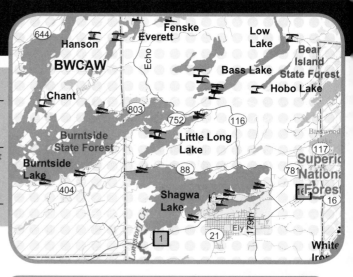

Area map page / coordinates: 17 / A-5

Watershed: Rainy headwaters

Surface water area / shorelength: 322 acres / 5.3 miles

Maximum / mean depth: 45 feet / 28 feet

Water color / clarity: Green tint / 17.0 feet (2010)

Accessibility: State-owned public access with concrete ramp on northeast shore, off the Echo Trail (Co. Rd. 116); portage access from Burntside (45 rods) and Bass Lake (320 rods)

47° 56' 20.80" N / 91° 54' 4.13" W

Accommodations: Resort, camping, picnicking, restrooms

FISH STOCKING DATA

year	species	size	# released
07	Walleye	Fingerling	3,900
09	Walleye	Fingerling	3,825

LENGTH OF SELECTED SPECIES SAMPLED FROM ALL GEAR
Survey Date: 06/16/2010

Number of fish caught for the following length categories (inches):

species	0-5	6-8	9-11	12-14	15-19	20-24	25-29	>30	Total
Black Crappie	-	1	8	1	-	-	-	-	10
Bluegill	641	541	6	-	-	-	-	-	1190
Green Sunfish	10	-	-	-	-	-	-	-	10
Hybrid Sunfish	2	1	-	-	-	-	-	-	3
Largemouth Bass	1	3	3	1	-	-	-	-	8
Northern Pike	-	-	-	6	9	1	-	-	16
Rock Bass	21	36	-	-	-	-	-	-	57
Smallmouth Bass	-	2	4	8	7	-	-	-	21
Walleye	-	1	5	1	19	23	3	-	52

FISHING INFORMATION

Little Long Lake is 322 acres with depths reaching to 45 feet. Adequate oxygen levels were measured down to 32 feet.

In 2010, the DNR surveyed these waters and found a lot of pros and a few cons. The pros are the fish population which was dominated by bluegills and walleyes. Bluegills averaged 6.4 inches and .21 pounds, which is decent. One practically platter-sized 10-inch bluegill was caught during the survey. Walleyes average 20.5 inches and 4.3 pounds. The bluegills and walleyes here are enough to make grown men giddy.

Other notable species here include largemouth and smallmouth bass, with one notable smallie measuring in at 18 inches. Black crappie numbers were down from past surveys.

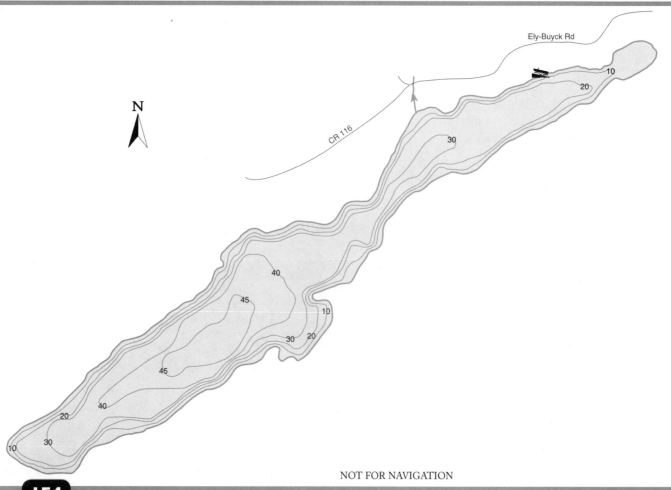

NOT FOR NAVIGATION

Source: Minnesota Department of Natural Resources, USGS

Johnson Lake

One Pine Lake

N

NOT FOR NAVIGATION

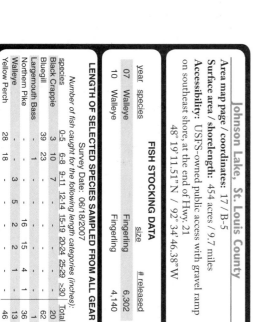

Johnson Lake, St. Louis County

Area map page / coordinates: 17 / B-5
Surface area / shorelength: 454 acres / 9.7 miles
Accessibility: USFS-owned public access with gravel ramp on southeast shore, at the end of Hwy. 21

48° 19'11.51"N / 92° 34'46.38"W

FISH STOCKING DATA

year	species	size	# released
07	Walleye	Fingerling	6,302
10	Walleye	Fingerling	4,140

LENGTH OF SELECTED SPECIES SAMPLED FROM ALL GEAR
Survey Date: 06/18/2007

Number of fish caught for the following length categories (inches):

species	0-5	6-8	9-11	12-14	15-19	20-24	25-29	>30	Total
Black Crappie	3	10	7	-	-	-	-	-	20
Bluegill	39	23	-	-	-	-	-	-	62
Largemouth Bass	-	1	-	-	-	-	-	-	1
Northern Pike	-	-	-	16	15	4	1	-	36
Walleye	-	3	5	2	2	1	-	-	13
Yellow Perch	28	18	-	-	-	-	-	-	46

One Pine Lake, St. Louis County

Area map page / coordinates: 17 / B-5
Surface area / shorelength: 355 acres / 4.0 miles
Accessibility: USFS-owned public access with concrete ramp on west shore, off Hwy. 21

47° 48'25.37"N / 91° 53'12.00"W

LENGTH OF SELECTED SPECIES SAMPLED FROM ALL GEAR
Survey Date: 07/30/2007

Number of fish caught for the following length categories (inches):

species	0-5	6-8	9-11	12-14	15-19	20-24	25-29	>30	Total
Black Crappie	8	21	6	3	-	-	-	-	38
Bluegill	138	34	7	-	-	-	-	-	179
Northern Pike	-	-	11	35	13	3	1	-	63
Pumpkin. Sunfish	13	13	-	-	-	-	-	-	26
Rock Bass	3	28	6	-	-	-	-	-	37
Smallmouth Bass	-	2	1	-	4	-	-	-	7
Walleye	-	24	38	22	22	2	-	-	108
Yellow Perch	18	36	13	-	-	-	-	-	67

SHAGAWA LAKE *St. Louis County*

Area map page / coordinates:	17 / A-5
Watershed:	Rainy headwaters
Surface water area / shorelength:	2,344 acres / 21.3 miles
Maximum / mean depth:	48 feet / 22 feet
Water color / clarity:	Green tint / 8.0 feet (2007)
Shoreland zoning classification:	General development
Management class / Ecological type:	Walleye / soft-water walleye

Accessibility: 1) County-owned public access with concrete ramp on northwest shore, off County Road 88
47° 55' 28.96" N / 91° 54' 45.71" W

Accessibility: 2) City-owned public access with sand ramp on south shore
47° 54' 16.37" N / 91° 52' 50.40" W

Accessibility: 3) State-owned public access with two concrete ramps on sout[h] shore, just west of Sandy Point
47° 54' 52.93" N / 91° 51' 25.49" W

Accessibility: 4) City-owned public access with gravel ramp on east shore
47° 55' 3.04" N / 91° 50' 16.48" W

Accommodations: Park, fishing pier, picnicking, restrooms

FISHING INFORMATION

Shagawa Lake is known as a walleye lake and for good reason. It might have something to do with the 2,300,000 or so fry that are stocked here every three years. It could also be the good numbers of catch-able fish present. Either way, the walleyes here have a high population and anglers are enjoying the bounty. These fish average 14.5 inches and 1.2 pounds. Early in the season, walleyes feed at the numerous bars reaching from the points around the lake. Outstanding spots on the south shore include Crossman Point and the small points east of it; Sandy Bar and Rocky Bay in the southeast corner are also producers. Clifford Noble, owner of Skube's Bait & Tackle, 1810 E. Sheridan St., Ely, MN, 218-365-5358, says the area near the Burntside River inlet is great walleye country in spring. The islands at the lake's center and west shore are always good, he says. Work them at 8- to 15-feet with crawlers on Lindy rigs. You can also try Lamb's Point and the bars and rocks off Miller Point. From May right through summer, fish drop-offs around Shipman Island and the small islets to Shipman's north.

White suckers were abundant and their numbers are high when compared to other lakes in this class. Sucker sizes averaged 14.9 inches and 1.6 pounds, which is considered normal.

Yellow perch numbers are higher than most lakes in this class and are even higher than past evaluations. Perch averaged 7.8 inches and .25 pounds. Growth rates are fast, especially for those aged three and older.

Only two smallmouth bass were caught in the most recent DNR survey, but they are considered "net shy" and are therefore not well represented in gill net studies. So, we turned to the pros, the locals, for their take on Shagawa's smallies. "There is a large population of smallmouth bass, some of which approach trophy size," said Noble. As might be expected in a walleye-smallmouth lake, there's plenty of structure to fish. Wherever you find walleyes on this lake, you'll also find smallmouths, which are becoming increasingly popular with fishermen. Bass can also be found at islands around the lake. While they are not as abundant as walleyes, they tend to be well-worth the effort of fishing them. A fun and productive way to chase smallies is to throw topwater lures near rocky shoreline early and late in the day. Poppers and chuggers work well, but fast moving walking baits like a Zara Spook or a Sammy can really draw vicious strikes.

During the 2007 DNR lake survey, northern pike numbers were higher than the median catch on this lake in previous surveys. The average northern pike measured 23.6 inches long and weighed 3.2 pounds. The overall growth rate of pike in Shagawa was considered faster than normal for the area.

Rusty crayfish are a large, aggressive species and have become fairly heavily populated in the lake. It is presumed they were introduced into the lake by anglers using them as bait.

Some of Shagawa's smallmouth bass may have tapeworm larvae and some yellow perch have had yellow grub in the past. These parasites do not infect humans and are removed during filleting or killed when cooked.

FISH STOCKING DATA

year	species	size	# released
07	Walleye	Fry	2,300,000
10	Walleye	Fry	2,430,000

NET CATCH DATA

Date: 08/06/2007	Gill Nets		Trap Nets	
species	# per net	avg. fish weight (lbs.)	# per net	avg. fish weight (lbs.)
Northern Pike	2.1	3.25	-	-
Rock Bass	-	-	-	-
Smallmouth Bass	0.2	2.3	-	-
Tullibee (Cisco)	0.7	1.89	-	-
Walleye	29.1	0.74	-	-
White Sucker	9.0	1.95	-	-
Yellow Perch	4.0	0.35	-	-

LENGTH OF SELECTED SPECIES SAMPLED FROM ALL GEAR

Number of fish caught for the following length categories (inches):

species	0-5	6-8	9-11	12-14	15-19	20-24	25-29	>30	Total
Northern Pike	-	-	-	-	4	10	3	2	19
Rock Bass	-	-	-	-	-	-	-	-	-
Smallmouth Bass	-	-	-	1	1	-	-	-	2
Tullibee (Cisco)	-	-	-	1	5	-	-	-	6
Walleye	-	60	72	75	48	6	1	-	262
Yellow Perch	4	18	14	-	-	-	-	-	36

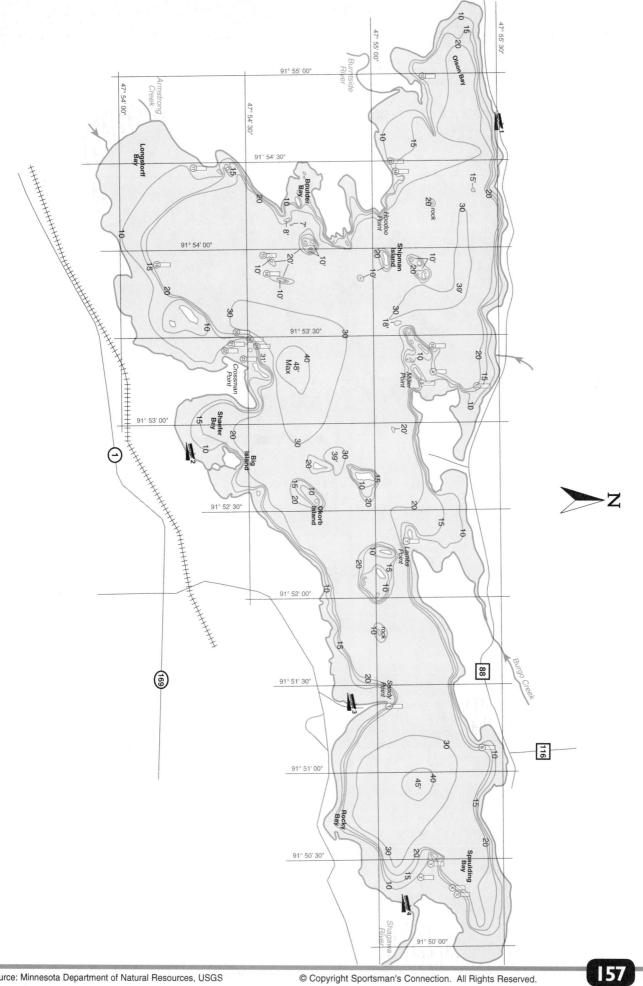

N

NOT FOR NAVIGATION

Source: Minnesota Department of Natural Resources, USGS

WHITE IRON LAKE   St. Louis County

Area map page / coordinates:	17 / A,B-6
Watershed:	Rainy headwaters
Surface water area / shorelength:	3,238 acres / 26.0 miles
Maximum / mean depth:	47 feet / 16 feet
Water color / clarity:	Brown stain / 5.0 feet (2010)
Shoreland zoning classification:	Recreational development
Management class / Ecological type:	Walleye / soft-water walleye

Accessibility: 1) State-owned public access with concrete ramp on north shore, one mile southwest off County Road 16 on County Road 447

47° 51' 42.05" N / 91° 49' 14.85" W

Accessibility: 2) County-owned public access on with concrete ramp on west shore, 1.5 miles east off Hwy. 1 on County Road 655

47° 53' 54.36" N / 91° 47' 2.76" W

Accommodations: Resorts, boat rental, camping, picnicking, restrooms

FISHING INFORMATION

Located southeast of Ely, White Iron Lake is fairly deep and moderately clear with decent weedbeds holding good numbers of forage fish. The result is good populations of walleyes, northern pike and smallmouth bass, as well as a few nice black crappies.

The lake was stocked with walleyes by the DNR until about 10 years ago, when it became apparent that there was sufficient natural production to maintain big populations. Clifford Noble owner of Skube's Bait & Tackle, 1810 E. Sheridan St., Ely, MN, 218-365-5358, says there's one hotspot that has to be pointed out, it's known as Silver Rapids and is the outlet of the Kawishiwi River. This is located on the northeast side, where a slow current passes through narrow Silver Rapids, often carrying walleyes and northern pike along. The fish are fairly easy to catch there and many of those landed are big adults like, walleyes of 3 or 4 pounds, and northern pike up to 20 and even 25 pounds. Not all the action is around the river; there are plenty of other early season walleye spots. Just check the map for the good points and small islands of the north bay to see where the walleyes will be located. The same is true of the south bay, particularly the east side of it which is loaded with islands, reefs, breaks, points and bars. Live bait, minnows, leeches and nightcrawlers fished on jigs, split shot rigs or under slip bobbers works well as do stickbaits like Rogues and Rapalas. As the water warms, live bait tends to work best in deeper water. Because of the strong forage base, a few walleyes attain lunker size, but because this popular lake is fished rather heavily, you're more likely to find eaters, with large fish weighing around 3-to 4-pounds. The DNR surveyed this lake in 2010 and found the walleye recruitment to be good with various year classes represented. The average size for White Iron Lake walleyes is about 14 inches long, weighing just over 1 pound. The growth rate was considered slower than normal compared to other area lakes.

Northerns are also on the large side in White Iron, where they have good weedbeds to patrol for ciscoes and white suckers. Spoons, spinnerbaits and Rapalas trolled at the outside edges of the weeds can be very effective in taking them. A very productive technique for catching pike early and late in the day or whenever you're faced with lowlight conditions is to bulge a spinnerbait. This technique is achieved by fishing with a spinnerbait which has a Colorado or Indiana blade. You quickly retrieve your spinnerbait just under the water surface creating a bulge just in front of your lure. If pike are near your lure, they'll crush it. Use a heavy leader since there are some large fish available in this lake. DNR data shows the average pike for this lake to measure nearly 2-feet long and weigh 3 pounds.

NO RECORD OF STOCKING

NET CATCH DATA

Date: 06/23/2010	Gill Nets		Trap Nets	
		avg. fish		avg. fish
species	# per net	weight (lbs.)	# per net	weight (lbs.)
Black Crappie	-	-	2.67	0.48
Bluegill	-	-	1.40	0.44
Northern Pike	2.67	3.41	0.93	2.09
Rock Bass	-	-	2.13	0.41
Tullibee (Cisco)	5.78	0.44	-	-
Walleye	13.22	1.29	0.80	1.37
White Sucker	2.78	1.86	0.60	2.62
Yellow Perch	7.89	0.18	2.93	0.16

LENGTH OF SELECTED SPECIES SAMPLED FROM ALL GEAR

Number of fish caught for the following length categories (inches):

species	0-5	6-8	9-11	12-14	15-19	20-24	25-29	>30	Total
Black Crappie	-	17	22	1	-	-	-	-	40
Bluegill	2	16	3	-	-	-	-	-	21
Northern Pike	-	-	1	2	15	10	9	1	38
Rock Bass	3	25	4	-	-	-	-	-	32
Tullibee (Cisco)	-	20	25	6	1	-	-	-	52
Walleye	-	8	26	61	18	16	2	-	131
White Sucker	-	1	4	2	24	3	-	-	34
Yellow Perch	39	64	12	-	-	-	-	-	115

Although both smallmouth bass and black crappies are available out of White Iron, they're not numerous. The DNR surveys show the smallmouth bass numbers to not be particularly high. The crappies are also low in numbers, but some of them are fairly stout.

Public access, with concrete ramp, is on the lake's northwest side.

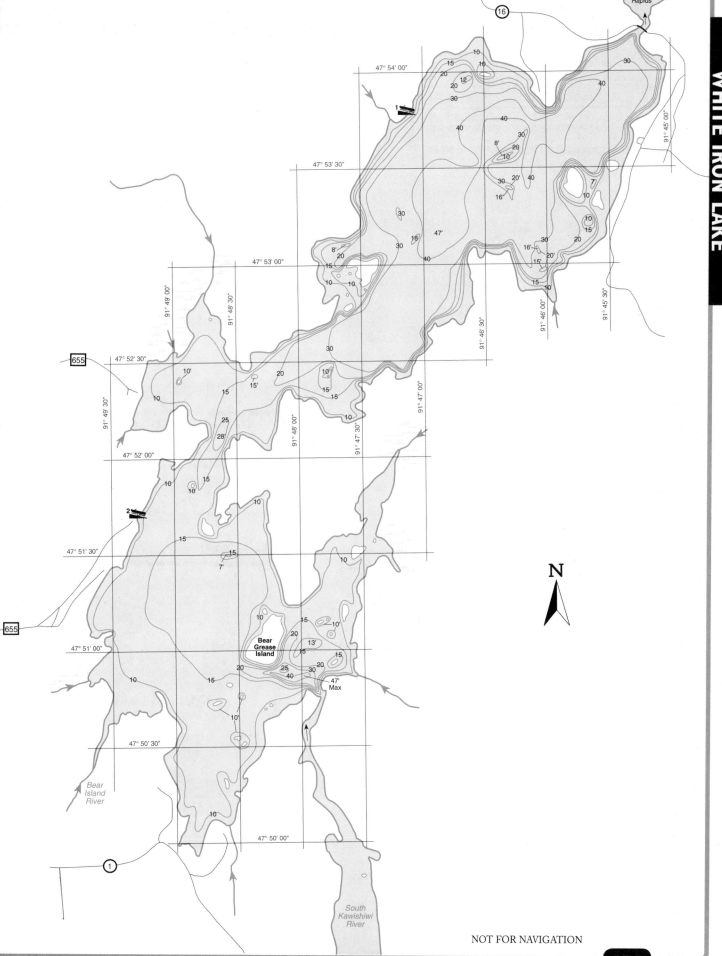

Silver Rapids

16

655

655

1

Bear Grease Island

47' Max

13'

Bear Island River

South Kawishiwi River

N

NOT FOR NAVIGATION

Muckwa Lake, St. Louis County

Area map page / coordinates: 17 / C-4
Surface area / shorelength: 147 acres / 2.9 miles
Accessibility: Carry-down accesses to south shore
47° 47' 46.63" N / 91° 59' 42.49" W

LENGTH OF SELECTED SPECIES SAMPLED FROM ALL GEAR
Survey Date: 08/09/2010
Number of fish caught for the following length categories (inches):

species	0-5	6-8	9-11	12-14	15-19	20-24	25-29	>30	Total
Walleye	-	-	24	4	83	14	1	-	126
Yellow Perch	41	17	22	-	-	-	-	-	80

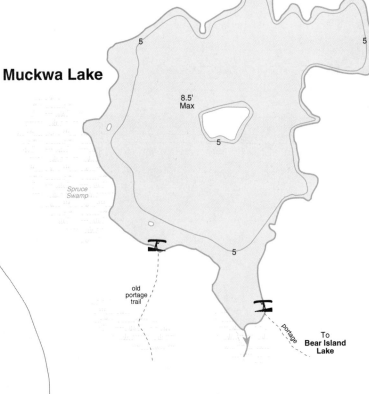

Muckwa Lake

Cub Lake, St. Louis County
Located in Bear Head Lake State Park

Area map page / coordinates: 17 / C-4
Surface area / shorelength: 8 acres / NA
Accessibility: Carry-down access (100-yard portage) down
steep hill from Bear Head Lake State Park road.
47° 47' 42.27" N / 92° 4' 37.32" W

FISH STOCKING DATA

year	species	size	# released
annual	Brook Trout	Yearling	~ 800

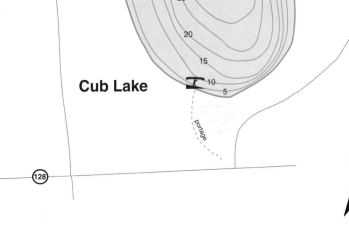

Cub Lake

N

Norberg Lake, St. Louis County
Located in Bear Head Lake State Park

Area map page / coordinates: 17 / C-4
Surface area / shorelength: 6 acres / NA
Accessibility: Carry-down public access (150-yard portage)
to north shore off Bear Head Lake State Park Road.
47° 47' 43.88" N / 92° 3' 54.79" W

FISH STOCKING DATA

year	species	size	# released
annual	Brook Trout	Yearling	~ 650

Norberg Lake

NOT FOR NAVIGATION

Source: Minnesota Department of Natural Resources, USGS

Perch Lake

Perch Lake, St. Louis County

Area map page / coordinates: 17 / C-5
Surface area / shorelength: 100 acres / 3.1 miles
Accessibility: Carry-down access (1/8-mile portage) to south shore from Cty. Rd. 903 off Co. Hwy. 21
47° 45' 21.18" N / 91° 55' 12.44" W

LENGTH OF SELECTED SPECIES SAMPLED FROM ALL GEAR
Survey Date: 07/17/2006
Number of fish caught for the following length categories (inches):

species	0-5	6-8	9-11	12-14	15-19	20-24	25-29	>30	Total
Bluegill	35	54	6	-	-	-	-	-	95
Hybrid Sunfish	14	1	-	-	-	-	-	-	15
Northern Pike	-	-	-	5	17	3	-	-	25
Walleye	-	4	11	23	47	4	-	-	89
Yellow Perch	7	15	-	-	-	-	-	-	22

N

13' Max

Whisper Lake, St. Louis County

Area map page / coordinates: 17 / C-5
Surface area / shorelength: 46 acres / 1.7 miles
Accessibility: Carry-down access (330-yard portage) from Perch Lake to north shore (47° 45' 11.71" N / 91° 55' 17.49" W); carry-down access (200 yard portage) from logging road to south shore (47° 44' 52.29" N / 91° 55' 24.98" W)

FISH STOCKING DATA

year	species	size	# released
08	Walleye	Fry	20,000
10	Walleye	Fry	20,000

LENGTH OF SELECTED SPECIES SAMPLED FROM ALL GEAR
Survey Date: 07/25/2006
Number of fish caught for the following length categories (inches):

species	0-5	6-8	9-11	12-14	15-19	20-24	25-29	>30	Total
Largemouth Bass	-	1	-	-	-	-	-	-	1
Walleye	-	-	6	3	-	-	-	-	9
White Sucker	-	1	4	11	22	-	-	-	38
Yellow Perch	-	10	-	-	-	-	-	-	10

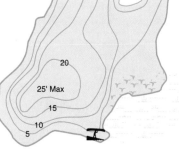

portage
To
Perch
Lake

25' Max

Whisper Lake

NOT FOR NAVIGATION

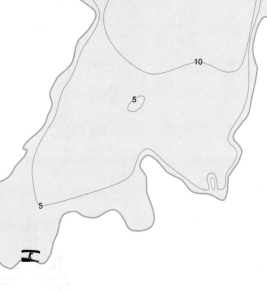

BEAR ISLAND LAKE St. Louis County

Area map page / coordinates:	17 / C-4,5
Watershed:	Rainy headwaters
Surface water area / shorelength:	2,362 acres / 21.3 miles
Maximum / mean depth:	62 feet / 19 feet
Water color / clarity:	Brown tint (bog stain) / 7.0 feet (2008)
Shoreland zoning classification:	Recreational development
Management class / Ecological type:	Walleye / soft-water walleye

Accessibility: 1) State-owned public access with concrete ramp on southwest shore, off County Road 490
47° 45' 34.74" N / 91° 59' 39.05" W

Accessibility: 2) County-owned public access with concrete ramp on south shore of Bear Island River arm, north on Co. Road 684 off CSAH 21
47° 46' 40.60" N / 91° 56' 47.12" W

Accessibility: 3) Township-owned public access with gravel ramp on north shore of Bear Island River arm, on Township Rd 4134, off CSAH 21
47° 47' 1.01" N / 91° 57' 5.97" W

Accommodations: Resorts, boat rental

FISHING INFORMATION

Bear Island is a large lake, boasting of 2,362 acres. The deepest depths reach down to 62 feet and water clarity goes to 10 feet. The Beaver River provides a major inlet on the lake. The spring walleye run occurs here. Beaver dams and rapids limit fish movement. The outlet at Beaver Island River also has limited fish movement during low waters, because of the old dam.

Several access points are available. The Minnesota DNR maintains the concrete access on the southwest shore off County Road 490. St. Louis County has a concrete access on the northeast end of the lake at the end of County Road 684. Finally, the township provides gravel access on the northeast bay off Township Road 4134.

The last DNR survey was conducted in May 2008. Overall, the fishery is in good shape, even with the neascus (black spot) present. Some of the perch sampled had yellow grub and some of the smallmouth had bass tapeworm. These parasites do not infect humans and in fact, are usually removed by filleting or killed during the cooking process. The mercury levels in walleyes and northern pike are a little on the high side and the DNR recommends no more than one meal per month of these Bear Island Lake species.

Bluegill numbers were in the top 75% of lakes in this class. They weighed .2 pounds and measured 6.3 inches, which is slightly below average. The largest bluegill caught during the survey was 8.4 inches. Growth rates are considered normal.

Rock bass numbers were also solid. The average rock bass was 6.7 inches.

Northern pike were in the fourth quartile for this lake and the median catch rate was higher than previous years. Pike averaged 23.9 inches and 3.3 pounds. Pike will usually respond to a plug or spinnerbait tossed to shore.

Walleye numbers were on par for lakes of this class. Growth is fast, with sizes averaging around 16 inches and 1.6 pounds. Troll green or black Rapalas off weeds for marble eyes. Use a bobber-and-minnow off reefs in 30 feet of water on cloudy days.

Smallmouth bass are generally not well represented in gill net testing; in this case, only 1.8 fish were caught per hour.

FISH STOCKING DATA

year	species	size	# released
05	Walleye	Fry	900,000
07	Walleye	Fry	900,000
09	Walleye	Fry	900,000

NET CATCH DATA

Date: 06/30/2008

	Gill Nets		Trap Nets	
species	# per net	avg. fish weight (lbs.)	# per net	avg. fish weight (lbs.)
Black Crappie	0.20	0.41	1.00	0.20
Bluegill	3.33	0.21	35.27	0.25
Burbot	0.07	2.87	-	-
Hybrid Sunfish	-	-	0.27	0.36
Largemouth Bass	-	-	0.53	0.28
Northern Pike	3.40	2.49	0.80	2.39
Pumpkin. Sunfish	-	-	1.47	0.15
Rock Bass	3.80	0.31	7.07	0.26
Smallmouth Bass	1.80	1.10	0.13	2.25
Tulibee (Cisco)	4.87	0.10	-	-
Walleye	5.73	1.16	0.53	1.74
White Sucker	2.33	1.45	0.80	2.57
Yellow Perch	1.87	0.23	1.00	0.21

LENGTH OF SELECTED SPECIES SAMPLED FROM ALL GEAR

Number of fish caught for the following length categories (inches):

species	0-5	6-8	9-11	12-14	15-19	20-24	25-29	>30	Total
Black Crappie	2	14	2	-	-	-	-	-	18
Bluegill	196	368	2	-	-	-	-	-	579
Burbot	-	-	-	-	-	1	-	-	1
Hybrid Sunfish	-	4	-	-	-	-	-	-	4
Largemouth Bass	3	3	1	1	-	-	-	-	8
Northern Pike	-	-	1	2	24	24	9	3	63
Pumpkin. Sunfish	15	7	-	-	-	-	-	-	22
Rock Bass	22	140	1	-	-	-	-	-	163
Smallmouth Bass	-	3	8	14	4	-	-	-	29
Tullibee (Cisco)	-	70	1	-	-	-	-	-	73
Walleye	-	13	17	34	19	9	2	-	94
White Sucker	-	2	8	13	20	4	-	-	47
Yellow Perch	8	25	10	-	-	-	-	-	43

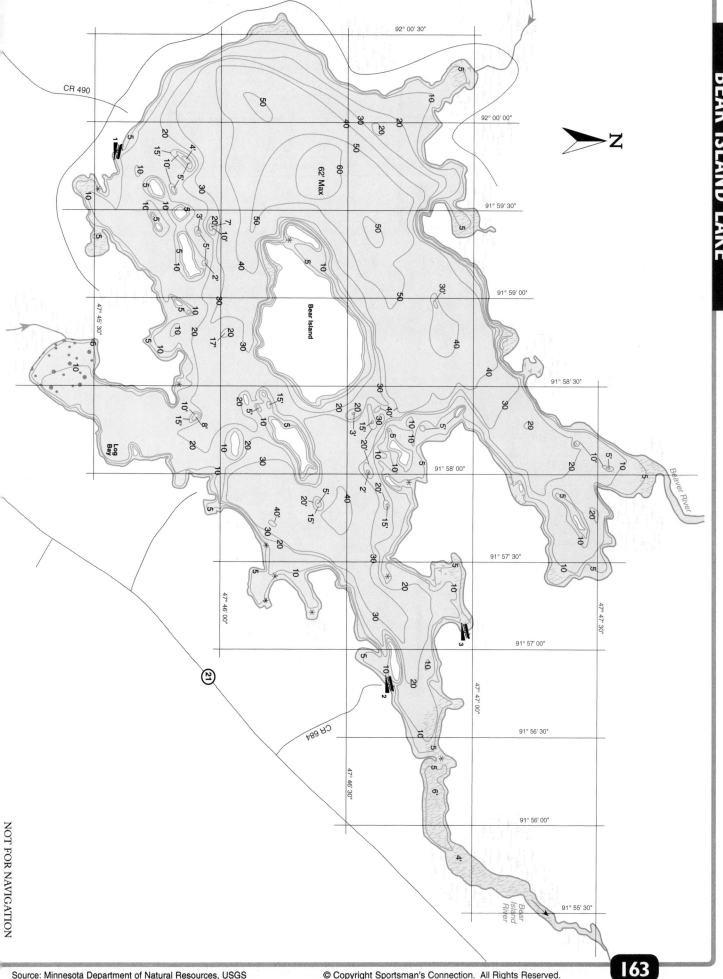

Bear Island

Log Bay

62' Max

CR 490

Beaver River

Bear Island River

CR 684

21

N

92° 00' 30"
92° 00' 00"
91° 59' 30"
91° 59' 00"
91° 58' 30"
91° 58' 00"
91° 57' 30"
91° 57' 00"
91° 56' 30"
91° 56' 00"
91° 55' 30"

47° 45' 30"
47° 46' 00"
47° 46' 30"
47° 47' 00"
47° 47' 30"

Source: Minnesota Department of Natural Resources, USGS

NOT FOR NAVIGATION

Twin Lakes, St. Louis County

Area map page / coordinates: 17 / B-4,5
Surface area / shorelength: 224 acres / 2.9 miles
Accessibility: USFS-owned public access with concrete ramp on north shore of West Twin, off USFS Rd 451; carry-down (1 mile portage) to East Twin from Mitchell Lake
47° 51' 23.12" N / 91° 57' 8.21" W

LENGTH OF SELECTED SPECIES SAMPLED FROM ALL GEAR
Survey Date: 06/19/2006
Number of fish caught for the following length categories (inches):

species	0-5	6-8	9-11	12-14	15-19	20-24	25-29	>30	Total
Green Sunfish	1	1	-	-	-	-	-	-	2
Largemouth Bass	2	-	1	3	1	-	-	-	7
Northern Pike	-	-	1	5	63	12	1	2	84
Pumpkin. Sunfish	2	-	-	-	-	-	-	-	2
Walleye	-	-	-	4	10	2	1	-	17
Yellow Perch	-	3	-	-	-	-	-	-	3

Twin Lakes

5
5
10
15
10
10
5
10
15
5
30
51' Max
50
40
30
20
20
5
15
10
10
*
5
10
15
16'
10
5
*
10
5
15
15

N

Sparrow (Purvis) Lake, St. Louis County

Area map page / coordinates: 17 / B-4
Surface area / shorelength: 53 acres / 1.6 miles
Accessibility: Carry-down access (1/8 mile portage) from county logging road to southwest shore
47° 49' 34.72" N / 92° 0' 26.52" W

FISH STOCKING DATA

year	species	size	# released
06	Walleye	Fry	50,000
08	Walleye	Fry	70,000
10	Walleye	Fry	50,000

LENGTH OF SELECTED SPECIES SAMPLED FROM ALL GEAR
Survey Date: 08/03/2009
Number of fish caught for the following length categories (inches):

species	0-5	6-8	9-11	12-14	15-19	20-24	25-29	>30	Total
Largemouth Bass	-	-	1	1	-	-	-	-	2
Northern Pike	-	-	-	1	11	1	-	-	13
Rock Bass	1	-	-	-	-	-	-	-	1
Walleye	-	-	-	-	5	2	-	-	7
Yellow Perch	-	1	-	-	-	-	-	-	1

3'
5
10
15
20
30
40
4'
50' Max
40
30
20
30
Taconite Trail
15
10
10
5
1'
5.5'

Sparrow Lake

NOT FOR NAVIGATION

Source: Minnesota Department of Natural Resources, USGS

Area map page / coordinates: 17 / B,C,D-5,6

Watershed: Rainy headwaters

Surface water area / shorelength: 5,628 acres / 54.5 miles

Maximum / mean depth: 25 feet / 12 feet

Water color / clarity: Brown stain / 5.0 feet (2003)

Shoreland zoning classification: Recreational development

Management class / Ecological type: Walleye-centrarchid / unclassified

Accessibility: 1) USFS-owned public access with gravel ramp in campground on north shore, southwest of Hwy. 1 bridge crossing
47° 48' 53.89" N / 91° 44' 38.38" W

Accessibility: 2) Carry-down public access by the dam, southeast of Hwy. 1
47° 48' 55.24" N / 91° 46' 56.71" W

Accessibility: 3) USFS-owned public access with concrete ramp in campground mid-lake, west shore, on USFS Rd. 429 off Hwy. 1
47° 45' 22.42" N / 91° 47' 2.30" W

Accessibility: 4) City-owned public access with concrete ramp on south shore, four miles northeast of Babbitt on FR 112 off County Road 623
47° 42' 59.40" N / 91° 53' 24.28" W

Accessibility: 5) County-owned public access with gravel ramp on south shore (Kramer Point), two miles north of Babbitt off County Road 407
47° 44' 7.90" N / 91° 56' 32.06" W

Accommodations: Resorts, camping, picnicking, restrooms

FISH STOCKING DATA			
year	species	size	# released
02	Walleye	Fry	3,000,000

NET CATCH DATA

Date: 08/25/2003

	Gill Nets		Trap Nets	
species	# per net	avg. fish weight (lbs.)	# per net	avg. fish weight (lbs.)
Black Crappie	0.6	0.22	-	-
Bluegill	0.2	0.61	-	-
Northern Pike	1.9	2.32	-	-
Rock Bass	0.5	0.39	-	-
Smallmouth Bass	0.1	2.20	-	-
Tullibee (Cisco)	7.1	0.64	-	-
Walleye	12.5	0.87	-	-
White Sucker	4.9	1.68	-	-
Yellow Perch	3.3	0.25	-	-

LENGTH OF SELECTED SPECIES SAMPLED FROM ALL GEAR

Number of fish caught for the following length categories (inches):

species	0-5	6-8	9-11	12-14	15-19	20-24	25-29	>30	Total
Black Crappie	4	4	1	-	-	-	-	-	9
Bluegill	-	2	1	-	-	-	-	-	3
Northern Pike	-	-	-	-	4	21	4	-	29
Rock Bass	-	7	1	-	-	-	-	-	8
Smallmouth Bass	-	-	-	-	2	-	-	-	2
Tullibee (Cisco)	-	56	17	26	7	-	-	-	106
Walleye	-	39	70	42	24	9	3	-	187
Yellow Perch	8	31	10	1	-	-	-	-	50

FISHING INFORMATION

The water in this picturesque lake is so dark it looks as though it could have been poured out of a root beer bottle. It's not very transparent, either, with average visibility being only 2 or 3 feet. Don't let that stop you from fishing Birch Lake, though. It's managed for walleyes and northern pike by the DNR and fishing can at times be excellent for both species.

Clifford Noble, owner of Skube's Bait & Tackle, 1810 E. Sheridan St., Ely, MN, 218-365-5358, says you'll find enough walleyes to keep you busy. Typical size is a 2-pound eater, and fish up to 10 pounds are pulled out fairly regularly. There's lots of gravel and rock, and the rock piles and points are the best places to fish for walleyes. In the western half of the lake, the shallows, rocks and islands south of Birch River Narrows are good for early-season action. You'll also want to try the rocks and reefs farther east. Marsyla Reef off Deer Island, and Blueberry Island, along with other outcrops on the lake's south shoreline often hold fish. In the east end, try the rocks along both shores and way down by the dam. Try a minnow or leech on a Lindy rig, slip bobber or a jig.

Northern pike fishing can be tremendous. While DNR data shows the average pike to weigh just over 2 pounds, Noble says fish in the 10-to 20-pound range are a real possibility. Birch has developed quite a reputation as a trophy pike lake, and that notoriety is well deserved. Early in the year, fish the bays with spinnerbaits, jerkbaits or minnows. During summer, fish deeper points and drop-offs with a large jig dressed with a minnow or soft plastic. There's also a good winter fishery for northerns. Big sucker minnows or fatheads work best then.

Black crappie populations in Birch are average for this area. Yellow perch are also available. According to DNR data, the average perch measures 7.7 inches long. The largest perch captured in the most recent DNR survey was 12.2 inches in length. Smallmouth bass also appear to be improving. The DNR feels the true abundance of smallmouth bass may be underestimated due to difficulties in capturing them in nets. The average smallmouth bass on Birch measured 15.7 inches long during the last DNR survey. Most amenities are available in nearby Ely. You'll find bait and tackle, food, lodging, plus souvenirs, and lots of specialty shops.

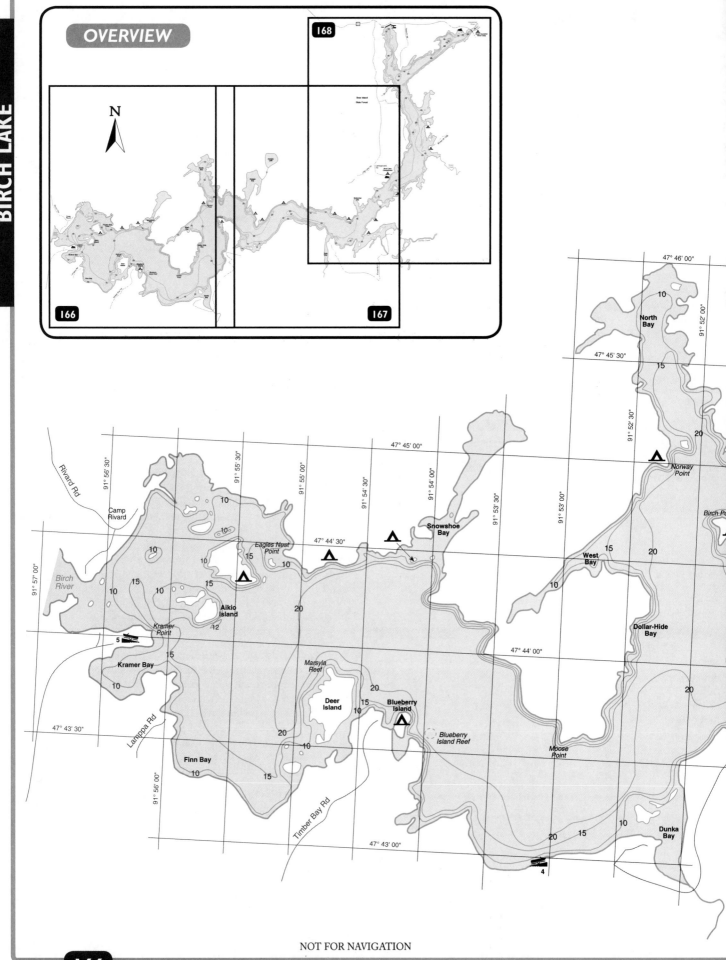

OVERVIEW

168

166

167

N

Deer Island
State Forest

Birch Lake
Campground

47° 46' 00"

91° 52' 00"

10

North
Bay

47° 45' 30"

15

91° 52' 30"

20

Norway
Point

47° 45' 00"

91° 56' 30"

Rivard Rd

91° 55' 30"

91° 55' 00"

91° 54' 30"

91° 54' 00"

Snowshoe
Bay

91° 53' 30"

91° 53' 00"

Birch Po

West
Bay

15

20

Camp
Rivard

91° 57' 00"

Birch
River

10

10

10

10

10

10

15

Eagles Nest
Point

47° 44' 30"

15

10

15

Dollar-Hide
Bay

20

15

15

20

10

Aikio
Island

12

Kramer
Point

5

15

Kramer Bay

10

Marsyla
Reef

20

47° 44' 00"

Deer
Island

20

15

10

Blueberry
Island

Blueberry
Island Reef

Moose
Point

20

47° 43' 30"

Lamppa Rd

91° 56' 00"

Finn Bay

10

20

10

15

15

Timber Bay Rd

47° 43' 00"

20

15

10

Dunka
Bay

4

NOT FOR NAVIGATION

Source: Minnesota Department of Natural Resources, USGS

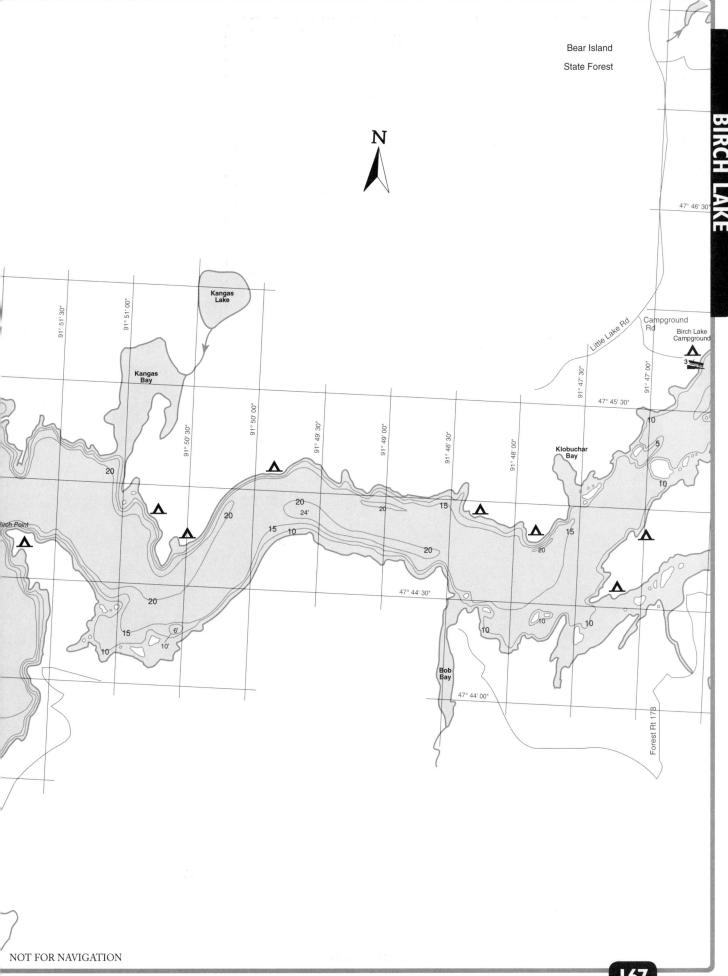

Bear Island
State Forest

N

47° 46' 30"

Kangas
Lake

91° 51' 30"
91° 51' 00"

Little Lake Rd

Campground
Rd

Birch Lake
Campground

Kangas
Bay

91° 47' 30"
91° 47' 00"

47° 45' 30"

91° 50' 00"

91° 49' 30"

91° 49' 00"

91° 48' 30"

91° 48' 00"

10

Klobuchar
Bay

5

91° 50' 30"

20

10

20

20

20

15

20

15

Birch Point

20
24'

15
10

20

15

15

20

20

15

20

10

47° 44' 30"

20

10

10

15

6'

10

10'

10

10

Bob
Bay

Forest Rt 178

47° 44' 00"

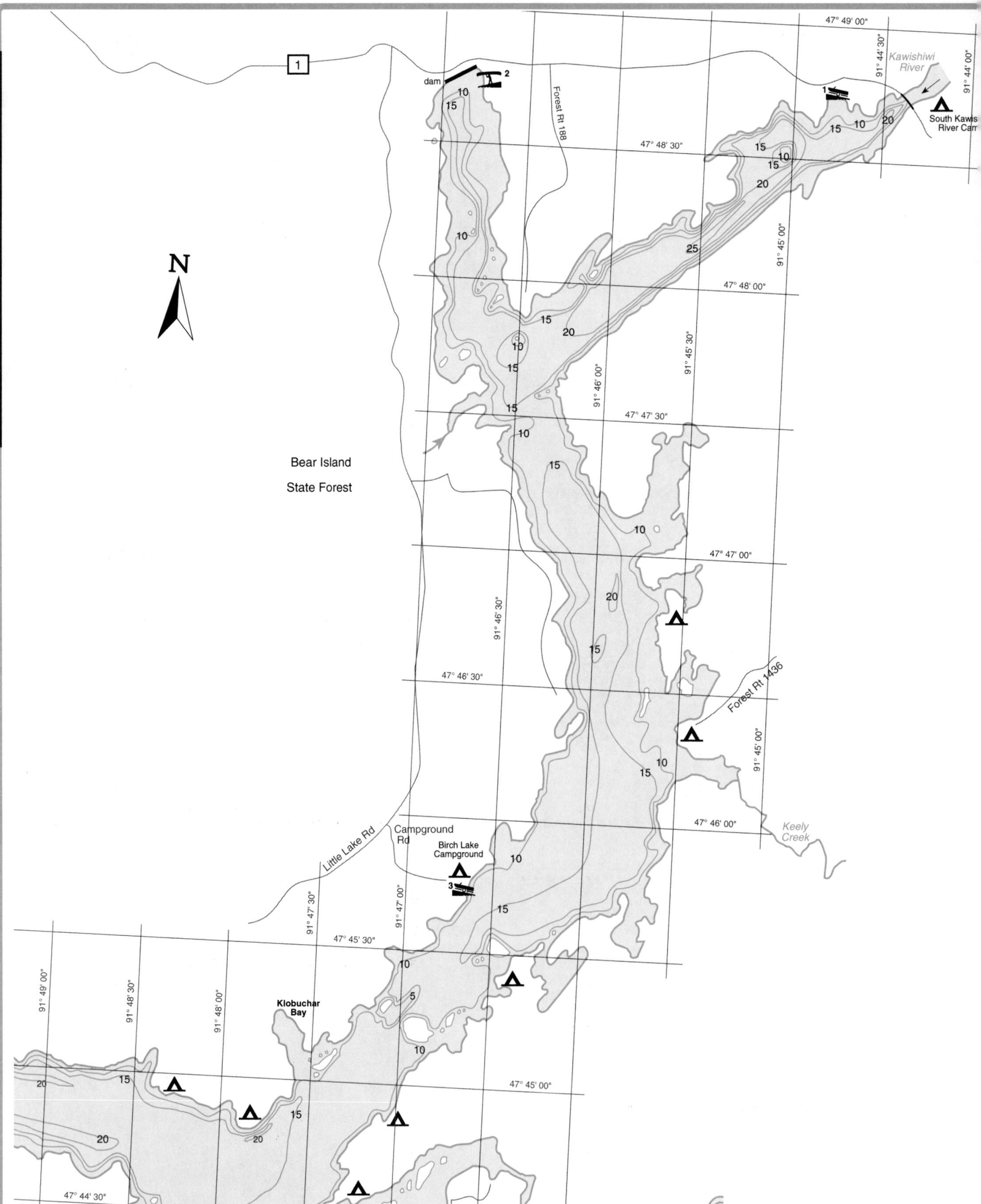

1

dam
2
10
15

Forest Rt 188

47° 49' 00"

91° 44' 30"

Kawishiwi
River

91° 44' 00"

1

15 10 20

South Kawis
River Cam

47° 48' 30"

15
10
15

20

N

91° 45' 00"

10

25

15 20

47° 48' 00"

91° 45' 30"

10

15

10

91° 46' 00"

15

Bear Island

State Forest

15

10

47° 47' 30"

15

10

47° 47' 00"

91° 46' 30"

20

20

15

Forest Rt 1436

91° 45' 00"

47° 46' 30"

15

47° 46' 00"

Keely
Creek

10
15

Little Lake Rd

Campground
Rd

Birch Lake
Campground

91° 47' 30"

91° 47' 00"

3

10

10

15

47° 45' 30"

10

5

Klobuchar
Bay

91° 49' 00"

91° 48' 30"

91° 48' 00"

10

47° 45' 00"

20

15

15

10

20

15

20

47° 44' 30"

Denley Creek

Bob
Bay

47° 44' 00"

10 10 10

Source: Minnesota Department of Natural Resources, USGS

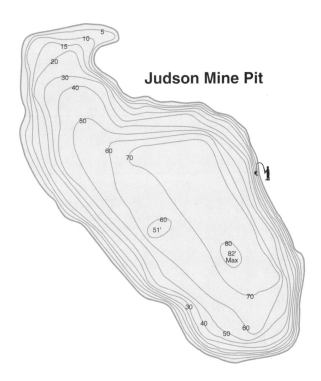

Judson Mine Pit

Judson Mine Pit, St. Louis County

Area map page / coordinates: 19 / C-4
Surface area / shorelength: 20 acres / NA
Accessibility: Hiking trail surrounding perimeter provides shorefishing access around entire lake
47° 29' 14.91" N / 92° 47' 13.99" W

FISH STOCKING DATA

year	species	size	# released
08	Rainbow Trout	Yearling	1,800
09	Rainbow Trout	Yearling	1,200
10	Rainbow Trout	Yearling	1,800

LENGTH OF SELECTED SPECIES SAMPLED FROM ALL GEAR
Survey Date: 09/18/2006
Number of fish caught for the following length categories (inches):

species	0-5	6-8	9-11	12-14	15-19	20-24	25-29	>30	Total
Green Sunfish	18	3	-	-	-	-	-	-	21
Rainbow Trout	-	-	-	7	2	-	-	-	9
White Sucker	-	2	16	15	39	-	-	-	72

N

Big Rice Lake, St. Louis County

Area map page / coordinates: 15 / D-6
Surface area / shorelength: 2,072 acres / 5.9 miles
Accessibility: USFS-owned public access with ramp on north shore, off Forest Road 256
47° 42' 12.21" N / 92° 29' 54.41" W

LENGTH OF SELECTED SPECIES SAMPLED FROM ALL GEAR
Survey Date: 06/12/1982
Number of fish caught for the following length categories (inches):

species	0-5	6-8	9-11	12-14	15-19	20-24	25-29	>30	Total
Northern Pike	-	1	-	5	11	1	4	1	23
Yellow Perch	-	46	26	3	-	-	-	-	75

Big Rice Lake

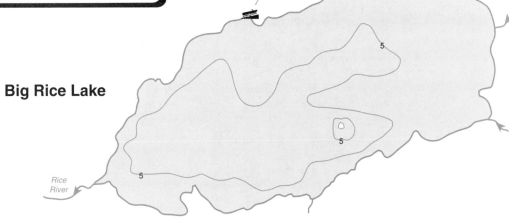

Rice River

NOT FOR NAVIGATION

DEWEY LAKE
St. Louis County

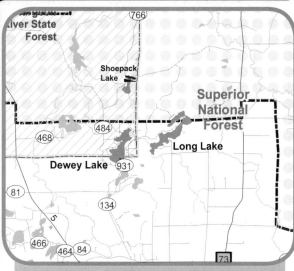

Area map page / coordinates: 18 / A-3

Watershed: St. Louis

Surface area / shorelength: 198 acres / 3.7 miles

Maximum / mean depth: 36 feet / NA

Water color / clarity: 12.5 feet (2007)

Accessibility: State-owned public access on southeast shore; 47° 35' 7.88" N / 92° 56' 27.13" W

Accommodations: Bordered by Sturgeon River State Forest

NOT FOR NAVIGATION

NO RECORD OF STOCKING

LENGTH OF SELECTED SPECIES SAMPLED FROM ALL GEAR
Survey Date: 07/23/2007
Number of fish caught for the following length categories (inches):

species	0-5	6-8	9-11	12-14	15-19	20-24	25-29	>30	Total
Black Crappie	1	14	2	-	-	-	-	-	17
Bluegill	53	29	-	-	-	-	-	-	82
Northern Pike	-	-	-	2	12	12	13	6	45
Pumpkin. Sunfish	5	3	-	-	-	-	-	-	8
Rock Bass	1	5	-	-	-	-	-	-	6
Tullibee (Cisco)	-	-	-	1	14	-	-	-	15
Yellow Perch	24	8	-	-	-	-	-	-	32

FISHING INFORMATION

Dewey Lake has a strong northern pike population, with averages falling in the 15-24 inch category, with one fish caught over 29 inches. According to the last DNR survey, the perch population is below state medians and cisco numbers are down. Bluegills, crappies and pumpkinseed sunfish are at normal populations.

Long Lake consists of 267 acres. The water is moderately stained with visibility to 7 feet. In 2004, the Minnesota DNR surveyed the lake and found a great bass-panfish lake. Black crappie catch rates were the highest ever surveyed, with the average crappie measuring 6.6 inches and weighing .17 pounds. Bluegills were also caught at the highest rates ever for this lake. However, increased numbers come with decreased sizes, as was evident by

the 5.3 inch average. Only 2 of the 198 sampled bluegills exceeded the 8 inch mark. Largemouth bass were electrofished during the assessment with good results. Although the abundance numbers were less than stellar, the sizes averaged 13.8 inches and 1.8 pounds, which is enough to make your rod do a little dance. Northern pike size structures were moderate at 23.9 inches. While the DNR report on Long Lake reflects a quality fishery, they do offer a word of caution. Lakeside development is on the rise here. Simple practices like not mowing to the water's edge, keeping all shoreline vegetation intact, not fertilizing lawns and maintaining septic systems will all help keep this fishery a good one.

LONG LAKE
St. Louis County

Area map page / coordinates: 18 / A-3

Watershed: St. Louis

Surface water area / shorelength: 267 acres / 6.2 miles

Maximum / mean depth: 38 feet / NA

Water color / clarity: 6.8 feet (2004)

Accessibility: Township-owned public access with concrete ramp on southeast shore

47° 35' 30.49" N / 92° 54' 57.41" W

Accommodations: None

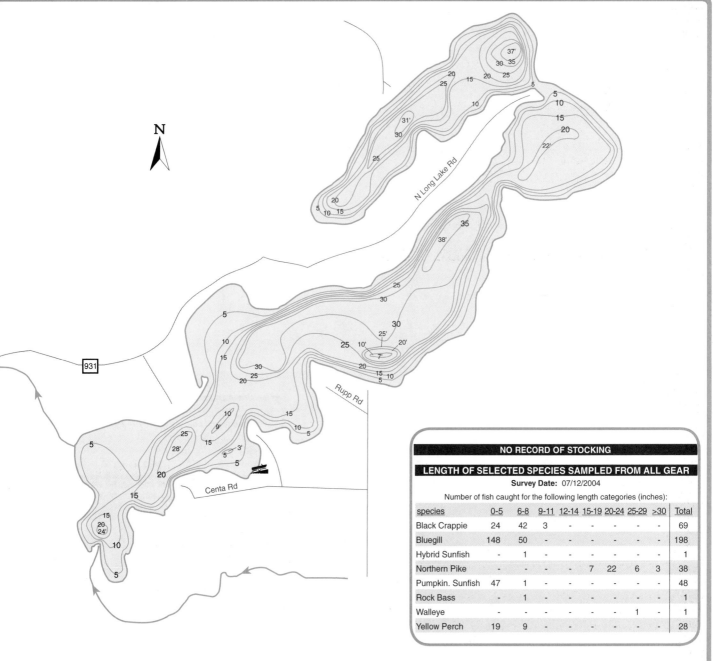

N

NO RECORD OF STOCKING

LENGTH OF SELECTED SPECIES SAMPLED FROM ALL GEAR

Survey Date: 07/12/2004

Number of fish caught for the following length categories (inches):

species	0-5	6-8	9-11	12-14	15-19	20-24	25-29	>30	Total
Black Crappie	24	42	3	-	-	-	-	-	69
Bluegill	148	50	-	-	-	-	-	-	198
Hybrid Sunfish	-	1	-	-	-	-	-	-	1
Northern Pike	-	-	-	-	7	22	6	3	38
Pumpkin. Sunfish	47	1	-	-	-	-	-	-	48
Rock Bass	-	1	-	-	-	-	-	-	1
Walleye	-	-	-	-	-	-	1	-	1
Yellow Perch	19	9	-	-	-	-	-	-	28

NOT FOR NAVIGATION

171

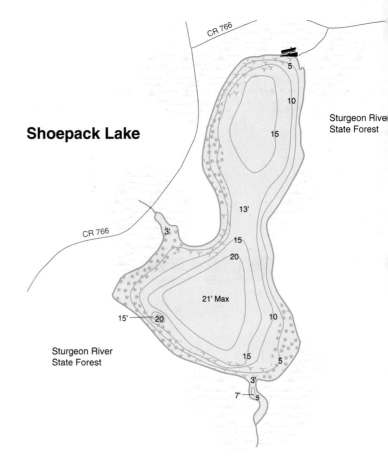

Shoepack Lake

Sturgeon River
State Forest

Sturgeon River
State Forest

N

Shoepack Lake, St. Louis County

Area map page / coordinates: 18 / A-3
Surface area / shorelength: 41 acres / NA
Accessibility: USFS-owned gravel ramp on north shore
47° 37' 12.31" N / 92° 56' 14.30" W

LENGTH OF SELECTED SPECIES SAMPLED FROM ALL GEAR
Survey Date: 07/14/1982
Number of fish caught for the following length categories (inches):

species	0-5	6-8	9-11	12-14	15-19	20-24	25-29	>30	Total
Black Crappie	1	9	4	-	-	-	-	-	14
Bluegill	5	20	-	-	-	-	-	-	25
Brown Bullhead	-	-	-	1	-	-	-	-	1
Northern Pike	-	-	1	3	6	3	-	1	14
Pumpkin. Sunfish	2	6	-	-	-	-	-	-	8
Yellow Perch	11	12	1	-	-	-	-	-	24

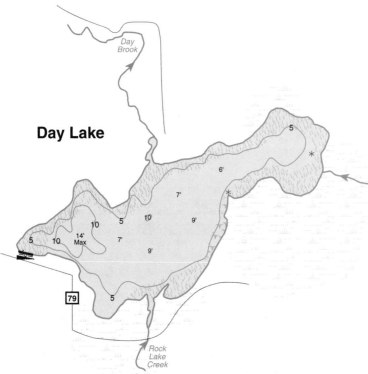

Day Lake

Day Brook

Rock Lake Creek

Day Lake, St. Louis County

Area map page / coordinates: 18 / B-2
Surface area / shorelength: 120 acres / NA
Accessibility: County-owned public access on southwest
shore; 47° 31' 44.45" N / 93° 1' 29.06" W

LENGTH OF SELECTED SPECIES SAMPLED FROM ALL GEAR
Survey Date: 08/21/1989
Number of fish caught for the following length categories (inches):

species	0-5	6-8	9-11	12-14	15-19	20-24	25-29	>30	Total
Black Crappie	58	19	-	-	-	-	-	-	77
Bluegill	35	3	-	-	-	-	-	-	38
Brown Bullhead	-	-	2	2	-	-	-	-	4
Northern Pike	-	-	-	1	29	7	2	-	39
Pumpkin. Sunfish	11	-	-	-	-	-	-	-	11
Rock Bass	1	-	-	-	-	-	-	-	1
Walleye	-	-	-	-	5	-	-	-	5
Yellow Bullhead	-	-	1	1	-	-	-	-	2
Yellow Perch	2	2	-	-	-	-	-	-	4

NOT FOR NAVIGATION

Source: Minnesota Department of Natural Resources, USGS

Longyear Lake

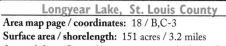

Longyear Lake, St. Louis County

Area map page / coordinates: 18 / B,C-3
Surface area / shorelength: 151 acres / 3.2 miles
Accessibility: Carry-down access on north shore of north basin (47° 29' 43.25" N / 92° 52' 35.17" W); also to northwest corner of the south basin (47° 29' 18.49" N / 92° 52' 37.20" W); fishing pier on east side of the north basin

FISH STOCKING DATA

year	species	size	# released
07	Walleye	Fry	155,000
09	Walleye	Fry	155,000

LENGTH OF SELECTED SPECIES SAMPLED FROM ALL GEAR
Survey Date: 09/07/2010
Number of fish caught for the following length categories (inches):

species	0-5	6-8	9-11	12-14	15-19	20-24	25-29	>30	Total
Black Bullhead	-	53	96	1	-	-	-	-	150
Black Crappie	2	-	2	-	-	-	-	-	4
Bluegill	-	19	-	-	-	-	-	-	19
Brown Bullhead	-	1	19	5	-	-	-	-	25
Hybrid Sunfish	-	1	-	-	-	-	-	-	1
Northern Pike	-	-	1	4	7	9	4	2	27
Pumpkin. Sunfish	6	-	-	-	-	-	-	-	6
Walleye	-	-	4	3	7	3	-	-	17
White Sucker	-	-	-	1	21	3	-	-	25
Yellow Perch	14	101	2	-	-	-	-	-	117

Chisholm

N

Carey Lake

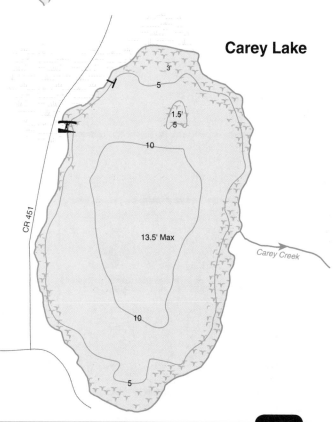

Carey (Dupont) Lake, St. Louis County

Area map page / coordinates: 19 / C-4
Surface area / shorelength: 139 acres / 1.5 miles
Accessibility: Carry-down public access to west shore
47° 25' 10.26" N / 92° 49' 50.40" W

FISH STOCKING DATA

year	species	size	# released
05	Walleye	Fingerling	4,482
07	Walleye	Fingerling	3,232
09	Walleye	Fingerling	2,169

LENGTH OF SELECTED SPECIES SAMPLED FROM ALL GEAR
Survey Date: 07/28/1997
Number of fish caught for the following length categories (inches):

species	0-5	6-8	9-11	12-14	15-19	20-24	25-29	>30	Total
Black Crappie	17	120	9	-	-	-	-	-	146
Bluegill	33	65	-	-	-	-	-	-	98
Northern Pike	-	-	-	-	8	8	7	3	26
Pumpkin. Sunfish	15	2	-	-	-	-	-	-	17
Walleye	-	-	2	5	2	3	-	-	12
Yellow Bullhead	-	-	1	1	-	-	-	-	2
Yellow Perch	12	3	-	-	-	-	-	-	15

NOT FOR NAVIGATION

Virginia (Bailey) Lake, St. Louis County

Area map page / coordinates: 19 / B-6
Surface area / shorelength: 31 acres / NA
Accessibility: City-owned public access with gravel ramp on south shore; electric motors only
47° 31' 31.13" N / 92° 32' 12.59" W

FISH STOCKING DATA

year	species	size	# released
07	Walleye	Fingerling	493
09	Walleye	Fingerling	442

LENGTH OF SELECTED SPECIES SAMPLED FROM ALL GEAR

Survey Date: 05/26/2010
Number of fish caught for the following length categories (inches):

species	0-5	6-8	9-11	12-14	15-19	20-24	25-29	>30	Total
Black Crappie	2	3	1	-	-	-	-	-	6
Bluegill	232	363	-	-	-	-	-	-	600
Hybrid Sunfish	-	11	-	-	-	-	-	-	11
Largemouth Bass	-	2	-	1	-	-	-	-	3
Northern Pike	-	-	1	4	18	12	10	1	46
Pumpkin. Sunfish	42	17	-	-	-	-	-	-	59
Rock Bass	14	9	-	-	-	-	-	-	23
Walleye	-	-	1	-	-	-	-	-	1
Yellow Perch	21	11	3	-	-	-	-	-	35

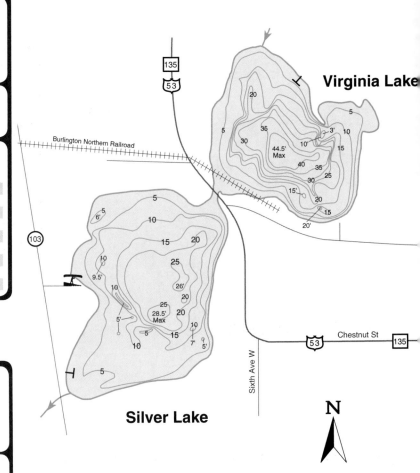

Silver Lake, St. Louis County

Area map page / coordinates: 19 / B-6
Surface area / shorelength: 44 acres / NA
Accessibility: Carry-down public access in city park on west shore; also fishing piers on northeast corner and south shore
47° 31' 27.04" N / 92° 32' 47.18" W

FISH STOCKING DATA

year	species	size	# released
07	Walleye	Fingerling	877
09	Walleye	Fingerling	784

LENGTH OF SELECTED SPECIES SAMPLED FROM ALL GEAR

Survey Date: 05/24/2010
Number of fish caught for the following length categories (inches):

species	0-5	6-8	9-11	12-14	15-19	20-24	25-29	>30	Total
Black Crappie	5	3	1	-	-	-	-	-	9
Bluegill	137	194	-	-	-	-	-	-	331
Hybrid Sunfish	-	5	-	-	-	-	-	-	5
Largemouth Bass	-	2	-	3	-	-	-	-	5
Northern Pike	-	-	-	-	-	4	6	-	10
Pumpkin. Sunfish	30	47	-	-	-	-	-	-	77
Rock Bass	-	3	4	-	-	-	-	-	7
Walleye	-	-	-	-	4	-	-	-	4
Yellow Bullhead	-	-	3	5	-	-	-	-	8

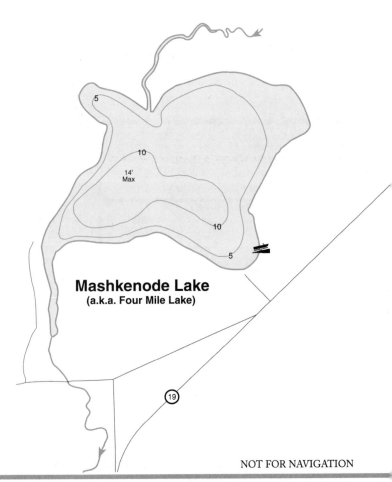

Mashkenode Lake, St. Louis County

Area map page / coordinates: 19 / B-5,6
Surface area / shorelength: 101 acres / NA
Accessibility: Carry-down public access to east and west shores; 47° 29' 35.44" N / 92° 35' 26.31" W

LENGTH OF SELECTED SPECIES SAMPLED FROM ALL GEAR

Survey Date: 06/18/2001
Number of fish caught for the following length categories (inches):

species	0-5	6-8	9-11	12-14	15-19	20-24	25-29	>30	Total
Black Crappie	14	19	12	2	-	-	-	-	47
Bluegill	67	104	-	-	-	-	-	-	171
Northern Pike	-	-	-	1	6	13	7	-	27
Pumpkin. Sunfish	49	2	-	-	-	-	-	-	51
Walleye	-	-	-	-	1	-	-	-	1
Yellow Perch	119	212	13	-	-	-	-	-	344

NOT FOR NAVIGATION

Source: Minnesota Department of Natural Resources, USGS

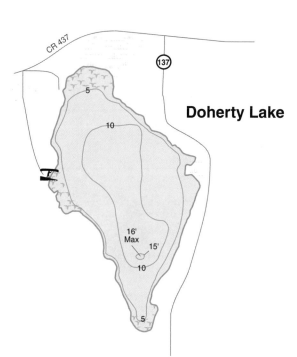

Doherty Lake

CR 437

137

5

10

16'
Max

15'

10

5

Doherty Lake, St. Louis County

Area map page / coordinates: 19 / C-5
Surface area / shorelength: 71 acres / NA
Accessibility: Carry-down public access to west shore
47° 28' 20.43" N / 92° 41' 29.82" W

LENGTH OF SELECTED SPECIES SAMPLED FROM ALL GEAR
Survey Date: 07/20/1981
Number of fish caught for the following length categories (inches):

species	0-5	6-8	9-11	12-14	15-19	20-24	25-29	>30	Total
Black Bullhead	-	1	-	1	-	-	-	-	2
Black Crappie	1	10	1	-	-	-	-	-	12
Bluegill	40	1	-	-	-	-	-	-	41
Brown Bullhead	1	5	7	-	-	-	-	-	13
Northern Pike	-	-	3	5	12	13	1	-	34
Pumpkin. Sunfish	22	1	-	-	-	-	-	-	23
Yellow Bullhead	1	30	14	1	-	-	-	-	46
Yellow Perch	1	1	-	-	-	-	-	-	2

N

Manganika Lake, St. Louis County

Area map page / coordinates: 19 / B-6
Surface area / shorelength: 158 acres / NA
Accessibility: Carry-down access to south shore
47° 29' 4.21" N / 92° 34' 23.09" W

LENGTH OF SELECTED SPECIES SAMPLED FROM ALL GEAR
Survey Date: 07/12/1989
Number of fish caught for the following length categories (inches):

species	0-5	6-8	9-11	12-14	15-19	20-24	25-29	>30	Total
Black Bullhead	18	10	-	-	-	-	-	-	28
Black Crappie	-	1	-	-	-	-	-	-	1
Brown Bullhead	-	-	-	2	-	-	-	-	2
Northern Pike	-	-	-	-	-	5	5	1	11
Yellow Perch	10	13	1	-	-	-	-	-	24

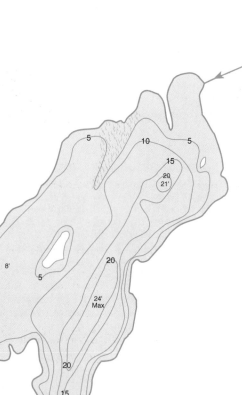

Manganika Lake
(a.k.a. Three Mile Lake)

5

10

5

15

20
21'

20

8'

5

20

24'
Max

20

15

10

5

NOT FOR NAVIGATION

WEST TWO RIVERS RESERVOIR *St. Louis County*

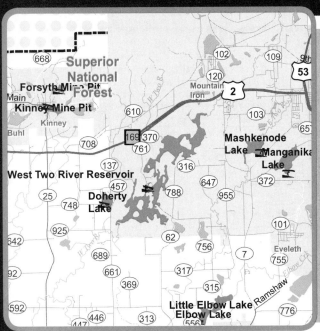

Area map page / coordinates:	19 / B,C-5
Watershed:	St. Louis
Surface water area / shorelength:	713 acres / NA
Maximum / mean depth:	27 feet / NA
Water color / clarity:	13.0 feet (2003)
Shoreland zoning classification:	NA
Management class / Ecological type:	NA / NA

Accessibility: City-owned public access with concrete ramp on west shore at the end of County Road 761 (Kane Road)

47° 28' 44.13" N / 92° 39' 48.25" W

Accommodations: Camping, picnicking, restrooms

FISHING INFORMATION

West Two Rivers Reservoir is a man-made creation that was formed to supply the MinnTac taconite processing facility with water in the 1960s. Since then, there have been a few winterkills. When tested through the ice, the oxygen levels have been low a number of times, making a repeat a possibility. Water quality is poor at times due to excessive nutrients, but that may diminish over time. Heavy algae blooms occur in the late summer.

There are five inlets on the reservoir, which drain local wetlands. The outlet flows to the St. Louis River and has a dam with a 25 foot head. There are lots of stumps and snags in these pike waters, so get to know the lake well and watch your lower unit. Doing so will keep you and your prop from getting bent.

During the 2003 DNR survey of the reservoir, fish populations were very high, showing high numbers of black bullhead, brown bullhead, northern pike, white sucker and good numbers of crappies.

Black bullhead numbers have decreased since their peak in 1979, but they are still the dominant species as far as quantities go. Brown bullhead numbers were in the fourth quartile for lakes of this class.

Northern pike numbers have remained stable over the years. During the DNR survey in 2003, there were 27 northerns caught. On average, they weighed 4.24 pounds and 19 of them fell into the 25-29 inch range. Doug Ellis, owner of the Virginia Surplus Store, 105 3rd Avenue, Virginia, MN, 218-741-0331, notes there are some real monster pike to be found. "You almost can't find anything under 5 pounds," Ellis says. Fish up to 24 pounds have been hauled out, and good numbers weighing in the teens are taken annually. This lake is just made for them. There's "so much structure" it's hard to pick a spot to fish, says Ellis. The lake's weak tea-color water is loaded with downed trees, brush and stumps, most of which hold fish. In addition, there are grassy points, pads, and virtually everything else to make West Two Rivers a pike angler's dream. Try fishing with a spinnerbait, lipless crankbait or a jerkbait. A bobber and large sucker minnow will also draw a few strikes.

Crappie anglers will find good numbers in the reservoir. The average crappie measured only 6 inches, but one whopper was 13.5 inches. With higher than average abundance levels, this is a good place for beginning anglers to catch crappie fever, a bug which can take hold and can last a lifetime. To catch a few crappie, make sure to bring along a supply of slip bobbers, small jigs and hooks. Crappies love to gobble up small minnows or leeches fished on a plain hook below a bobber. A small jig fished vertically will also take plenty of fish, especially when you fish them next to brush or any submerged cover.

White suckers have grown in abundance and size over the years, with an average of 17 inches.

The DNR observed neascus infections in half of the pike examined. Yellow perch also had neascus, as well as yellow grub parasites. These parasites are native to the area and do not infect humans. Filleting the fish often removes the parasites and cooking temperatures kill them.

NO RECORD OF STOCKING

NET CATCH DATA

Date: 06/09/2003

	Gill Nets		Trap Nets	
species	# per net	avg. fish weight (lbs.)	# per net	avg. fish weight (lbs.)
Black Bullhead	72.5	0.11	83.4	0.17
Black Crappie	8.5	0.12	10.0	0.20
Brown Bullhead	2.0	0.44	30.7	0.44
Green Sunfish	-	-	1.2	0.07
Hybrid Sunfish	-	-	0.1	0.19
Northern Pike	7.5	4.24	1.3	4.60
Pumpkin. Sunfish	-	-	3.9	0.06
White Sucker	17.5	1.96	5.1	2.26
Yellow Perch	32.0	0.10	0.4	0.07

LENGTH OF SELECTED SPECIES SAMPLED FROM ALL GEAR

Number of fish caught for the following length categories (inches):

species	0-5	6-8	9-11	12-14	15-19	20-24	25-29	>30	Total
Black Bullhead	73	226	-	-	-	-	-	-	299
Black Crappie	35	39	8	3	-	-	-	-	85
Brown Bullhead	-	29	150	-	-	-	-	-	179
Green Sunfish	11	-	-	-	-	-	-	-	11
Hybrid Sunfish	-	1	-	-	-	-	-	-	1
Northern Pike	-	-	-	-	-	6	19	2	27
Pumpkin. Sunfish	35	-	-	-	-	-	-	-	35
Yellow Perch	16	52	-	-	-	-	-	-	68

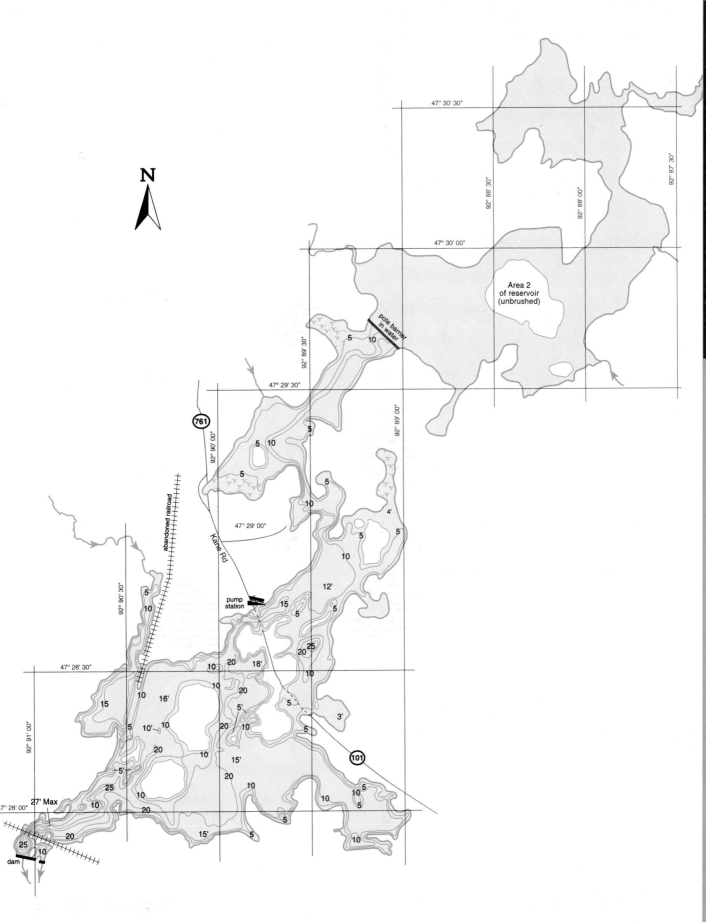

N

47° 30' 30"

92° 88' 30"

92° 88' 00"

92° 87' 30"

47° 30' 00"

Area 2
of reservoir
(unbrushed)

92° 89' 30"

pole barrier
in water

5   10

47° 29' 30"

761

5
10
92° 89' 00"

5

5

4'

5

5

5   10

5

10

92° 90' 00"

47° 29' 00"

Kane Rd

10

10

abandoned railroad

12'

pump
station

15

5

5

25

20

92° 90' 30"

5

10

10

20
18'

10

47° 28' 30"

10
10

20

15

10
16'

5'

20
5

3'

5

5   10   10
5

10
10
20

10

5

92° 91' 00"

20

15'

101

5'

20

10

5

25

10

10

10   5
10   5

5

27' Max

10
20

20
5

10

47° 28' 00"

15'

5'

10

dam

25   10

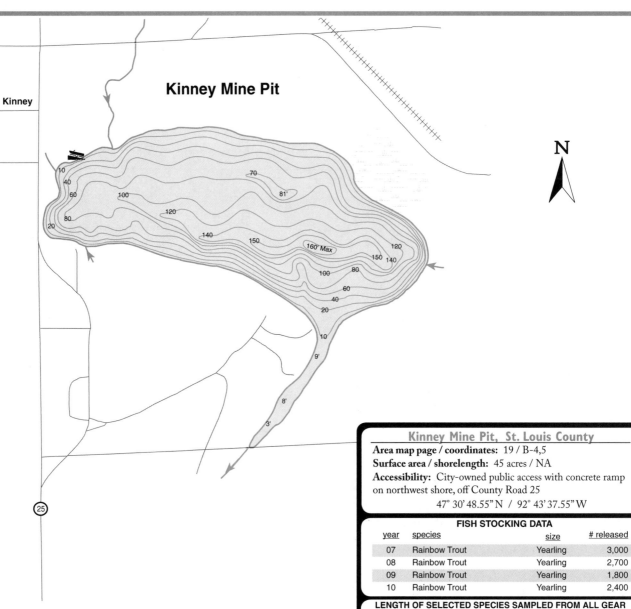

Kinney Mine Pit

Kinney

N

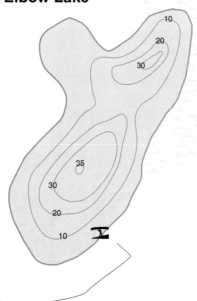

Little Elbow Lake

Kinney Mine Pit, St. Louis County

Area map page / coordinates: 19 / B-4,5
Surface area / shorelength: 45 acres / NA
Accessibility: City-owned public access with concrete ramp
on northwest shore, off County Road 25

47° 30' 48.55" N / 92° 43' 37.55" W

FISH STOCKING DATA

year	species	size	# released
07	Rainbow Trout	Yearling	3,000
08	Rainbow Trout	Yearling	2,700
09	Rainbow Trout	Yearling	1,800
10	Rainbow Trout	Yearling	2,400

LENGTH OF SELECTED SPECIES SAMPLED FROM ALL GEAR
Survey Date: 09/07/2010
Number of fish caught for the following length categories (inches):

species	0-5	6-8	9-11	12-14	15-19	20-24	25-29	>30	Total
Northern Pike	-	-	-	-	-	-	1	-	1
Rainbow Trout	-	-	-	14	6	-	-	-	20
Yellow Perch	-	14	-	-	-	-	-	-	14

Little Elbow Lake, St. Louis County

Area map page / coordinates: 19 / C-5
Surface area / shorelength: 5.8 acres / NA
Accessibility: Carry-down access via portage from Elbow
Lake to the west; also portage from Co. Rd. 315

47° 25' 47.87" N / 92° 27' 23.4" W

FISH STOCKING DATA

year	species	size	# released
annual	Rainbow Trout	Yearling	~ 240

LENGTH OF SELECTED SPECIES SAMPLED FROM ALL GEAR
Survey Date: 05/02/2005
Number of fish caught for the following length categories (inches):

species	0-5	6-8	9-11	12-14	15-19	20-24	25-29	>30	Total
Rainbow Trout	-	-	-	1	2	-	-	-	3

NOT FOR NAVIGATION

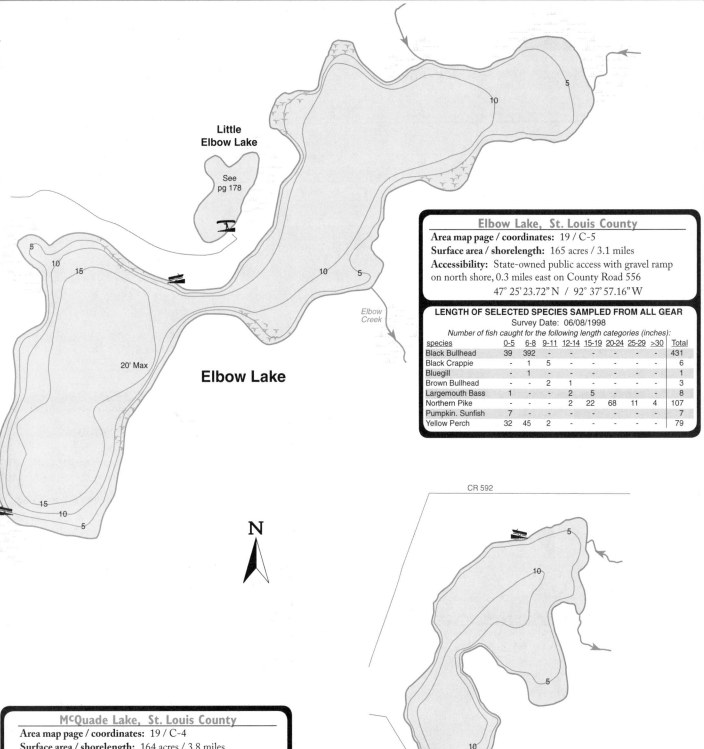

Little
Elbow Lake

See
pg 178

Elbow Lake

20' Max

Elbow
Creek

Elbow Lake, St. Louis County
Area map page / coordinates: 19 / C-5
Surface area / shorelength: 165 acres / 3.1 miles
Accessibility: State-owned public access with gravel ramp
on north shore, 0.3 miles east on County Road 556
47° 25' 23.72" N / 92° 37' 57.16" W

LENGTH OF SELECTED SPECIES SAMPLED FROM ALL GEAR
Survey Date: 06/08/1998
Number of fish caught for the following length categories (inches):

species	0-5	6-8	9-11	12-14	15-19	20-24	25-29	>30	Total
Black Bullhead	39	392	-	-	-	-	-	-	431
Black Crappie	-	1	5	-	-	-	-	-	6
Bluegill	-	1	-	-	-	-	-	-	1
Brown Bullhead	-	-	2	1	-	-	-	-	3
Largemouth Bass	1	-	-	2	5	-	-	-	8
Northern Pike	-	-	-	2	22	68	11	4	107
Pumpkin. Sunfish	7	-	-	-	-	-	-	-	7
Yellow Perch	32	45	2	-	-	-	-	-	79

CR 592

N

McQuade Lake

21'
20
15
17'
15
10
5

McQuade Lake, St. Louis County
Area map page / coordinates: 19 / C-4
Surface area / shorelength: 164 acres / 3.8 miles
Accessibility: State-owned public access sites on north (47°
25' 40.80" N / 92° 45' 55.30" W) and west shores (47° 25'
8.67" N / 92° 46' 24.39" W); both have earthen ramps

LENGTH OF SELECTED SPECIES SAMPLED FROM ALL GEAR
Survey Date: 07/17/2000
Number of fish caught for the following length categories (inches):

species	0-5	6-8	9-11	12-14	15-19	20-24	25-29	>30	Total
Black Crappie	4	2	5	-	-	-	-	-	11
Bluegill	7	17	5	-	-	-	-	-	29
Brown Bullhead	-	-	-	3	-	-	-	-	3
Northern Pike	-	-	-	1	21	12	7	1	42
Pumpkin. Sunfish	3	9	-	-	-	-	-	-	12
Walleye	-	-	-	-	6	2	-	1	9
Yellow Bullhead	-	-	1	1	-	-	-	-	2
Yellow Perch	3	2	-	-	-	-	-	-	5

NOT FOR NAVIGATION

MURPHY LAKE
St. Louis County

ELLIOTT LAKE
St. Louis County

Area map pg / coord: 19 / E-6

Watershed: St. Louis

Surface area: 354 acres

Shorelength: 5.3 miles

Max / mean depth: 24 feet / 9 feet

Water color / clarity: Brown tint / 5.7 feet (2009)

Shoreland zoning class: Rec. dev.

Mgmt class / Ecological type: Centrarchid / centrarchid

Accessibility: State-owned public access with concrete ramp on east shore, off County Road 327
47° 17' 45.96" N / 92° 29' 3.18" W

Accommodations: None

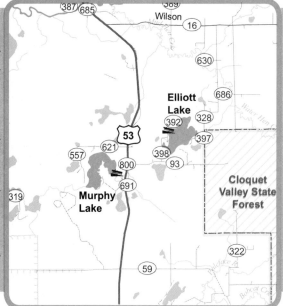

Area map pg / coord: 20 / E-1

Watershed: St. Louis

Surface area: 398 acres

Shorelength: NA

Max / mean depth: 13 feet / 7 feet

Water color / clarity: 9.0 ft. (2003)

Shoreland zoning class: Rec. dev.

Mgmt class / Ecological type: Walleye-centrarchid / centrarchid

Accessibility: State-owned public access with gravel ramp on west shore, off County Road 292
47° 18' 49.74" N / 92° 27' 4.55" W

Accommodations: None

FISH STOCKING DATA

year	species	size	# released
05	Walleye	Fingerling	16,827
07	Walleye	Fingerling	13,470
09	Walleye	Fingerling	8,427

NET CATCH DATA
Date: 08/10/2009

	Gill Nets		Trap Nets	
species	# per net	avg. fish weight (lbs.)	# per net	avg. fish weight (lbs.)
Black Bullhead	0.12	0.14	-	-
Black Crappie	1.25	0.28	2.27	0.22
Bluegill	2.50	0.17	18.91	0.10
Largemouth Bass	0.25	3.32	-	-
Northern Pike	3.88	3.47	0.91	4.92
Pumpkin. Sunfish	-	-	1.00	0.08
Walleye	0.88	1.94	0.18	5.50
White Sucker	1.12	2.30	-	-
Yellow Bullhead	0.75	0.92	0.55	1.06
Yellow Perch	6.12	0.16	0.18	0.11

LENGTH OF SELECTED SPECIES SAMPLED FROM ALL GEAR
Number of fish caught for the following length categories (inches):

species	0-5	6-8	9-11	12-14	15-19	20-24	25-29	>29	Total
Black Bullhead	-	1	-	-	-	-	-	-	1
Black Crappie	5	26	4	-	-	-	-	-	35
Bluegill	170	56	-	-	-	-	-	-	228
Largemouth Bass	-	-	-	-	2	-	-	-	2
Northern Pike	-	-	1	-	10	11	14	5	41
Pumpkin. Sunfish	11	-	-	-	-	-	-	-	11
Walleye	-	1	1	1	2	3	1	-	9
Yellow Bullhead	-	-	6	6	-	-	-	-	12
Yellow Perch	6	42	-	-	-	-	-	-	51

NO RECORD OF STOCKING

NET CATCH DATA
Date: 06/23/2003

	Gill Nets		Trap Nets	
species	# per net	avg. fish weight (lbs.)	# per net	avg. fish weight (lbs.)
Black Bullhead	0.2	0.53	-	-
Black Crappie	1.1	0.70	-	-
Bluegill	4.3	0.35	12.1	0.36
Brown Bullhead	8.4	0.99	1.9	0.78
Largemouth Bass	0.3	1.41	-	-
Northern Pike	10.1	1.74	1.2	1.06
Pumpkin. Sunfish	2.7	0.22	3.9	0.30
Walleye	0.8	3.27	0.1	4.28
White Sucker	2.1	2.61	-	-
Yellow Bullhead	3.9	0.57	2.2	0.65
Yellow Perch	3.0	0.37	2.2	0.51

LENGTH OF SELECTED SPECIES SAMPLED FROM ALL GEAR
Number of fish caught for the following length categories (inches):

species	0-5	6-8	9-11	12-14	15-19	20-24	25-29	>29	Total
Black Bullhead	-	1	-	1	-	-	-	-	2
Black Crappie	-	1	7	2	-	-	-	-	10
Bluegill	26	98	23	-	-	-	-	-	147
Brown Bullhead	-	2	34	57	-	-	-	-	93
Largemouth Bass	-	-	-	3	-	-	-	-	3
Northern Pike	-	-	1	10	63	21	1	4	100
Pumpkin. Sunfish	9	48	-	-	-	-	-	-	57
Walleye	-	-	-	1	1	6	-	-	8
Yellow Bullhead	-	7	43	4	-	-	-	-	54
Yellow Perch	1	12	30	1	-	-	-	-	44

FISHING INFORMATION

Located north of Cotton, near Highway 53, these two lakes have been receiving regular stockings of walleyes in an effort to establish fishable populations. There is a lot of good structure to fish on **Murphy Lake**, and heavy weed growth provides excellent largemouth bass cover. Walleye abundance was below average for similar lakes in this class, but they showed a fast growth rate. On average, you will find walleyes measuring around 17 inches. A stocking program also pumps several thousand walley fingerlings into Murphy in odd-numbered years.

Elliott Lake is bowl-shaped and is managed for largemouth bass and bluegills. According to the DNR survey in 2003, largemouth abundance was below average, but had fast growth rates, with the average four-year-old measuring 12.1 inches. Fish shoreline weeds for largemouth bass. Most of the lake's biggest bluegills are caught in summer months, while crappies are fished heavily during winter. Although northern pike showed a slower-than-average growth rate, they are above average in abundance and have a mean length of 19.5 inches.

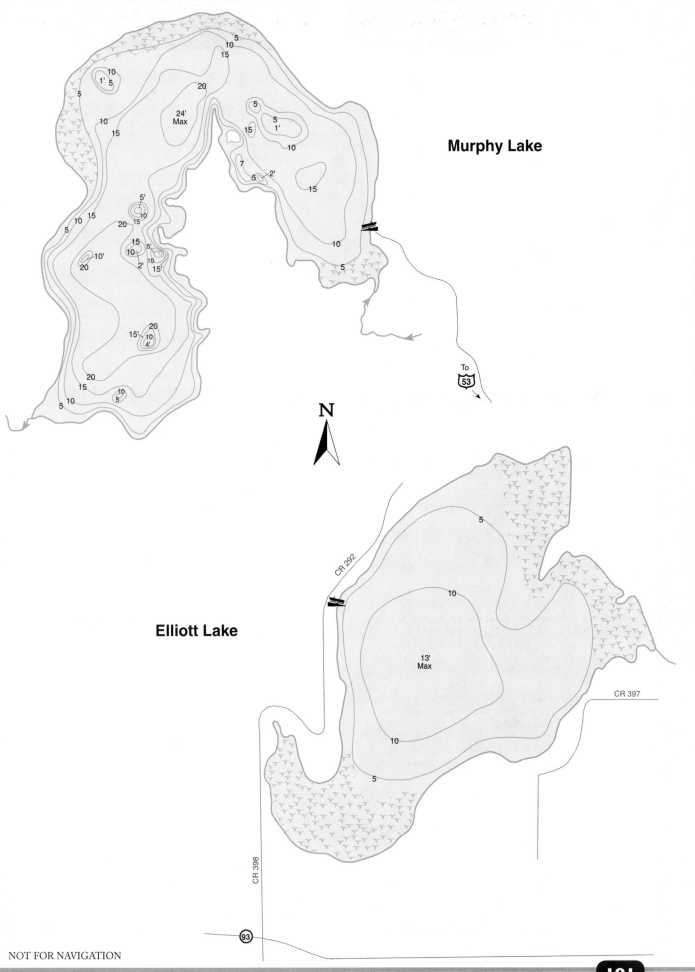

Murphy Lake

24'
Max

Elliott Lake

13'
Max

N

To
53

CR 292

CR 397

CR 398

93

NOT FOR NAVIGATION

Source: Minnesota Department of Natural Resources, USGS

ELY LAKE *St. Louis County*

Area map page / coordinates:	19 / C-6
Watershed:	St. Louis
Surface water area / shorelength:	709 acres / 8.1 miles
Maximum / mean depth:	70 feet / NA
Water color / clarity:	Clear / 16.0 feet (2008)
Shoreland zoning classification:	General development
Management class / Ecological type:	Walleye-centrarchid / centrarchid

Accessibility: State-owned public access with concrete ramp on north shore, off County Road 629

47° 27' 39.96" N / 92° 28' 30.18" W

Accommodations: Picnicking, restrooms

FISHING INFORMATION

Ely is a heavily developed 709-acre lake, with maximum depths of 70 feet. Water clarity goes down to 16 feet. Homes and cottages fill the shoreline on the dry side, while pondweeds and muskgrass cover it in the water. Lots of weeds provide lots of cover for bluegills, crappies, walleyes, and largemouth and smallmouth bass. Heavy recreational traffic means you'll want to fish early or late and during the week.

Bluegills dominated the net catches performed by the DNR, with a total of 562 caught during the most recent survey in August 2008. Sizes averaged 5.8 inches and .16 pounds, right at the median for similar lakes. Black crappie numbers were down but the size structure has remained consistent, with an average papermouth of 7.4 inches. The largest crappie captured during the survey was 10.2 inches.

The walleye population in Ely Lake has been very stable for more than 25 years, thanks to good growth rates and ongoing stocking efforts. In fact, walleyes have been stocked here for almost 100 years, beginning in 1912! On average, walleyes measure 15.6 inches and weigh 1.5 pounds. The population is naturally reproducing and continued stocking of fingerlings should only help grow the population.

Largemouth and smallmouth bass both exhibit normal growth rates by area standards. An average largemouth runs just over 10 inches, with one 19.8-inch specimen taken by survey nets. The biggest smallmouth was 16.5 inches, with a 10-inch fish closer to the average. Doug Ellis, owner of the Virginia Surplus Store, 105 3rd Avenue, Virginia, MN, 218-741-0331, says to look for bass on the rocks and reefs around mid-lake up north toward the public access site. You can also try fishing reefs and bars off the large point separating the lake's southern arm from the main lobe. When you are ready to move on, fish the bars west of the point near the eastern lobe.

A few northern pike were surveyed, with a median weight of about 7 pounds. Of the 8 pike that were caught, 7 of them measured 25 inches or longer. While the numbers may not be high, the quality sure seems to be. Ellis suggests fishing for big pike in weedlines in the bay near the seaplane base.

FISH STOCKING DATA

year	species	size	# released
03	Walleye	Fingerling	3,235
06	Walleye	Fingerling	7,984
09	Walleye	Fingerling	3,235

NET CATCH DATA

Date: 08/04/2008

	Gill Nets		Trap Nets	
species	# per net	avg. fish weight (lbs.)	# per net	avg. fish weight (lbs.)
Black Crappie	2.08	0.24	2.42	0.24
Bluegill	28.75	0.21	18.08	0.16
Green Sunfish	0.50	0.29	2.17	0.22
Hybrid Sunfish	4.33	0.28	7.50	0.19
Largemouth Bass	3.92	0.67	1.08	1.00
Northern Pike	0.58	6.52	0.08	3.76
Pumpkin. Sunfish	2.08	0.29	7.58	0.24
Rock Bass	4.67	0.28	3.58	0.15
Smallmouth Bass	1.42	0.91	1.25	0.20
Walleye	5.50	1.47	1.50	1.24
White Sucker	2.75	1.53	-	-
Yellow Perch	4.25	0.17	0.67	0.20

LENGTH OF SELECTED SPECIES SAMPLED FROM ALL GEAR

Number of fish caught for the following length categories (inches):

species	0-5	6-8	9-11	12-14	15-19	20-24	25-29	>30	Total
Black Bullhead	-	1	3	-	-	-	-	-	4
Black Crappie	17	26	11	-	-	-	-	-	54
Bluegill	201	351	-	-	-	-	-	-	562
Burbot	-	-	-	-	-	1	-	-	1
Green Sunfish	8	24	-	-	-	-	-	-	32
Hybrid Sunfish	43	99	-	-	-	-	-	-	142
Largemouth Bas	1	22	22	10	5	-	-	-	60
Northern Pike	-	-	-	-	-	1	3	4	8
Pumpkin. Sunfish	21	95	-	-	-	-	-	-	116
Rock Bass	41	56	2	-	-	-	-	-	99
Smallmouth Bass	4	14	6	5	3	-	-	-	32
Tullibee (Cisco)	-	-	-	1	-	-	-	-	1
Walleye	-	-	25	17	32	10	-	-	84
White Sucker	-	1	8	8	14	2	-	-	33
Yellow Bullhead	-	-	1	1	-	-	-	-	2
Yellow Perch	-	53	6	--	-	-	-	-	59

N

Eveleth
Lake Park

92° 30' 00"

47° 27' 00"

92° 29' 30"

47° 26' 30"

CR 628

70' Max

92° 29' 00"

47° 27' 30"

CR 396

92° 28' 30"

NOT FOR NAVIGATION

96

Fayal State Game Refuge

92° 28' 00"

92° 27' 30"

Source: Minnesota Department of Natural Resources, USGS

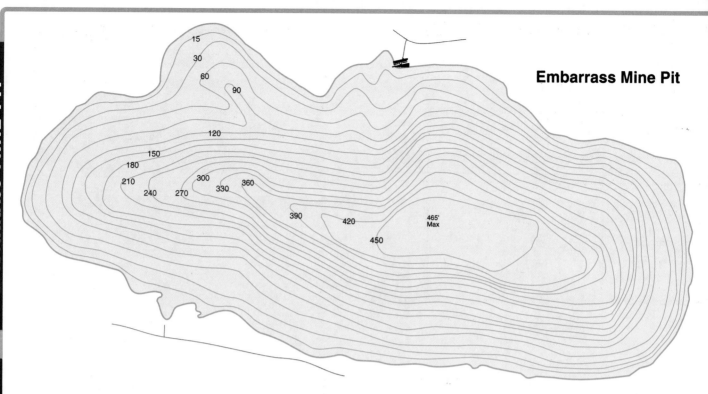

Embarrass Mine Pit

N

Embarrass Mine Pit, St. Louis County

Area map page / coordinates: 20 / B-2
Surface area / shorelength: 156 acres / NA
Accessibility: Township-owned public access with concrete ramp on north shore; 3 miles west of Aurora on Hwy. 135; one mile north on Co. Rd. 69 to public access road
47° 32' 24.94" N / 92° 16' 50.35" W

FISH STOCKING DATA

year	species	size	# released
07	Brook Trout	Yearling	1,550
08	Brook Trout	Yearling	1,534
09	Rainbow Trout	Yearling	1,550
10	Brook Trout	Yearling	1,600

LENGTH OF SELECTED SPECIES SAMPLED FROM ALL GEAR
Survey Date: 04/27/2005
Number of fish caught for the following length categories (inches):

species	0-5	6-8	9-11	12-14	15-19	20-24	25-29	>30	Total
Lake Trout	-	2	3	14	22	2	-	-	43
Rainbow Trout	-	-	-	5	-	-	-	-	5

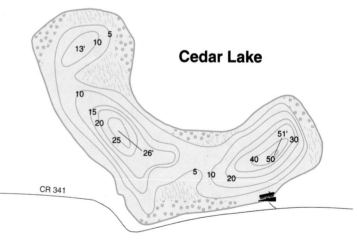

Cedar Lake

CR 341

Cedar Lake, St. Louis County

Area map page / coordinates: 20 / B-2
Surface area / shorelength: 32 acres / NA
Accessibility: County-owned public access with gravel ramp on southeast shore, off County Road 341
47° 29' 34.96" N / 92° 16' 29.39" W

FISH STOCKING DATA

year	species	size	# released
annual	Rainbow Trout	Fingerling	~ 2,000

LENGTH OF SELECTED SPECIES SAMPLED FROM ALL GEAR
Survey Date: 05/22/2007
Number of fish caught for the following length categories (inches):

species	0-5	6-8	9-11	12-14	15-19	20-24	25-29	>30	Total
Bluegill	61	455	-	-	-	-	-	-	516
Rainbow Trout	-	2	-	2	-	-	-	-	4

NOT FOR NAVIGATION

Source: Minnesota Department of Natural Resources, USGS

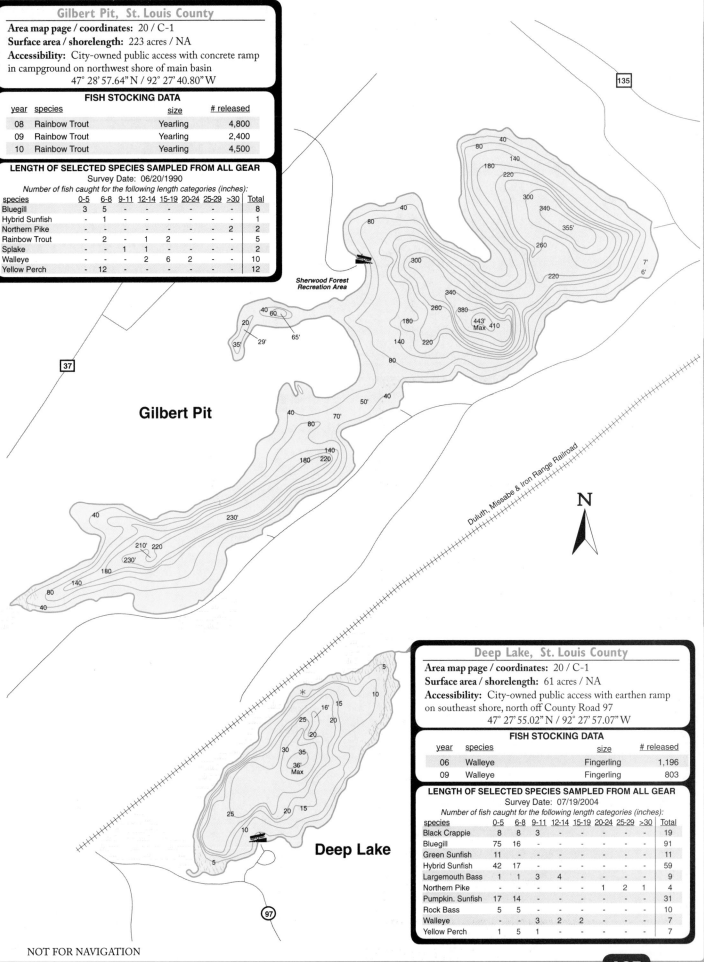

Gilbert Pit, St. Louis County

Area map page / coordinates: 20 / C-1
Surface area / shorelength: 223 acres / NA
Accessibility: City-owned public access with concrete ramp in campground on northwest shore of main basin
47° 28' 57.64" N / 92° 27' 40.80" W

FISH STOCKING DATA

year	species	size	# released
08	Rainbow Trout	Yearling	4,800
09	Rainbow Trout	Yearling	2,400
10	Rainbow Trout	Yearling	4,500

LENGTH OF SELECTED SPECIES SAMPLED FROM ALL GEAR
Survey Date: 06/20/1990
Number of fish caught for the following length categories (inches):

species	0-5	6-8	9-11	12-14	15-19	20-24	25-29	>30	Total
Bluegill	3	5	-	-	-	-	-	-	8
Hybrid Sunfish	-	1	-	-	-	-	-	-	1
Northern Pike	-	-	-	-	-	-	-	2	2
Rainbow Trout	-	2	-	1	2	-	-	-	5
Splake	-	-	1	1	-	-	-	-	2
Walleye	-	-	-	2	6	2	-	-	10
Yellow Perch	-	12	-	-	-	-	-	-	12

Sherwood Forest Recreation Area

Gilbert Pit

N

Deep Lake, St. Louis County

Area map page / coordinates: 20 / C-1
Surface area / shorelength: 61 acres / NA
Accessibility: City-owned public access with earthen ramp on southeast shore, north off County Road 97
47° 27' 55.02" N / 92° 27' 57.07" W

FISH STOCKING DATA

year	species	size	# released
06	Walleye	Fingerling	1,196
09	Walleye	Fingerling	803

LENGTH OF SELECTED SPECIES SAMPLED FROM ALL GEAR
Survey Date: 07/19/2004
Number of fish caught for the following length categories (inches):

species	0-5	6-8	9-11	12-14	15-19	20-24	25-29	>30	Total
Black Crappie	8	8	3	-	-	-	-	-	19
Bluegill	75	16	-	-	-	-	-	-	91
Green Sunfish	11	-	-	-	-	-	-	-	11
Hybrid Sunfish	42	17	-	-	-	-	-	-	59
Largemouth Bass	1	1	3	4	-	-	-	-	9
Northern Pike	-	-	-	-	1	2	1	-	4
Pumpkin. Sunfish	17	14	-	-	-	-	-	-	31
Rock Bass	5	5	-	-	-	-	-	-	10
Walleye	-	-	3	2	2	-	-	-	7
Yellow Perch	1	5	1	-	-	-	-	-	7

Deep Lake

NOT FOR NAVIGATION

185

EMBARRASS LAKE
St. Louis County

Area map pg / coord: 20 / B-2

Watershed: St. Louis

Surface area: 463 acres

Shorelength: 7.4 miles

Max / mean depth: 19 feet / NA

Water color / clarity: 5.0 ft. (2007)

Accessibility: 1) City-owned public access with concrete ramp in campground on west shore
47° 31' 47.19" N / 92° 19' 24.32" W

Accessibility: 2) State-owned public access with concrete ramp adjacent to inlet on north shore
47° 32' 8.85" N / 92° 18' 53.29" W

Accommodations: Fishing pier, picnicking

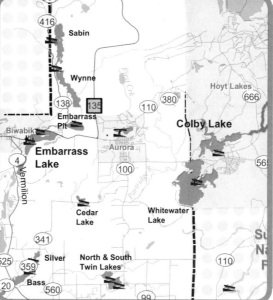

COLBY LAKE
St. Louis County

Area map pg / coord: 20 / B-3

Watershed: St. Louis

Surface area: 518 acres

Shorelength: 10.2 miles

Max / mean depth: 30 feet / 14 feet

Water color / clarity: 3.0 ft. (2010)

Shoreland zoning class: Nat. envt.

Mgmt class / Ecological type: Walleye-centrarchid / centrarchid-walleye

Accessibility: City-owned public access with double concrete ramp on south shore
47° 31' 20.10" N / 92° 9' 6.84" W

Accommodations: Camping

FISH STOCKING DATA

year	species	size	# released
08	Walleye	Fingerling	4,119
10	Walleye	Fingerling	3,672

NET CATCH DATA

Date: 08/27/2007

	Gill Nets		Trap Nets	
species	# per net	avg. fish weight (lbs.)	# per net	avg. fish weight (lbs.)
Black Crappie	0.7	0.22	3.0	0.48
Bluegill	2.3	0.38	7.1	0.29
Largemouth Bass	-	-	0.1	0.06
Northern Pike	5.4	1.25	1.1	1.48
Pumpkin. Sunfish	0.1	0.07	0.6	0.18
Walleye	5.9	0.79	0.7	0.64
Yellow Perch	1.6	0.47	0.4	0.59

LENGTH OF SELECTED SPECIES SAMPLED FROM ALL GEAR

Number of fish caught for the following length categories (inches):

species	0-5	6-8	9-11	12-14	15-19	20-24	25-29	>29	Total
Black Crappie	-	19	49	3	-	-	-	-	71
Bluegill	24	54	7	-	-	-	-	-	85
Largemouth Bass	1	-	-	-	-	-	-	-	1
Northern Pike	-	-	-	4	45	8	2	-	59
Pumpkin. Sunfish	4	2	-	-	-	-	-	-	6
Rock Bass	4	4	2	-	-	-	-	-	10
Walleye	-	12	18	12	15	2	-	-	59
Yellow Perch	1	3	13	1	-	-	-	-	18

NO RECORD OF STOCKING SINCE 1991

NET CATCH DATA

Date: 07/12/2010

	Gill Nets		Trap Nets	
species	# per net	avg. fish weight (lbs.)	# per net	avg. fish weight (lbs.)
Black Crappie	2.44	0.22	4.56	0.20
Bluegill	0.56	0.16	6.78	0.13
Channel Catfish	1.78	3.23	3.11	2.63
Hybrid Sunfish	-	-	0.11	0.46
Northern Pike	-	-	1.00	3.25
Rock Bass	-	-	0.11	0.09
Walleye	0.33	2.44	-	-
Yellow Perch	11.22	0.09	-	-

LENGTH OF SELECTED SPECIES SAMPLED FROM ALL GEAR

Number of fish caught for the following length categories (inches):

species	0-5	6-8	9-11	12-14	15-19	20-24	25-29	>29	Total
Black Crappie	4	54	3	-	-	-	-	-	63
Bluegill	42	22	-	-	-	-	-	-	66
Channel Catfish	-	-	1	1	19	20	3	-	44
Hybrid Sunfish	-	1	-	-	-	-	-	-	1
Northern Pike	-	-	-	-	1	11	8	2	22
Rock Bass	1	-	-	-	-	-	-	-	1
Walleye	-	-	1	-	1	1	-	-	3
White Sucker	-	1	6	5	8	2	-	-	23
Yellow Perch	71	27	1	-	-	-	-	-	101

FISHING INFORMATION

Embarrass Lake is located about one mile east of Biwabik. This shallow lake (less than 20 feet maximum) should suffer winterkill, but it is on the Embarrass River chain, and the moving water maintains sufficient oxygen to keep fish alive and well. Small, bog stained and close to town, this isn't one of the idyllic northern Minnesota lakes, but it does offer good fishing for smallish walleyes and northern pike, along with panfish of reasonable size. As a bonus, there also are some nice catfish to be had, says Doug Ellis, owner of Virginia Surplus Store, 105 3rd Ave., Virginia, MN, 218-741-0331. The shorelines are heavily weeded, and that's where you'll find crappies and bluegills. Local anglers take them with small minnows, worms or leeches under a slip bobber. It may take awhile, but eventually most fishermen find a school of one of these species and do reasonably well. The DNR keeps the lake well-stocked with walleye fingerlings and fry that show a good survival rate. In spring, says Ellis, fish for them in the sand and gravel around the public beach on the north side and around the railroad causeway, tossing small minnows. Later, fish the two points across from each other on the north and south shores at mid-lake and around Bradley Island in the east bay. Anglers fishing at night during summer use spinners or a Rapala in these areas with success. Walleyes are not large, but there are plenty of the 1.5- to 2-pounders available. There are also a fair number of northern pike. Use spinnerbaits, spoons, or crankbaits to take them. Be aware that Embarrass is very close to town and is often busy with swimmers and recreational boaters. Try to fish during weekdays to avoid the crowds. It's also a fine night-fishing lake. Public access is on the west side, off State 135. There's a concrete ramp.

Colby Lake has a solid population of northern pike, walleyes, bluegill, yellow perch and some largemouth bass. Look for walleyes near the island on the west side of the lake during summer months. You can also find them on the points. If you're after northern pike, bass or bluegills, fish the lily pads.

Biwabik

135

4

110

110

Embarrass Lake

Partridge River

Bradley Island

92° 10' 00"

47° 32' 30"

92° 09' 30"

Power Plant

Smolich Island

47° 31' 00"

92° 09' 00"

47° 32' 00"

Little Lake

47° 31' 30"

92° 08' 30"

Colby Lake

92° 08' 00"

N

92° 07' 30"

Partridge River

NOT FOR NAVIGATION

Source: Minnesota Department of Natural Resources, USGS

WHITEWATER LAKE St. Louis County

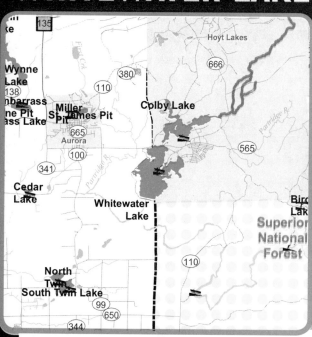

Area map page / coordinates:	20 / B-3
Watershed:	St. Louis
Surface water area / shorelength:	1,212 acres / 13.1 miles
Maximum / mean depth:	73 feet / 30 feet
Water color / clarity:	Green tint / 25.0 feet (2007)
Shoreland zoning classification:	Natural environment
Management class / Ecological type:	Walleye-centrarchid / centrarchid-walleye
Accessibility:	Three concrete ramps at Fishermans Point Campground on northeast shore
	47° 30' 18.19" N / 92° 10' 18.31" W
Accommodations:	Fishing pier, camping, picnicking, restrooms

FISHING INFORMATION

Whitewater is well known for producing good numbers of walleyes, including some specimens up to 12 pounds. According to local anglers, it also has some really nice crappies and bluegills and quite decent largemouth bass, some of which weigh as much as 5 pounds. In addition, there's the possibility of a large northern pike, though most are of the smaller "hammer handle" variety.

The lake was impounded in 1955 for use as a water storage reservoir for Erie Mining. Whitewater was formerly known as Partridge Lake. The inlet and outlet controls are now owned by Minnesota Power. Water losses due to groundwater seepage are substantial. The lake receives sewage treatment effluents from Hoyt Lakes.

The flats on the lake's southern end are where you'll find walleyes in summer. Troll with a crankbait or use live bait rigs or jigs tipped with a nightcrawler or leech. Walleyes were not in the lake when it was first investigated by the DNR in 1950. However, starting in 1956 through 1984 walleyes were stocked periodically. During the last DNR survey, the walleye population fell within the normal range. The average walleye sampled measured 13.5 inches long and weighed 1.15 pounds. The largest walleye captured measured 23.3 inches long. The overall growth rate was slower than normal by area standards.

You'll find northern pike at weedlines in the south end and in weeds near the sewage treatment plant in spring and summer. It's hard to go wrong firing out a flashy lure like a spinnerbait, jerkbait or lipless crankbait along weed edges. Northern pike numbers were higher than average during the last DNR survey. The average pike size was below normal, just 19.7 inches and 1.9 pounds. Even though the average pike isn't huge, the survey size was larger than the lakes historic average which has been 18.1 inches. The largest pike sampled measured 41.5 inches long.

Crappies will usually suspend off weedlines toward the north end in summer and around the big island near the public access site in winter. Crappie numbers were well below normal during the last DNR survey.

Yellow perch numbers were above average during the last DNR survey. Their numbers were high, but the overall size was pretty small. The average perch measured only 6.7 inches and weighed a light .15 pounds. The largest perch sampled measured 11.2 inches.

Panfish are also abundant on Whitewater. Bluegills, pumpkinseed and rock bass are all available. To catch any of these, fish weed edges with a slip bobber and a chunk of nightcrawler or a small leech. This method is very basic, but it is a tried and true method for catching panfish. Rock bass numbers were well above the average for the area. Their overall size fell into the average range.

A few of the gamefish sampled were infected with the parasite neascus (black spot). Some of the yellow perch were infected with yellow grub. Neither of these parasites can infect humans.

NO RECORD OF STOCKING

NET CATCH DATA

Date: 08/13/2007	Gill Nets		Trap Nets	
species	# per net	avg. fish weight (lbs.)	# per net	avg. fish weight (lbs.)
Black Bullhead	-	-	-	-
Black Crappie	1.6	0.18	-	-
Bluegill	9.2	0.15	-	-
Largemouth Bass	0.8	0.67	-	-
Northern Pike	5.3	2.84	-	-
Pumpkin. Sunfish	0.8	0.07	-	-
Rock Bass	5.3	0.19	-	-
Walleye	12.0	1.57	-	-
White Sucker	1.2	1.23	-	-
Yellow Perch	17.8	0.19	-	-

LENGTH OF SELECTED SPECIES SAMPLED FROM ALL GEAR

Number of fish caught for the following length categories (inches):

species	0-5	6-8	9-11	12-14	15-19	20-24	25-29	>30	Total
Black Bullhead	-	-	-	-	-	-	-	-	-
Black Crappie	11	4	4	-	-	-	-	-	19
Bluegill	59	51	-	-	-	-	-	-	110
Largemouth Bass	1	2	5	2	-	-	-	-	10
Northern Pike	-	-	3	4	14	26	11	6	64
Pumpkin. Sunfish	9	-	-	-	-	-	-	-	9
Rock Bass	28	35	-	-	-	-	-	-	63
Walleye	-	19	22	41	35	22	5	-	144
Yellow Perch	20	181	13	-	-	-	-	-	214

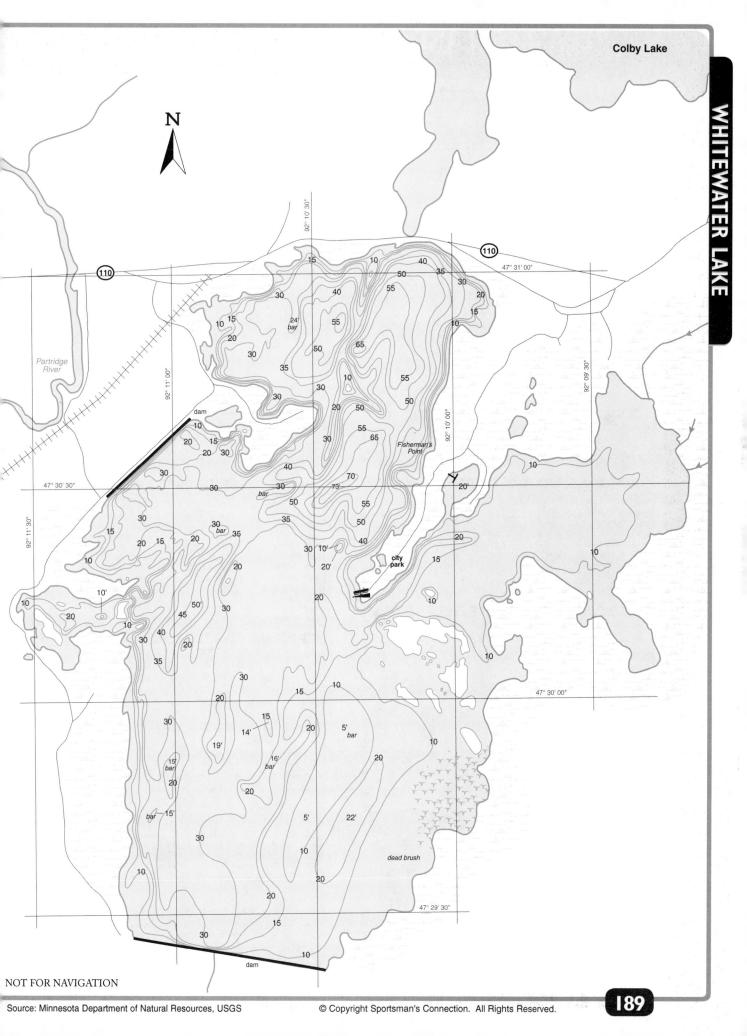

N

Partridge River

dam

Fisherman's Point

city park

bar
24' bar

dead brush

dam

92° 10' 30"
92° 11' 00"
92° 11' 30"
92° 10' 00"
92° 09' 30"

47° 31' 00"
47° 30' 30"
47° 30' 00"
47° 29' 30"

110

NOT FOR NAVIGATION

PLEASANT LAKE
St. Louis County

Area map pg / coord: 19 / D-6

Watershed: St. Louis

Surface area: 345 acres

Shorelength: 5.3 miles

Max / mean depth: 33 feet / 16 feet

Water color / clarity: Brown tint / 12.0 feet (2003)

Shoreland zoning class: Rec. dev.

Mgmt class / Ecological type: Walleye-centrarchid/centrarchid-walleye

Accessibility: State-owned public access with concrete ramp on north shore
47° 23' 54.42" N / 92° 28' 46.22" W

Accommodations: Private campground

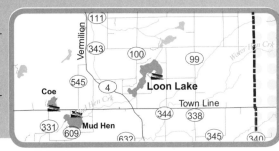

FISH STOCKING DATA

year	species	size	# released
05	Walleye	Fingerling	2,430
07	Walleye	Fingerling	2,055
09	Walleye	Fingerling	1,840

NET CATCH DATA

Date: 07/21/2003

	Gill Nets		Trap Nets	
species	# per net	avg. fish weight (lbs.)	# per net	avg. fish weight (lbs.)
Black Crappie	14.7	0.14	4.6	0.15
Bluegill	2.7	0.06	28.6	0.10
Largemouth Bass	0.7	1.99	1.0	0.66
Northern Pike	6.3	3.31	0.6	2.84
Pumpkin. Sunfish	0.1	0.21	2.6	0.11
Rock Bass	0.6	0.26	1.0	0.38
Walleye	0.7	1.49	-	-
Yellow Perch	1.0	0.10	0.1	0.10

LENGTH OF SELECTED SPECIES SAMPLED FROM ALL GEAR

Number of fish caught for the following length categories (inches):

species	0-5	6-8	9-11	12-14	15-19	20-24	25-29	>29	Total
Black Crappie	62	110	1	-	-	-	-	-	173
Bluegill	186	29	-	-	-	-	-	-	215
Brown Bullhead	-	-	3	2	-	-	-	-	5
Largemouth Bass	3	4	1	3	4	-	-	-	15
Northern Pike	-	-	-	-	8	30	22	2	62
Pumpkin. Sunfish	19	5	-	-	-	-	-	-	24
Rock Bass	3	11	-	-	-	-	-	-	14
Walleye	-	-	1	2	2	1	-	-	6
Yellow Bullhead	-	-	1	1	-	-	-	-	2
Yellow Perch	2	8	-	-	-	-	-	-	10

FISHING INFORMATION

Pleasant is a 345-acre lake, entirely surrounded by private property. There are three inlets; two drain local swamps and the third one is from Warren Lake. The local beaver population set up a housing project here, which inhibits fish movement. According to the DNR's last survey, pike averaged 23.7 inches and 3.3 pounds. Bluegill numbers are also high here, although they are not monsters, averaging 5.1 inches and .1 pounds. Crappies also have large quantities and relatively small size. Walleye numbers are low, but are of a decent size weighing 1.5 pounds and measuring 15.7 inches.

Loon is small, but deep. It has 271 acres and reaches 85 feet deep. The DNR's last assessment showed bluegill, yellow perch and northern pike as the dominant species. Walleyes, crappies, largemouth bass, bullhead, white

---

LOON LAKE
St. Louis County

Area map pg / coord: 20 / D-2

Watershed: St. Louis

Surface area: 271 acres

Shorelength: 5.1 miles

Max / mean depth: 85 feet / NA

Water color / clarity: Clear / 23.0 feet (2009)

Shoreland zoning class: NA

Mgmt class / Ecological type: Walleye-centrarchid / centrarchid-walleye

Accessibility: Township-owned public access with gravel ramp on south shore of eastern lobe
47° 23' 13.73" N / 92° 14' 46.22" W

Accommodations: None

FISH STOCKING DATA

year	species	size	# released
06	Walleye	Fingerling	2,540
08	Walleye	Fingerling	730
10	Walleye	Fingerling	1,260

NET CATCH DATA

Date: 07/13/2009

	Gill Nets		Trap Nets	
species	# per net	avg. fish weight (lbs.)	# per net	avg. fish weight (lbs.)
Black Crappie	4.67	0.32	1.11	0.38
Bluegill	11.83	0.12	49.22	0.18
Brown Bullhead	0.17	0.92	0.11	1.07
Hybrid Sunfish	-	-	2.67	0.35
Largemouth Bass	0.67	0.88	0.44	0.16
Northern Pike	5.50	2.38	0.78	1.80
Pumpkin. Sunfish	1.00	0.09	1.89	0.15
Rock Bass	-	-	2.56	0.15
Walleye	0.67	1.41	0.33	1.94
Yellow Perch	7.50	0.10	0.33	0.23

LENGTH OF SELECTED SPECIES SAMPLED FROM ALL GEAR

Number of fish caught for the following length categories (inches):

species	0-5	6-8	9-11	12-14	15-19	20-24	25-29	>29	Total
Black Bullhead	-	-	1	-	-	-	-	-	1
Black Crappie	4	18	16	-	-	-	-	-	38
Bluegill	207	301	-	-	-	-	-	-	514
Brown Bullhead	-	-	1	1	-	-	-	-	2
Hybrid Sunfish	1	23	-	-	-	-	-	-	24
Largemouth Bass	1	4	-	3	-	-	-	-	8
Northern Pike	-	-	1	1	16	13	8	1	40
Pumpkin. Sunfish	18	5	-	-	-	-	-	-	23
Rock Bass	12	11	-	-	-	-	-	-	23
Walleye	-	-	1	4	-	2	-	-	7
White Sucker	-	-	1	4	6	2	-	-	13
Yellow Perch	24	24	-	-	-	-	-	-	48

sucker and pumpkinseed were all present in fair numbers. The lake receives a modest stocking of walleye fingerlings in even-numbered years.

Both lakes' game fish populations were infected with neascus or yellow grub. These parasites pose no threat to humans and are killed during the cooking process. Mercury levels are moderately high in several species, with some falling into the no-more-than–one-meal-per-month category.

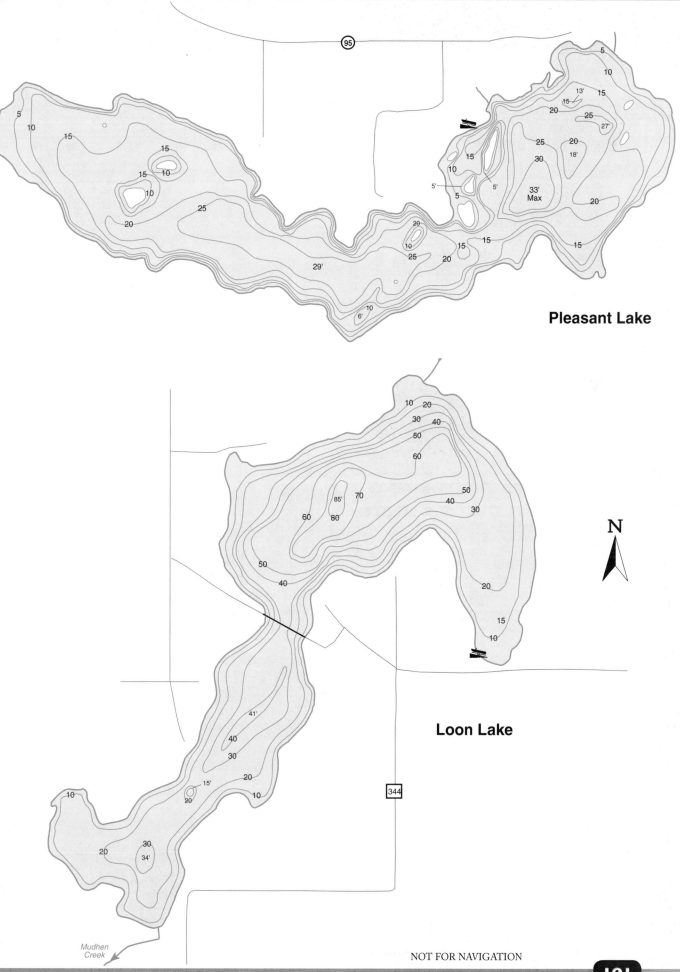

Pleasant Lake

Loon Lake

N

Mudhen
Creek

NOT FOR NAVIGATION

Source: Minnesota Department of Natural Resources, USGS

SABIN LAKE
St. Louis County

Sabin Lake

Superior National Forest

Wynne Lake

Embarrass Mine Pit

Miller Pit

St. James Pit

Biwabik

Embarrass Lake

Aurora

Area map page / coordinates: 20 / A-2

Watershed: St. Louis

Surface water area / shorelength: 314 acres / NA

Maximum / mean depth: 40 feet / NA

Water color / clarity: Brown stain / 5.0 feet (2006)

Accessibility: Public access with concrete ramp on west shore; 47° 35' 24.62" N / 92° 18' 12.94" W

Accommodations: Located in Superior National Forest, camping, picnicking, restrooms

NO RECORD OF STOCKING

LENGTH OF SELECTED SPECIES SAMPLED FROM ALL GEAR
Survey Date: 08/14/2006

Number of fish caught for the following length categories (inches):

species	0-5	6-8	9-11	12-14	15-19	20-24	25-29	>29	Total
Black Crappie	9	3	20	-	-	-	-	-	32
Bluegill	13	55	1	-	-	-	-	-	69
Channel Catfish	-	-	-	-	-	-	-	1	1
Golden Shiner	1	-	-	-	-	-	-	-	1
Northern Pike	-	-	1	6	21	9	1	-	40
Rock Bass	-	7	-	-	-	-	-	-	7
Tullibee (Cisco)	-	2	-	-	-	-	-	-	2
Walleye	-	5	24	18	10	2	-	-	59
White Sucker	-	1	1	16	59	1	-	-	78
Yellow Perch	41	49	13	-	-	-	-	-	104

FISHING INFORMATION

These Aurora-area lakes aren't really two separate bodies of water. Sabin (aka North Wynne) and Wynne are actually two bays of the same lake separated by a narrow neck which is quite navigable, both to fish and to those who fish for them. This isn't pristine, northern Minnesota water, like you would expect. It's dark, the color of tea, and moderately turbid; visibility is between 2 and 3 feet. This is not heavily used water. Recreation and fishing pressure both are light; the lake is mainly fished by locals. Both access sites are pretty good; you can get an 18-footer into the lake(s) without much trouble.

The Embarrass River flows through both lakes and directly effects the oxygen levels in the lakes. During times of heavier flowage, oxygen levels run deeper. Because of this, Sabin can see sustainable oxygen levels as shallow as 16 feet and as deep as 26 feet. Wynne's oxygen levels can vary from 28 feet to 45 feet. Fish move between the lakes, except when water levels are too low to allow navigation.

Cont'd on page 193

Source: Minnesota Department of Natural Resources, USGS

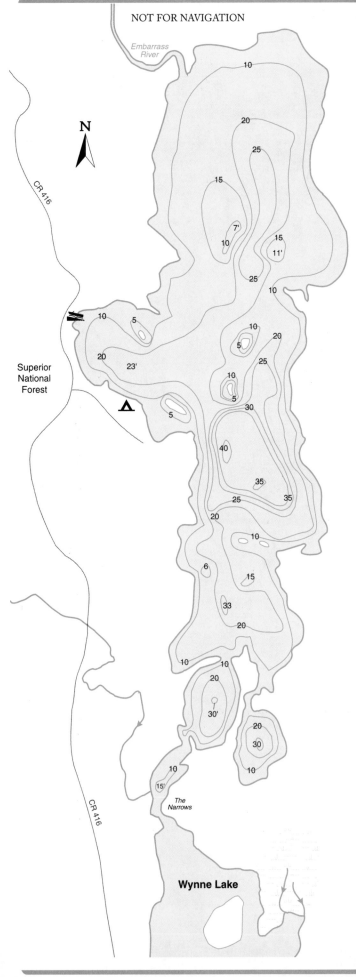

NOT FOR NAVIGATION

Embarrass River

N

CR 416

Superior National Forest

The Narrows

Wynne Lake

WYNNE LAKE
St. Louis County

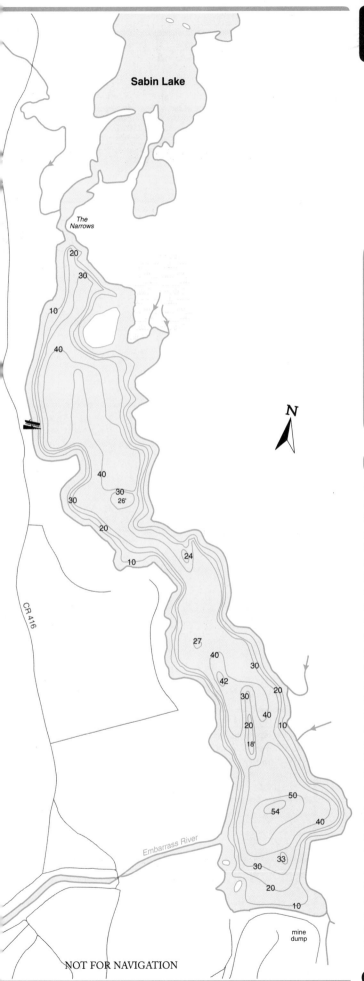

Sabin Lake

The Narrows

N

CR 416

Embarrass River

mine dump

NOT FOR NAVIGATION

Area map page / coordinates:	20 / A,B-2
Watershed:	St. Louis
Surface water area / shorelength:	278 acres / 5.4 miles
Maximum / mean depth:	54 feet / NA
Water color / clarity:	Brown stain / 6.0 feet (2006)
Accessibility:	State-owned public access with concrete ramp on west shore, mid-lake; 47° 34' 24.31" N / 92° 17' 57.10" W
Accommodations:	Located in Superior National Forest

NO RECORD OF STOCKING

LENGTH OF SELECTED SPECIES SAMPLED FROM ALL GEAR
Survey Date: 08/07/2006

Number of fish caught for the following length categories (inches):

species	0-5	6-8	9-11	12-14	15-19	20-24	25-29	>29	Total
Black Crappie	-	-	12	2	-	-	-	-	14
Bluegill	3	20	-	-	-	-	-	-	23
Northern Pike	-	-	2	2	9	4	-	-	17
Rock Bass	2	15	2	-	-	-	-	-	19
Tullibee (Cisco)	-	13	6	-	-	-	-	-	19
Walleye	-	5	12	4	3	3	-	-	27
White Sucker	-	-	2	4	9	-	-	-	15
Yellow Bullhead	-	1	1	-	-	-	-	-	2
Yellow Perch	10	10	3	-	-	-	-	-	23

FISHING INFORMATION

You'll find excellent numbers of walleyes in this double-basin lake, although the average size is nothing to write home about. Both lakes' walleyes averaged 11 inches in the last DNR survey, so focus your tales on quantity and you won't be telling any whoppers. Abundance was in the normal range for Wynne and above normal in Sabin. Growth rates were slow in both basins. For walleyes, the north end and the narrows produce early. Later, you'll want to troll the reefs and the first breaklines, paying particular attention to the 6- and 8-foot shallows on the west shore, just north of where the lake widens out. The 6-foot bar on the north end is a reliable producer, too, for walleyes and panfish, as well. For the former, live bait rigs or blue Rapalas seem to work best. Don't pass up on using spinner rigs and nightcrawlers if the walleyes are suspended off weedlines.

Northern pike, though about average in number, are a bit on the small side. The last DNR survey showed both basins to be fairly equal with their pike populations, although Wynne's pike seemed to grow slightly faster. The average 4-year-old on Sabin was 17 inches compared to Wynne's 19 inches. Even with this small-ish sized survey numbers, locals say anglers catch a few big ones every year. They claim a 10-pounder is not beyond the realm of possibility. In spring, look for pike in the north end, near the Embarrass River inlet; later, try weedlines in the bays with Silver Minnows or spinnerbaits. If the pike bite is tough, switch to a slip bobber and large minnow.

Nice-sized bluegills are found here, averaging 7.4- to 8-inches. The largest one caught in the DNR survey was 9.3 inches on Wynne and 9 inches on Sabin, both of which are respectable sizes. Growth rates were fast. Crawlers and small leeches do just fine for the panfish. Look for them in the shallow weeds in spring. Larger bluegills will move to deeper weedlines during summer months.

An occasional decent largemouth bass is taken, too, but that's the exception, rather than the rule. The area around the narrows is the most reliable fish-producer. Local anglers troll or drift chubs there much of the season. A topwater plug worked along shoreline cover both early and late in the day can produce a fish or two during summer months. Try a Carolina- or Texas-rigged soft plastic bait during midday to coax a summertime largemouth into biting.

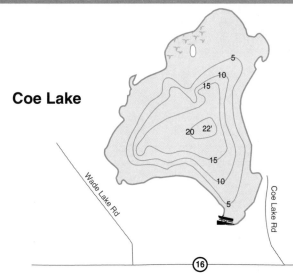

Coe Lake

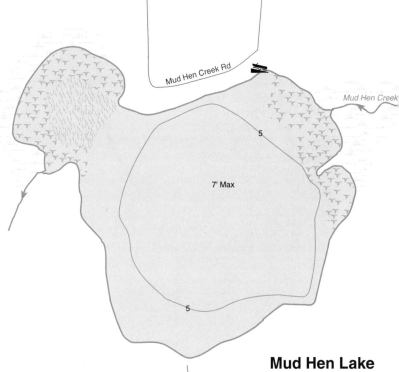

Coe Lake, St. Louis County

Area map page / coordinates: 20 / D-2
Surface area / shorelength: 55 acres / NA
Accessibility: Earth ramp public access to south shore
47° 22' 21.30" N / 92° 19' 16.99" W

LENGTH OF SELECTED SPECIES SAMPLED FROM ALL GEAR
Survey Date: 07/07/2008
Number of fish caught for the following length categories (inches):

species	0-5	6-8	9-11	12-14	15-19	20-24	25-29	>30	Total
Black Crappie	-	5	1	-	-	-	-	-	6
Bluegill	104	708	7	-	-	-	-	-	826
Largemouth Bass	-	7	4	5	-	-	-	-	16
Northern Pike	-	-	-	-	-	-	1	-	1
Walleye	-	-	-	-	-	1	-	-	1
Yellow Perch	2	24	2	-	-	-	-	-	28

Mud Hen Lake, St. Louis County

Area map page / coordinates: 20 / D-2
Surface area / shorelength: 161 acres / NA
Accessibility: State-owned public access with gravel ramp
on north shore, off County Road 16
47° 22' 10.49" N / 92° 18' 17.47" W

FISH STOCKING DATA

year	species	size	# released
08	Walleye	Fry	164,000
10	Walleye	Fry	165,000

LENGTH OF SELECTED SPECIES SAMPLED FROM ALL GEAR
Survey Date: 09/02/2008
Number of fish caught for the following length categories (inches):

species	0-5	6-8	9-11	12-14	15-19	20-24	25-29	>30	Total
Black Bullhead	-	4	11	-	-	-	-	-	15
Black Crappie	-	53	9	-	-	-	-	-	62
Bluegill	2	1	-	-	-	-	-	-	3
Northern Pike	-	2	-	-	22	44	9	2	79
Walleye	-	-	1	-	-	-	-	-	1
White Sucker	-	-	-	-	22	8	-	-	30
Yellow Bullhead	1	27	60	10	-	-	-	-	98
Yellow Perch	128	74	5	-	-	-	-	-	212

Mud Hen Lake

Section 14 (Leisure) Lake, St. Louis County

Area map page / coordinates: 20 / E-2
Surface area / shorelength: 140 acres / 3.3 miles
Accessibility: State-owned public access with concrete ramp
on southern tip, off Leisure Lake Road
47° 19' 25.88" N / 92° 19' 52.45" W

FISH STOCKING DATA

year	species	size	# released
04	Walleye	Fingerling	2,248
05	Walleye	Fingerling	3,000
09	Walleye	Fry	109,999

LENGTH OF SELECTED SPECIES SAMPLED FROM ALL GEAR
Survey Date: 08/25/2003
Number of fish caught for the following length categories (inches):

species	0-5	6-8	9-11	12-14	15-19	20-24	25-29	>30	Total
Black Crappie	16	16	10	1	-	-	-	-	43
Bluegill	17	96	2	-	-	-	-	-	115
Northern Pike	-	-	-	1	27	8	1	-	37
Pumpkin. Sunfish	-	19	1	-	-	-	-	-	20
Walleye	-	-	-	-	5	2	-	-	7

Section 14 Lake

NOT FOR NAVIGATION

Source: Minnesota Department of Natural Resources, USGS

Silver Lake, St. Louis County

Area map page / coordinates: 20 / C-2
Surface area / shorelength: 34 acres / 1.3 miles
Accessibility: Carry-down public access to southwest corner
47° 27' 31.27" N / 92° 19' 15.95" W

LENGTH OF SELECTED SPECIES SAMPLED FROM ALL GEAR
Survey Date: 07/11/1983
Number of fish caught for the following length categories (inches):

species	0-5	6-8	9-11	12-14	15-19	20-24	25-29	>30	Total
Black Crappie	9	62	4	-	-	-	-	-	75
Bluegill	28	47	-	-	-	-	-	-	75
Largemouth Bass	3	4	5	2	1	-	-	-	15
Northern Pike	-	-	-	-	2	6	1	-	9
Rock Bass	3	4	-	-	-	-	-	-	7

Silver Lake

CR 525

N

CR 359

CR 337

(4)

Bass Lake

Bass Lake, St. Louis County

Area map page / coordinates: 20 / C-2
Surface area / shorelength: 149 acres / 3.0 miles
Accessibility: State-owned public access with concrete ramp
on northeast shore, on E. Raymond Road off Farber Road
47° 27' 9.53" N / 92° 19' 25.74" W

FISH STOCKING DATA

year	species	size	# released
08	Walleye	Fingerling	449
10	Walleye	Fingerling	918

LENGTH OF SELECTED SPECIES SAMPLED FROM ALL GEAR
Survey Date: 06/14/2010
Number of fish caught for the following length categories (inches):

species	0-5	6-8	9-11	12-14	15-19	20-24	25-29	>30	Total
Black Crappie	3	16	6	-	-	-	-	-	25
Bluegill	766	232	-	-	-	-	-	-	1004
Brown Bullhead	-	2	14	4	-	-	-	-	20
Hybrid Sunfish	1	2	-	-	-	-	-	-	3
Largemouth Bass	2	10	-	2	-	-	-	-	14
Northern Pike	-	-	-	-	31	17	4	3	55
Pumpkin. Sunfish	12	17	-	-	-	-	-	-	29
Rock Bass	4	3	-	-	-	-	-	-	7
Walleye	-	-	-	1	-	4	1	-	6
White Sucker	-	-	-	-	2	2	-	-	4
Yellow Perch	-	3	-	-	-	-	-	-	3

Lost Lake, St. Louis County

Area map page / coordinates: 20 / C-1,2
Surface area / shorelength: 107 acres / NA
Accessibility: State-owned public access with gravel ramp
on southwest shore, off County Road 334
47° 25' 46.85" N / 92° 22' 9.21" W

LENGTH OF SELECTED SPECIES SAMPLED FROM ALL GEAR
Survey Date: 06/28/1999
Number of fish caught for the following length categories (inches):

species	0-5	6-8	9-11	12-14	15-19	20-24	25-29	>30	Total
Black Crappie	12	38	4	-	-	-	-	-	54
Bluegill	227	20	-	-	-	-	-	-	247
Largemouth Bass	10	15	-	2	1	-	-	-	28
Northern Pike	-	-	3	2	7	21	3	-	36
Pumpkin. Sunfish	47	4	-	-	-	-	-	-	51
Walleye	-	-	-	-	1	-	-	-	1
Yellow Perch	24	8	-	-	-	-	-	-	32

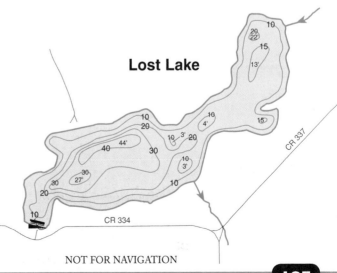

Lost Lake

CR 337

CR 334

NOT FOR NAVIGATION

195

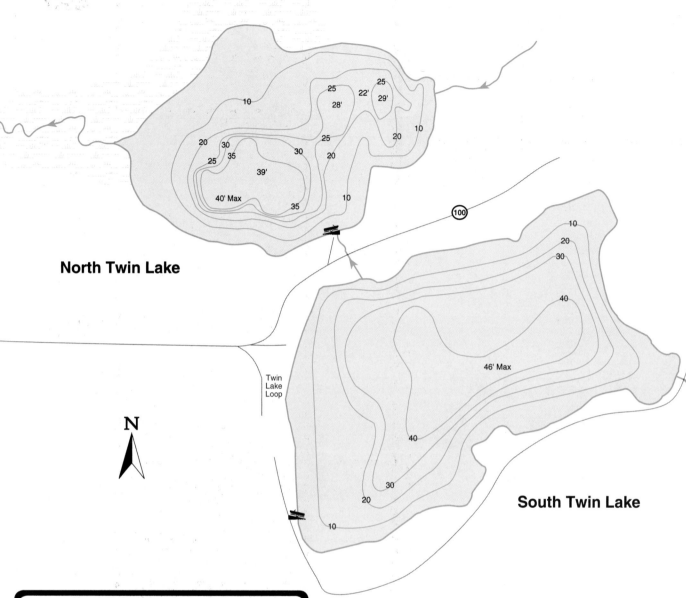

North Twin Lake

South Twin Lake

N

NOT FOR NAVIGATION

North Twin Lake, St. Louis County

Area map page / coordinates: 20 / C-2
Surface area / shorelength: 64 acres / NA
Accessibility: Township-owned public access with gravel ramp on south shore, off County Road 100
47° 26' 50.57" N / 92° 15' 4.45" W

FISH STOCKING DATA

year	species	size	# released
07	Walleye	Fingerling	932
09	Walleye	Fingerling	1,669

LENGTH OF SELECTED SPECIES SAMPLED FROM ALL GEAR
Survey Date: 06/26/2006
Number of fish caught for the following length categories (inches):

species	0-5	6-8	9-11	12-14	15-19	20-24	25-29	>30	Total
Black Bullhead	-	1	4	-	-	-	-	-	5
Black Crappie	-	34	32	-	-	-	-	-	66
Bluegill	19	39	1	-	-	-	-	-	59
Largemouth Bass	-	1	-	-	-	-	-	-	1
Northern Pike	-	1	2	4	8	5	3	-	23
Pumpkin. Sunfish	2	3	-	-	-	-	-	-	5
Walleye	-	1	1	3	7	1	1	-	14
Yellow Perch	16	20	1	-	-	-	-	-	37

South Twin Lake, St. Louis County

Area map page / coordinates: 20 / C-2
Surface area / shorelength: 106 acres / 1.9 miles
Accessibility: Township-owned public access with gravel ramp on south shore; 47° 26' 36.99" N / 92° 14' 34.36" W

FISH STOCKING DATA

year	species	size	# released
03	Walleye	Fingerling	641
05	Walleye	Fingerling	1,490
07	Walleye	Fingerling	1,260

LENGTH OF SELECTED SPECIES SAMPLED FROM ALL GEAR
Survey Date: 08/05/2003
Number of fish caught for the following length categories (inches):

species	0-5	6-8	9-11	12-14	15-19	20-24	25-29	>30	Total
Black Crappie	3	12	47	1	-	-	-	-	63
Bluegill	6	12	2	-	-	-	-	-	20
Brown Bullhead	-	3	2	-	-	-	-	-	5
Northern Pike	-	-	-	3	10	17	1	2	33
Walleye	-	1	4	13	-	1	-	-	19
Yellow Perch	11	33	-	-	-	-	-	-	44

Miller Pit, St. Louis County

Area map page / coordinates: 20 / B-2
Surface area / shorelength: 17 acres / NA
Accessibility: Carry-down access (50 yard portage) from parking area in Aurora to east shore of pit
47° 32' 4.87" N / 92° 14' 29.22" W

LENGTH OF SELECTED SPECIES SAMPLED FROM ALL GEAR
Survey Date: 06/25/1990
Number of fish caught for the following length categories (inches):

species	0-5	6-8	9-11	12-14	15-19	20-24	25-29	>30	Total
Bluegill	1	1	-	-	-	-	-	-	2

St. James Pit

First Creek

Miller Pit

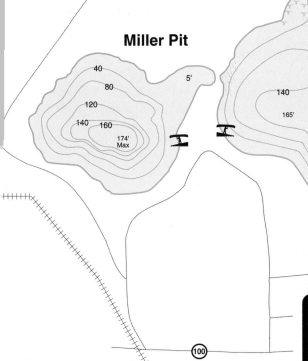

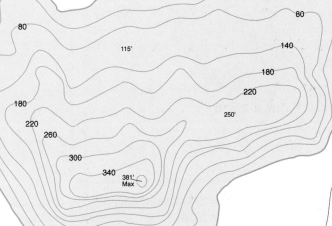

St. James Pit, St. Louis County

Area map page / coordinates: 20 / B-2
Surface area / shorelength: 100 acres / NA
Accessibility: Carry-down access (100 yard portage) from parking area in Aurora to west shore –
47° 32' 5.07" N / 92° 14' 26.34" W

FISH STOCKING DATA

year	species	size	# released
08	Rainbow Trout	Yearling	2,100
09	Rainbow Trout	Yearling	1,050
10	Rainbow Trout	Yearling	2,100

LENGTH OF SELECTED SPECIES SAMPLED FROM ALL GEAR
Survey Date: 06/05/1995
Number of fish caught for the following length categories (inches):

species	0-5	6-8	9-11	12-14	15-19	20-24	25-29	>30	Total
Brook Trout	-	-	1	1	-	-	-	-	2
Rainbow Trout	-	-	2	-	-	-	-	-	2

N

Bird Lake, St. Louis County

Area map page / coordinates: 21 / B-4
Surface area / shorelength: 16 acres / NA
Accessibility: Carry-down access across federal land from Hwy. 569 to south shore
47° 29' 12.10" N / 92° 3' 27.35" W

LENGTH OF SELECTED SPECIES SAMPLED FROM ALL GEAR
Survey Date: 06/18/1985
Number of fish caught for the following length categories (inches):

species	0-5	6-8	9-11	12-14	15-19	20-24	25-29	>30	Total
Black Crappie	24	-	-	-	-	-	-	-	24
Bluegill	18	-	-	-	-	-	-	-	18
Northern Pike	-	-	-	-	-	3	3	-	6

Bird Lake

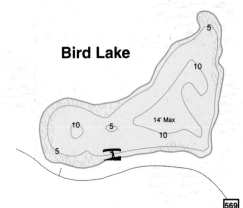

NOT FOR NAVIGATION

Source: Minnesota Department of Natural Resources, USGS

WHITEFACE RESERVOIR *St. Louis County*

Area map page / coordinates:	20 / E-3
Watershed:	St. Louis
Surface water area / shorelength:	4,567 acres / 51.4 miles
Maximum / mean depth:	33 feet / 10 feet
Water color / clarity:	Brown stain / 5.0 feet (2007)
Shoreland zoning classification:	Recreational development
Management class / Ecological type:	Walleye / hard-water walleye

Accessibility: 1) USFS-owned public access with gravel ramp on east shore o north peninsula separating middle and west basins, off County Road 265

47° 16' 56.62" N / 92° 11' 28.23" W

Accessibility: 2) Public access (owned by Minnesota Power) with concrete ramp on east shore of major south peninsula separating middle and east basins

47° 19' 40.36" N / 92° 8' 50.49" W

Accommodations: Camping

FISHING INFORMATION

Whiteface Reservoir is a walleye factory created when Minnesota Power dammed the Whiteface River to produce electric power. Whiteface doesn't get the pressure that Island Lake receives from area anglers, since it is a good 15 to 20 minutes farther up the road. However, one of the state's most scenic campgrounds lies on the lake's north shore, and this attracts tourists from all around the state and points beyond. During summertime highs, the reservoir spreads out over 5,000 acres, much of which is flooded forest. Lots of space and low fishing pressure gives fish and anglers plenty of elbow room.

Whiteface produces walleyes in several year classes with a typical fish running between 1- and 2-pounds. Anglers who know the lake, though, can find 2- to 3-pound walleyes with some regularity, and there's potential for bigger ones. Walleyes are fairly abundant here, with a mean length of 12.8 inches, which is slow compared to other Duluth area lakes. A total of 9 year classes were represented in the last DNR survey, with 1998 and 1999 being the strongest. The folks at Fisherman's Corner, 5675 Miller Trunk Highway, Hermantown, MN, 218-729-5369, suggest fishing jig-and-minnow combos around floating driftwood piles in bays. Don't be afraid to fish the shallows; you can sometimes catch walleyes down only 2 or 3 feet under driftwood. Whiteface's walleye population is healthy and provides some of the best walleye angling opportunities in the Duluth area.

Northern pike numbers are still below average, as they have been through the last 5 DNR investigations. Their size is average, with the mean length of 20.8 inches. Look for northern pike to hold in shallows early in the season. As the water warms, try steep drop-offs and points. Minnows, lipless crankbaits, jerkbaits and spinnerbaits are effective for taking pike.

Black crappies are slowly increasing in abundance and so are the angling opportunities for them. Catch rates were high and the average size is 9.8 inches. Shore anglers fare well on the dikes around the dam area, near the south end of the lake at the public access. If you have a yearning to chase crappies that run 2 pounds and more, try casting a minnow with no weight or bobber into the lily pads on a calm evening. You can try using a long spinning rod or even a canepole and present a small minnow or leech on a plain hook or tiny jig in the weeds. A vertical presentation is often the most productive for fooling crappies.

Bluegills fared well in the survey, too. Their abundance numbers are on the rise and the mean length was 7.3 inches. At the time of the survey, there

NO RECORD OF STOCKING				
NET CATCH DATA				
Date: 07/16/2007	Gill Nets		Trap Nets	
species	# per net	avg. fish weight (lbs.)	# per net	avg. fish weight (lbs.)
Black Crappie	1.3	0.25	2.9	0.44
Bluegill	0.3	0.55	2.9	0.45
Burbot	0.1	0.84	-	-
Northern Pike	1.2	1.58	0.8	3.84
Rock Bass	0.2	0.52	0.5	0.4
Walleye	9.6	0.60	1.8	0.96
White Sucker	2.7	2.12	0.4	2.58
Yellow Perch	1.6	0.41	0.4	0.32

LENGTH OF SELECTED SPECIES SAMPLED FROM ALL GEAR

Number of fish caught for the following length categories (inches):

species	0-5	6-8	9-11	12-14	15-19	20-24	25-29	>30	Total
Black Crappie	10	35	20	1	-	-	-	-	66
Bluegill	10	38	5	-	-	-	-	-	53
Northern Pike	-	-	1	2	18	7	2	2	32
Rock Bas	2	8	2	-	-	-	-	-	12
Walleye	1	40	59	48	21	-	1	-	170
Yellow Perch	5	11	13	1	-	-	-	-	30

were several specimens in the 8-inch-plus category. By now, there should be even more fish in that "preferred" size range. Use pieces of nightcrawler, or a small leech or wax worm to tempt bluegills. Shallow weeds are where you'll find many of them, but bigger bluegills will hold along deeper weed edges.

Four different access points are available in the lake. The gravel US Forest Service access site is located on the east side of the major north peninsula which separates the middle and west basins off County Road 628 at the Whiteface Reservoir Campground. A concrete public access, which is owned by Minnesota Power, is on the east side of the major south peninsula which separates the middle and east basins off County Road #265. An undeveloped back-in access is available for leased lots north of the USFS campground. Finally, an abandoned access is located on the west side of major peninsula on the south side off Cabin Circle Drive.

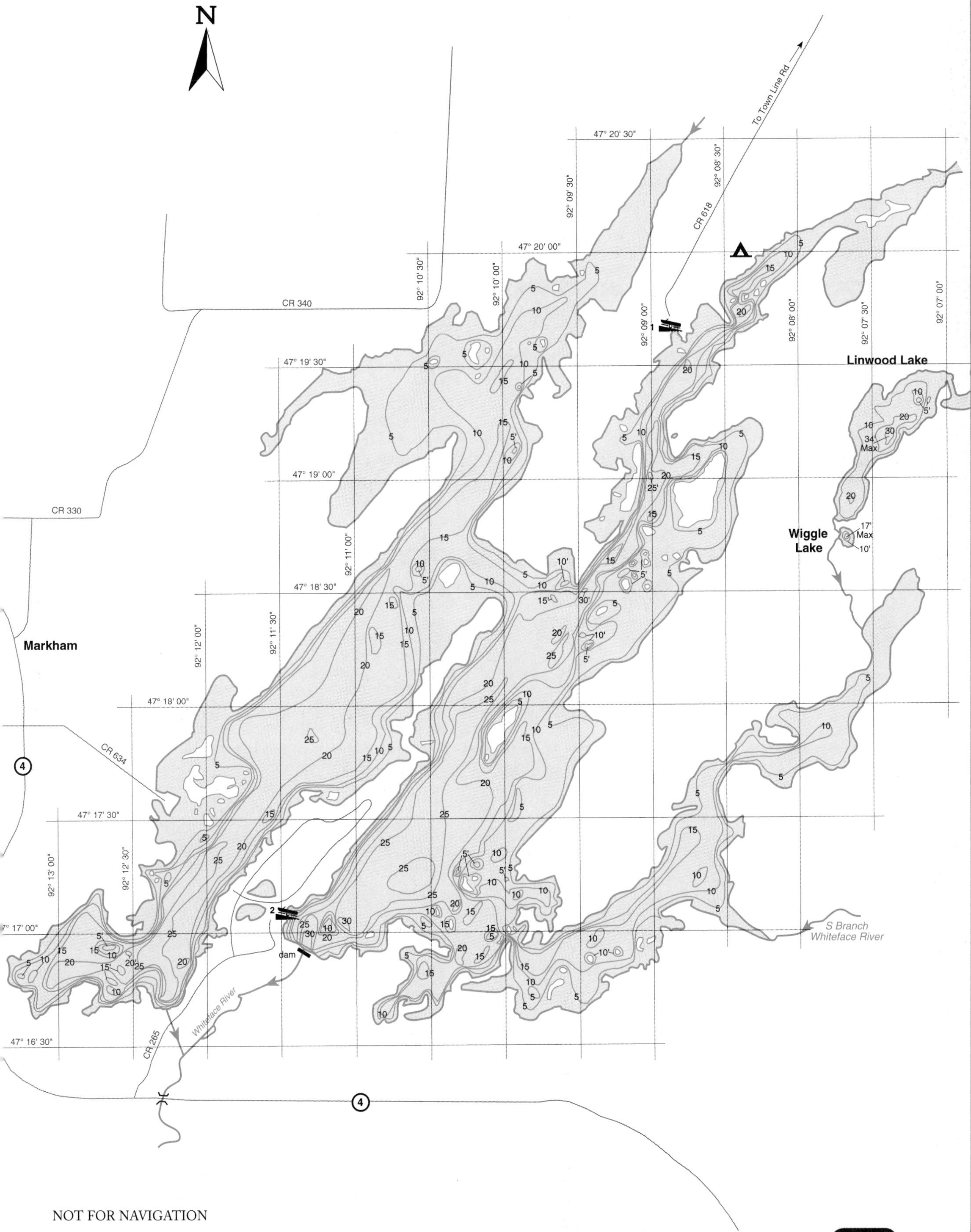

N

47° 20' 30"
47° 20' 00"
47° 19' 30"
47° 19' 00"
47° 18' 30"
47° 18' 00"
47° 17' 30"
47° 17' 00"
47° 16' 30"

92° 10' 30"
92° 10' 00"
92° 09' 30"
92° 09' 00"
92° 08' 30"
92° 08' 00"
92° 07' 30"
92° 07' 00"
92° 11' 00"
92° 11' 30"
92° 12' 00"
92° 12' 30"
92° 13' 00"

To Town Line Rd

CR 618
CR 340
CR 330
CR 634
CR 265

Markham

Linwood Lake

Wiggle Lake

34'
Max

17'
Max
10'

S Branch
Whiteface River

Whiteface River

dam

4

4

NOT FOR NAVIGATION

LINWOOD LAKE
St. Louis County

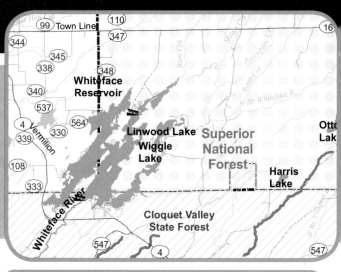

Area map page / coordinates: 20 / E-3

Watershed: St. Louis

Surface water area / shorelength: 251 acres / 3.8 miles

Maximum / mean depth: 34 feet / 9 feet

Water color / clarity: Light brown / 5.2 feet (1996)

Accessibility: Carry-down access across county or federal public land

Accommodations: None

FISH STOCKING DATA			
year	species	size	# released
99	Walleye	Fry	200,000
01	Walleye	Fry	200,000

LENGTH OF SELECTED SPECIES SAMPLED FROM ALL GEAR
Survey Date: 07/29/1996

Number of fish caught for the following length categories (inches):

species	0-5	6-8	9-11	12-14	15-19	20-24	25-29	>30	Total
Black Crappie	81	30	17	-	-	-	-	-	128
Bluegill	38	31	-	-	-	-	-	-	69
Northern Pike	-	-	1	2	14	12	4	2	35
Pumpkin. Sunfish	29	5	-	-	-	-	-	-	34
Walleye	-	-	1	7	9	6	3	-	26
Yellow Perch	4	4	-	-	-	-	-	-	8

FISHING INFORMATION

Linwood Lake can be tough to get into; the stream access from Whiteface is intermittent. However, federal and county land does abut the lake, so resourceful anglers who manage to drag in a canoe are rewarded with some pretty good action from this 251 acre lake.

Walleye fry were regularly stocked on this lake for about 20 years. According to the most recent DNR survey, walleye growth was better-than-average with four-year-olds reaching 14.9 inches. Size structure is excellent with 80% of the walleyes sampled measuring longer than 15 inches. Some natural reproduction is occurring on the lake.

Linwood Lake is best known for its panfish. Bluegills and crappies are abundant and decent-sized, with 46% of bluegills longer than 6 inches and 49% of crappies longer than 8 inches.

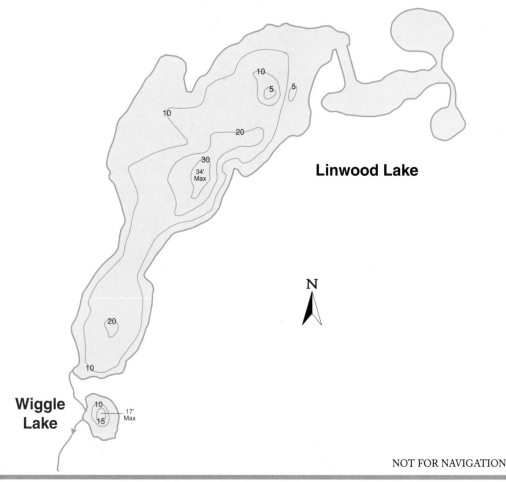

Linwood Lake

N

Wiggle Lake

NOT FOR NAVIGATION

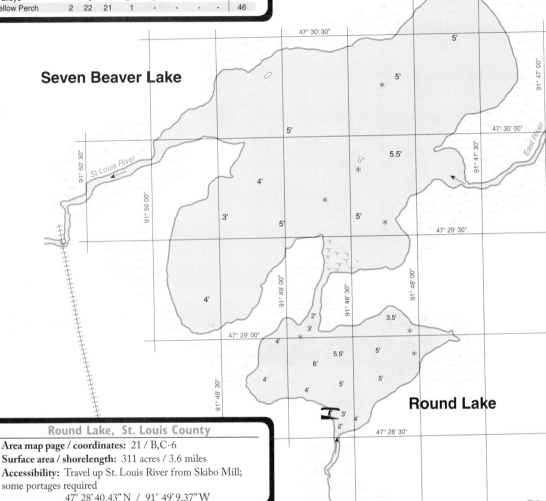

Seven Beaver Lake, St. Louis County

Area map page / coordinates: 21 / B,C-6
Surface area / shorelength: 1,410 acres / 8.8 miles
Accessibility: Travel up St. Louis River from Skibo Mill;
some portages required

LENGTH OF SELECTED SPECIES SAMPLED FROM ALL GEAR
Survey Date: 08/06/1986
Number of fish caught for the following length categories (inches):

species	0-5	6-8	9-11	12-14	15-19	20-24	25-29	>30	Total
Northern Pike	-	-	1	4	8	-	-	-	13
Walleye	-	3	1	21	5	-	-	-	30
Yellow Perch	2	22	21	1	-	-	-	-	46

Seven Beaver Lake

Round Lake

Pine Lake

N

Round Lake, St. Louis County

Area map page / coordinates: 21 / B,C-6
Surface area / shorelength: 311 acres / 3.6 miles
Accessibility: Travel up St. Louis River from Skibo Mill;
some portages required
47° 28' 40.43" N / 91° 49' 9.37" W

LENGTH OF SELECTED SPECIES SAMPLED FROM ALL GEAR
Survey Date: 08/06/1986
Number of fish caught for the following length categories (inches):

species	0-5	6-8	9-11	12-14	15-19	20-24	25-29	>30	Total
Black Bullhead	-	-	-	1	-	-	-	-	1
Northern Pike	-	-	-	2	3	-	-	-	5
Walleye	-	1	3	20	1	1	-	-	26
Yellow Perch	-	5	4	-	-	-	-	-	9

Pine Lake, St. Louis County

Area map page / coordinates: 21 / C-6
Surface area / shorelength: 450 acres / 3.9 miles
Accessibility: Carry-down access (100 yard portage) from
Hjalmer Lake Road (#419) to west shore
47° 27' 31.05" N / 91° 48' 6.73" W

LENGTH OF SELECTED SPECIES SAMPLED FROM ALL GEAR
Survey Date: 08/06/2007
Number of fish caught for the following length categories (inches):

species	0-5	6-8	9-11	12-14	15-19	20-24	25-29	>30	Total
Bluegill	499	132	4	-	-	-	-	-	635
Northern Pike	1	1	11	6	22	25	9	2	77
Pumpkin. Sunfish	121	34	-	-	-	-	-	-	155
Rock Bass	19	2	-	-	-	-	-	-	21
Walleye	-	6	5	5	23	8	3	-	50
Yellow Perch	38	106	7	-	-	-	-	-	151

NOT FOR NAVIGATION

Source: Minnesota Department of Natural Resources, USGS

OTTO LAKE
St. Louis County

Area map page / coordinates:	21 / E-4
Surface water area:	138 acres / 6.5 ft. secchi (1999)
Shorelength:	2.9 miles
Accessibility:	Carry-down access to south shore from FR 416 (old railroad grade)
	47° 19' 22.85" N / 91° 58' 23.93" W
Accommodations:	Camping

FISH STOCKING DATA

year	species	size	# released
97	Smallmouth Bass	Adult	100

FISHING INFORMATION

Otto Lake is a well-hidden treasure. It's accessible by a half-mile portage off County Road 416, where there's space to park three or four vehicles at the head of the trail. The portage is located across the road and is well-marked and fairly level. You can also get to the lake by hiking a few miles in from the Otto/Harris foot trail originating off County Road 416 parallel to Otto Lake, or you can try four-wheeling in up 416 from Highway 4 or down 416 from the Town Line Road to the trail that cuts into Harris. The "road" is prone to flooding from beaver dams, so make sure you have a winch. Although this lake is hard to reach, you'll find a pristine, undeveloped gem with three to four nice canoe campsites. The DNR had a walleye stocking program in place for a number of years, but it was unsuccessful. The focus was then switched to smallmouth bass, which have been stocked since 1995. In 1999, the DNR surveyed the lake to assess the effects of this shift and were encouraged by the results. Smallies are reproducing naturally, which indicates the population is not only surviving, but thriving.

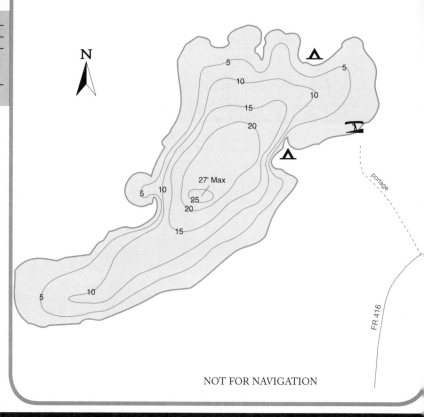

NOT FOR NAVIGATION

HARRIS LAKE
St. Louis County

Area map page / coordinates:	21 / E-4
Surface water area:	68 acres / 10.8 ft. secchi (2010)
Shorelength:	1.7 miles
Accessibility:	Carry-down access from FR 121 (off County Road 416) to southeast shore
	47° 17' 20.00" N / 92° 1' 33.04" W
Accommodations:	Camping

FISH STOCKING DATA

year	species	size	# released
05	Walleye	Fingerling	2,451
07	Walleye	Fingerling	2,268
09	Walleye	Fingerling	865

FISHING INFORMATION

Harris Lake is accessible via abandoned logging roads off County Road 4. While it is less than half the size of Otto Lake, it's only 68 acres, Harris has something Otto doesn't have: walleyes. The DNR stocking program seems to be taking hold here. Although they are down in abundance, the mean length is 14.8 inches and the growth rate is relatively fast with a 16.2 inch average for four year olds. Yellow perch and bluegill catch rates are average for lakes of this type. The northern pike abundance was considered low, but similar to the last two DNR surveys of this lake. When fishing a small lake like this, think finesse fishing tackle. Light line and small baits will tend to hook more fish than heavy gear will. Small inline spinners, crankbaits and live bait like leeches or nightcrawlers will attract most of the species swimming in this lake.

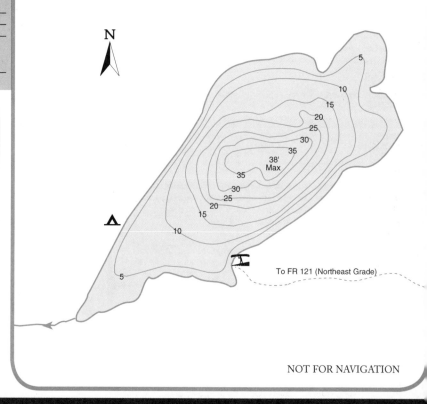

NOT FOR NAVIGATION

Source: Minnesota Department of Natural Resources, USGS

WOLF LAKE
St. Louis County

Area map page / coordinates: 21 / E-5 & 25 / A-5

Watershed: Cloquet

Surface area / shorelength: 456 acres / 8.4 miles

Maximum / mean depth: 12 feet / 5 feet

Water color / clarity: Brown stain / 3.3 feet (2001)

Accessibility: State-owned public access with concrete ramp on south shore, off County Road 547

47° 15' 23.53" N / 91° 57' 46.99" W

Accommodations: None

FISH STOCKING DATA

year	species	size	# released
00	Walleye	Fry	470,000

LENGTH OF SELECTED SPECIES SAMPLED FROM ALL GEAR

Survey Date: 08/24/2009

Number of fish caught for the following length categories (inches):

species	0-5	6-8	9-11	12-14	15-19	20-24	25-29	>30	Total
Black Crappie	1	14	20	1	-	-	-	-	36
Golden Shiner	3	1	-	-	-	-	-	-	4
Northern Pike	-	-	-	1	1	4	2	-	8
Pumpkin. Sunfish	3	8	-	-	-	-	-	-	11
Walleye	1	1	14	10	5	6	2	-	39
White Sucker	-	6	12	27	83	18	-	-	146
Yellow Perch	10	25	5	-	-	-	-	-	40

FISHING INFORMATION

Wolf Lake is a long, shallow, dark-stained lake full of stumps and marshy areas. It doesn't look like the type of lake that would hold walleyes, but it does, and apparently they are reproducing. The DNR has been stocking fry since 1990. According to the folks at the former Al's Bait & Tackle in Two Harbors, MN, most of the walleyes are small, although some are larger. The same can be said of the northern pike population. There is no shortage of fish for shore lunches. A larger northern in Wolf Lake will measure around 20 inches. There also are some nice crappies available, though they can be hard to find. The deep hole, about 12 feet deep, in the north end of the lake is productive for all species, as is the channel on the south end. Work the weedlines in these areas. Take time to look for the humps in these areas that don't show up on the map. These can be good fish holding areas. Crappies usually concentrate around the inlets and outlets in spring and move out to the deeper area as summer approaches. You can also try the extensive cover along the shoreline for them. Spring and summer fishing pressure for all species is moderate. The lake also gets some attention in winter, mainly for crappies. The gravel launch site is suitable for smaller boats. You'll want to watch your lower unit in the lake's south end, there are plenty of submerged stumps.

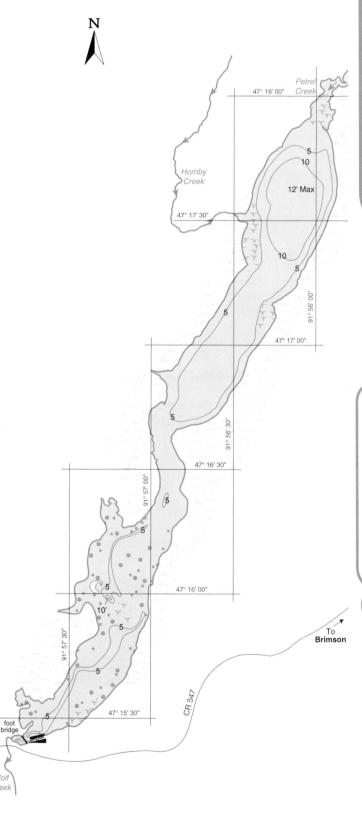

NOT FOR NAVIGATION

CADOTTE LAKE
St. Louis County

BASSETT LAKE

St. Louis County

CADOTTE LAKE

St. Louis County

BASSETT LAKE
St. Louis County

Area map pg / coord: 21 / D-5

Watershed: St. Louis

Surface area: 325 acres

Shorelength: 3.8 miles

Max / mean depth: 20 feet / 11 feet

Water color / clarity: 9.0 ft. (2003)

Shoreland zoning class: Rec. dev.

Mgmt class / Ecological type:
Walleye / soft-water walleye

Accessibility: USFS-owned public access with concrete ramp on west shore in campground

47° 22' 48.46" N / 91° 54' 57.07" W

Accommodations: Camping, picnicking, fishing pier, outhouse

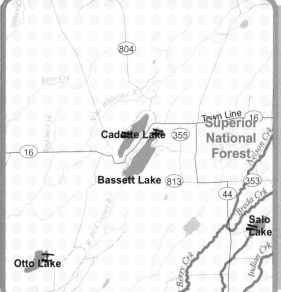

Area map pg / coord: 21 / D-5

Watershed: Cloquet

Surface area: 403 acres

Shorelength: 5.5 miles

Max / mean depth: 21 feet / 16 feet

Water color / clarity: 8.7 ft. (2006)

Shoreland zoning class: Rec. dev.

Mgmt class / Ecological type:
Walleye / soft-water walleye

Accessibility: Township-owned public access with concrete ramp on north shore

47° 22' 52.19" N / 91° 53' 38.27" W

Accommodations: Outhouse

NO RECORD OF STOCKING

NET CATCH DATA

Date: 07/28/2003

species	Gill Nets # per net	Gill Nets avg. fish weight (lbs.)	Trap Nets # per net	Trap Nets avg. fish weight (lbs.)
Bluegill	-	-	0.7	0.10
Northern Pike	0.4	3.21	0.1	0.22
Walleye	14.1	0.76	3.9	1.32
White Sucker	5.1	2.28	0.7	2.55
Yellow Perch	21.8	0.61	1.0	0.06

LENGTH OF SELECTED SPECIES SAMPLED FROM ALL GEAR
Number of fish caught for the following length categories (inches):

species	0-5	6-8	9-11	12-14	15-19	20-24	25-29	>29	Total
Bluegill	5	1	-	-	-	-	-	-	6
Northern Pike	-	-	1	-	2	1	-	1	5
Walleye	-	15	32	70	40	3	1	-	161
Yellow Perch	10	45	106	43	-	-	-	-	204

FISH STOCKING DATA

year	species	size	# released
03	Walleye	Fingerling	3,330
05	Walleye	Fingerling	12,551
07	Walleye	Fingerling	10,134

NET CATCH DATA

Date: 07/24/2006

species	Gill Nets # per net	Gill Nets avg. fish weight (lbs.)	Trap Nets # per net	Trap Nets avg. fish weight (lbs.)
Black Bullhead	-	-	0.3	0.07
Black Crappie	1.2	0.31	2.3	0.35
Bluegill	7.3	0.13	44.7	0.11
Northern pike	2.9	2.59	1.9	1.66
Pumpkin. Sunfish	2.0	0.05	12.3	0.05
Rock Bass	-	-	-	-
Walleye	7.0	2.21	0.9	1.48
White Sucker	8.4	2.1	3.0	2.66
Yellow Perch	120.2	0.13	8.0	0.13

LENGTH OF SELECTED SPECIES SAMPLED FROM ALL GEAR
Number of fish caught for the following length categories (inches):

species	0-5	6-8	9-11	12-14	15-19	20-24	25-29	>29	Total
Black Bullhead	2	1	-	-	-	-	-	-	3
Black Crappie	4	22	5	1	-	-	-	-	32
Northern Pike	-	-	3	2	9	25	3	-	42
Pumpkin. Sunfish	129	-	-	-	-	-	-	-	129
Rock Bass	-	-	-	-	-	-	-	-	-
Walleye	-	4	6	11	33	15	2	-	71
Yellow Perch	187	955	7	-	-	-	-	-	1149

FISHING INFORMATION

According to Dan Bohrer of the former Al's Bait & Tackle in Two Harbors, MN, not much has changed at Bassett Lake over the last few years, except the quality of largemouth bass fishing. "The bass population seems to be doing really well on Bassett," he said. "There are quite a few anglers fishing for them now. Some nice, solid fish are caught from this lake." Bass anglers would be smart to stock up on soft plastics when fishing Bassett. Basics are best when choosing plastics. Black, watermelon and green pumpkin tubes, lizards, worms and Senkos are good choices. Early in the day and season, fish these offerings around any shallow cover. You can then move to deeper weed edges to locate bass later in summer.

Bassett Lake has good fishing for keeper walleyes. Local anglers fish the sand bar along the west shore year around. Anglers also have good success by fishing steep shoreline drops. Some nice northern pike also roam Bassett, with 6- to 10-pound catches not being all that uncommon. Even 20-pound-class pike have been taken in recent years. Bassett also boasts of some saucer sized bluegills. Try the south end of the lake where weed growth is heaviest. This little lake is a favorite of locals. Bassett gets fairly heavy fishing pressure, both during open water months and in winter.

Cadotte Lake has a 27-site campground, complete with a swimming beach, plenty of parking and a fishing pier for those who don't have boats. Public access is via a concrete boat launch; it comes complete with dock.

The lake itself is very clear, making it difficult to fish. Like most clear lakes, you'll want to fish early morning, late evening and at night. Locals catch a lot of 1- to 1.25-pound walleyes along with some 4- to 5 –pounders. The last DNR lake survey indicated that the walleye population was above average for a lake of this type. Yellow perch are also very abundant in Cadotte, according to DNR figures. In the last DNR survey, the mean length for perch was 10.4 inches with a variety of sizes available. The growth rate was considered fast for the Duluth area. Perch provide a forage base for walleyes as well as angling opportunities. Northern pike are also present, but according to DNR statistics, not in very large numbers. One local angler noted that there also are giant bluegills, some of them being plate-sized 2-pounders! Fish weed edges and drop-offs for all species.

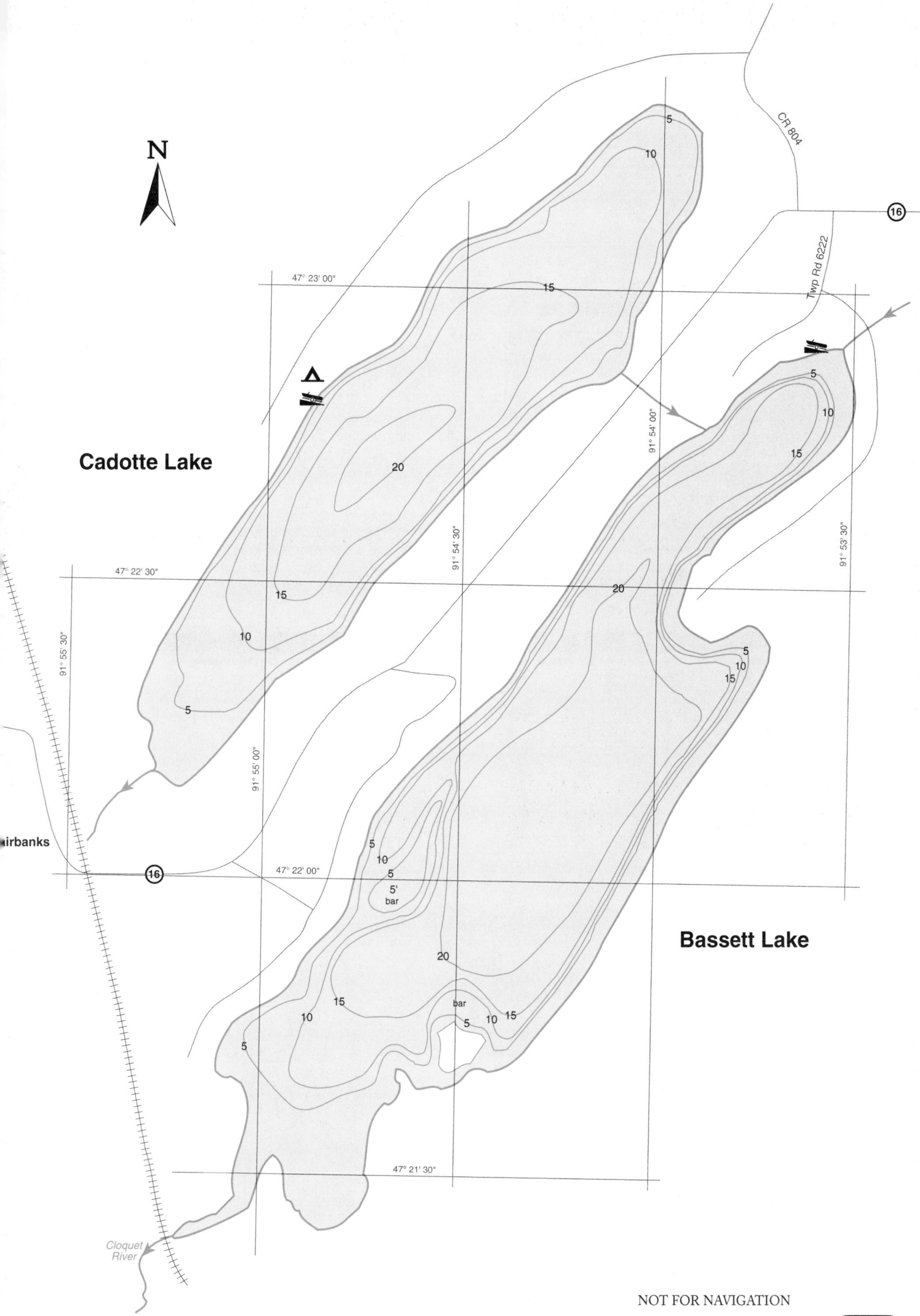

N

47° 23' 00"

CR 804

16

Twp Rd 6222

5

10

15

Cadotte Lake

20

5

10

15

91° 54' 00"

20

91° 53' 30"

47° 22' 30"

15

10

91° 55' 30"

91° 54' 30"

5

10

15

20

5

91° 55' 00"

5

irbanks

16

47° 22' 00"

5

10

5

5'
bar

Bassett Lake

20

15

10

bar

5

10

15

5

47° 21' 30"

Cloquet
River

NOT FOR NAVIGATION

205

BIG LAKE
St. Louis County

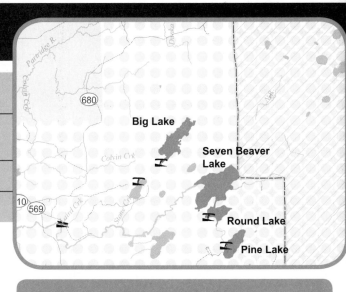

Area map page / coordinates: 21 / B-5,6

Watershed: NA

Surface water area / shorelength: 805 acres / 8.3 miles

Maximum / mean depth: 28 feet / NA

Water color / clarity: 9.0 feet (1993)

Accessibility: Carry-down access from state ATV trail to southwest shore
47° 30' 54.76" N / 91° 52' 0.21" W

Accommodations: None

NO RECORD OF STOCKING

LENGTH OF SELECTED SPECIES SAMPLED FROM ALL GEAR

Survey Date: 07/20/1993

Number of fish caught for the following length categories (inches):

species	0-5	6-8	9-11	12-14	15-19	20-24	25-29	>30	Total
Northern Pike	-	-	-	-	15	3	3	2	23
Rock Bass	1	29	-	-	-	-	-	-	30
Walleye	-	8	4	20	-	2	1	-	35
Yellow Perch	-	12	9	-	-	-	-	-	21

FISHING INFORMATION

Big Lake is not all that big by Minnesota standards, but it's big enough. The lake is 805 acres, has a maximum depth of 28 feet and water clarity down to 9 feet. There is access, one of which is reachable by ATV via the Cypress Railway at the west end of the lake. There is another tail that leads to the bay on the south end of the lake. This crosses private land via the Seven Beavers snowmobile trail. It is carry-in access only.

Northern pike and walleye dominate the fishery. Some large ones were found in the last DNR survey. For pike try a white or chartreuse spinnerbait worked parallel to submerged weeds. Fish the points and drop-offs with leeches, nightcrawlers or minnows to hook walleyes. The lake also boasts decent populations of rock bass, yellow perch and white sucker. Mercury levels can be high in pike caught here, so follow the DNR's consumption guidelines of no more than 1 meal per month for pregnant women or children. All others may eat it more frequently, as much as one meal per week.

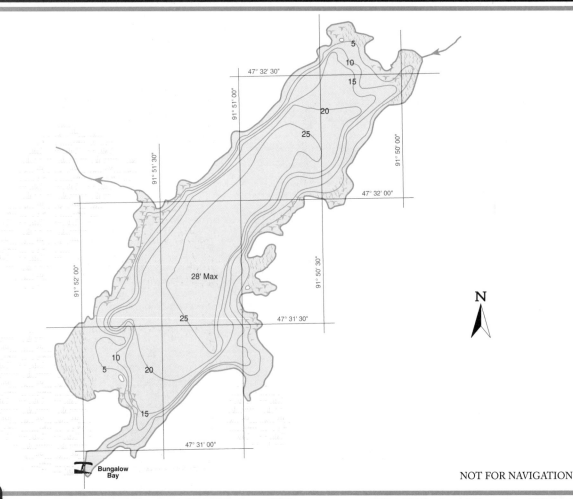

NOT FOR NAVIGATION

Loaine (Sand) Lake, St. Louis County

Area map page / coordinates: 25 / B-5
Surface area / shorelength: 27 acres / 1.8 miles
Accessibility: State-owned public access with gravel ramp on south shore, off Hwy. 266 on Loaine Truck Trail
47° 9' 53.80" N / 91° 52' 7.94" W

FISH STOCKING DATA

year	species	size	# released
05	Rainbow Trout	Yearling	3,400
06	Rainbow Trout	Yearling	3,278
07	Rainbow Trout	Yearling	2,626
08	Rainbow Trout	Yearling	2,606
09	Brown Trout	Adult	127
09	Rainbow Trout	Yearling	2,605
10	Brown Trout	Adult	99
10	Rainbow Trout	Yearling	1,942
10	Rainbow Trout	Adult	35

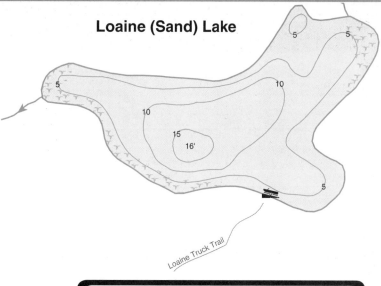

Loaine (Sand) Lake

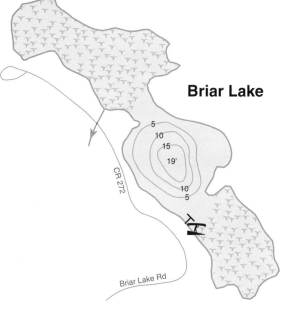

Briar Lake

N

Briar Lake, St. Louis County

Area map page / coordinates: 25 / D-5
Surface area / shorelength: 79 acres / 2.3 miles
Accessibility: Carry-down access to west shore off Briar Lake Road (County Road 272)
47° 4' 12.56" N / 91° 57' 38.35" W

FISH STOCKING DATA

year	species	size	# released
06	Rainbow Trout	Yearling	7,008
07	Rainbow Trout	Yearling	5,305
08	Rainbow Trout	Yearling	5,264
09	Brown Trout	Adult	256
09	Rainbow Trout	Yearling	5,252
10	Brook Trout	Adult	254
10	Brown Trout	Adult	200
10	Rainbow Trout	Yearling	3,959
10	Rainbow Trout	Adult	95

Mirror Lake, St. Louis County

Area map page / coordinates: 24 / E-3
Surface area / shorelength: 18 acres / 0.7 miles
Accessibility: Carry-down access on north shore, off Township Road 294
46° 58' 1.51" N / 92° 10' 19.02" W

FISH STOCKING DATA

year	species	size	# released
05	Splake	Yearling	1,858
06	Splake	Yearling	1,874
09	Walleye	Fry	20,000

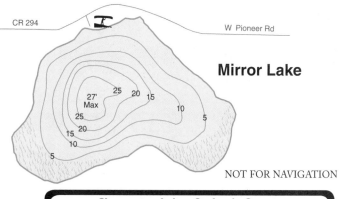

Mirror Lake

NOT FOR NAVIGATION

Clearwater Lake, St. Louis County

Area map page / coordinates: 24 / E-3
Surface area / shorelength: 15 acres / NA
Accessibility: Carry-down access to northwest shore off County Road 48
46° 58' 13.76" N / 92° 12' 57.86" W

FISH STOCKING DATA

year	species	size	# released
07	Rainbow Trout	Yearling	1,130
08	Rainbow Trout	Yearling	1,124
09	Brown Trout	Adult	57
09	Rainbow Trout	Yearling	1,124
10	Brook Trout	Adult	90
10	Brown Trout	Adult	50
10	Rainbow Trout	Yearling	835
10	Rainbow Trout	Adult	24

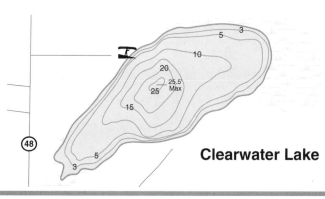

Clearwater Lake

Source: Minnesota Department of Natural Resources, USGS

WILSON LAKE
St. Louis County

WEST BASS LAKE
St. Louis County

EAST BASS LAKE
St. Louis County

	WILSON	WEST BASS	EAST BASS
Area map pg / coord:	24 / B-1	24 / B-1,2	24 / B-2
Watershed:	St. Louis	St. Louis	St. Louis
Surface area:	56 acres	162 acres	205 acres
Shorelength:	1.1 miles	2.3 miles	3.8 miles
Max / mean depth:	14 feet / 9 feet	27 feet / 15 feet	24 feet / 11 feet
Water color / clarity:	4.9 feet (2008)	12.0 feet (2004)	7.0 feet (2003)
Shoreland zoning:	Rec. dev.	Gen. dev.	Gen. dev.
Management class:	Centrarchid	Walleye-centrarchid	Walleye-centrarchid
Ecological type:	Centrarchid	Northern pike-sucker	Centrarchid-walleye
Accessibility:	Carry-down access off Cty. Rd. 224 on northeast shore	Carry-down access off Cty. Rd. 224 at outlet crossing	NA
	47° 12' 50.80" N 92° 21' 37.39" W	47° 12' 11.19" N 92° 21' 58.09" W	NA
Accommodations:	None	None	None

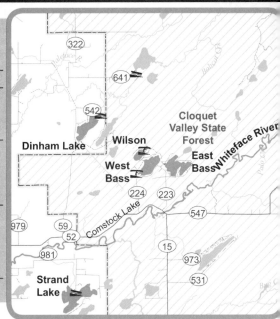

Wilson Lake

FISH STOCKING DATA			
year	species	size	# released
02	Walleye	Fingerling	1,673
04	Walleye	Fingerling	1,188
06	Walleye	Fingerling	633

LENGTH OF SELECTED SPECIES SAMPLED FROM ALL GEAR

Survey Date: 08/25/2008

Number of fish caught for the following length categories (inches):

species	0-5	6-8	9-11	12-14	15-19	20-24	25-29	>30	Total
Black Crappie	-	6	12	1	-	-	-	-	20
Bluegill	18	19	-	-	-	-	-	-	37
Largemouth Bass	-	1	3	4	1	-	-	-	9
Northern Pike	-	-	-	-	7	7	-	-	15
Rock Bass	2	3	-	-	-	-	-	-	5
Walleye	-	-	-	-	1	1	-	-	2
Yellow Perch	1	3	-	-	-	-	-	-	4

West Bass (aka Cameron) Lake

FISH STOCKING DATA			
year	species	size	# released
00	Walleye	Fingerling	4,218
02	Walleye	Fingerling	3,156
04	Walleye	Fingerling	5,881

LENGTH OF SELECTED SPECIES SAMPLED FROM ALL GEAR

Survey Date: 07/19/2004

Number of fish caught for the following length categories (inches):

species	0-5	6-8	9-11	12-14	15-19	20-24	25-29	>30	Total
Black Crappie	20	33	35	-	-	-	-	-	88
Bluegill	44	69	1	-	-	-	-	-	114
Northern Pike	-	-	1	1	15	31	8	1	57
Pumpkin. Sunfish	8	7	-	-	-	-	-	-	15
Rock Bass	4	10	1	-	-	-	-	-	15
Smallmouth Bass	-	-	-	1	3	-	-	-	4
Walleye	-	-	-	1	6	3	2	-	12
Yellow Perch	36	10	-	-	-	-	-	-	46

East Bass (aka Schubert) Lake

FISH STOCKING DATA			
year	species	size	# released
01	Walleye	Fingerling	1,047
04	Walleye	Fingerling	1,650

LENGTH OF SELECTED SPECIES SAMPLED FROM ALL GEAR

Survey Date: 07/16/2003

Number of fish caught for the following length categories (inches):

species	0-5	6-8	9-11	12-14	15-19	20-24	25-29	>30	Total
Black Crappie	14	3	3	-	-	-	-	-	20
Bluegill	120	72	-	-	-	-	-	-	192
Largemouth Bass	-	3	2	-	1	-	-	-	6
Northern Pike	-	-	-	-	14	7	1	-	22
Pumpkin. Sunfish	1	7	-	-	-	-	-	-	8
Rock Bass	13	29	5	-	-	-	-	-	47
Smallmouth Bass	-	-	1	6	6	-	-	-	13
Walleye	-	-	-	3	1	3	2	-	9
Yellow Perch	3	16	-	-	-	-	-	-	19

FISHING INFORMATION

Wilson is a 56-acre lake with a maximum depth of 14 feet. An earthen, back-in access is located off County Road 224 and has limited parking. The lake contains a good variety of fish, including northern pike, yellow perch, crappies and bluegills, all of which are of decent abundance and size. Walleyes and largemouth bass are the primary and secondary management species respectively. Walleye fry were stocked previously, but the DNR changed to fingerlings when the 2002 study showed the abundance to be lower than average compared to similar lakes.

East Bass (aka Schubert) Lake is an interesting fishery that receives little attention due to its access, or lack thereof. According to Deserae Hendrickson at the Minnesota DNR, the access to the lake now has no trespassing signs posted. "Our DNR Trails and Waterways division cannot definitively determine whether there is legal access at this site based on road right-of-way widths," Hendrickson said. "As a result, we have discontinued walleye fingerling stocking until better access can be acquired." Nice walleyes have been caught near the reefs, which are marked by buoys. There are also some nice 2- to 5-pound smallmouth bass to be found, along with largemouth, northerns, crappies and bluegills. Check with the DNR or local authorities before hitting this waterway to determine whether or not you can legally access it.

West Bass (aka Cameron) has available access, unlike its sister lake. The carry-down only access is off County Road #224, but has no parking. This 162-acre lake is primarily managed for walleyes and largemouth and smallmouth bass.

Wilson Lake

14'
Max

Anne Lake

27'
Max

West Bass Lake
(Cameron)

27'
Max

CR 224

CR 223

CR 815

(private road)

Bass Cove
Rd

N

East Bass Lake
(Schubert)

24'
Max

23'

NOT FOR NAVIGATION

Source: Minnesota Department of Natural Resources, USGS

HART LAKE
St. Louis County

L. COMSTOCK LAKE
St. Louis County

U. COMSTOCK LAKE
St. Louis County

UPPER COMSTOCK LAKE
St. Louis County

LOWER COMSTOCK LAKE
St. Louis County

HART LAKE
St. Louis County

	UPPER COMSTOCK	LOWER COMSTOCK	HART
Area map pg / coord:	24 / B-2,3	24 / B-2	24 / B-2,3
Watershed:	St. Louis	St. Louis	St. Louis
Surface area:	267 acres	161 acres	50 acres
Shorelength:	NA	NA	1.8 miles
Max / mean depth:	28 feet / 12 feet	30 feet / 12 feet	20 feet / 7 feet
Water color / clarity:	6.5 feet (2008)	4.7 feet (2000)	3.1 feet (2007)
Shoreland zoning:	Rec. dev.	Rec. dev.	Natural envt.
Management class:	Walleye-centrarchid	Walleye-centrarchid	Centrarchid
Ecological type:	Centrarchid-walleye	Centrarchid-walleye	Northern pike-sucker
Accessibility:	State-owned public access with gravel ramp on north shore	Via navigable channel from Upper Comstock Lake	Carry-down access by bridge on County Road 547
	47° 13' 27.42" N 92° 13' 11.97" W	NA	47° 12' 28.04" N 92° 12' 57.28" W
Accommodations:	None	None	None

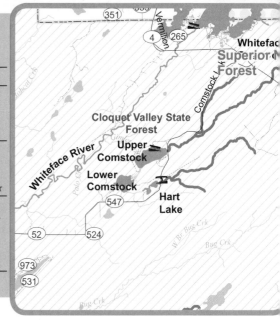

Upper Comstock Lake
FISH STOCKING DATA

year	species	size	# released
06	Walleye	Fry	540,000
08	Walleye	Fry	540,000
10	Walleye	Fry	540,000

LENGTH OF SELECTED SPECIES SAMPLED FROM ALL GEAR
Survey Date: 07/28/2008

Number of fish caught for the following length categories (inches):

species	0-5	6-8	9-11	12-14	15-19	20-24	25-29	>30	Total
Black Bullhead	2	-	-	1	-	-	-	-	3
Black Crappie	13	38	15	-	-	-	-	-	66
Bluegill	10	90	1	-	-	-	-	-	101
Northern Pike	-	-	-	-	12	12	4	1	29
Pumpkin. Sunfish	2	-	-	-	-	-	-	-	2
Rock Bass	-	1	-	-	-	-	-	-	1
Walleye	-	1	-	6	3	6	2	-	18
White Sucker	-	-	6	4	7	-	-	-	17
Yellow Perch	21	38	4	-	-	-	-	-	64

Lower Comstock Lake
FISH STOCKING DATA

year	species	size	# released
06	Walleye	Fry	121,000
08	Walleye	Fry	121,000
10	Walleye	Fry	121,000

LENGTH OF SELECTED SPECIES SAMPLED FROM ALL GEAR
Survey Date: 07/24/2000

Number of fish caught for the following length categories (inches):

species	0-5	6-8	9-11	12-14	15-19	20-24	25-29	>30	Total
Black Bullhead	-	-	1	1	-	-	-	-	2
Black Crappie	10	16	16	-	-	-	-	-	42
Bluegill	32	24	4	-	-	-	-	-	60
Brown Bullhead	-	-	1	-	-	-	-	-	1
Northern Pike	-	-	-	1	6	8	-	-	15
Pumpkin. Sunfish	6	4	-	-	-	-	-	-	10
Rock Bass	2	1	-	-	-	-	-	-	3
Walleye	-	-	2	2	7	2	1	-	14
Yellow Perch	25	21	-	-	-	-	-	-	46

Hart Lake
FISH STOCKING DATA

year	species	size	# released
03	Walleye	Fingerling	1,661
03	Walleye	Yearling	32

LENGTH OF SELECTED SPECIES SAMPLED FROM ALL GEAR
Survey Date: 06/25/2007

Number of fish caught for the following length categories (inches):

species	0-5	6-8	9-11	12-14	15-19	20-24	25-29	>30	Total
Black Crappie	1	7	5	-	-	-	-	-	13
Bluegill	19	25	1	-	-	-	-	-	45
Northern Pike	-	1	3	-	9	17	3	1	34
Pumpkin. Sunfish	9	2	-	-	-	-	-	-	11
Rock Bass	-	-	-	-	-	-	-	-	
Walleye	-	-	-	-	1	3	2	-	6
Yellow Perch	2	4	-	-	-	-	-	-	6

FISHING INFORMATION

These three little lakes lie in the Cloquet Valley Forest, north of Duluth. Each has something to recommend it. **Upper Comstock Lake** is best known for its bluegills, black crappies, and northern pike, according to the most recent DNR survey. Walleyes are stocked, although the catch rates have been steadily declining over the years. Crappies and bluegills were abundant with many keeper fish in the catch. Panfish are taken year around. Northern pike average 1 to 2 pounds, with an occasional lunker being taken.

Lower Comstock is much the same. Northerns are fairly plentiful and decent-sized with a handful exceeding 21 inches. Bluegills and crappies are above average in abundance. Bluegills measured above 6 inches 47% of the time and crappies exceeded 8 inches 53% of the time. Walleyes are lower in abundance than at other lakes of this type, according to the last DNR survey. However, the numbers did rise since the 1995 survey and their size is decent. In fact, most walleye here are at least 15 inches in length. Fry continue to be stocked in even-numbered years.

Hart Lake holds some decent northern pike, which average 22.3 inches, with a few measuring 39.8 inches, according to the last DNR survey. Anglers have also been lucky here with bluegills, crappies, walleyes, largemouth bass, rock bass and pumpkinseed, among others. The local beaver population literally floods the inlets and outlets with their condos. Watch for the occasional flood to occur.

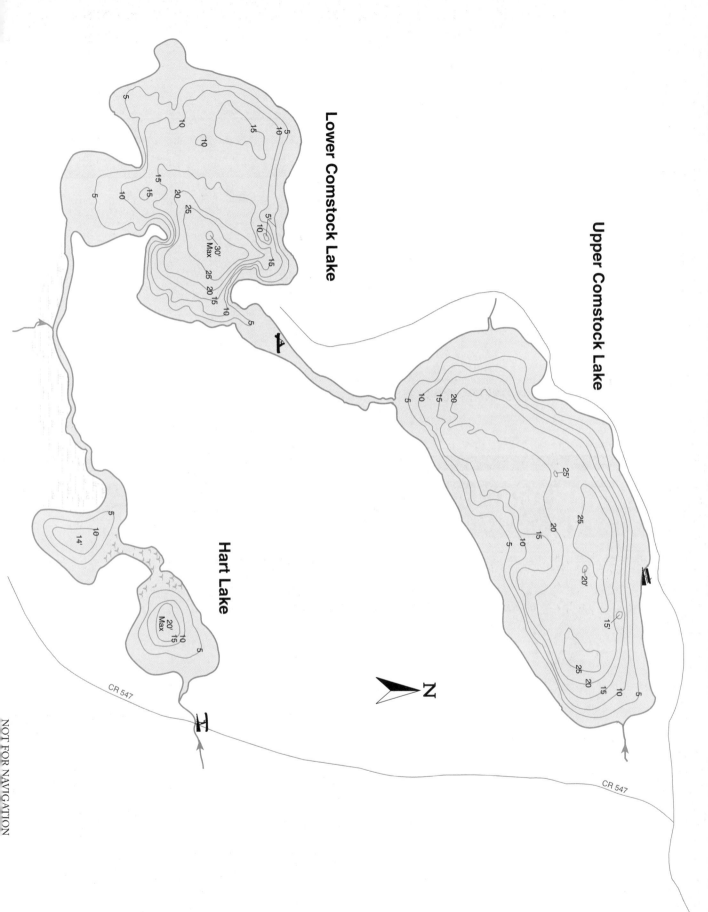

Lower Comstock Lake

Upper Comstock Lake

Hart Lake

5
10
15
10
5
10
15
10
15
20
5
15
10
5
25
30'
Max
15
25
20 15
10
5

14'
10
5

20'
Max
15
10
5

N

CR 547

CR 547

5
10
15
20
25
25
25
20
15
10
5
20
15'
25
20
15
10
5

Source: Minnesota Department of Natural Resources, USGS

NOT FOR NAVIGATION

STRAND LAKE
St. Louis County

Area map page / coordinates:	24 / C-1

Surface water area: 330 acres / 5.3 ft. secchi (2007)

Shorelength: 5.2 miles

Accessibility: Township-owned public access with gravel ramp on north shore, off County Road 973
47° 8' 47.69" N / 92° 24' 36.67" W

Accommodations: None

FISH STOCKING DATA			
year	species	size	# released
06	Walleye	Fry	660,000
08	Walleye	Fry	660,000
10	Walleye	Fry	330,000

FISHING INFORMATION

Strand Lake is a 330- acre lake with a maximum depth of 16 feet. The DNR stocked 660,000 walleye fry here in 2006, 2008 and half that in 2010. Strand has a very healthy walleye population, although the most recent DNR survey showed the percentage of keeper-sized fish was down from previous years. Casting jigs tipped with a leech or half a nightcrawler will hook walleyes from spring throughout summer. Also try trolling a spinner rig with a crawler or leech. Yellow perch numbers are up, with good numbers of fish measuring 9 inches or more. Small leeches, minnows or pieces of nightcrawler will draw strikes from perch. Black crappie numbers were down, but with sizes averaging over 8 inches, they showed the fastest growth rates in the entire Duluth area. Crappies are suckers for small minnows or leeches fished under a slip bobber. Look for crappies on deeper submerged weed edges during summer months.

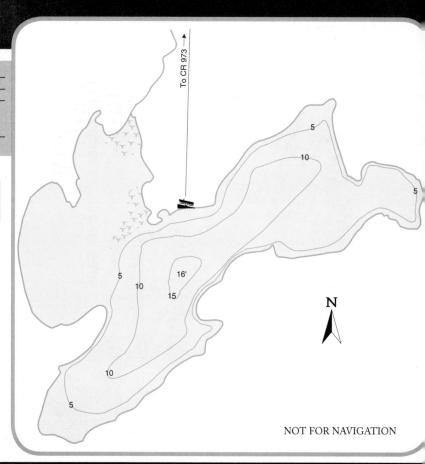

NOT FOR NAVIGATION

LEORA (ELORA) LAKE
St. Louis County

Area map page / coordinates:	24 / C-1

Surface water area: 269 acres / 9.1 ft. secchi (2003)

Shorelength: 2.8 miles

Accessibility: Public access with gravel ramp on south shore, off County Road 49
47° 5' 48.98" N / 92° 24' 35.27" W

Accommodations: None

FISH STOCKING DATA			
year	species	size	# released
06	Walleye	Fingerling	2,528
08	Walleye	Fingerling	8,315
10	Walleye	Fingerling	3,450

FISHING INFORMATION

Leora Lake, also known as Elora, is part of the Three Lakes chain. The walleye and largemouth bass populations are very strong here. Largemouth bass were caught at a rate of 42.5 fish per hour during the 2003 DNR survey. This is average for Duluth area lakes. Although the mean length decreased from the previous survey, the growth rate is considered fast. The mean length of the fish caught was 12 inches, which is the same size of a typical four year old. Largemouth bass hang out along the northeast shore and around the channel that runs into Dodo Lake on the southeast side. Walleye abundance increased, with all surveys showing average to above average abundance. Sizes have been on the rise, too, with mean lengths growing from 12.4 inches in 1998 to 17.2 inches in 2003. Most of the walleyes are caught in the north end of the lake. Northern pike abundance is also on the rise, but growth rates were slow. The average pike measured 20.4 inches

Three Lakes Rd

NOT FOR NAVIGATION

Source: Minnesota Department of Natural Resources, USGS

NICHOLS LAKE
St. Louis County

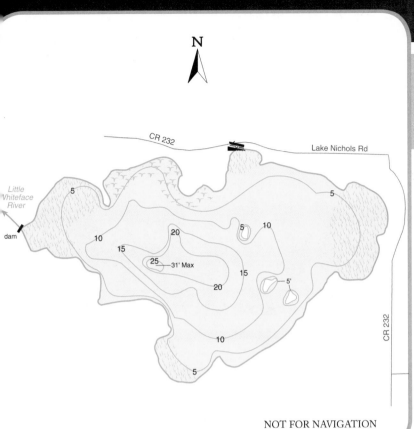

CR 232

Lake Nichols Rd

Little Whiteface River

dam

5

5

10

20

5

10

15

25 — 31' Max

15

20

5'

10

5

CR 232

NOT FOR NAVIGATION

Area map page / coordinates: 23 / C-6
Surface water area: 419 acres / 9.2 ft. secchi (2007)
Shorelength: 3.8 miles
Accessibility: State-owned public access with concrete ramp on north shore, off County Road 232
47° 5' 51.38" N / 92° 32' 10.98" W
Accommodations: None

FISH STOCKING DATA			
year	species	size	# released
04	Walleye	Fingerling	4,914
07	Walleye	Fingerling	4,665

FISHING INFORMATION

Nichols Lake is a decent all-around fishery providing many angling opportunities for the multi-species angler, although most of the fish caught are not picture-worthy. The lake was stocked with walleye fingerlings in 2004 and 2007. Although the 2002 DNR survey showed walleye abundance is below average compared to other lakes in this class, the growth rate is fast with an average length of 19.2 inches. Most of the water in this 419-acre basin is shallow and weedy, causing many of the walleyes to relate to weeds, rather than typical walleye structure. The areas around the islands provide some action early and late in the year, though. Bluegills are on the small side. Northern pike, bluegills and yellow perch are all average in abundance with slow growth rates. The crappie sample fared the best on this lake, with average abundance and average growth rates. Decent fish were sampled with the average crappie measuring 7.2 inches. The access site at Nichols is somewhat shallow and weed-choked.

DINHAM LAKE
St. Louis County

CR 542

Arizona Rd

N

5
10

10 5

15

20

20

25

20

15

10

5

NOT FOR NAVIGATION

Area map page / coordinates: 24 / A,B-1
Surface water area: 202 acres / 4.1 ft. secchi (2010)
Shorelength: 3.3 miles
Accessibility: State-owned public access with earthen ramp on northeast shore, off Township Road 542
47° 13' 52.05" N / 92° 23' 28.53" W
Accommodations: None

NO RECORD OF STOCKING

FISHING INFORMATION

Northern pike provide the best angling opportunity on Dinham Lake, according to the 2002 DNR survey. Strangely enough, the same survey showed they are average in abundance, but growth rates were not evaluated due to small sample size. Local anglers say the pike are too well fed on the lake's panfish to be readily catchable. Try hitting them early in morning or early evening. Flashy spinnerbaits, lipless crankbaits or a jerkbait are always good choices. Crappies and bluegills are found in good numbers, although they tend to be on the small side, averaging 7.3 and 5.2 inches respectively. A small slip bobber rigged with a single hook or a small jig tipped with a small leech or piece of nightcrawler will attract panfish. Walleyes are scarce, but a few of them are caught each year. This lake can be fished thoroughly in a single day, since it only covers 202 acres. The maximum depth here is 25 feet with the majority of the lake being less than 15 feet deep. There is a DNR public access in the northeast bay off Township Road 452.

213

BOULDER LAKE *St. Louis County*

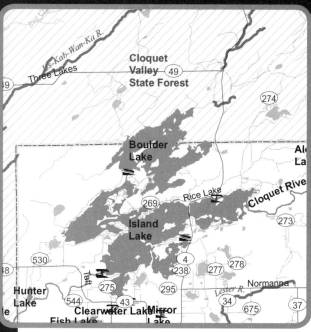

Area map page / coordinates:	24 / D-3

Watershed: Cloquet

Surface water area / shorelength: 3,260 acres / 26.9 miles

Maximum / mean depth: 18 feet / NA

Water color / clarity: Light brown / 6.5 feet (2008)

Shoreland zoning classification: Recreational development

Management class / Ecological type: Walleye / soft-water walleye

Accessibility: State-administered public access with concrete ramp on south shore, by the dam off Hwy. 269

47° 3' 6.55" N / 92° 12' 2.55" W

Accommodations: Resort, outhouse

FISHING INFORMATION

Boulder Lake was created when Minnesota Power dammed the Cloquet River system in the early 1920s. This reservoir covers 3,260 acres. The maximum depth is 18 feet, with 85% of the reservoir being shallower than 15 feet. Boulder doesn't receive the attention that the other big reservoirs in the area get, but it is one of the better lakes around for above-average-size walleyes. John Chalstrom, of Chalstrom's Bait and Tackle, 5067 Rice Lake Road, Duluth, MN, 218-726-0094, told us that of all the lakes he fishes in the area, Boulder is his favorite. The northwest side of Boulder is often referred to as Otter Lake (where the old river channel runs) by local fishermen. This is where Chalstrom says he catches most of his walleyes by still-fishing with 4-inch sucker minnows in 6-to 8-feet of water late in fall. There are usually some walleyes near the numerous small rock piles throughout the lake during spring and summer months. Try fishing rock piles with a slip bobber and a leech or crawler during summer. If there is a little wind to break up the surface of the lake, slip bobber fishing can be very productive. If you're having problems with small perch stealing your bait, switch to jumbo leeches. The bigger baits tend to hold up better to the onslaught of small fish. You can also fish these rock piles in early morning or evening hours by casting crankbaits or stickbaits over them. Walleyes hit these lures with a vengeance during low light hours. Veteran anglers talk of graphing "thousands of walleyes" while on Boulder, but they add that getting them to bite could be frustrating. A good yellow perch forage base creates considerable competition for the walleyes' attention. The last DNR survey showed walleyes didn't grow fast in Boulder, but their abundance was average compared to similar lakes.

Northern pike numbers are about average, though size is usually pretty small. However, you shouldn't let the small size dissuade you completely. Chalstrom says there are some real monster pike lurking in Boulder's dark water. Shore fishermen do well for them at the Boulder Lake dam, near the public access on the southeast shore. Try throwing sucker minnows or dead smelt on a bobber out from the dam. Shore fishing for northerns is also good where the Boulder Lake Dam Road runs along the lower southeast bay of the lake. You can toss spoons or spinnerbaits to weedlines. Don't be afraid to mix things up a bit and try a soft jerkbait. Rig them weedless and twitch them in and around deep weed edges. When pike are finicky, this lure can often draw strikes. Working these through weeds will give you fewer snags and headaches than spinnerbaits and spoons. The last DNR survey showed the northern pike abundance to be below average compared to similar lakes, although the average fish weighed better than 3 pounds.

There are some nice crappies around, too, but they can be tough to find. Try the shallows early in the year. Use a vertical presentation with a small

| | NO RECORD OF STOCKING | |

NET CATCH DATA				
Date: 07/14/2008		Gill Nets		Trap Nets
species	# per net	avg. fish weight (lbs.)	# per net	avg. fish weight (lbs.)
Black Bullhead	1.27	0.60	-	-
Black Crappie	1.80	0.46	-	-
Northern Pike	2.53	3.14	-	-
Pumpkin. Sunfish	0.20	0.16	-	-
Rock Bass	0.27	0.31	-	-
Walleye	8.87	0.80	-	-
White Sucker	4.73	1.82	-	-
Yellow Perch	6.53	0.30	-	-

LENGTH OF SELECTED SPECIES SAMPLED FROM ALL GEAR

Number of fish caught for the following length categories (inches):

species	0-5	6-8	9-11	12-14	15-19	20-24	25-29	>30	Total
Black Bullhead	-	5	12	2	-	-	-	-	19
Black Crappie	2	13	12	-	-	-	-	-	27
Northern Pike	-	-	-	-	11	17	6	4	38
Pumpkin. Sunfish	2	1	-	-	-	-	-	-	3
Rock Bass	-	4	-	-	-	-	-	-	4
Walleye	-	11	63	28	30	-	-	1	133
White Sucker	-	6	12	10	42	1	-	-	71
Yellow Perch	11	55	32	-	-	-	-	-	98

tube jig or a minnow. Try the areas near the inlets or the various small islands throughout the lake. Black crappies are in average abundance here.

In the past, the most abundant fish in the lake according to the DNR was the black bullhead. In fact, the bullhead population was so great, the DNR issued a permit to a commercial fisherman to remove bullheads from the lake. If you'd like to catch these stumpy catfish, fish the bottom with crawlers during early morning or evening hours. Anywhere along the dam face would be a good area to start your search for bullheads.

Boulder is one of the prettiest lakes in the area with numerous islands and miles of undeveloped, wooded shoreline. Although the lake is considered quite scenic, Adam Olson at Gander Mountain, 4275 Haines Road, Hermantown, MN, 218-786-9800, says caution is necessary when boating here. "The lake is a very good fishery overall," he said. "That aside, it's a prop shop owners dream. It can get very shallow and a lot of boaters lose or damage their props there every year. Just use some common sense when you're out there running your boat."

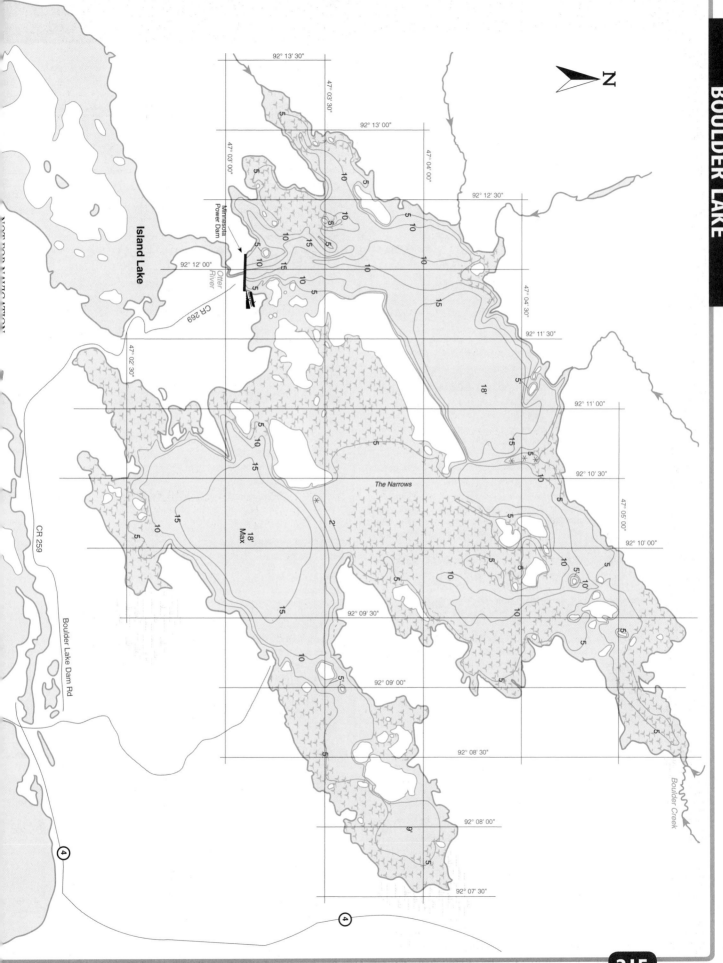

Island Lake

Minnesota Power Dam

Otter River

CR 269

The Narrows

18'

18' Max

2'

9'

CR 259

Boulder Lake Dam Rd

Boulder Creek

92° 13' 30"

92° 13' 00"

92° 12' 30"

92° 12' 00"

92° 11' 30"

92° 11' 00"

92° 10' 30"

92° 10' 00"

92° 09' 30"

92° 09' 00"

92° 08' 30"

92° 08' 00"

92° 07' 30"

47° 03' 30"

47° 04' 00"

47° 03' 00"

47° 04' 30"

47° 05' 00"

47° 02' 30"

N

4

4

ISLAND LAKE *St. Louis County*

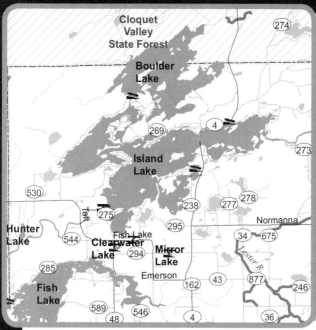

Area map page / coordinates:	24,25 / D,E-2,3,4
Watershed:	Cloquet
Surface water area / shorelength:	8,000 acres / 87.1 miles
Maximum / mean depth:	94 feet / NA
Water color / clarity:	Brown stain / 4.5 feet (2006)
Shoreland zoning classification:	Recreational development
Management class / Ecological type:	Walleye / soft-water walleye

Accessibility: 1) Public access (owned by Minnesota Power) with concrete ramp at dam on west shore, off Island Lake Dam Road (Co. Rd. 275)
46° 59' 27.84" N / 92° 13' 29.14" W

Accessibility: 2) Public (Abbott Road) access (owned by Minnesota Power) with concrete ramp on east shore of main basin, off County Road 4
47° 0' 44.62" N / 92° 8' 59.99" W

Accessibility: 3) Public (Hideaway) access (owned by Minnesota Power) wit concrete ramp on north shore of east basin, off County Road 4
47° 2' 7.21" N / 92° 7' 14.51" W

Accommodations: Parks, boat rental, camping, picnicking, restrooms

FISHING INFORMATION

Island Lake is the largest at 8,000 acres and most famous of the reservoirs and inland lakes in the Duluth area. Island Lake consists of two basins divided by the Highway 4 bridge. It's famous for its walleye fishing, and with good reason; it produces large numbers of 1-to 1 1/2 -pound fish. It usually takes a 9- to 10-pound walleye to win fishing contests periodically held on the lake, and you can count on several in this size range to be caught each year.

Scott Van Valkenburg, of Fisherman's Corner, 5675 Miller Trunk Highway, Hermantown, MN, 218-729-5369, told us that some people have a hard time fishing Island Lake because of its massive size and endless structure. In fact, much of the mid-lake structure doesn't hold fish. Van Valkenburg says the far west bay, near Otter River, always produces nice fish. The eastern bay, near the Cloquet River, offers great walleye fishing opportunities too, but only during spring. The last DNR survey in 2006 indicated the walleye population was average to above average in abundance. However, the growth rate was extremely slow.

Northern pike are also abundant in Island Lake, with the average running between 3 and 6 pounds. Van Valkenburg says several 20-pound pike have been taken in recent years. The latest DNR survey showed pike numbers to be above average.

Pound-plus crappies roam the lake, but they're tough to find. Patient anglers will search out suspended schools with their depth finders. The overall population is below average, but their growth and size was above average.

Smallmouth bass have been turning up in anglers' catches more frequently in recent years. The population abundance, according to the DNR, is above average. Overall mean length for smallies is 13.7 inches.

The DNR has been stocking the lake annually with muskies. Anglers have reportedly caught a few in recent years. Leech Lake strain muskie fingerlings have the potential of reaching 40 to 50 pounds. The mean length for Island muskies during the last DNR survey was 32.3 inches.

If you don't own or have access to a boat, don't worry. Shore anglers fare well at the base of the bridge and along the shore on both sides of the highway. The water depth drops fairly quickly under the bridge, where walleyes and crappies gather around the pilings. Some of the large walleyes caught each year are taken in this area from shore.

FISH STOCKING DATA

year	species	size	# released
06	Muskellunge	Fingerling	741
07	Muskellunge	Fingerling	1,848
07	Muskellunge	Adult	66
08	Muskellunge	Fingerling	2,546
09	Muskellunge	Fingerling	475
10	Muskellunge	Fingerling	2,020

NET CATCH DATA

Date: 06/06/2006

	Gill Nets		Trap Nets	
species	# per net	avg. fish weight (lbs.)	# per net	avg. fish weight (lbs.)
Black Bullhead	-	-		
Black Crappie	trace	0.49	1.6	0.5
Bluegill	-	-	0.7	0.55
Northern Pike	0.7	2.62	0.6	1.67
Pumpkin. Sunfish	trace	0.2	0.4	0.39
Rock Bass	2.7	0.45	1.6	0.4
Smallmouth Bass	0.5	1.46	0.5	0.86
Walleye	7.0	0.63	1.2	1.0
White Sucker	1.7	1.91	0.2	3.33
Yellow Perch	8.9	0.3	0.3	0.19

LENGTH OF SELECTED SPECIES SAMPLED FROM ALL GEAR

Number of fish caught for the following length categories (inches):

species	0-5	6-8	9-11	12-14	15-19	20-24	25-29	>30	Total
Black Bullhead	-	-	-	-	-	-	-	-	-
Black Crappie	2	16	14	1	-	-	-	-	33
Bluegill	-	12	1	-	-	-	-	-	13
Northern Pike	-	-	2	1	8	8	8	-	27
Pumpkin. Sunfish	-	8	-	-	-	-	-	-	8
Rock Bass	12	63	18	-	-	-	-	-	93
Smallmouth Bass	1	1	8	9	3	-	-	-	22
Walleye	-	42	72	48	15	5	1	1	184
Yellow Perch	2	135	71	1	-	-	-	-	209

ISLAND LAKE (east basin)

N
West Basin
Dam Rd
Minnesota Power picnic area
Minnesota Power Hideaway Recreation Area
CR 274
Cloquet River
EV
94' Max
92° 09' 00"
92° 08' 30"
92° 08' 00"
92° 07' 30"
92° 07' 00"
92° 06' 30"
92° 06' 00"
92° 05' 30"
92° 05' 00"
47° 01' 00"
47° 01' 30"
47° 02' 00"
47° 02' 30"

NOT FOR NAVIGATION

Source: Minnesota Department of Natural Resources, USGS

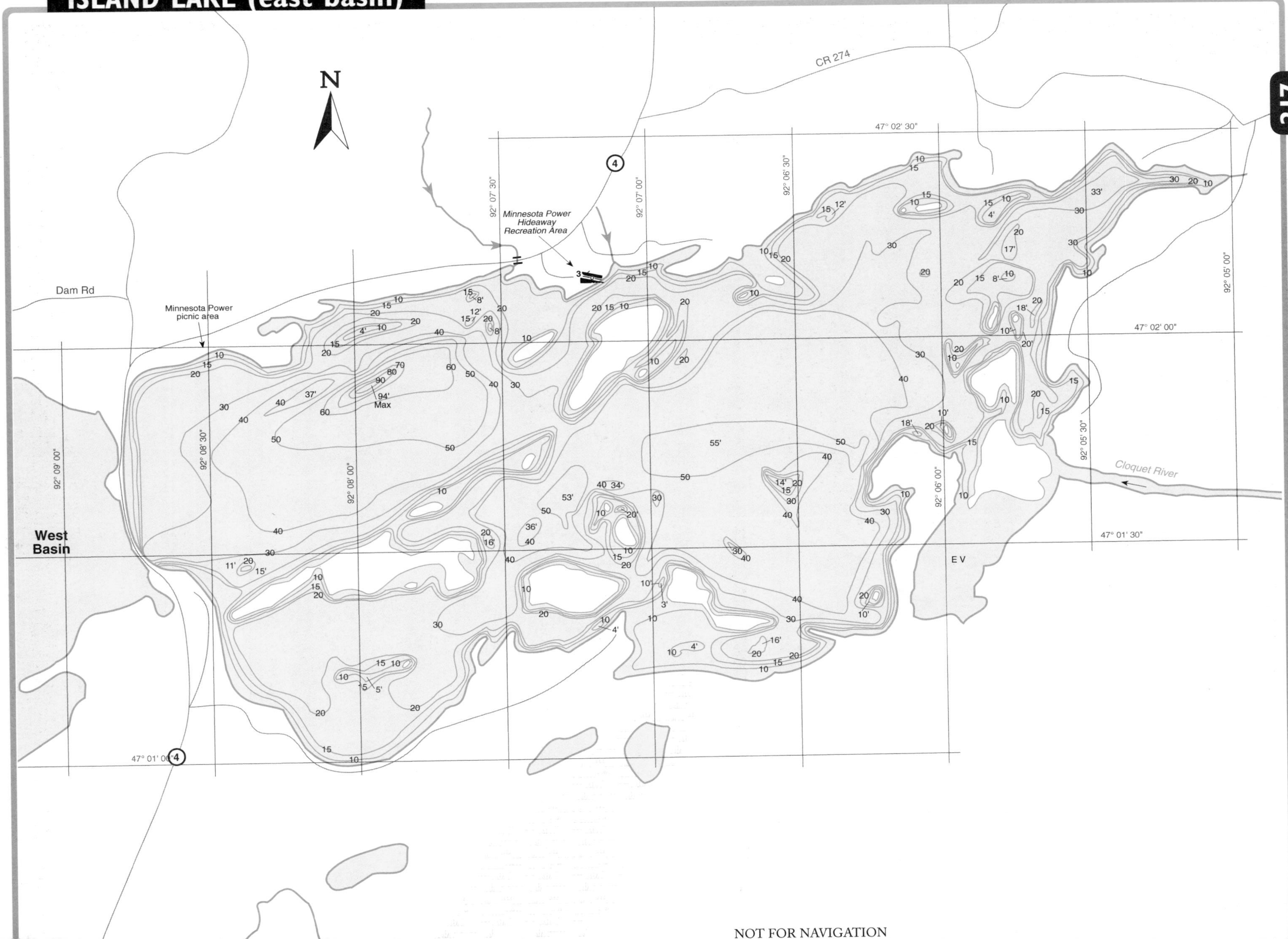

N

Morgan
Lake

Cook's
Lake

Apple
Lake

Boulder Dam Rd

Minnesota
Power Gate
(no thoroughfare)

W Island Lake Rd

North Dike Rd

East Cook Lake Rd

CR 215

48

48

Bear Island Rd

First Ave

dam

Cloquet River

Island Lake Dam Rd

Fredenberg Lake Rd

Island Beach
Campground

47° 02' 30"
47° 02' 00"
47° 01' 30"
47° 01' 00"
47° 00' 30"
47° 00' 00"
46° 59' 30"
46° 59' 00"
46° 58' 30"

92° 15' 30"
92° 15' 00"
92° 14' 30"
92° 14' 00"
92° 13' 30"
92° 13' 00"
92° 12' 30"
92° 12' 00"

NOT FOR NAVIGATION

Source: Minnesota Department of Natural Resources, USGS

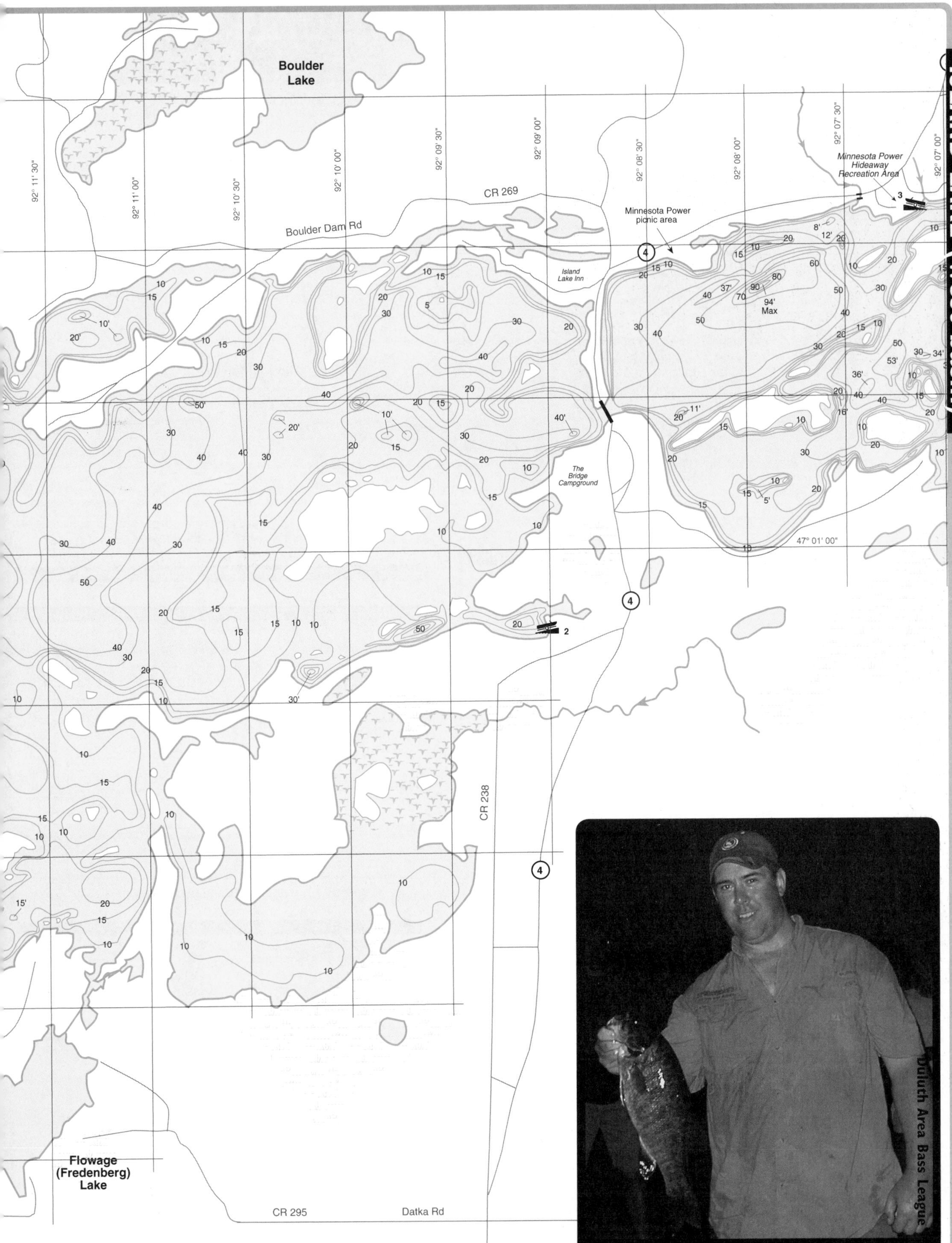

Boulder Lake
CR 269
Boulder Dam Rd
Minnesota Power picnic area
Island Lake Inn
The Bridge Campground
Minnesota Power Hideaway Recreation Area
94' Max
CR 238
Flowage (Fredenberg) Lake
CR 295
Datka Rd
92° 11' 30"
92° 11' 00"
92° 10' 30"
92° 10' 00"
92° 09' 30"
92° 09' 00"
92° 08' 30"
92° 08' 00"
92° 07' 30"
92° 07' 00"
47° 01' 00"
Duluth Area Bass League

This 3 lb 9 oz smallmouth took big bass honors at an evening tournament on Island Lake.

NOT FOR NAVIGATION

Source: Minnesota Department of Natural Resources, USGS

SALO LAKE
St. Louis County

INDIAN LAKE
St. Louis County

LITTLE STONE LAKE
St. Louis County

LITTLE STONE LAKE

St. Louis County

INDIAN LAKE

St. Louis County

SALO LAKE

St. Louis County

	SALO	INDIAN	LITTLE STONE
Area map pg / coord:	21 / D-6	25 / A-5	25 / A-6
Watershed:	Cloquet	Cloquet	Cloquet
Surface area:	141 acres	57 acres	183 acres
Shorelength:	2.1 miles	1.7 miles	3.6 miles
Max / mean depth:	20 feet / 7 feet	19 feet / 9 feet	17 feet / 9 feet
Water color / clarity:	Brown tint / 6.0 feet (2006)	Brown / 4.5 feet (2009)	13.6 feet (2007)
Shoreland zoning:	Rec. dev.	Rec. dev.	Rec. Dev.
Management class:	Walleye-centrarchid	Northern pike	Centrarchid
Ecological type:	Centrarchid-walleye	Northern pike-sucker	Centrarchid
Accessibility:	USFS-owned public access with concrete ramp on west shore	State-owned public access with concrete ramp on east shore	County-owned public access with gravel ramp on southwest shore
	47° 20' 10.21" N 91° 49' 39.58" W	47° 16' 17.73" N 91° 50' 59.22" W	47° 13' 45.06" N 91° 49' 35.94" W
Accommodations:	Picnicking, dock, outhouses	Camping, picnicking	None

Salo Lake

FISH STOCKING DATA

year	species	size	# released
05	Walleye	Fingerling	8,229
07	Walleye	Fingerling	5,734
09	Walleye	Fingerling	6,324

LENGTH OF SELECTED SPECIES SAMPLED FROM ALL GEAR
Survey Date: 06/19/2006

Number of fish caught for the following length categories (inches):

species	0-5	6-8	9-11	12-14	15-19	20-24	25-29	>30	Total
Black Bullhead	-	-	2	-	-	-	-	-	2
Black Crappie	7	7	8	-	-	-	-	-	22
Bluegill	28	38	-	-	-	-	-	-	66
Northern Pike	-	-	1	2	4	10	5	3	25
Pumpkin. Sunfish	6	2	1	-	-	-	-	-	9
Smallmouth Bass	-	-	-	1	-	-	-	-	1
Walleye	-	-	1	3	-	-	-	-	4
Yellow Perch	9	21	-	-	-	-	-	-	30

Indian Lake

NO RECORD OF STOCKING

LENGTH OF SELECTED SPECIES SAMPLED FROM ALL GEAR
Survey Date: 06/22/2009

Number of fish caught for the following length categories (inches):

species	0-5	6-8	9-11	12-14	15-19	20-24	25-29	>30	Total
Black Bullhead	1	1	-	-	-	-	-	-	2
Black Crappie	5	26	13	-	-	-	-	-	44
Bluegill	20	27	-	-	-	-	-	-	47
Northern Pike	-	-	-	-	14	19	3	1	37
Pumpkin. Sunfish	7	1	-	-	-	-	-	-	8
Walleye	-	-	-	-	6	4	3	-	13
White Sucker	-	-	3	4	41	-	-	-	48
Yellow Perch	10	13	2	-	-	-	-	-	25

FISHING INFORMATION

These are good little fishing lakes in the Brimson area. The folks at the former Al's Bait & Tackle in Two Harbors, MN, said **Indian Lake** has a lot of northern pike in the 1.5- to 3-pound class and produces one or two a year in the teens, poundage-wise. Walleyes are tough to find, and they're usually in the 1- to 2-pound class. Crappies, sunfish and yellow perch are also available with average sizes generally running in the small- to medium-range. Fish shorelines and weed edges for all species. The lake is small, but it receives relatively heavy fishing pressure because of its campground. There are 25 campsites with fire pits, picnic tables, outhouses, water pumps and a nice swimming beach.

Salo Lake is a pretty little lake that doesn't receive much fishing pressure. Crappies get most of the attention, but there is also a fair walleye population, one buoyed by DNR stocking. Decent northern pike fishing is also available. A few nice largemouth and smallmouth bass are caught every year.

Little **Stone Lake**'s walleye fishing has been on the rise and there are nice largemouth bass, northern pike and bluegills found near the ample cover and structure. Most locals fish the lake for crappies and bluegills. The folks at the former Al's Bait & Tackle said this is a great lake to take kids fishing. Little Stone is fishable from shore, with a good mix of species and sizes. Fish weed edges and submerged wood. Be sure to watch your lower unit, if you take your boat out.

Little Stone Lake

FISH STOCKING DATA

year	species	size	# released
05	Walleye	Fingerling	8,356
07	Walleye	Fingerling	3,627
09	Walleye	Fingerling	2,170

LENGTH OF SELECTED SPECIES SAMPLED FROM ALL GEAR
Survey Date: 07/30/2007

Number of fish caught for the following length categories (inches):

species	0-5	6-8	9-11	12-14	15-19	20-24	25-29	>30	Total
Black Crappie	33	22	7	-	-	-	-	-	62
Bluegill	291	239	-	-	-	-	-	-	530
Largemouth Bass	-	1	-	-	-	-	-	-	1
Northern Pike	-	-	2	4	14	18	7	1	46
Pumpkin. Sunfish	20	4	-	-	-	-	-	-	24
Walleye	-	-	-	-	1	4	1	-	6
Yellow Perch	7	6	-	-	-	-	-	-	13

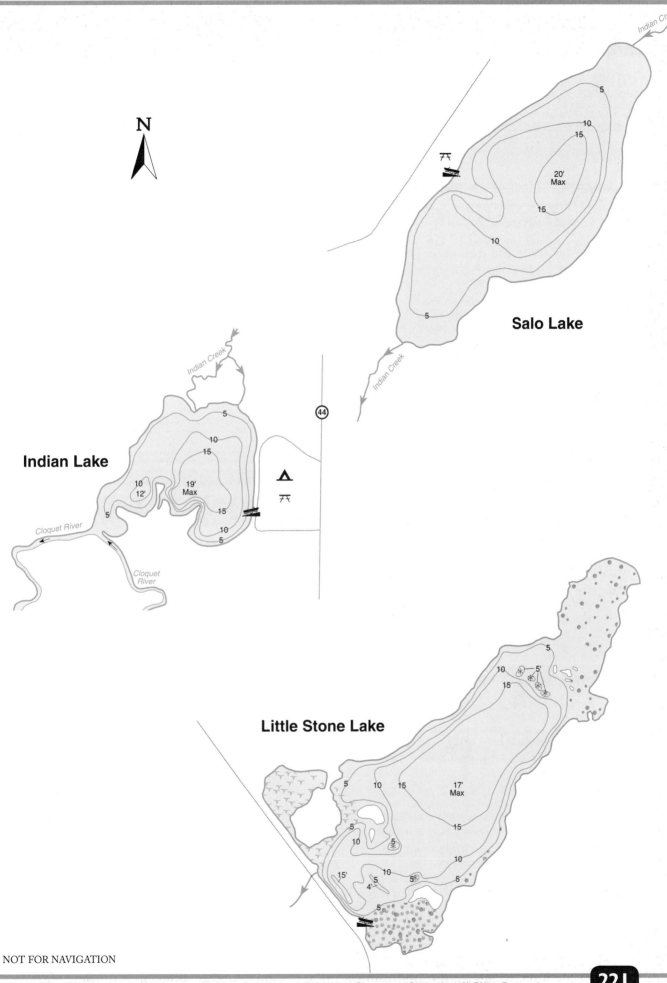

Salo Lake

20'
Max

Indian Lake

19'
Max

12'

Little Stone Lake

5'

17'
Max

15'

4'

Indian Creek

Cloquet River

Cloquet River

N

44

NOT FOR NAVIGATION

Source: Minnesota Department of Natural Resources, USGS

BEAR LAKE
St. Louis County

Area map page / coordinates: 25 / B-5
Surface water area: 61 acres / 5.0 ft. secchi (1965)
Shorelength: 1.8 miles
Accessibility: Access with concrete ramp on southwest shore, off Bear Lake Trail
47° 12' 27.37" N / 91° 55' 17.94" W
Accommodations: State campground

NO RECORD OF STOCKING

FISHING INFORMATION

According to Dan Bohrer at the former Al's Bait & Tackle in Two Harbors, MN, Bear Lake is basically known as a northern pike and panfish lake, but there are a few walleyes and some decent largemouth bass available.

One of the easiest ways to catch northern pike throughout the year is to throw something flashy at them. Spinnerbaits or jerkbaits fished just under the surface will trigger strikes from these aggressive predators.

Anglers attempting to hook a few walleyes would be wise to stick with a slip bobber and bait here. Since walleye numbers aren't very high, fishing with a leech, minnow or nightcrawler could not only help you catch a few walleyes, but it should also entice other fish like bass or panfish. To reach the public access from Highway 44, turn off on North Bear Lake Road and go 3 miles to the public access sign; take a left and go 1/8 mile. The ramp is quite decent and will accommodate boats to 18 feet.

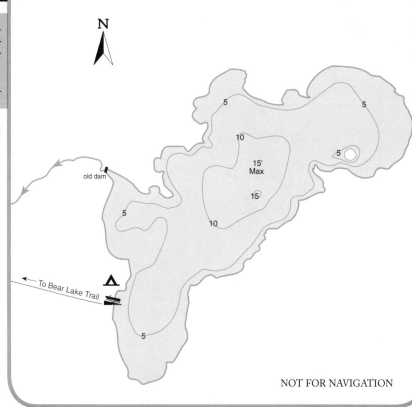

NOT FOR NAVIGATION

MOOSE LAKE
St. Louis County

Area map page / coordinates: 25 / B-5
Surface water area: 62 acres / 9.5 ft. secchi (2001)
Shorelength: 1.4 miles
Accessibility: Carry-down access from Cry. Rd. 44 to east shore; 47° 11' 39.64" N / 91° 53' 3.00" W
Accommodations: None

FISH STOCKING DATA			
year	species	size	# released
99	Walleye	Fry	110,000
01	Walleye	Fry	110,000

FISHING INFORMATION

Moose Lake is a 62-acre lake with a maximum depth of 17 feet. Water clarity is decent, reaching down to 9.5 feet. While there is no designated public access, there is land at the east side of the lake which is county-owned due to tax forfeit. Fishing pressure is light here owing to limited public access and low shoreline development.

Walleye fry have been stocked here bi-annually. However, very few walleyes have been sampled from this lake by the DNR. Of the whopping 6 that were caught over the course of two surveys, only one was aged to the same year as walleye stocking occurred. The 2 walleyes caught by the DNR in 2001 were in the 20- to 24-inch category.

The mean length of 22.1 inches for northern pike is considered large. Black crappies were also large measuring 8.2 inches and 8 of the crappies sampled were over 9 years old.

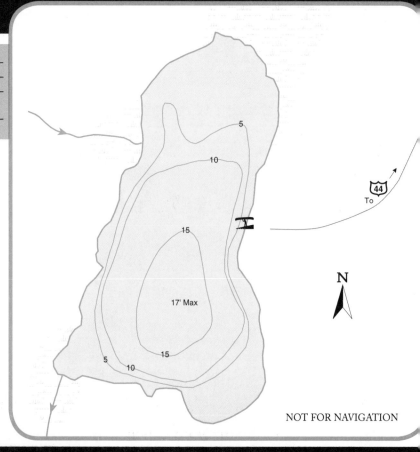

NOT FOR NAVIGATION

Source: Minnesota Department of Natural Resources, USGS

WHITE LAKE
St. Louis County

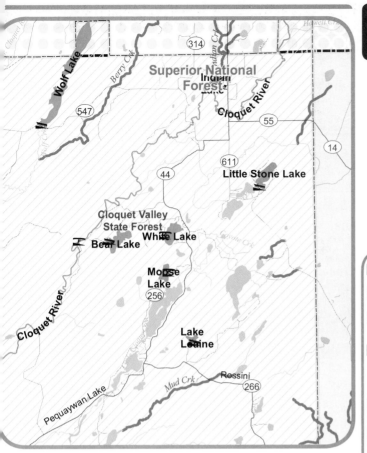

Area map page / coordinates:	25 / B-5
Watershed:	Cloquet
Surface area / shorelength:	123 acres / 2.2 miles
Maximum / mean depth:	34 feet / 12 feet
Water color / clarity:	7.5 feet (2007)

Accessibility: State-owned public access with gravel ramp on southwest shore, off White Lake Road

47° 12' 35.49" N / 91° 53' 9.76" W

Accommodations: None

FISH STOCKING DATA

year	species	size	# released
06	Walleye	Fingerling	2,299
08	Walleye	fingerling	7,560
10	Walleye	Fingerling	3,000

LENGTH OF SELECTED SPECIES SAMPLED FROM ALL GEAR
Survey Date: 08/17/2007

Number of fish caught for the following length categories (inches):

species	0-5	6-8	9-11	12-14	15-19	20-24	25-29	>30	Total
Black Crappie	5	8	37	2	-	-	-	-	52
Largemouth Bass	-	-	-	3	-	-	-	-	3
Northern Pike	-	-	-	-	1	6	6	1	14
Pumpkin. Sunfish	15	33	-	-	-	-	-	-	48
Rock Bass	10	22	9	-	-	-	-	-	41
Walleye	-	4	10	3	29	1	-	-	47
Yellow Perch	3	31	-	-	-	-	-	-	34

FISHING INFORMATION

White Lake is by no means a big body of water. At 123 acres, it is small enough to fish thoroughly in one day. While you're out there, you'll find walleyes, black crappies, northern pike, yellow perch and largemouth bass.

Walleyes are the primary management species on this lake. During the most recent DNR lake survey, the walleye population was considered average for similar lakes in the area. The mean length was 12.8 inches, which is considered small. The management of walleyes has changed through the years from stocking fingerlings then fry then fingerlings again. At this time the DNR plans on continuing stocking the lake, unless it is deemed ineffective. There are some steep drop-offs along the eastern shore which should be fished during summer months. Try bottom bouncers and spinners or a live bait rigged tipped with a jumbo leech or a nightcrawler. According to Dan Bohrer of the former Al's Bait & Tackle in Two Harbors, MN, nothing much has changed on this lake in the last few years. "The fishing has stayed about the same here," he said. "The walleyes are there, but they're generally just eaters."

Black crappies are in average abundance here with a mean length of 8.9 inches. Anglers can have success fishing for crappies along weed edges in spring and steeper drops in summer. Ice fishing is also productive for crappies. Black crappie numbers declined significantly in the last DNR survey. The DNR is investigating this situation to determine whether walleye management is negatively impacting the crappies.

Northern pike anglers will find fish here. Their population is average according to the DNR, but their mean length, 23.5 inches, was considered large. Look for northerns anywhere along the various weed edges. If you want to try for a large specimen, fish deeper structures during summer. Use a heavy jig-and-minnow combo or try a bass flipping jig and dress a fluke or similar soft plastic minnow imitator on the back. Use your electronics to find fish and pop either of these combos along the bottom. You'll find out quickly if the pike want to play.

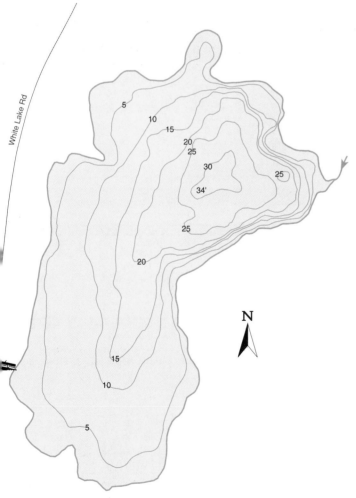

White Lake Rd

N

NOT FOR NAVIGATION

ALDEN LAKE LITTLE ALDEN LAKE SPRING LAKE
St. Louis County *St. Louis County* *St. Louis County*

	ALDEN	LITTLE ALDEN	SPRING
Area map pg / coord:	25 / D-4	25 / D-4	25 / D-4
Watershed:	Cloquet	Cloquet	Cloquet
Surface area:	180 acres	81 acres	98 acres
Shorelength:	2.8 miles	1.9 miles	2.6 miles
Max / mean depth:	29 feet / 6 feet	29 feet / 11 feet	25 feet / 3 feet
Water color / clarity:	6.2 feet (2001)	9.0 feet (2001)	8.5 feet (2008)
Shoreland zoning:	Rec. dev.	Natural envt.	Rec. dev.
Management class:	Walleye-centrarchid	NA	Walleye-centrarchid
Ecological type:	Centrarchid	NA	Centrarchid
Accessibility:	Via navigable channel from the Cloquet River	Via navigable channel from the Cloquet River	Carry-down access to east shore across public land
	NA	NA	47° 4' 7.93" N 91° 59' 49.52" W
Accommodations:	None	None	None

Alden Lake

NO RECORD OF STOCKING

LENGTH OF SELECTED SPECIES SAMPLED FROM ALL GEAR
Survey Date: 07/30/2001

Number of fish caught for the following length categories (inches):

species	0-5	6-8	9-11	12-14	15-19	20-24	25-29	>30	Total
Black Crappie	-	9	6	2	-	-	-	-	17
Bluegill	1	17	3	-	-	-	-	-	21
Northern Pike	-	-	2	2	-	5	-	-	9
Pumpkin. Sunfish	1	4	-	-	-	-	-	-	5
Rock Bass	1	2	3	-	-	-	-	-	6
Smallmouth Bass	-	-	2	6	-	-	-	-	8
Walleye	-	2	6	7	9	2	-	-	26
Yellow Perch	31	40	5	-	-	-	-	-	76

Little Alden Lake

NO RECORD OF STOCKING

LENGTH OF SELECTED SPECIES SAMPLED FROM ALL GEAR
Survey Date: 08/06/2001

Number of fish caught for the following length categories (inches):

species	0-5	6-8	9-11	12-14	15-19	20-24	25-29	>30	Total
Black Crappie	-	1	6	1	-	-	-	-	8
Bluegill	16	28	-	-	-	-	-	-	44
Northern Pike	-	-	2	8	11	6	2	-	29
Pumpkin. Sunfish	11	7	-	-	-	-	-	-	18
Rock Bass	1	-	1	-	-	-	-	-	2
Smallmouth Bass	1	-	-	1	2	-	-	-	4
Walleye	-	-	2	6	4	1	1	-	14
Yellow Perch	6	9	-	-	-	-	-	-	15

FISHING INFORMATION

Alden and Little Alden Lakes are part of the Cloquet River flowage, and while there is no designated public access on either, the lakes can be entered from the river. The river system provides the Aldens with a wide variety of species that migrate in and out at their whim.

Big Alden is primarily managed for walleyes. In the latest DNR survey, growth rates were slow, but abundance levels were average. Yellow perch stats were similar. Walleyes seem to be doing well, with all year classes represented in the survey. Northern pike, black crappies and bluegills were all found to be below average in abundance, but with larger than average sizes. Quality is the key here, not quantity.

The DNR stats on **Little Alden** showed similarities among the species. Northern pike and yellow perch were found to be average in abundance and size. Black crappies were below average in abundance, but the mean length was a whopping 10 inches. Bluegills were average in abundance, size and growth rates.

Spring Lake, unlike Big and Little Alden Lakes, has a gravel access in the north shore. Black crappie growth rates were fast and the size structure was good, with 81% of the crappies sampled measuring longer than 8 inches. Walleye stocking programs started on this lake with a mixture of yearlings, fingerlings and adults being stocked. The program has since concentrated on fingerlings.

Spring Lake

FISH STOCKING DATA

year	species	size	# released
05	Walleye	Fingerling	5,337
07	Walleye	Fingerling	2,398
09	Walleye	Fingerling	3,013

LENGTH OF SELECTED SPECIES SAMPLED FROM ALL GEAR
Survey Date: 08/18/2008

Number of fish caught for the following length categories (inches):

species	0-5	6-8	9-11	12-14	15-19	20-24	25-29	>30	Total
Black Bullhead	76	57	-	-	-	-	-	-	137
Black Crappie	-	5	3	1	-	-	-	-	9
Bluegill	2	2	-	-	-	-	-	-	4
Northern Pike	-	1	-	1	11	3	1	-	17
Pumpkin. Sunfish	31	2	-	-	-	-	-	-	33
Walleye	-	-	-	-	1	-	-	-	1
White Sucker	-	2	4	5	31	2	-	-	45
Yellow Perch	-	7	3	-	-	-	-	-	10

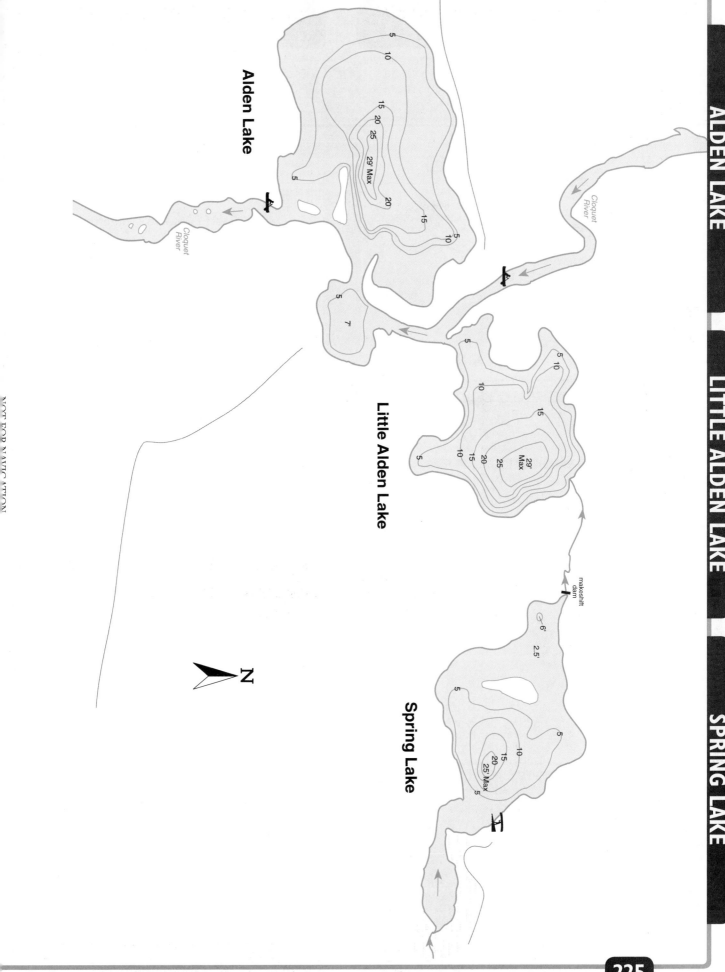

Alden Lake

Little Alden Lake

Spring Lake

N

Source: Minnesota Department of Natural Resources, USGS

PRAIRIE LAKE
St. Louis County

Area map pg / coord: 26 / C-3

Watershed: Prairie-Willow

Surface area: 794 acres

Shorelength: 1.8 miles

Max / mean depth: 47 feet / NA

Water color / clarity: 5.0 ft. (2010)

Shoreland zoning class: Rec. dev.

Mgmt class / Ecological type:
Walleye / soft-water walleye

Accessibility: State-owned public access with concrete ramp on east bay
46° 47' 19.24" N / 92° 53' 8.97" W

Accommodations: Outhouse, dock

WEST TWIN LAKE
St. Louis County

Area map pg / coord: 27 / C-6

Watershed: St. Louis

Surface area: 121 acres

Shorelength: NA

Max / mean depth: 18 feet / NA

Water color / clarity: 10.5 ft. (2010)

Shoreland zoning class: Rec. dev.

Mgmt class / Ecological type:
Centrarchid / northern pike-sucker

Accessibility: Carry-down public access in county park on west shore
46° 48' 6.24" N / 92° 35' 33.07" W

Accommodations: County park

PRAIRIE LAKE — FISH STOCKING DATA

year	species	size	# released
06	Walleye	Fry	1,275,000
08	Walleye	Fry	1,345,000
09	Walleye	Fry	1,275,000

NET CATCH DATA
Date: 08/30/2010

species	Gill Nets # per net	Gill Nets avg. fish weight (lbs.)	Trap Nets # per net	Trap Nets avg. fish weight (lbs.)
Black Crappie	7.67	0.27	3.75	0.40
Bluegill	0.17	0.17	2.92	0.27
Largemouth Bass	-	-	0.08	0.07
Northern Pike	2.17	3.39	1.50	2.89
Rock Bass	0.75	0.51	0.42	0.43
Walleye	2.58	0.65	0.33	1.43

LENGTH OF SELECTED SPECIES SAMPLED FROM ALL GEAR
Number of fish caught for the following length categories (inches):

species	0-5	6-8	9-11	12-14	15-19	20-24	25-29	>30	Total
Black Bullhead	-	-	1	-	-	-	-	-	1
Black Crappie	6	113	16	1	-	-	-	-	137
Bluegill	4	33	-	-	-	-	-	-	37
Largemouth Bass	1	-	-	-	-	-	-	-	1
Northern Pike	-	-	1	1	9	14	16	3	44
Pumpkin. Sunfish	2	1	-	-	-	-	-	-	3
Rock Bass	1	10	3	-	-	-	-	-	14
Walleye	-	2	13	14	5	1	-	-	35
White Sucker	-	2	1	7	16	8	-	-	34
Yellow Perch	49	38	2	-	-	-	-	-	89

WEST TWIN LAKE — FISH STOCKING DATA

year	species	size	# released
05	Walleye	Fry	205,000

NET CATCH DATA
Date: 06/28/2010

species	Gill Nets # per net	Gill Nets avg. fish weight (lbs.)	Trap Nets # per net	Trap Nets avg. fish weight (lbs.)
Black Crappie	0.50	0.17	5.73	0.20
Bluegill	0.50	0.16	8.36	0.22
Northern Pike	4.50	1.60	1.00	2.22
Smallmouth Bass	0.50	2.23	-	-
Walleye	2.25	3.71	1.00	4.54

LENGTH OF SELECTED SPECIES SAMPLED FROM ALL GEAR
Number of fish caught for the following length categories (inches):

species	0-5	6-8	9-11	12-14	15-19	20-24	25-29	>30	Total
Black Crappie	39	15	11	-	-	-	-	-	65
Bluegill	15	78	-	-	-	-	-	-	94
Hybrid Sunfish	10	-	-	-	-	-	-	-	10
Northern Pike	-	-	-	3	16	7	3	-	29
Pumpkin. Sunfish	107	-	-	-	-	-	-	-	107
Smallmouth Bass	-	-	-	1	1	-	-	-	2
Walleye	-	-	-	-	3	14	3	-	20
Yellow Perch	5	8	-	-	-	-	-	-	13

FISHING INFORMATION

Prairie Lake is a good-sized lake boasting of 794 acres and a maximum depth of 47 feet. Because it connects to the Mississippi River watershed, it is home to a diverse fish community that includes black crappie, bluegill, northern pike, walleye and yellow perch. A good area for walleyes is off Big Island in the western section of the lake. Fish steeper drops near the south side of the island. There are also some nice ones along the north shore of the bay, near the public access. Most of the walleyes are 1- to 1 1/2 -pounders, but there's a chance at some 5-pound-plus fish. The best action seems to be early in the day. Northern pike tend to be on the small side here, with the average length being around 20 inches and a few measuring 25 inches. Try fishing for pike along shorelines and off the river outlet on the southwest shore. Work weedbeds near the cattails. For a change of pace, try

fishing for tullibee (also known as Ciscoes). Only a few lakes in the Duluth area have this specie and sport netting is open.

West Twin is a small lake with two public access locations on its west side. The maximum depth here is 18 feet, but only 4% of the lake reaches that far. The rest of the lake is 15 feet or shallower. The lake has was last stocked in 2005, when 205,000 walleye fry were released. Walleye abundance is average and fast growth rates are occurring, according to the latest DNR survey. The majority of the northern pike sampled were in the 15-19 inch range, with no collected specimen busting the 30-inch mark. You can catch crappies all around the lake. Focus on the area around the public access early in the season. As water warms, they suspend in deeper water off the islands.

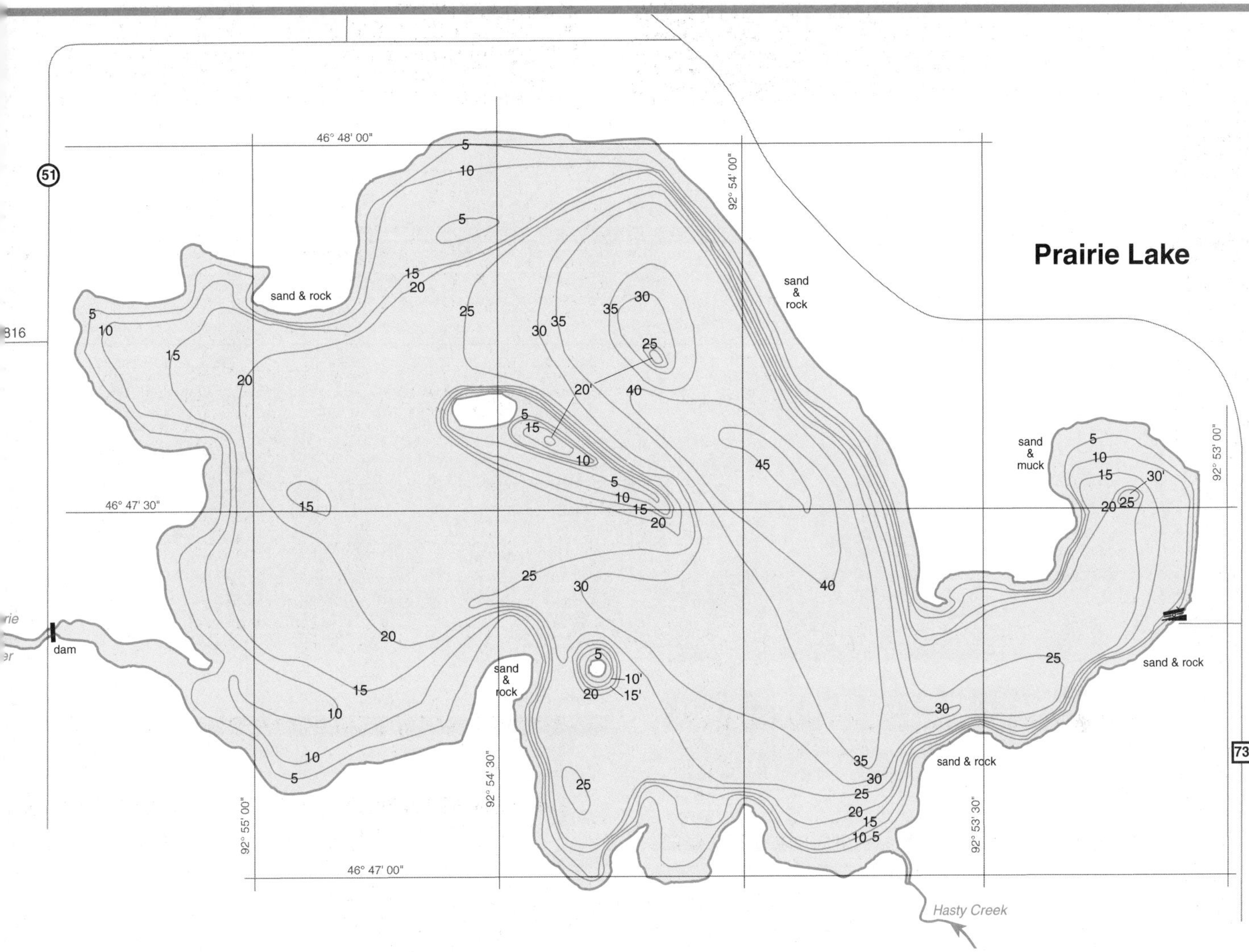

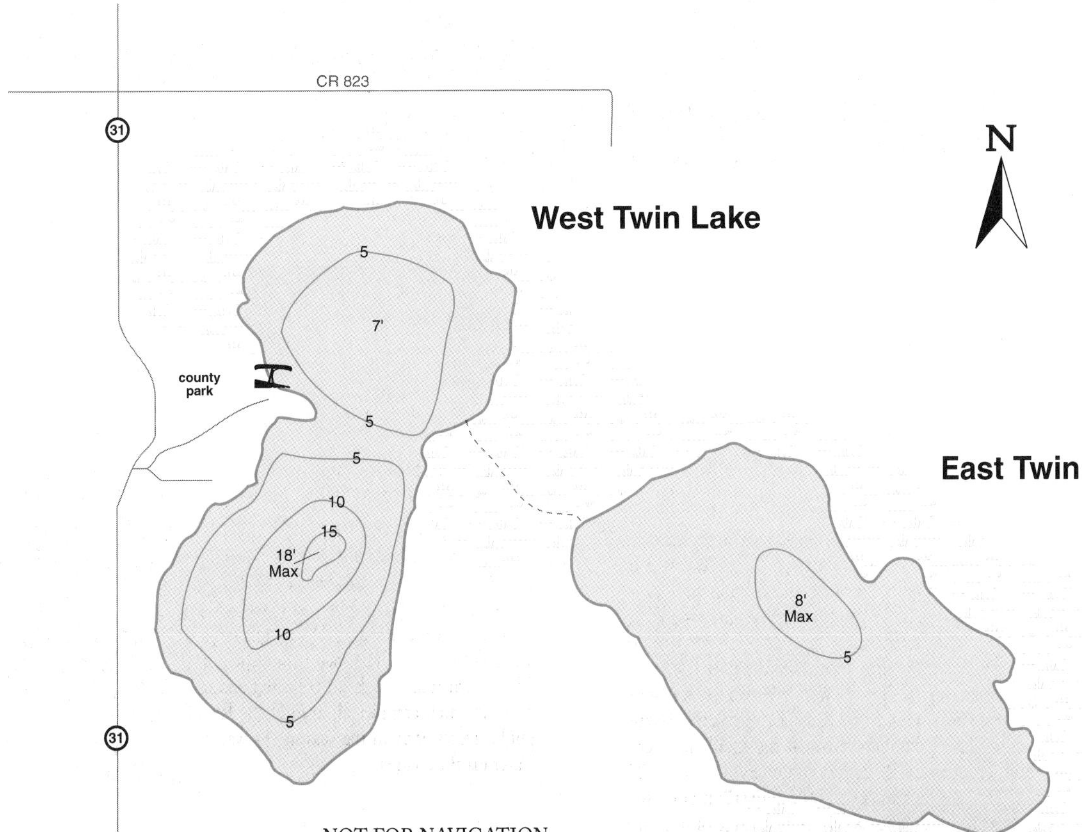

Prairie Lake

46° 48' 00"

92° 54' 00"

92° 53' 00"

46° 47' 30"

92° 54' 30"

92° 55' 00"

92° 53' 30"

46° 47' 00"

51

316

sand & rock

sand & rock

sand & muck

sand & rock

sand & rock

sand & rock

sand & rock

dam

rie
er

73

5
10
5
15
20
25
30 35 35 30
30 35
25
20'
40
45
5
15
10
5
10
15
20
25
30
20
15
10
5
10
5
20
15
10
5
5
10'
15'
25
30
35
30
25
20
15
10 5
40
5
10
15
20 25
30'
25
5
10
15
20
30

Hasty Creek

CR 823

31

West Twin Lake

N

5
7'
5
5
10
15
18'
Max
10
5

county
park

East Twin Lake

8'
Max
5

31

NOT FOR NAVIGATION

Source: Minnesota Department of Natural Resources, USGS

PIKE LAKE *St. Louis County*

Area map page / coordinates: 28 / B-2

Watershed: St. Louis

Surface water area / shorelength: 488 acres / 4.9 miles

Maximum / mean depth: 62 feet / 28 feet

Water color / clarity: Green tint / 13.75 feet (2009)

Shoreland zoning classification: General development

Management class / Ecological type: Walleye / soft-water walleye

Accessibility: Township-owned public access with earthen ramp on east shore off Martin Road

46° 51' 54.99" N / 92° 16' 59.76" W

Accommodations: Private club beach and amenities

FISHING INFORMATION

Pike Lake, located just north of Duluth, with its shoreline of birch trees and fine homes, is popular with recreational boaters and anglers alike. Scott Van Valkenburg owner and operator of Fisherman's Corner, 5675 Miller Trunk Highway, Hermantown, MN, 218-729-5369, is probably as familiar with this body of water as anyone. He says many popular freshwater gamefish can be found here, including walleyes, northern pike, largemouth bass, crappies and bluegills.

Many of the walleyes tend to run on the small side, but a DNR program has helped create a wide range of year classes. Most are caught from early June through the summer months and can be found off the large point on the south shore and along other steep drop-offs. Work the 16- to 20-foot depths, focusing on any subtle bottom structure changes and weedlines. Fish a little shallower in spring. The standard live bait approaches will work, as will trolling crankbaits and spinner rigs. After the DNR survey in 2004, it was determined the walleye population is average compared to similar lakes in the area. An ongoing stocking program continues, with nearly 500,000 fry introduced in even-numbered years.

According to Van Valkenburg, Pike Lake has some of the biggest northerns in the area. They're caught off the point and in the area adjacent to the AAA Auto Club beach area, as well as near the weedline, which runs pretty deep, due to clear water. Northern pike seem to bite best in early spring and again in July. Spinnerbaits, crankbaits and large minnows will all attract their fair share of pike. The most recent DNR survey, conducted in 2009, showed the abundance of northern pike to be below average compared to other lakes of a similar type. However, all captured fish were at 30 inches long.

Bluegills run from 1/2 to 1 pound and can be found in shallows when they move to spawning beds in late spring. Bluegill abundance was below average according to DNR statistics. Both size and growth rates were average.

You'll find largemouth bass shallow earlier in the year and in morning and evening in summer months. They tend to move to deeper water near weedlines during the day in summer. Soft plastics are a good bet when chasing bass. Texas rigged tubes, worms or creature baits will work under most conditions. You can also try your luck with the topwater bite.

FISH STOCKING DATA			
year	species	size	# released
06	Walleye	Fry	494,000
08	Walleye	Fry	495,000
10	Walleye	Fry	494,000

NET CATCH DATA				
Date: 08/17/2009	Gill Nets		Trap Nets	
species	# per net	avg. fish weight (lbs.)	# per net	avg. fish weight (lbs.)
Black Crappie	1.33	0.60	0.56	0.47
Bluegill	9.00	0.31	6.44	0.23
Largemouth Bass	0.33	1.31	-	-
Northern Pike	0.22	11.96	0.44	16.55
Rock Bass	4.67	0.31	6.00	0.18
Walleye	13.00	1.51	-	-
White Sucker	8.22	1.56	7.78	2.84
Yellow Perch	51.11	0.14	1.89	0.15

LENGTH OF SELECTED SPECIES SAMPLED FROM ALL GEAR								
Number of fish caught for the following length categories (inches):								
species	0-5	6-8	9-11	12-14	15-19	20-24	25-29	>30	Total
Black Crappie	-	3	14	-	-	-	-	-	17
Bluegill	11	127	1	-	-	-	-	-	139
Largemouth Bass	-	-	-	3	-	-	-	-	3
Northern Pike	-	-	-	-	-	-	-	6	6
Pumpkin. Sunfish	8	7	-	-	-	-	-	-	15
Rock Bass	37	59	-	-	-	-	-	-	96
Walleye	-	2	7	35	60	11	2	-	117
White Sucker	-	2	12	26	85	19	-	-	144
Yellow Perch	83	386	8	-	-	-	-	-	477

Crappies will be in many of the same areas you'll find bass earlier in the year. They'll suspend over deeper water later in the year. Small minnows or jigs work early on and leeches become a factor for catching crappies during summer.

There is also a good population of yellow perch. The population is considered above average. Length and growth rates are average. This lake is very popular with recreational users. Try to fish during weekdays, if possible, to avoid crowds.

NOT FOR NAVIGATION

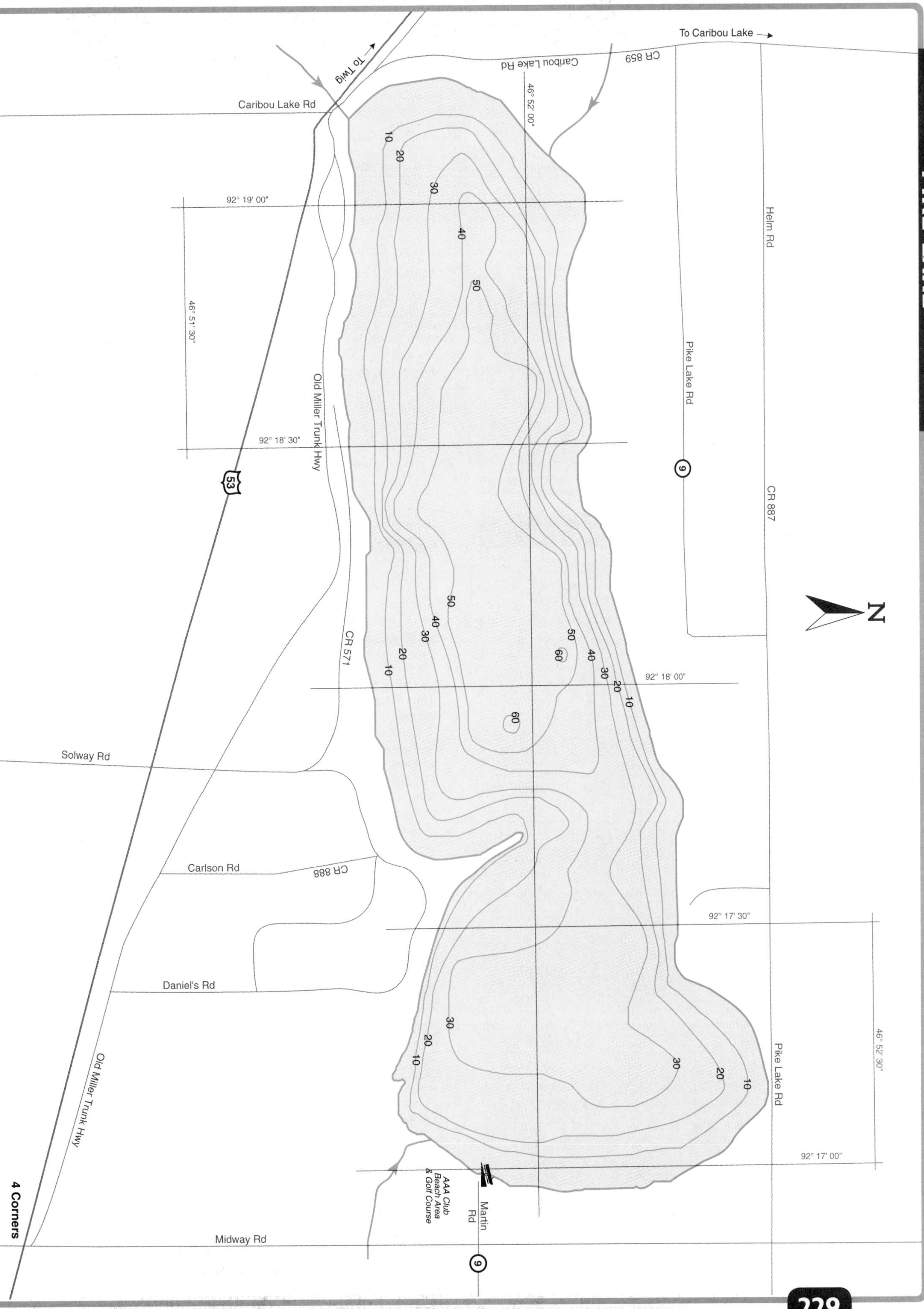

To Caribou Lake →

Caribou Lake Rd

CR 859

Caribou Lake Rd

Helm Rd

46° 52' 00"

92° 19' 00"

46° 51' 30"

92° 18' 30"

53

Old Miller Trunk Hwy

Pike Lake Rd

9

CR 887

10
20
30
40
50

N

46° 52' 00"

CR 571

50
40
30
20
10

50
60
40
30
20
10

60

92° 18' 00"

Solway Rd

Carlson Rd

CR 888

Daniel's Rd

92° 17' 30"

46° 52' 30"

30
20
10

30
20
10

92° 17' 00"

Old Miller Trunk Hwy

AAA Club
Beach Area
& Golf Course

Martin
Rd

Midway Rd

4 Corners

9

Source: Minnesota Department of Natural Resources, USGS

CARIBOU LAKE St. Louis County

Area map page / coordinates:	28 / A,B-2

Watershed: Cloquet

Surface water area / shorelength: 539 acres / 5.4 miles

Maximum / mean depth: 21 feet / 9 feet

Water color / clarity: 7.0 feet (2010)

Shoreland zoning classification: General development

Management class / Ecological type: Walleye-centrarchid / centrarchid

Accessibility: 1) Township-owned public access with earthen ramp, east shore
46° 53' 39.91" N / 92° 18' 4.01" W

Accessibility: 2) State-owned public access with concrete ramp, north shore
46° 53' 59.56" N / 92° 19' 25.18" W

Accessibility: 3) County-owned public access with earthen ramp, southwest
46° 53' 40.41" N / 92° 19' 25.41" W

Accommodations: None

FISHING INFORMATION

Caribou Lake is considered one of the area's best largemouth bass lakes. The folks at Fisherman's Corner, 5675 Miller Trunk Highway, Hermantown, MN, 218-729-5369, say most of the fishing on Caribou Lake is for northern pike, crappies and bluegills. Although the lake has been stocked with walleyes in recent years, these fish are hard to find. The last DNR lake survey showed the average walleye was about 20 inches long. This survey also produced three walleyes over 25 inches in length.

Northern Pike fishing is good all season with average length, according to DNR statistics, being near 20 inches. A 20-pound-class fish is caught each year, according to the folks at Fisherman's Corner. Try fishing for them and their smaller brothers and sisters around the edges of the many weed beds. For fast action, throw a spinnerbait with a brightly colored skirt and blades. White or chartreuse are good color options. If the area you're fishing is too weedy to work a spinnerbait, try a weedless spoon or a soft jerkbait rigged weedless. Of course, a bobber floating a minnow is always a good choice when fishing slows down.

Crappies run two or three to the pound and can be caught along shallow weedlines early in the year. A slip float and a small minnow or tiny tube jig will hook their fair share of crappies. During summer months, crappies tend to move to deeper weed edges. Use your electronics to locate inside turns, pockets or holes along deeper weeds. Present the same offerings you did earlier in the year, but add small leeches to your arsenal.

Largemouth bass have been averaging 2 pounds, but an occasional 4- to 6-pound fish is caught. Mid-June through summer is the best time for them. Most of the anglers are practicing catch and release, which explains the good average size and the possibility of a trophy bass. Caribou can get very weedy in summer, but a weed cutter is used to help keep the situation under control. Prior to the thickest weeds appearing, try casting a spinnerbait along weed edges and near shallower cover. As summer progresses, fish with a soft plastic like a Texas rigged tube or worm. A weightless Senko rigged

weedless can also produce bass in thick weeds. Stick with darker colors like green pumpkin or watermelon. If you want to try for the biggest bass in the lake, find a dense area of matted weeds. These areas can often hold big bass during the heat of summer. Use a flipping stick and spool your reel with heavy line; braided line is a good choice here. Tie on a weedless frog and cast it on top of matted weeds. Use a slow retrieve with plenty of pauses, especially near or in any openings. The strikes may not be plentiful, but they'll often be explosive.

FISH STOCKING DATA

year	species	size	# released
05	Walleye	Fingerling	31,453
07	Walleye	Fingerling	18,965
09	Walleye	Fingerling	24,703

NET CATCH DATA

Date: 07/19/2010

	Gill Nets		Trap Nets	
species	# per net	avg. fish weight (lbs.)	# per net	avg. fish weight (lbs.)
Black Crappie	5.44	0.23	7.08	0.19
Bluegill	4.11	0.20	21.83	0.18
Hybrid Sunfish	0.33	0.21	0.17	0.48
Largemouth Bass	0.78	1.78	-	-
Northern Pike	11.44	2.07	1.42	2.26
Pumpkin. Sunfish	4.00	0.22	2.58	0.16
Rock Bass	0.11	0.73	0.50	0.42
Walleye	1.33	1.43	0.42	4.81
White Sucker	0.11	3.29	-	-
Yellow Perch	5.33	0.11	0.17	0.12

LENGTH OF SELECTED SPECIES SAMPLED FROM ALL GEAR

Number of fish caught for the following length categories (inches):

species	0-5	6-8	9-11	12-14	15-19	20-24	25-29	>30	Total
Black Crappie	32	87	15	-	-	-	-	-	134
Bluegill	153	144	-	-	-	-	-	-	299
Hybrid Sunfish	2	3	-	-	-	-	-	-	5
Largemouth Bass	-	-	1	4	2	-	-	-	7
Northern Pike	-	-	1	3	48	51	15	2	120
Pumpkin. Sunfish	41	26	-	-	-	-	-	-	67
Rock Bass	2	3	2	-	-	-	-	-	7
Walleye	-	-	4	5	2	3	3	-	17
White Sucker	-	-	-	-	1	-	-	-	1
Yellow Perch	16	34	-	-	-	-	-	-	50

N

To 53

CR 885

CR 859

92° 19' 30"

46° 53' 30"

92° 19' 00"

46° 54' 00"

46° 54' 30"

3

2

5

5

10

5

5

10

10

10

10

10

10

10

10

15

15

5

10

5

15

15

20

21' Max

92° 18' 30"

CR 885

92° 18' 00"

1

Shady Lane

Industrial Rd

Kehtel Rd

CR 885

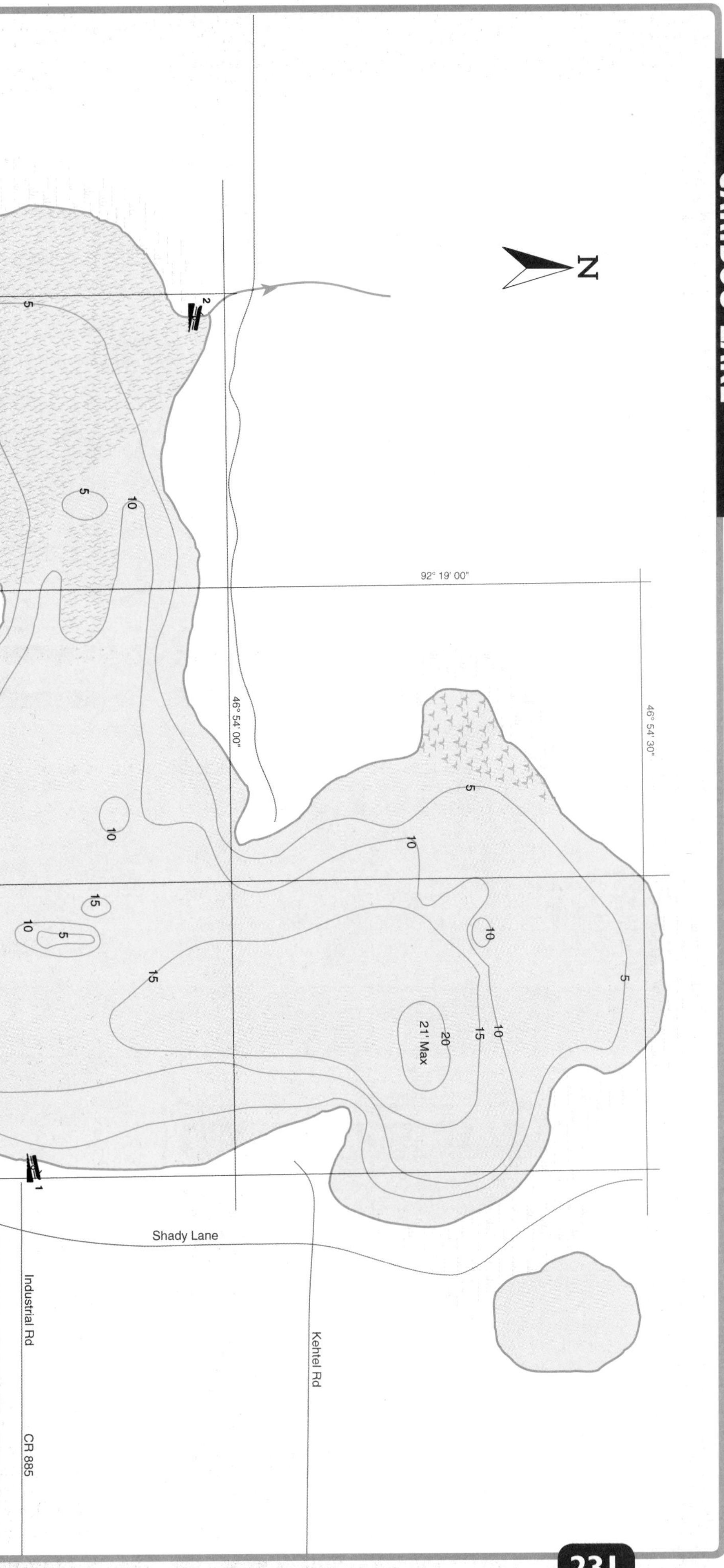

This angler was happy to pose
with his first bass of the season

Eric McPhee

Source: Minnesota Department of Natural Resources, USGS

BIG GRAND LAKE
St. Louis County

Area map pg / coord: 28 / B-1

Watershed: Cloquet

Surface area: 1,659 acres

Shorelength: 7.3 miles

Max / mean depth: 24 feet / 7 feet

Water color / clarity: Light brown / 11.5 feet (2010)

Shoreland zoning class: Gen. dev.

Mgmt class / Ecological type: Warm-water gamefish / bullhead

Accessibility: State-owned public access with gravel ramp, north shore

46° 52' 58.67" N / 92° 24' 27.74" W

Accommodations: None

LITTLE GRAND LAKE
St. Louis County

Area map pg / coord: 28 / B-1

Watershed: Cloquet

Surface area: 176 acres

Shorelength: 2.8 miles

Max / mean depth: 58 feet / 15 feet

Water color / clarity: NA / 13.0 feet (2008)

Shoreland zoning class: Rec dev.

Mgmt class / Ecological type: Walleye-centrarchid / centrarchid-walleye

Accessibility: Carry-down access at creek on north shore

NA

Accommodations: None

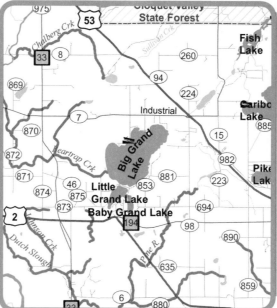

FISH STOCKING DATA			
year	species	size	# released
05	Walleye	Fry	1,925,000
07	Walleye	Fry	3,000,000
09	Walleye	Fry	3,019,999

LENGTH OF SELECTED SPECIES SAMPLED FROM ALL GEAR

Survey Date: 08/30/2010

Number of fish caught for the following length categories (inches):

species	0-5	6-8	9-11	12-14	15-19	20-24	25-29	>30	Total
Black Bullhead	-	1	133	-	-	-	-	-	134
Black Crappie	8	39	26	-	-	-	-	-	73
Bluegill	26	79	1	-	-	-	-	-	107
Brown Bullhead	-	-	143	3	-	-	-	-	146
Hybrid Sunfish	-	2	-	-	-	-	-	-	2
Largemouth Bass	-	-	-	5	4	-	-	-	9
Northern Pike	-	-	14	2	24	17	7	1	65
Pumpkin. Sunfish	38	35	-	-	-	-	-	-	73
Rock Bass	1	-	-	-	-	-	-	-	1
Walleye	-	-	-	-	3	6	2	-	11
White Sucker	-	-	-	1	16	16	-	-	33
Yellow Perch	46	104	6	-	-	-	-	-	156

NO RECORD OF STOCKING

LENGTH OF SELECTED SPECIES SAMPLED FROM ALL GEAR

Survey Date: 08/25/2008

Number of fish caught for the following length categories (inches):

species	0-5	6-8	9-11	12-14	15-19	20-24	25-29	>30	Total
Black Bullhead	1	16	65	-	-	-	-	-	82
Black Crappie	1	25	16	-	-	-	-	-	42
Bluegill	15	27	-	-	-	-	-	-	42
Brown Bullhead	-	2	44	-	-	-	-	-	46
Largemouth Bass	3	1	2	1	1	-	-	-	8
Northern Pike	-	-	-	2	28	27	5	-	63
Pumpkin. Sunfish	3	13	-	-	-	-	-	-	16
Rock Bass	2	9	3	-	-	-	-	-	14
Smallmouth Bass	-	-	-	1	8	-	-	-	9
Walleye	-	-	-	-	2	2	-	-	4
White Sucker	-	-	-	-	12	17	-	-	29
Yellow Perch	3	11	-	-	-	-	-	-	14

FISHING INFORMATION

The staff at Fisherman's Corner, 5675 Miller Trunk Highway, Hermantown, MN, 218-729-5369, say **Grand Lake** is loaded with small 1.5- to 2-pound-class northern pike and a few larger ones. If you want a tussle with one of them, toss a spinnerbait along weed edges or float a minnow under a bobber.

Walleye fishing can be good if you learn the lake, though. Try fishing shallow bars early in the season. These can be spotted by locating reeds above the water line. Live bait such as minnows, leeches or nightcrawlers is your best bet. Rig your bait on a jig, split shot rig or a slip bobber. Make sure to fish all parts of the bars. Later in the year, troll with un-weighted spinners tipped with leeches or crawlers to keep the bait above heavy weed growth. Experiment a bit by adding small weights ahead of the spinner to keep your offering just ticking the tops of the submerged vegetation.

Crappie fishing is best in late spring and some fish in the .75- to 1.25-pound range are mixed in with smaller ones. Fishing pressure dies down in the summer on Grand Lake due to heavy weed growth.

Little Grand also has some nice crappies, walleyes and a few northern pike. According to the folks at Fisherman's Corner, it's a tough lake to fish because, unlike Big Grand, which has rather dark water, Little Grand is deep and relatively clear. Make sure to fish Little Grand during low-light conditions to up your odds for success.

Baby Grand Lake offers mainly black bullheads. There are some hammer-handle northerns, decent-size crappies, some 1-pound largemouth, bluegills and yellow perch, but they're all pretty scarce. This lake's maximum depth is only 8 feet and isn't overly productive.

Big Grand Lake

N

Harnell Park

To Hwy 7
Dickerman Rd

46° 53' 30"
46° 53' 00"
46° 52' 30"
46° 52' 00"

92° 25' 30"
92° 25' 00"
92° 24' 30"
92° 24' 00"
92° 23' 30"
92° 23' 00"

Bear Trap Creek

CR 881

Klimek Rd

46° 51' 30"

Little Grand Lake

58' Max

CR 878

CR 853

Baby Grand Lake

8'

46° 51' 00"

CR 694

Seville Rd

WILD RICE LAKE St. Louis County

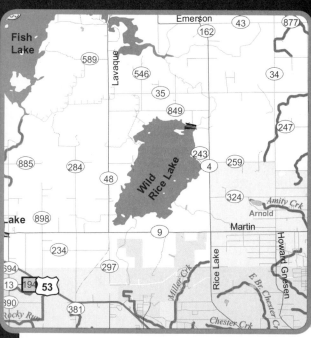

Area map page / coordinates: 28 / A,B-3

Watershed: Cloquet

Surface water area / shorelength: 2,372 acres / 12.9 miles

Maximum / mean depth: 12 feet / 7 feet

Water color / clarity: Brown stain / 3.5 feet (2009)

Shoreland zoning classification: Natural environment

Management class / Ecological type: Walleye / hard-water walleye

Accessibility: Public access (owned by Minnesota Power) with concrete ramp just west of dam on northeast shore off County Road 247

46° 54' 36.10" N / 92° 9' 54.76" W

Accommodations: Outhouses

FISHING INFORMATION

Wild Rice Lake, located just north of Duluth off Rice Lake Road (Highway 4), is another reservoir created by Minnesota Power when it dammed the Beaver River. This lake covers 2,372 acres and has a maximum depth of 12 feet. Unlike the other Duluth-area reservoirs, Wild Rice is generally lacking in obvious structure. In fact, its bottom is almost bowl-like. However, the abundant walleyes find plenty of subtle structure in the form of rocks and sunken timber to hide near. Anglers have good success, especially early in the season catching walleyes by working this structure with a jig-and-minnow combination or slip bobber rig tipped with a leech, nightcrawler or minnow. John Chalstrom, owner of Chalstrom's Bait and Tackle, 5067 Rice Lake Road, Duluth, MN, 218-726-0094, suggests fishing the stumps on the south side early in the season. In addition to live bait-fishing, try casting crankbaits and stickbaits in this and other areas. Move around the lake and pay attention to any subtle changes in bottom structure to locate fish schools. Some of the rocks shown on the map are good areas to try. The overall walleye population has increased in abundance in recent years. The most current DNR survey conducted in 2009 showed the abundance of walleyes to be up nearly two-fold from the 2004 survey, with good numbers of fish in the 20- to 24-inch range.

Yellow perch abundance, however, showed a marked decrease in overall numbers from the previous survey. To catch perch, fish the same structures you'd fish walleyes. Actually, it's pretty common to catch a few larger perch while you're chasing walleyes. If you want to specifically target the perch, just downsize your offerings.

The northern pike abundance was above average for Minnesota lakes . The mean length was around 22 inches with good numbers of fish in the 25- to 29-inch range present. The lake isn't known for its northern pike fishing, but every once in a while a 14- to 15-pound northern is taken. Flashy spinnerbaits, lipless crankbaits or jerkbaits will attract pike, as will a sucker minnow fished under a bobber. Think weed edges when looking for pike. For a fun diversion, use a large bass-style topwater lure instead of the typical subsurface offerings. Fish your topwater lure at sunrise to draw explosive strikes. Most pike won't be giants, but the ferocity of a pike strike on top of the water is worthwhile regardless of fish size.

Anglers in search of black crappies will find an average population here with a mean length of 9.3 inches. The DNR says the crappie growth is fast on Wild Rice compared to other lakes in the area.

NO RECORD OF STOCKING				
NET CATCH DATA				
Date: 07/27/2009	Gill Nets		Trap Nets	
species	# per net	avg. fish weight (lbs.)	# per net	avg. fish weight (lbs.)
Black Crappie	2.27	0.47	5.00	0.63
Bluegill	1.67	0.16	11.12	0.07
Northern Pike	7.33	2.87	0.94	2.71
Pumpkin. Sunfish	1.80	0.09	3.81	0.07
Rock Bass	1.20	0.27	0.69	0.30
Walleye	17.53	1.58	2.00	4.33
White Sucker	3.33	2.92	0.62	4.17
Yellow Perch	3.53	0.17	1.06	0.15

LENGTH OF SELECTED SPECIES SAMPLED FROM ALL GEAR

Number of fish caught for the following length categories (inches):

species	0-5	6-8	9-11	12-14	15-19	20-24	25-29	>30	Total
Black Crappie	-	25	84	5	-	-	-	-	114
Bluegill	183	15	-	-	-	-	-	-	203
Northern Pike	-	-	1	-	23	65	27	9	125
Pumpkin. Sunfish	80	4	-	-	-	-	-	-	88
Rock Bass	9	18	2	-	-	-	-	-	29
Walleye	-	7	2	120	105	50	11	-	295
White Sucker	-	-	-	-	45	15	-	-	60
Yellow Perch	34	24	12	-	-	-	-	-	70

Be careful when you motor around this impoundment, though. There are many lower-unit-eating rocks in the channel from the public access and around the shoreline in the main lake. Due to its close proximity to town, Wild Rice gets a lot of boat anglers. Shore fishing is also popular, particularly at the dam and along the shoreline near the public access. Kids can cash in on some fast action with small sunfish below the dam on the Beaver River. Chalstrom notes that the lake can get so engulfed by weeds by mid-July it becomes very difficult to fish until the fall.

N

CR 849

92° 11' 00"

92° 10' 30"

92° 10' 00"

Beaver
River

Rice Lake Dam Rd

46° 54' 30"

5

dam

46° 54' 00"

92° 12' 00"

92° 09' 30"

5

5

5

5

10

11'

10

46° 53' 30"

92° 12' 30"

dead
trees

10

5

5

46° 53' 00"

92° 13' 00"

5

5

46° 52' 30"

dead
trees

46° 52' 00"

dead trees

48

4

9

Martin Rd

Rice Lake Rd

NOT FOR NAVIGATION

HUNTER LAKE
St. Louis County

Area map page / coordinates:	24 / E-2
Surface water area:	64 acres
Shorelength:	1.6 miles
Accessibility:	Access by boat from Cloquet River
	NA
Accommodations:	None

NO RECORD OF STOCKING

FISHING INFORMATION

Hunter Lake is part of the Cloquet River system and its diverse fishery. Although there are no designated public access sites, you can get in by boat from the Cloquet River. Fishing pressure is light, due to poor accessibility. There hasn't been a DNR survey since 1965. Anglers fish for walleyes, northern pike, crappies and channel catfish, but you can also find pumpkinseed, bluegills, bullheads largemouth and smallmouth bass. Al Anderson, DNR Assistant Area Manager, says you'll find solid populations of channel catfish using Hunter Lake along with some walleyes, northern pike, smallmouth bass and other river species like white suckers and redhorse. "Hunter Lake hasn't been surveyed in over 40 years," said Anderson. "However, since there have been recent surveys on the Cloquet River with stations set up close to Hunter Lake, you can expect to find a decent fishery there. The channel catfish are what are really providing a good fishing opportunity lately." A slip bobber rig baited with a nightcrawler or a leech are good bets for catching channel catfish. In fact, a slip bobber and bait is a good bet for catching pretty much anything that swims in this little offshoot of the Cloquet River.

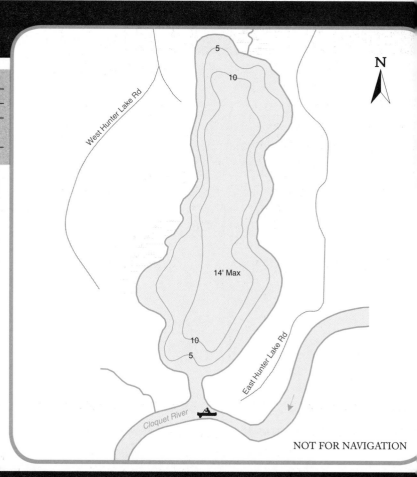

NOT FOR NAVIGATION

SIDE LAKE
St. Louis County

Area map page / coordinates:	28 / A-2
Surface water area:	44 acres
Shorelength:	1.1 miles
Accessibility:	Access by boat from Cloquet River
	NA
Accommodations:	None

NO RECORD OF STOCKING

FISHING INFORMATION

Try the deep hole where the river enters Side Lake for all species. Angling for walleyes can be good early in the season before heavy weed growth occurs. Walleye populations vary with river level fluctuations. Try jigging minnows or trolling spinners with nightcrawlers for walleyes early in the season. Leeches are more productive later in the year. Northern pike can be caught by casting big spoons or spinnerbaits to the submerged weeds. According to Al Anderson, DNR Assistant Area Manager, catfish angling is particularly good in this area. "While we haven't done a survey on Side Lake since 1992, I've done surveying on the Cloquet River," he said. "Since this lake is connected to the river, the fish you find there are in the lake. The channel catfish are doing very well. Any average fish is 15 inches long with some over 20 inches in length." Anderson offers a cautionary word about transporting invasive species out of this lake. "Right now there is definitely a problem beginning with exotic species coming into our waterways," he said. "To prevent transporting these species, we recommend you clean off your boat with hot water like a pressure wash and don't transfer water or minnows from one lake to the other."

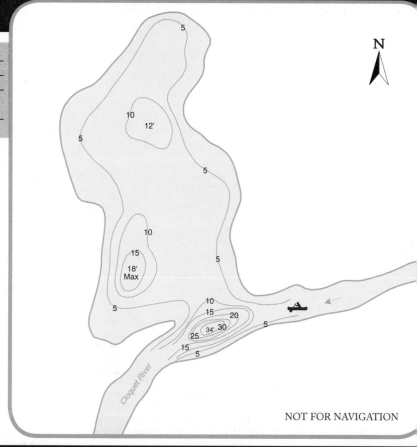

NOT FOR NAVIGATION

Source: Minnesota Department of Natural Resources, USGS

rea map page / coordinates: 28 / A-2,3

Vatershed: Cloquet

urface water area / shorelength: 3,258 acres / 99.9 miles

Iaximum / mean depth: 37 feet / NA

Vater color / clarity: 4.3 feet (2010)

horeland zoning classification: Recreational development

Ianagement class / Ecological type: Walleye / soft-water walleye

ccessibility: 1) State-administered public access with concrete ramp on north hore, just east of dam off Township Road 285

46° 57' 31.75" N / 92° 16' 11.17" W

ccessibility: 2) State-owned public access with concrete ramp on northwest hore, off County Road 15

46° 56' 31.71" N / 92° 18' 7.60" W

ccommodations: Resorts (2) with concrete launch facilities

NO RECORD OF STOCKING

NET CATCH DATA

	Gill Nets		Trap Nets	
Date: 08/02/2010		avg. fish		avg. fish
species	# per net	weight (lbs.)	# per net	weight (lbs.)
Black Crappie	1.67	0.50	6.93	0.50
Bluegill	1.27	0.34	13.47	0.26
Largemouth Bass	0.33	1.49	0.07	0.20
Northern Pike	4.27	1.76	1.80	3.67
Pumpkin. Sunfish	2.40	0.20	1.67	0.14
Rock Bass	0.93	0.34	1.27	0.25
Walleye	5.73	1.42	0.73	3.03

LENGTH OF SELECTED SPECIES SAMPLED FROM ALL GEAR

Number of fish caught for the following length categories (inches):

species	0-5	6-8	9-11	12-14	15-19	20-24	25-29	>30	Total
Black Crappie	9	22	98	-	-	-	-	-	129
Bluegill	40	180	1	-	-	-	-	-	221
Channel Catfish	-	-	-	-	1	-	-	-	1
Hybrid Sunfish	-	3	-	-	-	-	-	-	3
Largemouth Bass	-	1	-	5	-	-	-	-	6
Northern Pike	-	-	-	8	42	24	13	3	91
Pumpkin. Sunfish	38	22	-	-	-	-	-	-	61
Rock Bass	6	26	1	-	-	-	-	-	33
Walleye	-	8	9	19	52	7	2	-	97
White Sucker	-	15	10	11	123	18	-	-	177
Yellow Perch	56	119	3	-	-	-	-	-	178

FISHING INFORMATION

Fish Lake, located in Fredenburg Township, is one of the more popular lakes in the Duluth area, and for good reason. Walleyes, crappies, bluegills and northern pike are found in good numbers and sizes. The reservoir was created in the early 1920s when Minnesota Power dammed Beaver River. It stretches over 3,200 acres.

Local anglers say the walleye fishing has been good, although, as in most lakes, some years are better than others. Walleyes average just over a pound and are caught around the many islands and in the flats as water warms in summer. As fall turns to winter, walleyes begin moving into the high banks area and into the narrows on the north side of the lake. Scott Youngstrom at the Fredenberg Minno-ette, 5109 Fish Lake Road, Fredenberg, MN,

218-721-4800, says walleyes are the most popular fish for anglers to chase on Fish Lake. "I'd have to say that most of the folks going out are trying for walleyes," he says. "Of course, that doesn't mean they'll always catch them. The fishing has been pretty good for walleyes though." Like many northern Minnesota lakes, it's a good idea to break out the live bait rigs and slip bobbers when fishing for walleyes. Leeches and nightcrawlers top the list during warm weather months and minnows are best when water temperatures drop. Don't forget your trolling gear, too. There are plenty of flats, submerged humps and points to pull crankbaits and spinner rigs over throughout warm weather periods.

Crappie fishing along the high banks area is an autumn ritual for anglers who take advantage of the schools of 1/2-pound to pound-plus slabs that move in at that time. Youngstrom says there are some nice crappies to be caught. When the DNR last surveyed Fish Lake, their data showed the crappie population to be near its highest levels. If you're targeting crappies, think live bait or jigs or a combo of both. Keep your presentation vertical by using a slip bobber or a long pole to present your offerings.

There are also some plump bluegills to be found throughout the weedbeds. The bays on the southwest end of the lake are a good place to try for them. Youngstrom says there are some big bluegills to be caught in Fish Lake. Try fishing with a fly rod and a popper in shallows for bluegills. This is especially productive in spring and early summer when bluegills are in the shallows in some stage of spawning. They're very aggressive at this time and will often crush a popper twitched overhead.

Decent northerns round out the fishery. Most are found throughout the lake's shorelines and weedbeds. Get down into deeper, cooler water during summer months for the larger ones. Youngstrom says the overall northern pike fishing hasn't been fabulous over the last few years. "Anglers just aren't catching many pike," he says. "The fish are there, but the food fish are very abundant and pike just seem to not be chasing what anglers are giving them." Try fishing for northern pike early and late in day. Use fast and flashy lures such as spinnerbaits, buzzbaits, or lipless crankbaits. You can also finesse a few pike with a soft jerkbait like a fluke.

Anglers do well fishing from shore along the County Road 48 bridge area for walleyes, northern pike, crappies and bluegills throughout the year, especially during spring and fall when migration occurs.

N

Beaver River

Fish Lake Dam

high banks

92° 15' 00"

92° 15' 30"

10
15
20
25
8'
5
bar
5'
27
20
5'
rock
pile
23'
20'
dam
1
20'
20'
10
92° 16' 30"
92° 16' 00"
5
10
15
18'
15
10
16'
10
92° 17' 00"
5
5
10
92° 17' 30"
Bachelor Rd
2
46° 56'
15
5'
20
25
10
5'
30'
12'
15
10
15
bar
5
10
10
15
10
15
5
5
5
5
10
92° 14' 30"
10
12
15
20'
10
5
10
5
5
10
5
10
16 '
15
Little
Moose
10
15
5
10
10
46° 56' 00"
5
5
46° 55' 30"
5
46° 55' 00"

Source: Minnesota Department of Natural Resources, USGS

Fredenberg

48 Fish Lake Rd 43

CR 285

46° 58' 00"

CR 294 Pioneer Rd

92° 12' 30"

48

92° 12' 00"

Rd

Pontoon Bay

Hi Banks Resort

barrel

5 10

3'

15 15

15

10

15

10

15

5 5

10

5

15

13'

5 12'

16

10

5

10

5

10

46° 57' 30"

92° 11' 00"

5

Blue Max Resort

5

10

11'

Eagle's Nest Resort

92° 13' 30"

92° 13' 00"

92° 14' 00"

46° 57' 00"

10

92° 11' 30"

5

92° 10' 30"

5

10

46° 56' 30"

10

5

LaVaque Rd

30"

West Lismore Rd

48

To 53

NOT FOR NAVIGATION